HUGO BLACK

and the

SUPREME COURT

A Symposium

Hugo L. Black

Photography by Glogau, Washington, D.C.
(1967)

HUGO BLACK

and the

SUPREME COURT

A Symposium

Edited by

Stephen Parks Strickland

THE BOBBS-MERRILL COMPANY, INC.

A Subsidiary of Howard W. Sams & Co., Inc.

PUBLISHERS

INDIANAPOLIS • KANSAS CITY • NEW YORK

Copyright © 1967 By the Bobbs-Merrill Company, Inc.
Library of Congress Catalog Card No. 67-18209
Printed in the United States of America
All Rights Reserved

FOR TAMARA

Contents

Foreword

Looking out from a third-story window of the Essex Building in Queens' College, you can see, through day and into dusk, little groups of Cambridge undergraduates, moving along Silver Street, punting on the river, going in for lunch at the pub, carrying notebooks to and from lecture rooms on Mill Lane. It is a long way, over much salt water, to rural Alabama or even to Washington. Yet one feels that these young people, who for the most part know, and doubtless need to know, so little about so many American public men, ought to know about Hugo Black.

It would be tempting to start by trying to explain to them, or inviting them to guess with you, how it happened, whether it was more than chance, that this prophetic judge who for thirty years, some of them bitterly discouraging, has read condemnation on racialist law and on tyranny over opinion, began and remains an American Southerner, essentially and to the roots. But that ought to come later, after they understood the first thing about the man's work. It might be catching rhetoric, but it would not go to the heart of the matter, to begin with vignettes of steadfastness in darker days—with the *Dennis* dissent, for example. Yet again, something more fundamental is wanted.

Randolph Paul, in this volume, has reminded us of Chesterton's saying, that the most important thing about a man is his philosophy. The meetings and meanings of biography, the glow of occasional and steady courage, need to be led across the Atlantic by an account of the most important thing about the man. Hugo Black's philosophy is rich and subtly shaded. But the main outlines of the philosophy he has brought to and developed within his principal work are comprehensible, in Cambridge as in Washington and in Alabama. Making these outlines comprehensible to the Cambridge undergraduate would entail much filling in of background, unnecessary to the dominantly American readers of this book, but I think the essence could at last be conveyed; the young man on his way from Mill Lane would understand the chief among the many things we honor in Hugo Black, and would know a little more about America.

First, Hugo Black in his life-work partakes of and illustrates the view, deep-rooted in American thought, that law is a pathway to the good life, that the best hope of the nation is to be worked out through law, that our highest political goals are expressible and expressed in law. Other peoples have lived through law in this way; still others have not. The American mode, as it seems from his opinions to be accepted by Hugo Black, sees text as quest, sees the Preamble to our Constitution as reaching forward to suffuse the whole with a purpose in whose presence narrowness cannot live: "In order to . . . secure the blessings of liberty to ourselves and our posterity . . . no Bill of Attainder shall be passed."

Secondly, Hugo Black accepts (perceiving, I have no doubt, that the people also accept) the judicial function of review for constitutionality as a normal and proper means of making real our national decision to live through law. Having seen what his duty as a judge is defined to be, he does not hang back from it with a constant and perpetual *nolo episcopari*.

Seeing the Constitution, then, as chief among our means to the pursuit of happiness through law, and to the securing through law of liberty for ourselves and for the even remoter posterity of 1787, Hugo Black has addressed himself to his judicial task of interpretation with a clearly discernible view of what Marshall called "the genius and character of the whole government." The grand strategy of Hugo Black's constitutionalism has two aspects: he sees government as possessing ample, perhaps even yet hardly explored powers to act in the pursuit of the happiness of all, and he sees these powers as bindingly limited, with something like the same amplitude, against any entry into certain broad reserved areas of human dignity and freedom.

Our Constitution grants powers, mostly to Congress. There is a puzzling substyle in American legal culture which likes to spin out endless restricting glosses on plain language. "Regulation" does not include "prohibition." Commerce may not be regulated "indirectly." With all of this, Hugo Black will have nothing to do. The power to regulate commerce amply covers all measures Congress may take to deal with the exchange and movement of goods, services and people. The power to tax stands in no shadow of restrictive meaning. One of this book's clearest messages is that for all his thirty years on the Court, Black has expounded a philosophy of congressional power which leaves no room for second-guessing by the Court on the questions of what is good for the country and what is the expedient way to seek that good. It is not that he sees Congress as above the Constitution, or the Court as no authorized expounder, but rather that he believes, with Marshall, that the Constitution, as a matter of law, gives powers adequate to arising national need. He thinks the Framers wrought well. And he has chosen, in upholding particular congressional actions, to expound, for Congress and for the people, modern applications of the Marshallian thought, teaching in his opinions that the national power usurps nothing when it acts on national need.

Yet, as this symposium also reminds us, the Constitution looks another way, too. Having created this great engine of power, it decrees that it shall not be used in certain ways. Hugo Black does not see these prohibitions as inconveniences, as hard sayings to be reduced by successive paraphrase, by tacit reservation, to the point of making no more trouble. He sees them as defining, in vital part, the "genius and character of the whole government." And he reads them (as he reads the commerce clause) with that spirit which giveth life. If Congress may not "abridge" the freedom of speech, why ought not the word "abridge" be read with the same latitude, with the same room for historical development to answer need, as the word "regulate" in the empowerment of Congress to regulate commerce?

There is no paradox in this. The creation of great power, with simultaneously created safeguards against its entry into forbidden ground, is entirely familiar, in institutions and in physical arrangements. Reliance, for freedom, on the intrinsic general weakness of government may once have been less obviously misplaced than it would be today. In any case, it is certain that Hugo Black believes, with the plainest textual warrant, that our Constitution rejected that reliance. He looks upon the great power of government and finds it filled with potential for happiness; he would not seek freedom by making government weak. But he has also taught, once more by the plainest words of the text he so much reveres, that there are closes of personality, walled gardens of human dignity, where this power may not enter.

Justice Black, at eighty-one, is a tennis player. (Here, I think, the ears of the Cambridge undergraduate would prick up, and he would start asking questions to be sure he understood.) You drive the ball hard, for you are playing to win. If your opponent is on one side, you try to put your shot in the other corner. If he is at the net, put it over his head. If you can make it spin, make it spin.

But you must not drive it out of bounds.

No man alone makes a style, creates a mode. Even within the Court, Hugo Black has sat with others who faced the same way. Yet, when the list is made up of those men through whom has chiefly been worked out this nation's resolve to live greatly through law, to make a way by law for the prevailing of its democracy, to use law to increase general happiness, and yet steadfastly to express through law its respect for the individuality of man, Hugo Black's name will surely be among a very few of highest honor.

Cambridge, England

Winter 1967   *Charles L. Black, Jr.*

Acknowledgments

One must rely upon so many people for assistance in producing a book of this kind that perhaps only those who have been involved in similar undertakings can appreciate my sense of indebtedness.

First of all, I am deeply grateful to the contributors of the new studies of Justice Black that appear here, because, to a man, they interrupted other important endeavors to participate in this symposium. Of those contributors I am especially grateful to Professor Swisher, who not only provided a chapter for me but, before that, provided the opportunity for my original study of Justice Black and then offered counsel and encouragement as that seed was nurtured into a book. John Frank also offered early encouragement and George Kaufmann provided pertinent and important criticisms and assisted in reading the galley proofs.

I also wish to express my appreciation to the authors and the journal editors and association officers who permitted me to use materials that previously appeared elsewhere. Their kind consents are reflected in the paragraphs about the authors and their work.

Justice Black deserves a special word. In the course of my research, questions developed to which answers could not readily be found in his opinions or anywhere else in print. When I first asked for an interview to seek needed facts, I was a stranger to him; he was not aware that some of the participants were men he knew until late in the course of the project; and even as the effort came to a close, he had no guarantee that my intentions were objective. Nonetheless, from the time of my first request over a year ago down to a recent telephone inquiry about a minor point, he answered my questions without questioning me—an unusual and admirable attitude, in my view.

Mrs. Frances Lamb, the Justice's secretary, was very helpful as were several of the Judge's previous law clerks, including John W. Vardaman. So, too, was Miss Amelia Beck of the Supreme Court Clerk's Office. Regardless of the condition of the chapter manuscripts when first presented to her, Miss Elizabeth Beverly was always ultimately able to turn out a beautifully typed version for the publisher. Miss Olive Mills' keen eye and good editorial judgment have made my own writings much more acceptable than they were when I first asked her to look at them. My secretary, Mrs. June Speigelman Ducaud, agreeably and efficiently assisted me on a number of occasions and in a variety of ways as the book progressed. My colleague, Harry A. Marmion, read several of the galley proofs and offered useful suggestions. And I have had consistent and generous support, editorial and otherwise, from David B. Cox of Bobbs-Merrill. To all of these, and to other unspecified helpers, I express my thanks.

There are three persons whose assistance to me in this effort can neither be adequately described nor overly praised. My friend and former student, David Lamar Hill, helped with the research, checked citations, and performed other chores. Others might have done these things, but no one I know could have done them with equal speed and efficiency or with such good cheer. That meant much. William Holmes Brown, Jr., once more proved the scope and resiliency of his friendship by providing so many services that I cannot begin to recount them all here. He will understand if I simply say that he gave me generous moral, logistical, and redactorial aid, and all manner of good ideas besides. My wife, Tamara Gunsard Strickland, has been my strongest supporter in this undertaking from beginning to end. That will occasion no surprise for anyone who knows her. But even I now have a reinforced awareness of her uncommon talents: she not only read and re-read manuscripts and proofs, to the final product's great advantage, but always calmed me down, cheered me up, and spurred me on, as appropriate, to meet frequent needs.

Finally, both the scholarly and managerial aspects of this project have reminded me again of my debt to my parents, Kelly Parks Strickland and Alice Winn Peeples Strickland. Two of the most important lessons they tried to impart to me in my youth were those of patience and persistence. As I finish this book I can only be thankful that the lessons "took" as well as they did and that, maybe because my youth was not so long ago, they have lasted at least until now.

Stephen Strickland

Washington, D.C.
April 1967

Contributing Authors

DANIEL M. BERMAN is Professor of Government at the American University and Executive Director of the Institute on American Freedoms. He received his B.A. from Rutgers University, his M.A. from the University of Wisconsin, and his Ph.D. from Rutgers for a dissertation on "The Political Philosophy of Hugo L. Black." He has written articles on Black for several law journals, and contributed to and edited a special issue of the *American University Law Review* dedicated to Justice Black on the occasion of his seventy-fifth birthday. His books include *A Bill Becomes A Law: Congress Enacts Civil Rights Legislation; In Congress Assembled: The Legislative Process in the National Government; It Is So Ordered: The Supreme Court Rules on School Segregation;* and *Milestones: Toward Legal Recognition of Negro Equality.*

CHARLES L. BLACK, JR. since 1956 has been the Henry R. Luce Professor of Jurisprudence at the Yale University Law School. A native of Texas, he received his B.A. and M.A. from the University of Texas. His LL.B. is from Yale, and he has practiced law in New York City. In addition to his teaching career at Yale, he has been a member of the faculties of Columbia University Law School and the Salzburg Seminar in American Studies. For the first half of the 1966-67 academic year, he was visiting professor at Cambridge University, England. In addition to his many articles in legal and other periodicals, he is the author of a number of books, including *The People and the Court; The Occasions of Justice;* and *Perspectives in Constitutional Law.* He has appeared as counsel in a number of Supreme Court cases involving civil rights and school segregation, and is also a specialist in admiralty law.

IRVING DILLIARD, a native of Illinois, has had three principal careers, as a journalist, as an educator, and as an author. After graduating from the University of Illinois, he became a cub reporter for the *St. Louis Post-Dispatch* where subsequently he wrote editorials for thirty years. Since 1963 he has been Ferris Professor of Journalism and Senior Fellow of the Council of Humanities at Princeton University, and twice has served on the faculty of the Salzburg Seminar. Books he has edited include *The Spirit of Liberty: Papers and Addresses of Learned Hand;* and *One Man's Stand For Freedom: Mr. Jutice Black and The Bill of Rights,* and his articles on the Supreme Court and several of its Justices have appeared in a number of literary magazines and law journals. He is the recipient of honorary doctoral degrees from Brandeis, Southern Illinois, and Washington Universities, Colby and MacMurray Colleges, and the New School for Social Research. From 1961 to 1967 he served as a trustee of the University of Illinois.

JOHN P. FRANK is a native of Wisconsin and received three of his degrees—B.A., M.A., and LL.B.—from the University of Wisconsin. His J.S.D. is from Yale. He has been a professor of law at Indiana University as well as at Yale, and has been in the private practice of law in Arizona since 1954 though he has continued to teach occasional law courses such as those he offered at the summer session of the University of Washington in 1966. A member of the Wisconsin and Arizona bars, he was law clerk to Justice Black for the October 1942 term. His book, *Mr. Justice Black,* appeared in 1949 and he has continued to write about the Justice for various law journals. Others of his books include *Cases on the Constitution; Marble Palace: The Supreme Court in American Life; Lincoln As A Lawyer; Justice Daniel Dissenting;* and *The Warren Court.*

GEORGE KAUFMANN, a member of the New York, District of Columbia, and Supreme Court Bars, has been engaged in the private practice of law in Washington, D.C., since 1958. Specializing in labor relations and appellate practice, he has appeared before the Supreme Court in numerous cases. In 1950 he received his B.A. from the College and, in 1954, his J.D. from the Law School of the University of Chicago. He was managing editor of the *University of Chicago Law Review*. Recently he has written about the Supreme Court for the *Washingtonian* Magazine.

W. WALLACE KIRKPATRICK is Associate Dean of the National Law Center of the George Washington University, having joined the faculty of that institution in 1961. He received his B.A. degree with high honors from Harvard, spent a year at Oxford, and subsequently was graduated from the Harvard Law School with honors. He spent more than twenty years as an attorney in the Antitrust Division of the Department of Justice, serving as First Assistant of the Division for several years and as sometime Acting Assistant Attorney General. Interruptions in that career were for tours of duty as the chief United States legal officer in Berlin and as a Naval officer. The main portion of his chapter in this volume was written for the special 1967 issue of the *U.C.L.A. Law Review* honoring Justice Black, where his article bore the title "Mr. Justice Black and Antitrust." The historical background which he uses to introduce his treatment of antitrust herein is largely taken from his "Crossroads of Antitrust and Union Power," which appeared in the December 1965 issue of the *George Washington Law Review*.

The late RANDOLPH PAUL was called, at the time of his death in 1956, "the ablest tax lawyer in the United States." He received his B.A. degree from Amherst College, his LL.B. from the New York University Law School, and as a practicing attorney was a member of the New York, New Jersey, and District of Columbia Bars. But he was a scholar, teacher, and presidential adviser as well as a tax attorney, serving as special tax consultant to President Roosevelt, special assistant to President Truman, and general counsel of the Department of the Treasury from 1942 to 1946. Sometime lecturer at Harvard and Yale Law Schools, his books include *Studies in Federal Taxation; Taxation For Prosperity;* and *Taxation in the United States*. His chapter in this volume originally appeared in longer form in the *Yale Law Journal* in February 1956 under the title "Mr. Justice Black and Federal Taxation." It was among the last articles he produced. Tax law events of the intervening years which are relevant to the main thrust of Mr. Paul's study have been noted in the present chapter by the editor.

CHARLES A. REICH received his undergraduate degree from Oberlin and his law degree from Yale, and has been on the Yale Law School faculty since 1960. His special area of concentration is Constitutional Law. During the 1953 Supreme Court term, he clerked for Justice Black and subsequently he practiced law in Washington, D.C., and New York. The author of a number of journal articles, his recent exploration, in the *Yale Law Journal,* of the problem of how community and societal planning and individual liberty can both be accommodated in a free society has generated widespread interest. Professor Reich's chapter in this book first appeared as a section of an even more extensive study, "Mr. Justice Black and the Living Constitution," in the February 1963 issue of the *Harvard Law Review.* (© Harvard Law Review Association, 1963.) The article was originally written to mark Justice Black's seventy-seventh birthday and his completion of twenty-five years on the Supreme Court.

STEPHEN PARKS STRICKLAND, like Justice Black a native of Alabama, received his B.A. degree in 1956 from Emory University, where he was a member of Phi Beta Kappa and where he began studies in Constitutional Law. His M.A. is from the Johns Hopkins University where he is presently a candidate for the Ph.D. degree. His studies there were commenced under a Congressional Staff Fellowship of the American Political Science Association, awarded him after six years service on Capitol Hill as an administrative assistant to a congressman and chief clerk of a committee of the House of Representatives. His initial study of Justice Black won the 1965 McCoy Prize at Johns Hopkins and a subsequent version appeared in the Winter 1966 issue of the *Federal Bar Journal* under the title, "Mr. Justice Black: A Reappraisal." A staff associate of the American Council on Education and executive secretary of its Committee on Sponsored Projects, he is the editor of and contributor to a forthcoming book, *Sponsored Research in American Universities and Colleges,* and the author of a number of articles relating to federal research activities.

CARL BRENT SWISHER has taught constitutional law at the Johns Hopkins University since 1937, the year that Justice Black was appointed to the Supreme Court. Since 1938 he has held the Thomas P. Stran Chair of Political Science there. A native of West Virginia, he received his B.A. and M.A. degrees from Pomona College and his Ph.D. from the Brookings Graduate School in Washington, D.C., in 1929. Thereafter he served as a Fellow of the Brookings Institution, taught at Columbia University, and served as special assistant to the United States Attorney General. His books include *Stephen J. Field: Craftsman of the Law; Roger B. Taney; American Constitutional Development;* and *The Supreme Court in Modern Role.* Distinguished lecturer series have taken him to the University of Chicago, University College—London, Boston University, and Whittier College, and he, too, has taught at the Salzburg Seminar. The recipient of honorary doctoral degrees from Pomona and Oberlin Colleges and from West Virginia Wesleyan University, he has served as president of both the Southern Political Science Association and the American Political Science Association.

Introduction

On January 29, 1925, H. L. Black, attorney, of Birmingham, Alabama, made his first appearance before the United States Supreme Court. He was there to argue the case of *Lewis v. Roberts*. The man he represented was a Negro convict, Henry Lewis, who with others like him had been "leased" by the State of Alabama to a mining company to work underground in its coal mines. Because of the company's negligence, an accident occurred in which Lewis was seriously injured and he won a $4,000 judgment in a damage suit against the company. Before the award was paid, however, the company declared bankruptcy. Lewis then filed a claim against the company's estate for the amount due him. But the company's trustee argued, and the Federal District Court agreed, that the only kinds of claims the estate was required to pay under the Bankruptcy Act were those involving debts owed to anyone with whom the company had had a contractual agreement. The debt owed Henry Lewis was not based on any kind of contract; thus Lewis did not have to be paid.

William Howard Taft was Chief Justice at that point in time, and Joseph McKenna and Oliver Wendell Holmes were the Supreme Court's senior justices in length of service. They would be gone twelve and a half years later when the Hugo Black appearing before them that day would himself be appointed to the Court. Gone, too, would be Justice Edward T. Sanford who had made possible the young Birmingham attorney's appearance in the *Lewis* case and whose opinion for the Court in the case was to give Black one of the most important achievements in his career as a lawyer. Also sitting on the 1925 Court was Willis Van Devanter, whose own seat would be taken in 1937 by the man here serving as counsel for the petitioner. Four justices—James C. McReynolds, George Sutherland, Pierce Butler, and Louis D. Brandeis—would still be on the Court when the October 1937 term began. For the first three, it would be a rare occasion indeed when they were again swayed by the arguments of Hugo Black.

His line of reasoning was supported by stronger precedents than those offered by counsel for the mining company, and the Court had no difficulty deciding in Lewis' favor. But Black had not agreed to take the case, without fee, because it would be an easy victory. He had involved himelf in the matter because he was offended at the devastating injustice that would be done to a poor and injured man—and to any others who afterwards might find themselves in similar straits—if the decisions of the District and Appellate Courts were allowed to stand.

That the Supreme Court found the relevant issues easy to resolve is evidenced by the fact that its opinion was unanimous, brief, and relatively promptly announced. Yet it was actually the kind of case the Court of that era would have preferred not to hear in the first place. Its significance was quite limited: it dealt not with a constitutional issue but with the interpretation of a relatively minor statute; it affected not great segments of society but, at best, only a small handful of citizens. Except that the decision being appealed was in direct conflict with other interpretations of the Bankruptcy Act by other Federal Courts of Appeal, the Supreme Court almost certainly would have refused to review the case. If the appeal had been based only on the plight of Henry Lewis, it would have been denied.

The Judges Bill enacted later in the same year provided Congressional approval for the Supreme Court to exercise greater selectivity in arranging its docket. Had that bill already become law, Lawyer Black would have had even more difficulty in getting the Court to issue a writ of certiorari. He had enough trouble as it was. Specifically, he had asked that Lewis' petition proceed *in forma pauperis* so that, in view of the petitioner's impoverished station, the Court itself might bear the expenses of preparing and presenting the case. The Court Clerk balked. There were few precedents for such a course. He would agree only to Black's taking up the matter directly with Mr. Justice Sanford who was responsible for overseeing the Fifth Judicial Circuit. In his conference with the

Justice from Tennessee, the young Alabama lawyer was persuasive: the case would be placed on the docket, Black himself would present oral arguments, and the Court would pay
the incidental costs.

Victory in his first Supreme Court appearance must have
seemed, later on, especially fortunate. As it turned out, *Lewis
v. Roberts* was also the last case he argued before the Court.
The next year, in 1926, he began his arduous but ultimately
successful race for the United States Senate. In his new role,
the *Lewis* case continued to have great meaning for him. As
Carl Swisher points out, once in the Senate, Black favored
legislation that would encourage the Supreme Court to hear
cases of great importance to the individuals involved, regardless of their importance to the nation at large. And as George
Kaufmann suggests, Black never forgot the difficulties he had
in 1925 with the Court Clerk who, in his eyes, was more concerned with procedural precedents than with the pursuit of
justice. Certainly Hugo Black as a member of the Supreme
Court has encouraged the use of *in forma pauperis* proceedings
so that lack of money might not stand in the way of a poor
citizen's having his case heard by the highest court in the
land, if such it merited.

That, of course, is only one of the ways in which Black—
to borrow Irving Dilliard's phrase—has left his own clear
impress on our life and law. It is the examination of that
impress, the analysis of that impact, that is the purpose of
this volume.

Three decades have passed since President Franklin D.
Roosevelt made his first appointment to the Supreme Court.
He had been forced to wait until six months after his second
term began for the opportunity to make it. Until then, the
Court had blocked one New Deal plan after another. That
"nine old men" could veto social and economic reforms which
had received overwhelming approval by the people in two
elections meant, to F.D.R., a thwarting of the procedures of
democracy. He declared war on the Court. As John Frank
suggests, who gained the victory depends on how the term is
defined. In either case, when the smoke of battle cleared, there
had been one crucial change in the situation: a vacancy had
occurred on the Court. The President seized the chance with

characteristic purpose; he appointed someone he could count on. The appointee was Hugo Lafayette Black, the Senior Senator from Alabama whose firm New Deal convictions, though lacking a label, predated the New Deal itself.

Because Roosevelt's first Supreme Court appointment followed so closely after the fight over the "Court-packing plan," it was bound to bring controversy regardless of the appointee himself. It did not help matters that the new appointee, as a Senator, had been one of the strongest supporters of that plan. His considerable talents were undisputed. He was universally recognized as a brilliant and unrelenting investigator of activities he disapproved and a zealous and effective promoter of causes he believed in. But were his intellectual qualities the kind which fitted a man for high judicial office? As Randolph Paul and Carl Swisher indicate, Black's suitability to sit on the Supreme Court was sharply questioned, from several sides, on the basis of his legal experience and his temperament. And as Daniel Berman reminds us, the rediscovered fact of Black's previous membership in the Ku Klux Klan soon brought the controversy to a new level of intensity.

The appointment did not go undefended, of course. Black's Senate colleague and frequent ally in legislative battles, George Norris, thought the President had made an ideal choice. The Senator from Nebraska stated publicly that "The scales of justice in his hands will bring renewed hope to millions of our common people. . . ."

When the Court plan and appointment storms subsided, and as the new Justice's conceptions about law and the role of the Court began to be revealed in his judicial performance, Roosevelt had reason to feel that, in light of his own goals, he had used the proper tactics generally and had made precisely the right appointment. The Court's previous predictable hostility to almost any New Deal proposal quickly, quietly faded away. The particular appointment had broader significance, however. Beginning with his earliest opinions, Black prodded the Court into new postures: not only a posture of restraint in passing on the "wisdom" of legislation enacted by state legislatures as well as by the Congress, but also a posture of more active concern for protecting and even extending the rights of individuals.

In the years of Black's Supreme Court service, times and issues have changed and changed again. And always changing with them, it is said, is the Supreme Court. But how? In what regard, and to what degree? Black remains on the Court as its Senior Associate Justice. He has come to be called by some the Court's chief philosopher. How great has his influence really been? What have been his most important roles? How has he reacted to philosophies of colleagues and predecessors, to recurrent issues and new demands?

In attempting to answer these and similar questions, this symposium focuses on Black, the Judge. Personal elements have of course affected the judicial career. Hence, where they are significant to the main theme, Black's rural Alabama childhood, his extensive self-education, his record as a local prosecutor and police court judge, his enthusiasms and successes as a Senator, and his affiliation with the Klan, are related. One personal element is not examined and for that reason deserves a special word. I speak of the element of personal relationships among members of the Supreme Court. The tradition that ours is a government of laws, not men, has never been taken to mean, I think, that personalities, singly or in special combinations, have not affected the evolution of statutes and the way they are interpreted. The suggestion that changes in personnel on the Supreme Court have affected Justice Black's over-all work is an eminently reasonable one. On another level, there is enough evidence to the contrary to prevent a prudent analyst from asserting that personal friendships and animosities do not occasionally affect alliances in cases. The point is that this particular kind of environmental factor has not been explored here. The clashes of opinions and philosophies described should be taken as that and nothing more. In my own chapter, for example, I have emphasized Justice Black's repeated attacks on the judicial philosophy most consistently and most eloquently articulated in the opinions of the late Justice Felix Frankfurter. Frankfurter's attacks on the Black approach, also alluded to, are equally famous. In this symposium at least, there is no implication that such "attacks" had personal motivation or reflected personal animosities. If anything, Justice Black had not only a keen appreciation of Justice Frankfurter's mind and abilities but a personal fondness for the man as well. To illustrate further, one of Black's close personal friends on the Court at present is John Harlan, the colleague with whom he probably disagrees more frequently than any other in deciding cases. In parallel, the companionships pointed up in the discussions that follow are those relating to the comradeship of conviction. The best evidence is that Justice Black respects both the colleagues with whom he agrees and those with whom he disagrees.

Two other points should be made. First, although most of Black's special concerns in law are discussed either in separate chapters or in the course of other discussions, the approach here has been selective rather than all-inclusive. Other areas of law could have been highlighted to provide insights, similar to those we offer, about the way the Justice thinks.

Second, our subject has sometimes been reported paradoxically. No other Supreme Court member has urged a more active role for the Court in certain areas; in other areas, no justice has been more critical of judicial usurpation. Black has been variously described as a States' Righter and as a proponent of powerful central government. He has been viewed by some as being restricted by his literalist interpretation of the Constitution; others have noted, whether with approval or disapproval, his expansionist tendencies in interpreting constitutional provisions as well as statutes. The authors of this volume have not been distracted by the paradoxes alleged by others. They have mainly relied on root sources for their interpretations. Nonetheless, especially because of the alternate examination of broad and narrow aspects of the Judge, the participants in this symposium do not always present their findings in dimensions and shadings that match. Further, the career under scrutiny has indeed been unusually long and rich and, as Charles Reich reminds us, there is much about Black's philosophy that he has not explicitly revealed. I would submit that admirable consistency has characterized the way that Black has approached both the law and his own work; yet nothing is more obvious about his thirty-year tenure on the Court than that he has grown and, at least in that way, changed. His deepest Socratic conviction, the bedrock of his personal philosophy, is a dedication to democracy; but his Socratic mode of procedure has included a willingness to review his own position on issues and, when shown a more intelligent answer, to change.

Differences of emphasis and of interpretation in this volume, that is to say, reflect the complexities of the man who is the object of the study as well as the inevitable subjective differences of the students. In final analysis, however, most of the perspectives merge. The distinctive impresses Hugo Black has made on discrete areas of the law ultimately reflect related parts of a larger judicial philosophy. Particular examples of judicial performance reveal, when seen together, a single belief about the nature of the Constitution and the way judges should treat it. The authors hope the reader will find in our aggregate endeavor a clear and comprehensive portrait of this extraordinary Judge, whose career has so greatly affected the law, and through the law, the lives of his contemporaries and of those to follow.

Stephen Parks Strickland

Washington, D.C.
April 1967

CHAPTER ONE

History's Panorama and Justice Black's Career

CARL BRENT SWISHER

AS he rounds out three decades of service on the Supreme Court it is apparent that Hugo Black will be one of the justices of greatest length of service in the Court's entire history. Like the few other justices who have served longer and the many who have served for shorter terms, he will have had a career shaped not only by his own character, personality, background, and endeavors but also by the historical events and sequences which prompted, conditioned, or curbed the work of the Court during the time span of his membership. Justice Holmes once suggested that much of the greatness attributed to Chief Justice Marshall might be principally the product of the fact that Marshall was *there* at the time when great events invited the kind of forceful judicial performance by which he made his imprint. Chief Justice Taney won high repute during nearly twenty years of service and then, with the ignominy brought by the Dred Scott case and the racial crisis culminating in the Civil War, fell into such disrepute that his reputation has been only gradually rescued in a succeeding century.

To illustrate further, for the period of his service as associate justice from 1910 to 1916, Charles Evans Hughes is little remembered except by specialized students of the Supreme Court, and the Chief Justice of that period, Edward D. White,

Notes appear at pages 275-278.

is no better remembered. But Hughes gained a prominent place in history for his service as Chief Justice from 1930 to 1941, when stormy events were shaping the nation's future and involving the Supreme Court in the ordeal of the depression and the New Deal. A man always of greatness or potential greatness, he had the opportunity during the 1930's to steady the helm of the Court as Justices divided sharply over critical issues and as an unprecedented attack was made on the Court by the Franklin D. Roosevelt administration in strategic defense of the New Deal. During this period—some years of which Hugo Black spent as an active and aggressive member of the Senate and some as a member of the Court— Hughes partly won victories and partly suffered frustration in the face of events not predictable at the time of his appointment to the Chief Justiceship and otherwise beyond his control.

Like the Hughes Chief Justiceship of eleven years, the Black associate Justiceship of thirty years has been conditioned by stormy and oftentimes unpredictable events, events which not only have determined the issues to be raised in litigation but which, as well, have done much to shape the thinking of the Justices deciding the cases and writing the opinions. While in Black's case the multiple crises have been met by a man firmly established in attitude, philosophy, and character, such crises have nevertheless given content to his strategy in particular cases and sequences of cases. At the time of his appointment, the Court's greatest and most immediate challenge was the task of constitutional adjustment to the revolution of the New Deal. This adjustment especially included the need for a rationale for the vastly increased exercise of government power over property; the rationale was shortly provided in terms of getting "back to the Constitution" from which the Court in earlier years had allegedly departed. The subsequent concentration of power in the federal government for waging World War II, when added to the "positive government" characteristic of the New Deal, worked not merely temporary but also permanent changes in the scope of governmental activities in world relations as well as in internal affairs. The judiciary, like the political branches of the government, was then to feel the turbulence of a nation's conflicting desires: on the one hand for return to normalcy after the war and, on the other, for continuation of an active role in preventing war's recurrence. That role, assumed through membership in the United Nations, itself underwent change with the developing "cold war" with the Communist world and, once more, conditioned the atmosphere in which constitutional principles were to be interpreted.

Of the essence of New Deal and wartime constitutional interpretation was acceptance of the fact of change in the character of the economy. The growth of mass production industrialism brought increasing contrasts with the simpler forms of production and with the economic organization and thinking which were characteristic of our beginning years as a nation. The concept of property, possessing elements of sanctity long recognized in Supreme Court decisions, shifted from identity with things primarily fixed and tangible to rights so intermixed with the rights of competing claimants—the rights of people in the mass as distinguished from possessors of formal title—that much of the property right's absoluteness gave way to relativity. But the fact of relativity had to be recognized specifically by courts and the law, so seemingly fundamental was the position of property as a characteristic of our national heritage.

Even as the courts in general accepted, more and more, government's placement of limitations on rights of property, the Supreme Court found itself increasingly involved with protecting the rights of individuals and groups threatened by the growing power and anonymity of government. These rights ranged all the way from those of freedom of speech and press to rights of the accused, rights to freedom from racial discrimination, and rights to political equality in legislative districting. The preoccupation of the Court, that is to say, was with the people and their rights as people, rights without which people could be only cogs in the increasingly complex social mechanism. With the positive operations of the government the Court had little to do. Positive policy was made in the business and professional world and in the Legislative and Executive branches of government; the Court interfered to prevent evils on the basis of constitutional or statutory authority, but not more than incidentally did it direct policy or make positive choices.

So it is that ours remains a free society, in that choices are made by representatives of the people who are judicially restrained only within the pattern of the law. Throughout the history of the Supreme Court, of course, there has been debate over the proper limits of its restraining power. When in 1923 the Court denied its own authority to pass on the constitutionality of expenditures out of the general funds in the treasury,[1] some thought the decision marked the beginning of the end of judicial power.[2] For money is a source of great power, yet government with complete freedom to tax or borrow and spend could be checked only peripherally by the judiciary. For example, the judiciary has little to say about the present expenditure of the more than seventy billion dollars annually —more than half the national budget—that goes for defense purposes. Indeed, it has little to say about most of the civil budget as well. Thus a great deal gets done, a great deal of basic policy gets made, before the protective sphere of the judiciary is reached. The Legislative and Executive branches decide whether and how to prepare for national defense, for development of the economy, for programs of social welfare. Ordinarily the courts simply decide whether statutes are constitutional or are correctly interpreted. Yet in the exercise of this limited area of restrictive power, such authority as belongs to the judiciary is focused on the preservation of constitutional principles. In the light of the totality of power exercised by the federal government, the exercise of judicial authority may seem but a sideline responsibility. But performance of the judicial task may involve expression of the essence of American democratic ideals, and by some Justices, including Justice Black, that task is often so conceived.

A Senator's View of the Court

Hugo Black's experience as a Senator reflected both the impact of past history on his own thinking and constituted history which conditioned his later performance as a Justice. In 1930, while letting more outspoken Senators such as George Norris and William Borah spearhead the attack, he voted against confirmation of Charles Evans Hughes as Chief Justice of the Court from which Hughes had resigned in 1916 to run as a Republican candidate for the presidency in opposition to Woodrow Wilson. Black did not publicly give his reasons for opposition. They may have been at least partially those of a Democrat critical of Hughes' earlier departure from the Court for partisan reasons. More probably Black's reasons were those of his fellows who had been attacking federal courts generally for their conservatism and who feared that, particularly because of Hughes' recent professional connections with big business interests, he was likely to be biased in favor of capital and against labor and the common people.

During the middle 1930's Black had reason to be critical of courts. They had used their injunctive power to restrain the public development and sale of electric power in the Tennessee Valley under the plan which Black, along with Senator Norris, had sponsored. Consequently, in 1935 he introduced a bill to require submission to the Supreme Court, within ten days, of the record in any case in which an inferior court had set aside an act of Congress. Asked for advice concerning this bill so vitally affecting its work load, the Court sent to a meeting of the Senate Judiciary Committee three of its members, Chief Justice Hughes and Justices Willis Van Devanter and Louis D. Brandeis, with the Chief Justice acting as spokesman. Hughes opposed the Black bill. He argued that it was not needed to insure prompt review of decisions properly to be appealed to it, that it would not speed the process of litigation, and—a reason with which Black was not impressed —that it would "impose a very heavy burden on the Supreme Court."[3] The bill was not passed.

Continued obstruction of the TVA program by inferior courts, even in the face of a Supreme Court decision finding part of the program constitutional,[4] no doubt added to Black's reasons for supporting President Roosevelt's plan to pack the Supreme Court with members sympathetic to the New Deal. In debate he emphasized what he saw as the need for granting more writs of certiorari—for getting more cases reviewed by the Supreme Court because of their importance to the litigants themselves, as distinguished from need of the nation at large to have legal questions determined by the Court. In so urging, Black showed no signs of disturbance at the fact that he was taking a position counter to the purpose of the Court-sponsored "Judges Bill" of 1925 which Congress had enacted to enable the Court to winnow the cases on its overloaded docket and limit its review activity to issues of importance to the country as distinguished from particular litigants.

In defending the Court-packing plan, Black argued that a President had a right to appoint to the Court men sharing his views of the public interest. He tried to show—by argumentative strategy resembling his later occasional strategy as a Justice—that former President William Howard Taft, before his appointment as Chief Justice, had taken the same position. Taft had published an article supporting Warren G. Harding for President, partly on the ground that Harding would make better appointments to the Supreme Court than would his Democratic opponent. "There is no greater domestic issue in this campaign," Taft had written, "than the maintenance of the Supreme Court as the bulwark to enforce the guarantee that no man shall be deprived of his property without due process of law."[5]

What Taft must have meant, explained Black, was that "the due process clause of the Constitution of the United States was what the Judge construing it thought it was." What Taft further implied, said Black, was that he wanted judges who would "construe the due-process clause to mean what he, Mr. Taft, thought it ought to mean." This meant that Taft advocated appointment of judges who, "in interpreting this elastic due-process clause, which means one thing to one citizen and another thing to another citizen, have the philosophy which is the prevailing sentiment of the country." In Black's rephrasing, Taft had said that "the great domestic issue in a Presidential campaign was the economic philosophy and predilections of the Judges who were to sit in the Supreme Court and make final and unappealable decisions as to national policies, by the application of those predilections to the due-process clause of the Constitution."[6] Black professed admiration for Taft and his conception of the basis of judicial appointments, though not of his public policies; he thought it quite appropriate that President Roosevelt as well as a Republican President should have the privilege of appointing judges to support his economic predilections—in this instance the principles of the New Deal. At that point in time, Black had doubts about the merits of life appointments for judges. About this specific subject he became silent once his own appointment had taken place, though certain other of his suspicions about judges seem to persist. As for the expansion or contraction of the meaning of due process clauses depending on the ends judges sought to attain, he came to regard it as an abuse of judicial power and sharply criticized his brethren when they seemed to him to be using such tactics.

New Colleagues and New Law

In the light of Black's critical and realistic approach to the courts and the judicial process while in the Senate, it could be predicted at the time of his appointment to the Court in 1937 that he was likely to stand out as an alien, not only among the extreme conservatives, but also among the so-called liberals less hostile to the New Deal. Surviving conservatives, after the retirement of Justice Van Devanter whom Black replaced, were James C. McReynolds, appointed by President Wilson in 1914, and George Sutherland and Pierce Butler, appointed by President Harding in 1922. The three of them had enjoyed the warm approval of Chief Justice Taft, who had been so deeply concerned about the kind and caliber of appointments. With none of these ultraconservative Justices, all steeped in laissez-faire and rigidified beliefs concerning the nature and sanctity of private property and concerned about growing paternalism in government, was Black likely to have much in common. With the departure of Van Devanter, the three had already witnessed the beginning of obsolescence for their mode of thinking. They could but face the future with gloom.

At the middle of the Court in terms of legal and social philosophy stood Hughes and Owen J. Roberts, a Hoover appointee, aligning themselves now with the conservatives and now with the liberals in divisions over the exercise of governmental regulatory power. While on occasion Black would align himself with them in the decision of cases, this Democratic crusader against monopolies and power lobbies, and for serv-

ices such as the TVA and for the rights of labor, was unlikely
to have close affinity with them.

The three so-called liberals were Brandeis, appointed by
President Wilson in 1916, Harlan F. Stone, appointed by President Coolidge in 1925, and Benjamin N. Cardozo, appointed
by President Hoover in 1932. Black had had some contact
with Stone as a result of work he had done for the Department
of Justice while Stone was Attorney General. He probably
knew Stone better than any other member of the Court, but
Stone had maintained reserve even as he offered friendship and
counsel. And soon he was to be worried about Black's tendency
to strike out in behalf of positions without full argument and
due consideration of precedents. With the elderly Brandeis,
aristocratic and wealthy Jewish lawyer, socially minded judge
and citizen, deeply reverent toward the Court and the judicial
process, Black never established a close relationship. The same
was true as to Cardozo, sensitive and gentle and literary and by
this time in poor health, with the days of his great achievements behind him.

Justice Black gave little heed to the discomforts of his initial
aloneness on the Court. In a personal interview a decade
after he joined the Court, he remarked that, as was the custom
with beginners, he had at first been assigned only easy cases
in which to act as official spokesman. The assignments were
made on Saturdays and he wrote these official opinions on
Sundays. As a result, a great deal of time was left for concentration on dissenting opinions; and of these, he wrote a great
many with considerable fervor in those early years. In doing
so Black not only steered away from the ultraconservatives but
often eschewed the company of the liberals as well. During the
term beginning in October 1937, he voted in dissent sixteen
times, and on twelve of these occasions he stood alone.[7] He
boldly challenged the formula for rate making adhered to by
a majority of the Court since 1898,[8] a formula soon to be
largely abandoned as a test of constitutionality. Dealing with
another point ignored by the majority, he attacked the doctrine
of the existence of a body of federal common law applied by
federal courts in diversity of citizenship cases without reference
to the relevant law of the states[9]—a position likewise soon to
be taken by the majority of the Court.[10] It was in such bold

taking of positions without firm reference to arguments in the cases at hand or to the status of precedents that Black disturbed Justice Stone and others of his brethren who were more concerned with legal niceties.[11] Even more boldly, and this time without any real prospect of ultimate success, Black challenged the position taken half a century earlier that a corporation was a person within the meaning of the Fourteenth Amendment and as such was entitled to the protection of due process of law.[12]

While this crusading innovator was jarring the nerves of his more sedate brethren, further changes in the personnel of the Hughes Court came rapidly. Justice Sutherland retired in January 1938, to be replaced immediately by Stanley Reed, the Solicitor General who had presented many of the government's New Deal cases before the Court. Though less colorful and less aggressive than Black, Reed could be expected in general to look favorably on New Deal policies and measures. Justice Cardozo died in 1939, to be replaced by Felix Frankfurter of the Harvard Law School, who had intimate connection with New Deal programs and personnel. But Frankfurter was devoted, as Black was not, to the niceties, the finer shadings of judicial performance, and was later to become known as a leading advocate of "judicial self restraint" on the part of the courts.

The same year brought the replacement of Justice Brandeis by William O. Douglas, chairman of the Securities and Exchange Commission and formerly a professor at Yale Law School. An ardent New Dealer and civil libertarian, a critic of bigness in business and of the exercise of arbitrary power by government, Douglas was to be for some years a close associate of Black and the one colleague to remain on the Court with him long after others had departed.

Justice Butler was replaced in 1940 by Frank Murphy, then Attorney General of the United States and a former governor of Michigan. Murphy had a deep commitment to civil liberties and throughout his nine-year period on the Court was to be the most vigorous defender of the rights of individuals. When Justice McReynolds retired in 1941, he was replaced for a year by James F. Byrnes of South Carolina, who after brief judicial service resigned to aid the administration in its war effort.

Byrnes was replaced on the Court by Wiley B. Rutledge, dean of the law school at Washington University, St. Louis, who served until 1949, and who was always closely associated with Justice Murphy in the defense of civil liberties.

At the retirement of Chief Justice Hughes in 1941, only Justices Stone and Roberts remained of his pre-1937 associates. Roberts remained until 1945, finding himself more and more isolated among the newcomers. To replace Hughes, Stone, who was a Republican and a Coolidge appointee, was promoted to the Chief Justiceship. At the same time Robert H. Jackson, then Attorney General, a New Dealer, and a defender of the Roosevelt plan to pack the Court, was added to the membership. By this time Justice Black, who had begun as the lone representative of a new regime, found himself surrounded by men largely bearing the New Deal stamp. There were, to be sure, differences among them from the outset, and some very sharp differences were to develop between Black and some of the others, particularly Justices Frankfurter and Jackson.

But whatever the differences among them, the New Deal Justices were concerned with revitalization of constitutional thinking. The pattern of judicial decisions was to be brought more into harmony with the necessities of the times. The new approach had both positive and negative aspects. On the positive side, it marked recognition of the fact that government must often promote and manage, that it must make choices not merely between right and wrong, as in the exercise of police powers, but between alternatives not intrinsically good or bad. Positive guidance of the social order was provided partly through exercise of the taxing, borrowing, and spending powers, which (at least as to spending from the general funds in the treasury) were largely beyond the scope of judicial power.[13] Among the tendencies requiring rationalization by the Court was the expanding use of the commerce power as a source of major control of enterprise of many kinds, extending far beyond the scope of the control permitted in earlier years. This expansion began toward the end of the term preceding that at which Justice Black joined the Court.[14] Thereafter it was extended to regulation of hours, wages, and working conditions of labor, to control of agricultural production through limitations on shipments in interstate commerce, to regulation or dissolution of holding companies, to oversight of sale of securities in the interstate market, and to many other areas. The New Deal Justices had little trouble finding grounds to support such exercise of positive power, even though they did have more than the expected amount of trouble in agreeing on the writing of opinions.

For the judiciary, the negative aspect of the New Deal was implied in the positive aspect. Courts were to remember, as Justice Stone had reminded in 1936, that they were not "the only agency of government that must be assumed to have the capacity to govern."[15] Courts were not to convert their essentially negative function into performance aimed at dominance of government policy.[16] Courts, having the last word in constitutional interpretation, were to engage in constant self-scrutiny to insure the practice of self-restraint. Black's previous implied position to the contrary, judges were to view with skepticism the tendency to work their own predilections into the status of constitutional principles. In the interpretation of the Constitution and statutes, the benefit of doubt was to be given to positions taken by the "political" branches of government in which, by contrast with the judiciary, public policy was rightly to be made.

Commitment to judicial self-restraint was perhaps mainly an attitude towards novel federal legislation stemming from the depression and the New Deal response. But the attitude also extended, consistently, to state action. With respect to certain categories of cases, this meant a whole new constitutional approach and the overruling of many past decisions. For example, "substantive due process" in economic matters had evolved over a number of decades not merely to insure correct "process" but to prevent substantive action deemed detrimental to property. With the establishment of the New Deal Court, substantive due process for the protection of property rights virtually disappeared from the texts of opinions and eventually largely disappeared from the arguments of counsel. Subsequently, when not running into conflict with federal programs in the field, states found themselves before a judicial green light in the exercise of powers of regulation of business and industry, in sharp contrast with the earlier restrictions of due process of law the Court had imposed on them.

Yet there were important limits to the removal of judicial fetters on both state and federal action. Even as the Supreme Court gave approval to unprecedented regulation of property, it was showing increased sensitivity to the rights of the accused and to personal and civil rights of various other kinds, with incidental if vigorously expressed differences among the Justices as to the rightful scope of the Court's intervention— giving rise to still further controversy over judicial self-restraint and judicial activism. More significant at this point, however, in a partly chronological treatment of the Black Court, is the shading of the constitutional problems of the New Deal period into those of the period of World War II.

The Effects of War on the Judicial Process

By contrast with its impact on political functions, war tends to crowd judicial functions into the background. It is not that dockets are less crowded or that judges have less to do. The reverse is more likely to be true. But in time of war people are less tolerant of the slowness and carefulness of judicial processes, and a smaller percentage of issues vital to public policy are likely to be entrusted to the judiciary. Even so, war also tends to give rise to peculiar judicial responsibilities, both for the war period and for the years to follow. During World War II it was only natural that the broadening of governmental powers via taxing and spending and the regulation of commerce should be extended under the war powers. The repercussions of the combination traveled far down into the pattern of civilian life as a result of the widened scope of immunity from judicial control. The Supreme Court refused to take over from Congress responsibility for determining prices to be paid to would-be profiteers; it also refused to interfere with price restraints when Congress did not see fit to provide for them. When without adequate legislation the government sought by suit to recover from a steel company the exorbitant profits it made on a government contract, the Court, speaking through Justice Black, held that protection of the government's bargaining position was the responsibility of Congress and not of the courts.[17] On the other hand, when Congress did exercise its authority by providing for the renegotiation of war contracts under which exorbitant profits might have been collected, the Court unanimously refused to interfere with this alleged invasion of the right of the protesting corporation to the full benefits of its initial contract.[18]

Current trends in constitutional development were further advanced during the war period in that the Court used the war situation as a means of devitalizing the concept of "fair return on a fair value" as a measure of the power of government to delimit prices. It held, for example, that a nation that could demand the lives of its men and women in war was not obligated on the domestic front to allow to each landlord the privilege of charging prices to insure a fair return on the value of his property—in the face of the protest of Justice Roberts that in the given situation the statute created "personal government by a petty tyrant instead of government by law."[19]

As against the pre-New Deal Court's restrictive attitude toward the delegation of legislative power to the executive, the new Court had already begun shifting to broader concepts, and during the war it still further relaxed restrictions.[20] In the international area it allowed extensive disposition of rights of private property by mere executive agreement and without respect to the treaty power.[21] The eventual curb on the Executive branch came only during the Korean war period when the Court, speaking through Justice Black, denied the power of the President to seize and operate steel mills for the national defense in the absence of a statute authorizing such action.[22]

With regard to the restriction of property rights and the enhancement of executive power, the Court during the war period followed a natural course of development stemming from the New Deal. But it had no immediate body of knowledge or precedent for dealing with personal rights or the rights of the accused in such a period. World War I certainly provided no precedent for determining the rights of the Japanese-American minority on the American West Coast. No parallel existed for trial by military commission of military

agents of the enemy sent secretly to the United States to operate
out of uniform as saboteurs. No precedent had been established for determining when and how military tribunals of the
victors might punish the leaders of defeated enemy forces, or
for determining the rights of such defendants at the time
of trial. Such limited precedents as were to be found anywhere in this area were to be derived from the Civil War
period when the whole body of circumstance was very different from that of the 1940's.

Members of the Supreme Court thus approached war issues
without the sureness of touch which most of them had in
interpreting the Constitution merely to meet peacetime needs
of an increasingly industrialized and interrelated society. While
the Justices had strong convictions about the rightness of the
American cause and about the constitutional power to wage
war to a successful conclusion, they had not placed the exercise
of war powers into a consistent pattern of overall constitutionality. Most of them, indeed, probably accepted the
traditional assumption that war marked an aberration in the
normal pattern of American life; that the exercise of war
powers, while of course constitutional in the immediate context of a particular war that had to be waged, must not be
allowed to corrupt the stream of peacetime development.
While a loyal judiciary must not obstruct the waging of the
war, it must also refrain from ratifying procedures not consistent with our democratic system, geared primarily to a
regime of peace.

So it was that the Court, with eight sitting members, unanimously upheld the right of the Executive branch to provide
for military trial of saboteur members of the forces of the
enemy, while concealing great differences among the Justices
as to the nature and source of the power exercised.[23] With
evidence of painful qualms the Court allowed the military
to enforce a curfew against Japanese-Americans in critical
West Coast areas.[24] With Justice Black as its spokesman, it
went further in *Korematsu v. United States*[25] by upholding
military removal of such Americans from the areas involved.
The several opinions—the opinion of the Court, a concurring
opinion and three dissenting opinions—showed obvious discomfort on the part of the Court. Justice Black cautiously

limited the Court's holding to "the exclusion order as of the time it was made and when the petitioner violated it." Justice Roberts protested on one set of grounds and Justice Murphy on another; Justice Jackson pointed to the heart of the judicial problem by urging that the Court not put itself in a position wherein it must either uphold questionable military measures taken in the heat of the conflict, thereby reading into them constitutional acceptability, or find them unconstitutional and thereby perhaps jeopardize the war effort. He sought a carefully delimited middle ground: "if we cannot confine military expedients by the Constitution, neither would I distort the Constitution to approve all that the military may deem expedient."[26]

It was not clear that the Court had escaped the dilemma highlighted by Justice Jackson, for all Justice Black's caution and the concurring comment of Justice Frankfurter that "To find that the Constitution does not forbid the military measures now complained of does not carry with it the approval of that which Congress and the Executive did."[27] As for the constitutionality of wholesale detention of Japanese-Americans in detention camps, the Court never had to pass upon it. The only case approaching the subject involved detention not of such persons generally but of a woman who had already received a loyalty clearance. In this instance the Court avoided the constitutional question by holding that the relevant statute and executive orders did not authorize such detention.[28]

The ugly subject of treason gave rise to painstaking research and argument, in one case resulting in a five to four decision.[29] The principal demonstration from all the effort involved in that case was that evidence must be very clear indeed if such a conviction was to be upheld. As during World War I, it often seemed expedient for the government to seek punishment not for treason but for some other offense not directly specified in the Constitution, such as sedition or espionage. In any event, more revealing of the Court's determination to curb the operations of military tribunals in civilian areas was a holding, through Justice Black, that the suspension of the privilege of the writ of habeas corpus in Hawaii and the partial continued use of military tribunals in basically civil matters had been unduly extended beyond the period of the local military crisis. Civil courts and their procedural safeguards were indispensable to our system of government, wrote Justice Black, in interpreting the Hawaiian Organic Act. Military tribunals had no such standing. The military was always to be kept in subordination to the laws of the country.[30]

In a saboteur case near the beginning of the war, the Court had established the precedent of determining the propriety of a military tribunal's jurisdiction without passing on the merits of the military action once jurisdiction had been established. It rendered the same service after the war when a military tribunal in the Philippines, then American territory, tried and convicted for war crimes General Tomoyuki Yamashita, the commander of the Japanese forces in the Philippines. However, it denied leave to file petitions for habeas corpus from an *international* military commission in Tokyo set up to try war criminals, holding that the tribunal was not an American tribunal even though American officers played a part in it, and that it was therefore not in any way subject to the Supreme Court's jurisdiction.[31] Even though the Court had for a time carried on its work without the services of one of its members, Justice Jackson, in order that he might participate in the Nuremberg trials in the European war theater, it would not admit such kinship with any non-American tribunal as to justify a right of appeal. Neither would the Court inquire into the jurisdiction of a strictly American tribunal operating in a foreign country on a habeas corpus petition from members of the German armed forces who had never been domiciled in the United States. The petitioners in such a case had been tried and convicted, by an American military commission, for carrying on war in China against the United States after surrender by the German high command. Here the military tribunal operated on foreign soil against non-Americans, so that no rights subject to the jurisdiction of an American civil tribunal were found to exist.[32] The Supreme Court, speaking through Justice Jackson, was careful to distinguish also between the rights of American citizens and aliens dealt with abroad, noting that Americans had rights stemming from citizenship itself and not merely from the location of the military agency. Three dissenting Justices, however, led by Justice Black, contended that the right to equal justice through the civil courts extended not only to American citizens but to all persons everywhere who were subject to trial by American military tribunals. It remains to be seen whether the majority or the minority position will mark the course of the future.

It is clear that amid the uncertainties of the war situation the Supreme Court tried hard to preserve basic rights of persons while avoiding embarrassment to American military operations. Even so, with the perspective of post-war years, discomfort was felt over some of the wartime decisions. Chief Justice Earl Warren remarked in 1962 that the Japanese-American curfew and removal cases had been regarded in some quarters as "aberrational." He noted, further, that the determination of military necessity had been in the hands of the Executive branch and not of the courts, and that because of the limitations under which the Supreme Court must sometimes operate in situations involving the military, other agencies of government must bear primary responsibility for determining whether particular actions were consonant with the Constitution. "To put it another way," said the Chief Justice, "the fact that the Court rules in a case like *Hirabayashi* that a given program is constitutional, does not necessarily answer the question whether, in a broader sense, it actually is."[33] He voiced the traditional American belief that "War is, of course, a pathological condition for our Nation."[34] He seems to have assumed—and to have found the assumption verified in the experience of World War II—that the Supreme Court as well as other agencies of government was affected by that national pathological condition. While Justice Black, a participant in the wartime decisions as Chief Justice Warren was not, published no such criticism of the Court's wartime handiwork, it may well be, in the light of his growing absolutism with respect to the Bill of Rights, that he has come to feel much as does the Chief Justice.

The Fear of Subversion

Growing in part out of World War II were the problems of enforcement of loyalty and prevention of subversion of American institutions. The grim period of witch hunting which reached its peak in the early or middle 1950's was personalized in the name of the late Senator Joseph McCarthy of Wisconsin who from his senatorial office led a crusade against Communists said to have infiltrated the federal government and various other institutions. But the movement was not exclusively that of a single effective demagogue and might well have occurred in some dimension had McCarthy never appeared on the scene. Contributing factors were the unspent emotions whipped up for the winning of the war, the confusion and uncertainty which followed that as any other war, the disillusionment with the achievement of idealistic war aims, the dropping of an "iron curtain" against the West by the Communist powers, the frustrating military involvement in Korea, and perhaps even the slowness of some people both in and out of government to recognize the renewed rivalry between the Communist powers and the West—to accept it and be properly watchful of alien and hostile influence and espionage within the government. In any event, the country found itself the host of a kind of crusade against an enemy that was seen everywhere and yet was hard to find, that was said to be engaged in subversion at critical points throughout the governmental structure and the business, labor, and educational institutions throughout the land.

For the Supreme Court, the strictly legal question was one of correct interpretation of the Constitution and statutes amid this popular crusade against a subversive enemy. For observers the question might be phrased somewhat differently. Would the Court bend with the sentiments of the times, as it tended to do in time of war, or would it hold itself as aloof as possible in exercise of judicial self-restraint, or would it wave the banner of freedom in terms of the Bill of Rights and stand firmly against all encroachments on traditional liberties?

Despite the lack of extreme differences among the Justices appointed by Presidents Roosevelt and Truman, it was inevitable that they should differ about degrees of protection given by the Court and about matters of legal phrasing. It was likewise inevitable that debate would be renewed over the implications of the clear and present danger doctrine which had its initial statement by Justice Holmes in a World War I case decided in 1921.[35] The rule announced then was that the power of Congress to suppress speech and publication, curbed by the First Amendment, depended on whether the prohibited words were so used as to create a clear and present danger of bringing about evils Congress had an inherent right to prevent. Although the decision in the case was unanimous—upholding the restriction there involved—the Court was not thereafter able to agree fully on the meaning of the rule. While it was an attractive symbol for moderate liberals, including many admirers of Justices Holmes and Brandeis, it was disapproved by judges and others at both extremes of the legal-political spectrum. Justice Black seemed to use it without reluctance in 1941 in a five-to-four decision protecting the right to criticize a decision of a California court. What finally emerged from the several cases making use of the doctrine was "a working principle that the substantive evil must be extremely serious and the degree of imminence extremely high before utterances can be punished."[36] Black eventually rejected it altogether as not consistent with the absolute prohibitions of the First Amendment.[37]

Part of the concern of liberals lay in the fear that, with the rising tensions of the cold war, the rule might provide an entering wedge for restraint of individual freedom which, if allowed in any degree, could not be kept within bounds. Conservatives, on the other hand, saw "clear and present" as requiring very broad interpretation so that a sufficient scope for government control could be rationalized. In the 1951 *Dennis* case decision, upholding the conspiracy conviction of a group of Communist leaders, the Court, with no majority opinion, left the doctrine in utter confusion. Here Chief Justice Vinson, who had succeeded Chief Justice Stone in 1946, challenged the absolutist claim made in the name of the First Amendment. "Nothing is more certain in modern society," he contended, "than the principle that there are no absolutes, that a name, a phrase, a standard has meaning only when associated with the considerations which gave birth to the nomenclature. . . . To those who would paralyze our government in the face of impending threat by encasing it in a semantic straitjacket we must reply that all concepts are relative."[38]

While Chief Justice Vinson spoke for only four of the six Justices who voted to uphold conviction, it is to be noted that even Justice Douglas, in dissent, admitted that "The freedom to speak is not absolute."[39] Justice Black's dissenting opinion noted the majority's repudiation of the clear and present danger doctrine and then indicated his belief that the doctrine did not implement the full protection implicit in the Bill of Rights. He saw the decision of the Court as watering down the First Amendment "so that it amounts to little more than an admonition to Congress."[40]

Similar differences on the Court appeared in other areas. In a case holding notice and hearing not necessary for deportation of an alien enemy, Justice Black dissented and expressed the belief that "because of today's opinion individual liberty will be less secure tomorrow than it was yesterday."[41]

Still other cases brought the cold war conflict into Court. In a dissent against requirement of non-Communist affidavits of labor union leaders, Justice Black proclaimed that "Fears of alien ideologies have frequently agitated the nation and inspired legislation aimed at suppressing advocacy of these ideologies. At such times the fog of public excitement obscures the ancient landmarks set up in our Bill of Rights. Yet then, of all times, should this Court adhere most closely to the course they mark."[42] Embroilment in controversy over the "Attorney General's list," a list of allegedly subversive organizations used to stigmatize the loyalty of government employees and others, caused further strife on the Court, with inconclusive results as far as future challenges to loyalty would be concerned.[43]

In the thick of the cold war controversy was the Committee on Un-American Activities of the House of Representatives, a hardy perennial of its kind dating from the 1930's and in all periods finding subversives, usually Communists, in every agency and every situation investigated. In the cold war atmosphere the Committee received more attention and larger appropriations and was able to create more discomfort for more people by its free-wheeling methods of investigation and exposure, being matched only by a similar committee of the Senate headed for a time by Senator McCarthy himself. Of course, investigating agencies in other departments of the government and in the states were also somewhat similarly engaged.

If for no other reason than that it takes time to get controversial issues before it, the Supreme Court played little part in appraising the work of such committees during the more intense portion of the McCarthy crusade. When cases dealing with the scope and methods of legislative investigation finally came to the Court, it was headed by a new Chief Justice. Earl Warren, appointed by President Eisenhower in 1953, was more devoted to civil liberties than Chief Justice Vinson had been, though he lacked the fervor of now departed Justices Murphy and Rutledge. The Warren Court found difficult the task of leaving open the route to effective legislative inquiry while at the same time curbing the grossness of trial by inquiry and the making of political capital out of sensational disclosures. In the *Watkins*[44] case in 1957, Chief Justice Warren, speaking for a majority of the Court, stated a broad denial of the power of a Congressional committee to expose for the sake of exposure and to compel testimony without showing the pertinency of the questions to the inquiry the committee was authorized to make. Justice Frankfurter joined with a more cautious concurring opinion and Justice Clark, appointed in 1949 by President Truman, at the time when Justices Murphy and Rutledge left the Court, criticized the majority opinion for "its mischievous curbing of the informing function of Congress."[45]

Liberals cheered by the *Watkins* decision had their hopes chilled two years later in the *Barenblatt*[46] case. The previous minority became the majority and upheld another investigation. The Court did not here reject the pertinency requirement but did find relevancy and power to investigate. Justice Harlan, a 1955 Eisenhower appointee, and increasingly an advocate of conservative positions, spoke for the Court. Where Congress had the power to investigate, he contended, a congressional purpose of exposure was not to be taken as showing that there was no legislative purpose. As for rights under the First Amendment, he concluded that "the balance between the individual and the governmental interests here at stake must be struck in favor of the latter, and that therefore the provisions of the First Amendment have not been offended."[47]

Justice Black attacked use of the device of balancing where the absolutes of the First Amendment were involved and predicted that unless the Court returned to the position that the Bill of Rights meant what it said "our great charter of liberty will be more honored in the breach than in the observance."[48] As for the contention that the rights protected were to be balanced against the necessity for survival, he believed that the free play of ideas was itself essential to that survival. If we began to punish speech then "we cannot honestly proclaim ourselves to be a free Nation and we have lost what the Founders of this land risked their lives and their sacred honor to defend."[49]

Differences in the Court's delineations of the scope of power to be allowed to legislative investigating committees have continued throughout the Black period. On the whole the Congressional right to investigate has not been seriously curbed. Yet again and again the Court has found ways of defeating punishment for contempt when witnesses have refused to answer questions put to them. Justices operating from opposite sides of the issue have achieved an uncertain though persistent equilibrium which leaves government largely free but which eventually if only partially protects the questioned persons who, refusing to answer, become the accused and sometimes the convicted. Whether or not "balancing of values" is an appropriate concept, it is hard to avoid the belief that it is a kind of balancing process that shapes the law as it is expounded by the Court.

Emerging Perspectives of Law and Rights

The first half of Justice Black's thirty years on the Court seems to fall into distinct periods: The New Deal, World War II, and the McCarthy period. The later years lend themselves less well to such periodization. The reason for the difficulty may be simply that we are too close to these years to see them in perspective, or it may be that the diversity of subject matter is too great ever to permit of such breaking into periods. Quite possibly these later years belong in a period which also includes the years immediately ahead of us and which will in due time end in some clearly discernible transition.

In any event, some significant parallel developments do characterize these later years. They include(increased emphasis on the constitutional rights of the accused, new lines of demarcation between governmental activity and the province of religion, vigorous assertion of rights of racial equality, assertion of equal rights in legislative apportionment between rural and urban areas, and renewed concern about antitrust enforcement amid ever more rapid consolidation of various forms of economic enterprise.) Decisions in these fields have involved new controversies over judicial activism and judicial self-restraint.

A further generalization can be offered about the recent cases in these fields, a generalization that seems now to have special significance even though it could have been made in similar words about almost any period in the history of the Court, even as far back as the regime of Chief Justice Marshall. We are very much aware of the vast difference between our times and those in which the Constitution and its early amendments were drafted, and of the difficulty of using the intentions of the Framers as a basis for decisions on constitutional questions today. We are aware that if ours is to be a living Constitution it must be a Constitution that grows and adapts to changing conditions, and that it must grow and adapt by a process of interpretation in which the Supreme Court is the final interpreter. But because today's conditions are so different from those confronting the Framers, and even from the conditions surrounding many of the judicial precedents to be taken into account, the Supreme Court sits less and less as a mere interpreter of pre-existing constitutional law. Rather it sits as a kind of continuing constitutional convention which has no need ever of directly referring its amendments back to the people or to the states for ratification. Furthermore, while there is usually some rationalization of new departures in terms of established constitutional principles, decisions in the designated fields sometimes read like fiat determinations made without reference either to documented history or to clearly expressed principle.

This generalization, to repeat, could be made or have been made by a person living in almost any period of American history but it seems especially authentic today amid current awareness of social turmoil and transition. Its validity for the present is perhaps increased by the simple fact that we are at a greater distance from the founding period than ever before, and by the apparent fact that changes are coming thicker and faster than at any previous time in our history. We as a people are moving further and further away from our historical base; indeed, we are increasingly different as a people, as a society, as an economy. Even the abstract principles of liberty and equality and social organization, which we call on to implement the opportunity of each person to live his own life to the fullest extent and with greatest possible richness, must be given legal content in terms of today's possible pattern of living. George Washington, Benjamin Franklin, Thomas Jefferson, James Madison, and Chief Justices Marshall and Taney have only limited guidance for us when it comes to applying principles enunciated in their times to the conditions of the 1960's. We sense that Justice Black and his brethren must often proceed pretty much on their own, for all their obeisance to the founding fathers and to past precedents; and we watch them with anxiety and with readiness to protest, to demand that Congress "impeach Earl Warren" or that in some way the Supreme Court be "kept in its place"—a place which we ourselves cannot define except for some reference to some mythical "good old days" which we assume must have existed some time. This is not to imply that the Court is always right and the critics always wrong, but rather to suggest that both the Court and its critics are apt to find it expedient sometimes to pretend to a certainty they do not feel, and thus occasionally to sound forth with unbecoming shrillness.

The realm of the rights of the accused could be characterized as one of peculiar difficulty for the Court at the mid-sixties were it not that formidable difficulties appear in other realms as well. Organized crime has built itself into an industry involving billions of dollars with financial permeation far down into the body of legitimate business. Crime in the streets and individual crime generally have increased in appalling degrees. Yet it is also true that the increase in crime has led to the building up of law enforcement machinery likewise almost to industrial proportions. State and local police and prosecutors, and the various groups of federal policing and investigatory agencies and prosecuting officers, have accumulated a body of knowledge and skills for manipulating people or acquiring information of dimensions that overwhelm the private individual on whom their activities are brought to bear. On the whole the power of government is dominant save as crime becomes organized and interconnected with legitimate social mechanisms, including governmental agencies themselves.

It is in the light of the fact that law enforcement machinery is at once inadequate to deal with organized crime and too large and impersonal and ruthless to deal with individuals acting alone that the courts must interpret the powers and the prohibitions of the Constitution. Since the development of skills and techniques for dealing with crime must be left largely to the political branches of government, the power of the Supreme Court, here as in many other spheres, expresses itself uniquely in cutting clear the rights to be protected. So it is that in recent years the Court has revealed increased sensitivity to the rights involved in search and seizure, in arrest with or without warrant, in requirements as to prompt arraignment, in use of confessions directly or indirectly coerced, in right to counsel, and in many other areas. Restrictions on the states as well as on the federal government are involved. While Justice Black has not been able to persuade a majority of his brethren that the adoption of the Fourteenth Amendment in and of itself made all provisions of the first eight amendments directly applicable to the states,[50] much the same result has been achieved indirectly by the expansion of the due process clause of the Fourteenth Amendment to include much of the content of the first eight amendments. The First Amendment, for example, which begins with the provision that "Congress shall make no law" is also read as if it said that "No state shall." Additionally, the passive voice restrictions of other amendments, hitherto held applicable only to the federal government,[51] are in large part now read as directly applying to the states.

In recent years the Supreme Court has been tightening restrictions on both the federal government and the states in the realm of trial procedures and of procedures for the collection of evidence that may be used in court. In 1963, for example, in *Gideon v. Wainwright*,[52] Justice Black won a battle he had lost in 1942, in that he was authorized to say for the Court that the Sixth Amendment right to counsel extended via the Fourteenth Amendment in state cases not only to capital offenses but to those that were noncapital as well. As a specific result of this decision a man convicted of breaking into a poolroom was able, with the aid of highly competent counsel, to win an acquittal at a new trial.[53]

Again, in 1964 in *Escobedo v. Illinois*,[54] the Court by a five to four vote overturned a conviction based in part on the results of questioning after the accused had been denied a request for consultation with his attorney. Then in 1966 the Court, by a division that again was in part five to four, in *Miranda v. Arizona,* held that the Fifth Amendment prohibition of use of coerced confessions was violated when conviction was based on use of evidence gotten by police interrogation without access to counsel and proper warning to the accused that he was entitled to remain silent.[55]

The *Miranda* decision was important not only for its specific holding but also for what Justice Harlan in dissent called "the Court's new constitutional code of rules for confessions,"[56] and what Justice White, also in dissent, called "the Court's constitutional straitjacket which forecloses more discriminating treatment by legislative or rule-making pronouncements."[57] In that case, Chief Justice Warren, speaking for a majority that included Justice Black, noted that the *Escobedo* case had been subject to spirited debate with a variety of judicial and scholarly interpretations, with extensive citations for illustration. The Court had agreed to hear the *Miranda* case and others decided with it "in order further to explore some facts of the problems, thus exposed, of applying the privilege against self-incrimination to in-custody interrogation, and to give concrete constitutional guidelines for law enforcement agencies and courts to follow."[58]

The elaborate discussion which followed, dealing not merely with the specific cases but with the rules to be followed in questioning prisoners, warning of right to silence and right to counsel and other matters, did indeed have much the appearance of a code, as described by the dissenters. It stood as a major legislative endeavor by a tribunal with primarily judicial responsibilities. The judicial presentation of such a code, coupled with the fact that as a matter of expediency the newly declared body of (presumably always existing) constitutional law was not allowed to be applied retroactively, highlighted the change in the recent era of the pattern of performance by the highest Court in the land. More and more the Court seemed to be struggling toward the position of a positive agency of government, an agency defining rights and duties in advance of individual clashes under the adversary system by which our courts have traditionally operated. In determining the rights of the accused it is apparent that the Court in Justice Black's later years is becoming a very different tribunal from the one we have hitherto known—though it is again to be noted that some of the critical decisions and lines of strategy have been determined by the narrow margin of five to four.

Extending the Constitution

While issues involving the rights of the accused forced themselves on the Supreme Court by virtue of changes in the social order, the Court during the same period seems to have reached out for the opportunity to make changes in a very different field, that of church-state relations or the place of religion in a society increasingly subject to the overall supervision of government. In this field it has not gone to the extent of drafting a code, as it seemed to do in the *Miranda* case discussed above, but it has greatly elaborated the body of judge-made rules said to stem from the First Amendment with its guarantee of freedom of religion and its prohibition of the establishment of religion. Here again, despite the frequent use of judicial opinions of early American history—or of "law office" history at any rate—the constitutional holdings of the Court are not to be seen as clearly and necessarily dictated either by the Framers or by the authors of early precedents. For example, nothing in the minds of Constitution-makers or early judges determined that state relief contributions must be distributed in such a way as to avoid discrimination against persons unwilling to work on Saturdays because of their religious beliefs.[59] Here, as in other areas, the Court projected its decision outward from the Constitution but projected it so far as to be beyond the scope of considerations of religion that may have been in the minds of the Framers.

Where religion is concerned, the Court in the Black period seems to have launched upon a program of *laissez-faire,* and this at a time wherein *laissez-faire* with respect to property has become obsolete. Freedom of religion is to be pressed to its extreme at the same time that governmental connection with religion is to be kept at a minimum. Our forefathers would no doubt have been amazed to be told that in the 1960's a Sunday closing law could be upheld only because it provided a uniform day of rest and recreation and not because of the values inherent in our religious heritage[60]—that such a measure would have been unconstitutional if grounded in religious purposes. With Justice Black as an ardent participant the Court has extended the establishment clause beyond the strict establishment of a church or a religion, according to the customs of the eighteenth century and earlier, and has applied it to all government aid for any religious purpose whatsoever, however nondiscriminatory. Committing itself to this broad interpretation of the clause, the Court then faced the necessity of determining whether government aid given where religion was some place in the offing was aid actually to religion or merely to persons having incidental religious interests—as in the instance of payment of bus fares for children getting secular education in parochial schools.[61] Some would no doubt say that the thinking was more his own than that of the founding fathers when in 1962 Justice Black said for the Court that "The First Amendment was added to the Constitution to stand as a guarantee that neither the power nor the prestige of the Federal Government would be used to control, support or influence the kinds of prayer the American people can say."[62]

It remains to be seen whether the Court in this area has read the book of the times better than the books of history or, in either case, whether it has served the needs of the people by its line of interpretation. In any event, this much must be said in defense of the Court: For all its ability to postpone action on troublesome issues until it has had time to look at them critically, basic issues do have to be faced eventually and decisions have to be made whether or not they stand up under the scrutiny of critics in future years.

The racial issue, a persistent one in American constitutional history, reached crisis dimensions after World War II. Nonwhite races surged forward in other parts of the world and achieved importance in world opinion, and American Negroes, shaken out of their static condition by the war itself, by the process of industrialization, and by development of educated leadership, began to make effective demands for equal treatment and political influence. Without indicating and perhaps without knowing the full extent of the constitutional revolution in the offing, the Court in 1950 undermined the separate but equal doctrine which had prevailed since 1896. Speaking unanimously through Chief Justice Vinson, it found a lack of equality between separate law schools maintained by a state for white and colored people, doing so in such a way as to cast doubt on the feasibility of any linkage between equality on the one hand and racial segregation on the other, at least at the level of higher and professional education.[63]

It is a familiar story that four years later in the *Brown*[64] case, and other cases decided with it, argued first before the Vinson Court and then before the Court now spoken of in the name of Chief Justice Warren, the issue had to be dealt with at the level of elementary education. Unable to find in the history of the Fourteenth Amendment intention one way or another as to outlawing segregation in education, Chief Justice Warren, speaking for a unanimous Court as Vinson had done earlier, built on the Vinson precedent and looked to the impact of segregation on the isolated persons. The conclusion was that "Separate educational facilities are inherently unequal." At the same time, in a District of Columbia case to which the equal protection clause did not apply, the Court read the same barrier to segregation in education into the due process clause of the Fifth Amendment, remarking that "Classifications based solely upon race must be scrutinized with particular care, since they are contrary to our traditions and hence constitutionally suspect."[65]

With the Supreme Court's finding in the *Brown* case that separate educational facilities were inherently unequal, and that state separation violated the equal protection clause, it was only natural that segregation in public transportation and recreation should likewise be challenged on the same ground. The Court had come under immediate fire for its alleged lack of legal ground for the *Brown* holding and its resort to what it called "psychological knowledge." Perhaps for this reason, it did not in these adjacent areas attempt to demonstrate, as it had done in the field of education, that segregation in transportation and in various forms of recreation was inherently unequal. Instead, by per curiam dispositions of cases appealed to it, the Court merely cited the *Brown* case in affirming or reversing lower court decisions with the implication that the same inherent inequality here prevailed. As a result of this approach, the appearance of fiat performance, as distinguished from reasoned application of legal precedents, was heightened.[66]

It is, of course, impossible to estimate the variety of personal ingredients that went into the Court's unanimous decision in the *Brown* case, whereby the Court assumed leadership, for a time, in the reduction of racial inequities and the improvement in race relations, which leadership ought to have been taken by the Legislative and Executive branches of the government. In any event, as Congress by the Civil Rights Act of 1964 and the Executive by various activities assumed their rightful role, it became apparent that some members of the Court were conscious of other rights involved in racial controversies. Against a background of demonstrations, riots, and sit-in performances, Justice Black pointed out in an interview in 1962 that while the primacy of the Bill of Rights is to be stressed, we do have a system of property that limits the rights of nonpossessors. He recognized, for example, the right of a man to make a speech against the Supreme Court, but not the right to invade the home of a member of the Court for the purpose of making the speech there.[67] With Justices Harlan and White in a 1964 case, Black dissented from the Court's refusal to enforce trespass laws against Negro demonstrators trying to coerce a restaurant into serving them. He contended that "none of our prior cases has held that a person's right to freedom of expression carries with it a right to force a private property owner to furnish his property as a platform to criticize the property owner's use of that property."[68]

Later, while concurring with the Court that Congress had the power to outlaw segregation in a motel[69] and a restaurant[70] serving interstate commerce, he protested at the eagerness of his brethren in extending a federal statute backward to invalidate convictions under state laws for prior sit-in demonstrations. While he had apparently abandoned none of his commitment to equal racial rights as against segregation at the hands of government, he may have welcomed the opportunity to stress the variety and complexity of the body of rights to be protected by the law. In other words, he showed awareness of a responsibility for keeping in broad judicial perspective the manifold facets of law, in contradistinction to judicial sponsorship or favoritism in limited areas such as that of desegregation.

Although some saw the *Brown* decision of 1954 as a kind of Magna Carta for the Negro, with the elimination of all major race problems swiftly to follow, it is now apparent that the decisions of that year and of the ensuing decade dealt only with the beginning of the task of resolution. The ultimate judgment of the Court's actions will probably be arrived at not so much in terms of orthodox and unorthodox conceptions of the proper role of the judiciary as in terms of our ultimate experience at working out legal and practical solutions, not yet in sight, of interracial problems. If the judiciary itself engages in a reappraisal of its own past performance in segregation cases, the reappraisal is likely to be delayed long enough that it will be made not by the judges responsible for the initial decisions but by successors appointed and living through periods greatly different from the period of the 1950's—as was the case of the Court's reappraisal in 1954 of the separate-but-equal doctrine of 1896.

In 1962 the Supreme Court entered the "political thicket" of reapportionment[71] against which Justice Frankfurter warned it in 1946 and which it had then refused to enter.[72] Its change of attitude was compelled, once again, by mounting evils with which the states and the political branches of the federal government had failed to cope. The evils were inherent in the problems of rapid continuing urbanization in the United States, and extended to transportation, education, public health, welfare of the poor, and most other aspects of town and city life. Solution of those problems required recognition, imagination, and money in large quantities. In Congress and in the state legislatures, control tended to remain where it had traditionally been, in representation from rural areas; and rural domination almost always meant lack of adequate knowledge and understanding and, particularly, willingness to spend in the appropriate way the funds necessary to prevent the further decay of the hearts of cities, to arrest the multiple social and economic diseases of city life. Nevertheless, except in the minds of the most naive, there was no assurance that giving city people adequate legislative representation would necessarily bring the solution of urban problems. But it did seem clear that a solution would not be reached without such representation.

The 1962 decision of the Supreme Court having opened the door to litigation over equality in representation, suits were instituted in most of the states, involving representation either in state legislatures, or in congressional districts over which states were allowed to share jurisdiction with Congress. The several cases reaching the Supreme Court resulted in holdings that unequal representation in state legislatures denied equal protection of the laws. Without requiring absolute numerical equality, the decisions went most of the way toward acceptance of the rule of "one man, one vote." Said Chief Justice Warren for the Court in a major case, "The Equal Protection Clause demands no less than substantially equal state legislative representation for all citizens, of all places as well as all races."[73]

The equal protection clause would have provided a sufficient basis for invalidating congressional districting to the extent that inequality was the product of state action. It was at least theoretically possible, however, that Congress would take congressional representation into its own hands, and the equal protection clause did not extend to the federal government. As early as his dissenting opinion in 1946, Justice Black had taken the position that not only the equal protection restriction on the states, but also the constitutional requirement that representatives were to be chosen by the "people of the several states," made it necessary that all votes for members of Congress have approximately equal weight.[74] In 1964 he spoke for a majority of the Court in finding unconstitutional a Georgia apportionment scheme for election of congressmen. The decision was reached not on the basis of the equal protection clause but on the ground that Article I required that all votes for congressmen in a given state have approximate equality. While a constitutional historian has contended that in doing so Justice Black "mangled constitutional history,"[75] the task was performed to the satisfaction of six members of the Court. In any case, here as in other important cases, the Supreme Court was undoubtedly making as well as employing history.

The Supreme Court's plunge into the "political thicket" and its allegedly distorted use of history are not likely to determine final popular judgment of the Court's decision, whatever the reactions of that minority chiefly concerned with the purity of the judicial process. For those not concerned primarily with legal discipline as such, the question of greatest concern will be whether the newly given equality of legislative representation brings solution of crying urban problems. And yet, it is quite possible that the decisions here mentioned and others related to them, despite their stirring a momentary sense of outrage in some quarters and delight in others, will drift into the background of popular attention as their implementation becomes a matter of legislative and administrative routine. They may even be overshadowed by a growing belief that solutions depend less on mere numerical equality than upon the devising of new techniques and machinery, both locally and in federal-city relations, for the correction of urban ills. Most probably the routes followed will be multiple, will involve a merging of methods and techniques and beliefs, so that the effects of particular decisions will not be subject to clear delineation and the strategies by which the Court reached those decisions will become increasingly less relevant and ever more obscure.

From Constitution to Seminal Statutes

As with any comparable period in constitutional history, Justice Black's term on the Supreme Court is to be appraised primarily in terms of the *constitutional* interpretation afforded. However, particularly in recent decades, a great deal of the work of the Court has involved interpretation of broadly phrased regulatory or prohibitory statutes. Such statutes are often almost of the nature of constitutions; they call for the same resort to fundamental principles and beliefs as does the Constitution itself and require comparable study of the history of enactment and enforcement. Included with their subsequent amendments are the Interstate Commerce Act, the Sherman and Clayton Antitrust Acts, the Federal Trade Commission Act, the Railway Labor Act, the Federal Communications Act, the Securities and Exchange Act, the Federal Power Commission Act, the National Labor Relations Act—or Labor-Management Relations Act—and many others. Statutes overlap and interrelate, and agencies set up under them often have conflicting or at least competing jurisdiction. In deciding cases involving rivalries between such agencies, the attitudes of justices toward the agencies and their assignments seem to influence decisions. By contrast with the often prevailing assumption, for example, that the agencies most to be trusted are those well grooved in tradition, such as the Interstate Commerce Commission, Justice Black once remarked in conversation that there was something to be said for the argument that the only good administrative agency was a new agency. His point was that governing bodies, and particularly regulatory agencies with some fostering responsibilities, tend over the years to develop special constituences of their own and consequently tend to lose sight of the broader public interest initially meant to be served.

There does, at any rate, seem to be a difference in zeal between largely prohibitory agencies such as the Federal Trade Commission and the Antitrust Division of the Department of Justice on the one hand, and on the other hand agencies such as the Interstate Commerce Commission and the Board of Governors of the Federal Reserve System and the Comptroller of the Currency, which have fostering responsibilities for given businesses or industries or other activities. Whereas the former tend to exercise the negative powers of policing or to become somewhat comatose in their activities, the latter may take on as their own the interests of the groups to be regulated and conduct themselves accordingly.

A current illustration involving the Supreme Court lies in the field of antitrust enforcement, with particular reference to bank mergers. Whereas Congress over the years has given to the Justice Department and to the Federal Trade Commission the bulk of responsibility for coping with combinations in restraint of trade, control with respect to bank mergers is given, in varying situations, to the Federal Reserve System, the Comptroller of the Currency, and the Federal Deposit Insurance Corporation. For many years, attempts have been made in Congress to confer upon the Justice Department clearer antitrust jurisdiction over the highly technical field of banking which hitherto it had been assumed not to have. Coinciding with the beginning of the Kennedy administration in 1961, the Antitrust Division, with supporting appropriations from Congress, began to build up its personnel and to intensify antitrust activities in the face of a swelling tide of mergers in many fields. The Supreme Court, with gradually changing personnel, gave support to this movement by favorable decisions. Encouraged, the Antitrust Division instituted cases challenging bank mergers, in the face of the approval of such mergers by one or more of the fostering agencies. With protests from a Court minority led by Justice Harlan, the majority of the Court found both the Clayton Act and the Sherman Act applicable to bank mergers.[76] Congress, under special pressure from banking interests, modified the law where these interests were concerned, while the decisions of the Court, in this and other segments of the antitrust field, seemed to be aimed at slowing down the growth of corporate bigness.

The antitrust approach of a majority of the Court was articulated by Justice Black in 1966 as follows: "From this country's beginning there has been an abiding and widespread fear of the evils which flow from monopoly—that is the concentration of economic power in the hands of the few."[77] The purpose of the several antitrust measures, drafted in terms of such sentiment, was "to prevent economic concentration in the American economy by keeping a large number of small competitors in business."[78] Such antitrust sentiment, voiced at various times by Justices Black, Douglas, Brennan, and others, has no doubt existed in a high degree and continues to exist on the Court and in the country. Yet it runs counter to other sentiment, or at any rate to other events, which may well mark the wave of the future. The process of business combination, whether by merger or otherwise, continues in the face of the opposition. It is at times delayed in individual situations and periods by antitrust activity and antitrust decisions, but the integration of the American economy into ever larger units seems to be in prospect. This is not to say that the delaying action taken by the Department of Justice and the Court has no value but is merely to indicate that from the perspective of coming generations of citizens and judges the antitrust movement may come to be seen as a mark of antiquity. Here again, however, full and fair evaluation of the performance of Justice Black and his brethren must await the future.

The Personal Dimensions of History

Established since 1945 as the senior associate Justice on the Court, Justice Black is perhaps now less affected by personnel changes among his brethren than he might have been in earlier years. Yet new colleagues bring new ideas and approaches and new alignments in decisions, so that new appointments are always matters of concern. In the sequence of Chief Justices, he has served under Hughes, Stone, Vinson, and Warren. Stone, who never became fully reconciled to what he thought was Black's somewhat cavalier way of dealing with precedents and questions not fully argued before the Court, died in 1946. He was replaced by a Truman appointee and fellow Democrat, Fred M. Vinson of Kentucky. In a personal way Black got along well with his fellow southerner but found him a relativist in a very different philosophical camp. Vinson was succeeded in 1953 by Earl Warren, a liberal Republican and former Governor of California. Warren, similarly adventurous if lacking the precision of thought and dynamic force of Black, has provided companionship particularly in the field of civil liberties and antitrust enforcement. While there has been no succession to the almost exclusive preoccupation with civil rights represented down to 1949 by Justices Murphy and Rutledge, somewhat close have been William J. Brennan, Jr., appointed by President Eisenhower in 1956, Arthur Goldberg, a Kennedy appointee, who after a three year period beginning in 1962 left for the United Nations, and Abe Fortas, appointed in 1965 by President Johnson. The retirement of Justice Frankfurter in 1962 removed a powerful presence and a frequent critic of Black positions, leaving Black unquestionably the Court's outstanding figure. John M. Harlan, appointed in 1955, reflects Frankfurter's concern about judicial self-restraint, and in business matters is apt to be joined by Potter Stewart, another Eisenhower choice, appointed in 1958, but Harlan wields little of the influence of the scholarly professor whose mantle he seeks to carry. Byron White, appointed in 1962 by President Kennedy, takes positions not clearly defined in terms of the alignments so important to Justice Black but is in general not likely to be classified along with him.

Such changes in personnel, along with dynamic changes in the course of current history, inevitably affect the atmosphere in which Justice Black operates and, in ways often intangible, condition his own work. Not to be discounted even though not subject to precise measurement or even to precise characterization are the effects of Justice Black's lengthening term of service, which has educated his approach to the law and the Court's role in the later years. By contrast with his isolation, his aloneness, during his first term on the Court, he has been for a score of years the senior member and is second to none in the deference received. Yet it is an intriguing fact that his performance remains highly individual in character. This seems to be true in the strategy and phrasing of his majority opinions as well as in his concurring and dissenting opinions. And it is to be noted that during the middle 1960's his dissenting opinions, in number and vigor and independence, carry reminders of those of his first year. While his current differences with his brethren appear to stem in considerable part from differing ways of looking at the Bill of Rights in the context of other constitutional rights, it is too soon to appraise the current panoramic scene as fairly as we can that of the earlier part of his three decades on the Court. In any event, on many public issues he now stands deeply committed, with his commitments permanently registered in the United States Reports. Even though changing circumstances and the presentation of new issues, or of old issues in new forms, may call for deviation or elaboration on particular points, Black is probably in large part encased within the framework of the positions he has already taken. Or, perhaps more fundamentally, he operates within the framework of the person and the jurist he has allowed himself or compelled himself to become according to terms of the era that was destined to be his. He is very much a product, as well as a prominent maker, of the history of his times.

CHAPTER TWO

The New Court and The New Deal

JOHN P. FRANK

HIS thirtieth year on the Supreme Court is a great milestone in Justice Black's career as America's senior warrior for individual liberty. Yet this is not at all the career which President Roosevelt expected of Hugo Black when he appointed the senior Senator from Alabama to the Court in 1937. That Black would become a great civil libertarian was predicted by the thoughtful; it required no change in his outlook. But the fact remains that his concern for civil liberties, which has seemed to dominate heavily his work for the last half of the thirty years, was not the purpose of the appointment in the first place. Black was appointed first and foremost to be, in political and economic terms, a New Dealer on the Court.

The shift of career emphasis has been so gradual that contemporary commentators have fallen into the practice of speaking of Black's libertarianism as though this were the whole of him. That shift is illustrated in three comments made over a wide spread of years in the Lawyers Guild publication:

1. In a review of Black's first year on the Court, a 1938 commentator analyzed his major opinions, which were in the fields of rate regulation, taxation, and other aspects of substantive due process. The writer summarized Black's point of view thus:

> Legislators, administrative officials, even juries, should be allowed a freer hand. Somewhat paradoxically he is bold in the assertion of lack of [judicial] power.[1]

Notes appear at pages 279-287.

Black's economic-constitutional views were compared to Chief Justice Taney's. The writer anticipated that Black would be on the Bench for most of "the next thirty years," and predicted that he would lead the way back to a Taney approach to constitutional law.

2. Eighteen years later, the same publication noticed Black's seventieth birthday. By this time, Black's work in the field of civil liberties had become substantial. The shift from a primary service to the New Deal to a primary service to old freedoms was well underway, and this inspired the main tone in the chorus of good wishes. A perceptive essayist, noticing this, said:

> Currently Justice Black's fame as a libertarian has tended to obscure his egalitarian drives. Future historians will bring it into balance. For his contributions to this area, both as legislator and as judge, have helped to build into the social and economic structure reforms so vital to the little people that they will in time be seen to be as important as his striving to keep the country from straying from the paths of freedom.[2]

3. In 1960, the same publication had an essay on Black's seventy-fourth birthday. The title was *Justice Hugo Black— First Amendment Fundamentalist*. The text said, very correctly: "The popular image of Black is as distinct as that of any Justice in the history of the Court. He is our First Amendment Fundamentalist."[3]

The preoccupation with Black, the civil libertarian, is reasonable; for the past fifteen or more years this has been perhaps the most important part of his work. But to make it exclusive would be to see less than the whole man. For Hugo Black was not only the first New Dealer to go to the Court; he remains the senior New Dealer in American public life.

The shift in focus does not mean that the Justice himself is a changed man. Black recently teased himself about consistency of view, reminding an audience that his classmates at the University of Alabama Law School in 1906 noted of him in their yearbook that "this fellow seems to possess but one idea, and that is a wrong one."[4] In the field of civil liberties, he has been a "one idea man" with a lifetime pattern of extraordinary consistency, particularly in the area of fair criminal procedure and of freedom of speech.[5]

The new emphasis then, reflects not a change in Black but a change in the problems confronting the country. For example, the late Senator McCarthy of Wisconsin was not yet even a cloud on the horizon when Black went to the Court. Besides, there were civil liberties issues from the beginning of his Court service, and Black took a decided hand in dealing with them. Three of his greatest civil rights triumphs came in his first five years on the Court when he began his long series of right to counsel opinions.[6]

Yet civil liberties were at the margin of the important issues in the 1930's when lusty battles were raging over Franklin D. Roosevelt and his New Deal. The Hugo Black on the Supreme Court today is properly thought of as the inheritor of the tradition of Thomas Jefferson and James Madison, but the Black who went to the Court was also the special inheritor of the tradition of John Peter Altgeld and of the elder Bob LaFollette, whose son was his close companion in the Senate. The Black of the appointment was George Norris's most effective Democratic ally. The Black whom F.D.R. sent to the Court in 1937 was, in sum, the hard-hitting, infinitely energetic representative of the Populist-Progressive-New Deal tradition in America.

Major concerns of the era of his appointment, as well as what his own friends and supporters thought of him, are reflected in a rave editorial from the *Philadelphia Record,* a good enough synthesis of the 1937 point of view to warrant an extensive quotation:

A Great Nomination

The President has made a great nomination to the Supreme Court. Senator Hugo L. Black, of Alabama, is an outstanding liberal, a man of wide knowledge and acute understanding. He will make a splendid judge. Senator Black is, in fact, the first nominee since Louis D. Brandeis and one of the few Supreme Court nominees in our history who does not come from the bench or the corporations but from an active career in public service. . . .

He clashed with the big Navy lobby in 1929. He dug out the yellow-dog contract decision that blocked confirmation of John J. Parker for the Supreme Court in 1931. He fathered the 30-hour-week bill in 1933, and despite lack of administration support, put it through the Senate by a vote of 53-40 before it was sidetracked by the N.R.A. He exposed the ocean and air subsidy scandals. He uncovered the fake telegram campaign against the Utility Holding Company Act. He put the spotlight on the Liberty League-Hearst-Crusader combination of Tory stooges and Fascist termites working to undermine American democracy in the last campaign. He has been more liberal than the White House on many issues. . . .

He is cosponsor of the new Federal minimum-wage and maximum-hour bill and he has not hesitated to meet southern objections head-on. "These wages," he said, "make southern industry prosperous—for its owners. But the dividends go North. . . ."

His fight against the Power Trust and for Government operation of Muscle Shoals began long before the New Deal. He has demonstrated his courage. He attacked Heflin in 1928, and voted to seat Bankhead instead of the Alabama demagogue in a contested election. He blocked immediate consideration of two of the President's appointments to the Maritime Commission recently when they were charged with being antiunion. Though Black's name is sure to invoke protest from the Tories, they will find it hard to block his confirmation. He is a Senator. He is a southern Democrat. He is a small-town Baptist. He is no professor or brain truster. But a product of Main Street America.

Politically, the President has made a shrewd choice. He has also made a wise one. Hugo Black's liberalism will wear well.[7]

Hugo Black's transfer from the United States Senate to the United States Supreme Court was no gentle transition from the world's greatest gentlemen's club to the calm of the Marble

Palace. Indeed, President Roosevelt sent his first appointee
over to the Court, in an atmosphere of shot and shell, as if it
were an enemy position to be occupied. For the appointment
fight was the last real battle in Roosevelt's war with the
Supreme Court and Black was the President's one-man army
of occupation.

The Senate Inheritance

The years 1929 to 1932 signified the failure of the old order.

> Whether it was true in fact, it was true in popular
> belief that the control of American life had been turned
> over to the businessman; and in 1932 the people de-
> manded an accounting. They forced the old political
> order into bankruptcy and were ready to enforce drastic
> changes in the economic order. So the old barriers
> against trade unions, against social legislation, against
> state interference in, and competition with, business
> broke down, the more easily in that the pressure against
> them was now at least a generation old.[8]

Mr. Roosevelt himself summarized the problems of the day
in September of 1932 when he said:

> A glance at the situation today only too clearly indicates
> that equality of opportunity as we have known it no
> longer exists. Our industrial plant is built; the problem
> just now is whether under existing conditions it is not
> overbuilt. Our last frontier has long since been reached,
> and there is practically no more free land. More than
> half of our people do not live on the farms or on the
> lands and cannot derive a living by cultivating their
> own property. There is no safety valve in the form of a
> Western prairie to which those thrown out of work by
> the Eastern economic machines can go for a new start.
> We are not able to invite the immigration from Europe
> to share our endless plenty. We are now providing a
> drab living for our own people. . . . The independent
> business man is running a losing race. . . . If the process
> of concentration goes on at the same rate, at the end of

another century we shall have all American industry controlled by a dozen corporations, and run by perhaps a hundred men. But plainly, we are steering a steady course toward economic oligarchy, if we are not there already.[9]

To do something about it after he was elected, the President proposed a massive legislative program. In the first hundred days of the 1933 session, he and a cooperative Congress hammered out the first action program in American history directed at economic depression and the social evils which accompanied it:

9 March	Emergency Banking Act
20 March	Economy Act
31 March	Civilian Conservation Corps
19 April	Gold standard abandoned (ratified 5 June)
12 May	Federal Emergency Relief Act
12 May	Agricultural Adjustment Act
12 May	Emergency Farm Mortgage Act
18 May	Tennessee Valley Authority Act
27 May	Truth-in-Securities Act
13 June	Home Owner's Loan Act
16 June	National Industrial Recovery Act
16 June	Glass-Steagall Banking Act
16 June	Farm Credit Act

In the years following, the list grew mightily.[10]

Hugo Black was elected for his second term as Senator simultaneously with Mr. Roosevelt's election to his first term as President. Black swiftly became a major force for the President's program; indeed, as the *Philadelphia Record* editorial suggests, he was at times ahead of it. Black's bill to restrict hours of labor to thirty a week led the way for what became the Fair Labor Standards Act of 1938, the last major piece of New Deal legislation. Without his Lobby Investigation, the Public Utility Holding Company Act of 1935 would never have passed; it was Black's exposure of the utility interests' corruption of newspapers, and of their false flood of spurious letters and telegrams against the legislation, which got the bill through.[11]

President Roosevelt helped the country out of the depression but his accomplishments did not delight all of his fellow citizens. In 1935 and 1936, opposition to the President reached a point of frenzy;[12] and in the politically embattled country of the election year, the New Dealers gave at least as good as they got. We know in retrospect that it was an uneven war; the President was reelected in 1936 by the most overwhelming vote in a hundred years. But public opinion polling had not reached a point of efficiency that made his reelection predictable, and the fight of 1936 was fought as though it might go either way.

Black was very much in the middle of that fight.[13] An extraordinarily able public speaker, he was used extensively around the country. In this very bitter battle, the Supreme Court seemed clearly to the New Dealers to be siding with the enemy. Vital elements of the New Deal program had been invalidated by the Court; others were severely menaced. Even state legislation dealing with elementary economic problems had been held unconstitutional.

With the President's overwhelming reelection in 1936, it was apparent that either the Court or the New Deal would have to give, and the President had no doubt about which it should be. In 1937 he called upon Congress to authorize him to appoint up to six additional Justices. Black was, once more, a leading supporter of the President. He made a series of speeches in behalf of the Court plan, and the speeches, both on the floor of the Senate and around the country, leave us with an extraordinarily clear picture of his conception of the proper role of the Supreme Court and of a Supreme Court Justice—on the eve of his own appointment.

By Justice Black's thirtieth year on the Supreme Court, we have moved so far from the mechanistic theory of constitutional interpretation that it is by now difficult to realize that it was only recently the dominant concept of constitutional interpretation in the United States. Charles Beard has told us that when he began the study of constitutional law in 1902,

[A] Justice of the Supreme Court, in the theory of the classroom, seemed to be a kind of master mechanic. Indeed, as I heard the budding lawyers and judges talk,

I was often reminded of a machine once used in the
Bank of England to test the coins deposited day by day.
When a coin was gently placed on its delicately balanced
receptacle, the machine trembled for a second or two
and then dropped the coin, right or left, into the proper
chest as sound or spurious according to its monetary
merits.[14]

The view that there was range in constitutional interpretation,
a wide permissive area of choice in which the economic,
social, and political preconceptions of the judge would necessarily influence the ultimate determination, was still the minority view of a few iconoclasts like Professors Thomas Reed
Powell at Harvard or Douglas Maggs at Duke. As late as 1936,
Justice Roberts had been able to say for a majority of the
Supreme Court, in validating the Roosevelt administration's
agricultural program, that in a constitutional case the whole
duty of the Court was "to lay the article of the Constitution
which is invoked beside the statute which is challenged and
to decide whether the latter squares with the former."[15]

Black was with the iconoclasts. He saw it as "no charge
against the integrity of any prospective judge that with reference to economic predilections after he goes on the bench he
will still be the same man that he was before he went there."[16]
As he further saw it, the dominant bloc of the Court was
espousing and reading into the Constitution its own economic
philosophy which had been overwhelmingly rejected by the
country. Referring to that majority bloc, he said,

It is proper to add that the political and economic constitutional interpretations of these five Justices followed
along the direct trail of the dominant interpretations
since Justice Field succeeded in overturning previous
constitutional principles many years ago.[17]

His repeated theme was that the economic philosophy of the
Court's majority of the moment was "contrary to the letter
and spirit of our Constitution."[18]

Black argued that the Court and its members showed a
"distinct line of demarcation" on all cases relating to property

as against all matters concerning human rights and human interest,[19] and by this he meant that the Court was wrongly deciding cases relating to economic programs. As he saw it, the general social philosophy of the anti-New Dealers outside the Court had

> led us to business chaos and in the direction of social and political disintegration. It brought starvation wages; health-breaking long hours of work; child labor in mills; business to bankruptcy; and farmers to crushing mortgages that could not be met with 5-cent cotton, 10-cent corn, 20-cent wheat, and other farm prices in proportion.[20]

The Roosevelt administration had sought to deal with those crises of American economic life, and the Court, by reading its economic philosophy into the Constitution, was barring these reforms, said the Senator. The Court was blocking sensible public utility rate regulation. It was blocking reasonable business regulations. It was grossly unfair to organized labor, particularly by holding that the yellow-dog contract could not be barred.

Black attacked the course of decisions both generally and specifically. He believed that Congress could provide work for the jobless, that Congress and state legislatures could improve working conditions, that they could prohibit overly long hours and provide minimum wages, that they could control agricultural prices, that the Congress could develop the rivers of America both for flood control purposes and to provide public power.

Speaking more generally, he attacked the entire concept of substantive due process of law:

> A bare majority of the members of the Supreme Court of the United States have been for a number of years assuming the right on their part to determine the reasonableness of State and Federal laws. The Constitution never gave that majority any such power.[21]

So far as Black was concerned, the people of America had chosen the program of the New Deal by forty-six states to two and they would not be stayed. "The time has arrived when those who favor fitting laws to modern needs in order to correct and cure social and industrial injustices must face their problem squarely and fairly." He had a specific remedy to propose: the country needed "new ideas on the bench."[22]

When Black went on the Supreme Court he carried with him several firm intellectual convictions which were to affect his own work and the work of the Court:

1. He recognized that there were clear areas of the law where judicial interpretation was clearly proscribed. But he also recognized that there were large areas in which the law's answers to particular questions were very uncertain. In those areas, he realized that, to an undefined degree, judges would necessarily decide the cases and determine the law in the light of the economic, social, and philosophical predilections they took with them to the bench.

2. He was committed to certain specific approaches to constitutional interpretation. For example, he was committed absolutely to the proposition that it was never the business of judges to pass upon the *reasonableness* of legislation. He rejected totally substantive due process.

3. On the affirmative side, Black was committed to a concept of Congressional constitutional power broad enough to deal with the economic needs of the nation, and he took a comprehensive view of which economic needs could be dealt with. The government could regulate:

    a. Labor relations.
    b. Labor conditions, including wages and hours.
    c. Agricultural conditions, including all factors that related to the production and pricing of farm products.
    d. Any other matters which related to the control, prevention, or avoidance of economic depression.
    e. The complete development of national resources, including the development of public power.
    f. All phases of marketing, including security.
    g. Whatever was needed to insure a competitive economic order.

4. His strong belief was that it was the proper business of government "to correct and cure social and industrial injustice,"[23] and that this broad charter included regulation of industrial accidents and their consequences, with the Supreme Court having a duty to give broad and effective interpretation to industrial accident legislation.

These, then, were the "new ideas"—some of them not really so new—that Black took as the first representative of the New Deal to the Supreme Court. Had they represented the totality of his thought, his mark would have been less lasting. With the passage of time, some of the specific problems covered in this list would have taken care of themselves, as indeed many largely did.

But there was something more. Though Black was a New Dealer, he was not a doctrinaire New Dealer, limited to the concepts of the program as it then existed. Far more important than his specific ideas and convictions was a mind unabashed by change. His basic attitude had been expressed in 1934 when the Senate debated the confirmation of Rexford Tugwell as Undersecretary of Agriculture. There had been a good deal of mealymouthed support for Tugwell in the Senate by Senators who were really a little embarrassed about the appointment because of Tugwell's alleged radicalism. This was not Black's stance. He said:

> It is my intention to vote for Dr. Tugwell, because I am for him. I am for the views he has expressed, as I understand those views to be written in his books. I am for him because I believe that he is one man who is not content with looking backward, who for every thought he has in mind is not bowed down by slavish precedents. I am for him because he dared to express his unbelief in some of the theories which have been announced by theorists of the past, and because he does not accept a principle of political economy which has been announced and which has been organized and which has been accepted in the past merely because it has been accepted in the past.[24]

The spirit with which Black went to the Court as a New Dealer was one of solid determination to do a job. What he had said only a few months before in the Senate in behalf of his own wage-hour bill has a certain direct appositeness to the constitutional revolution about to come:

> We have waited too long for it already—at what cost in dollars and cents as well as in flesh and blood no one will ever know.
>
> Now we are through waiting. The Democratic Party has promised the country this kind of legislation. The President has pledged it. The mandate of the election has ordered it.
>
> And at long last the American people are going to have it![25]

The American people were going to have what the Democratic Party had promised, what the President had pledged, and what the election of 1936 had demanded, and Hugo Black was going to do all within the power of one man to help give it to them.

The Eclipse of Substantive Due Process

The conservative forces of American politics had, in one way, won an important victory in the Court fight. True, while the President had not obtained his bill, the Court even before the Black appointment had conducted a strategic retreat by upholding both minimum wage legislation and the National Labor Relations Act.[26] Yet in form, at least, the President had lost. The appointment of an extreme New Dealer to fill the vacancy left by the retirement of conservative Justice Willis Van Devanter robbed the victors of their fruits. Their hostility rose to a passionate howl when the *Pittsburgh Gazette* began an attack on Black's pre-1926 Klan membership, an attack elaborated upon by Daniel Berman in the next Chapter of this volume.

The attack on Black's past associations became the violent tail of the Court fight storm. Riding in the same wind was an attack on Black's competence. The two great bodies of work before the Court are constitutional interpretation and statutory interpretation, with their ancillary areas of procedure and jurisdiction. Black could be expected to be comfortable with statutes. He might, however, be predicted to be much less comfortable with the Constitution, with its vast encrustation of history and judicial precedents, and with jurisdiction and procedure. Indeed, it was widely anticipated by the opinion-shaping critics of the country, and particularly by the press, that he would be wholly incompetent.

The most remarkable feature of Black's switch from Senate to Court was the surefootedness of his transfer. Thirty years later, those who follow the Court are unanimously aware that Black needs a ghostwriter about as badly as Shakespeare or John Marshall; the always pleasant but fundamentally minor role of his law clerks in his professional life is well documented.[27] But even the critics of the 30's who were impressed with his early opinions could not swiftly admit their own errors of anticipation; thus it was initially speculated that Black's beginning work must have been done by some off-the-Court ghostwriter such as his intimate friend and a principal New Deal advisor, Thomas Corcoran.[28]

The first five years did have bobbles, but they were astonishingly few. None were on the New Deal side, in the area of economic problems. Nor did Black make any early mistakes in the basic civil liberties questions of freedom of speech or press or fair trial.[29]

Isolated instances of conceptual error are mentioned in the footnotes to demonstrate their rarity. The striking feature of the first two years is how ready and equipped Black was to take his definitive positions. Nowhere is this better demonstrated than in the field of substantive due process, and the related matter of judicial superintendence of utility rate-making.

The most astonishing single creation of the Supreme Court in the fifty years preceding Black's appointment had been the development of substantive due process. Under this concept, the Court could review the "reasonableness" of state and federal legislation. In determining the validity of social and regulatory legislation, the Court balanced the public interest against private property rights. It held, for example, that state regulation of health and labor conditions under the police power could not unduly infringe on private property and its use. This concept of the essential substantive right of private property and its use, including the sanctity of private contracts, necessitated a judicial review of legislative decisions which in any way affected the property and contracts of individuals and businesses and resulted in the invalidation of wage and hour legislation and other social legislation as well.

Substantive due process had become the principal constitutional tool of the *laissez-faire* social order, and coupled with the narrow interpretation of the Commerce Clause it meant that neither the state nor the federal government could deal effectively with what to Black were the shrieking needs of the age. Justice Holmes had already protested. Referring to the "constitutional rights of the states," Holmes had said, "As the decisions now stand, I see hardly any limit but the sky to the invalidating of those rights if they happen to strike a majority of this Court as for any reason undesirable."[30]

Black knew this constitutional story when he was appointed. It was at the heart of his attack on the Supreme Court during the Court fight.[31] The difference between Holmes and Black was that while Holmes wanted to temper the abuses of substantive due process, Black wanted to abolish it. Substantive due process, whether it be regarded as a "creation" or a "concoction" of the Supreme Court, is wholly judge-made, and so is its subdivision, constitutional review of utility rates. Black's position in the Court fight had been that the power of the Court to pass upon the reasonableness of legislation did not exist at all.[32]

His attack was along three lines. First, he said that the "persons" covered by the due process clause meant only natural persons and did not cover corporations. It was not hard to demonstrate historically that when the country adopted the Fourteenth Amendment "the people were told that its purpose was to protect the weak and helpless human beings and were not told that it was intended to remove corporations in any fashion from the control of state governments."[33] Nonetheless, in 1886 under Chief Justice Morrison Waite, the Supreme Court had extended the provision to corporations.[34] Black would reverse the 1886 decision. As a practical matter, this would largely end substantive due process, since almost always in the rate field and usually in the regulatory field, it was corporations which invoked the protection of the clause.

In the cases involving the setting of public utilities rates, the earlier decisions of the Waite Court held rate-making to be unreviewable under the due process clause; under Black's philosophy the entire structure of judicial review of the constitutionality of rates would be abolished. He joined with Justices Douglas and Murphy in re-invoking those cases which "emphatically declared price fixing to be a constitutional prerogative of the legislative branch, not subject to judicial review or revision."[35] The prevalence of the Black view today has resulted in the virtual abolition of the federal constitutional law of rate-making.[36]

In dealing with the economic regulatory legislation, Black both attacked the theory that the Court might review the reasonableness of legislation and also argued that in any given case, the legislation was clearly reasonable. An early illustration of this position is found in *Polk Co. v. Glover*.[37] In that case it was held that a challenge to the validity of Florida legislation governing cans used in shipping citrus juice must be tried. Black dissented alone on the ground that there was nothing to try. "Even according to the presently prevailing interpretation of the Due Process Clause," he thought, there was nothing wrong with this statute. He saw no need for the trial court to weigh and pass upon the relative judgment, poise, and reasoning ability of the one Florida legislator who had voted against the law, as contrasted with the ninety-four legislators and the Governor who favored it; and the wisdom of this policy rested with the legislature of Florida subject to the veto power of Florida's governor. The dissent in *Polk Co. v. Glover*[38] is the law today and it represents one of the great triumphs of Black, the New Dealer.

This is not to say that the demise of substantive due process has been due solely to Justice Black. First of all, the whole concept was badly overage and ripe for interment. Second, any development in the course of Supreme-Court-made law requires at least five Justices, and as the New Dealers came to the bench, they commonly had the same point of view on substantive due process. Justice Douglas in particular put in strong strokes against the dying doctrine. But along with the Douglas opinion in the *Olsen*[39] case, the two major opinions on substantive due process of the past thirty years are Black's, *Lincoln Federal* in 1949 and *Ferguson v. Skrupa* in 1963.[40] *Lincoln Federal* dealt with the validity of state legislation prohibiting yellow-dog contracts, or contracts by which employees were barred from joining labor unions; and the issue in *Ferguson v. Skrupa* was whether a state could regulate the business of "debt adjusting," a specialized type of financial counseling.

In *Lincoln Federal*, Black for the Court spoke of the basic decisions and principles of substantive due process as having been "deliberately discarded" and said that the Court has "consciously returned closer and closer to the earlier Constitutional principle that states have power to legislate against what are found to be injurious practices in their internal commercial and business affairs, so long as their laws do not run afoul of some specific federal Constitutional prohibition, or of some valid federal law." The reference to "specific federal Constitutional prohibition" is the key to the matter— "due process" is clearly unspecific. In *Ferguson v. Skrupa* in 1963, Black had the ultimate pleasure of declaring the law to be what in 1937 he had told the Senate it ought to be:

> A bare majority of the members of the Supreme Court of the United States have been for a number of years assuming the right on their part to determine the reasonableness of state and federal laws. The Constitution never gave that majority any such power.

Senator Black, March 24, 1937.

> The doctrine that prevailed in [several cases] that due process authorized courts to hold laws unconstitutional when they believe the legislature has acted unwisely has long since been discarded. We have returned to the original Constitutional proposition that courts do not substitute their social and economic beliefs for the judgment of legislative bodies, who are elected to pass laws.

Mr. Justice Black, *Ferguson v. Skrupa*, April 22, 1963.

Not since the day Black joined the Court has any state economic regulation been invalidated on the grounds of denial of substantive due process. As a practical matter, "no claim of substantive economic rights would now be sustained by the Supreme Court."[41]

The only emergence of substantive due process in contemporary times with any substantial judicial support is *Griswold v. Connecticut*,[42] the Connecticut birth control case. Justices Harlan and White voted to invalidate the Connecticut statute against the use of birth control materials on substantive due process grounds. Justice Douglas for the Court expressly rejected substantive due process, relying instead on a right of privacy said to be within a penumbra of the Bill of Rights. Justice Goldberg relied principally upon a conception of Ninth Amendment rights.

Black was unable to see any important functional difference among the three positions, the one outspokenly resting on substantive due process and the other two relying upon what seemed to him re-emergences of the same basic concept that, one way or another, the Court could review the reasonableness of legislation. To dramatize that the case was for him an acid test of due process principles, he made explicit that the Connecticut law was totally offensive to him; he subscribed to Justice Stewart's opinion which emphasized the absurdity of the law. Black made clear that if the case could have been put into a First Amendment posture in which the doctor was punished for engaging in free speech with his patient, he would have considered the problem quite differently. But so far as he was concerned, the Court has simply no power at all to review "the wisdom and value of legislative policies and to hold unconstitutional those laws which they believe unwise or dangerous." While he reasserted his belief in the principle of judicial review, he said:

> I do not believe that we are granted power by the Due Process Clause or any other Constitutional provision or provisions to measure Constitutionality by our belief that legislation is arbitrary, capricious or unreasonable, or accomplishes no justifiable purpose, or is offensive to our own notions of "civilized standards of conduct."

Black demonstrated that the cases relied upon by Justices White and Goldberg had themselves been opinions of Mr. Justice McReynolds which had been based on substantive due process cases, many of which had been overruled by name by the Court. So far as Black was concerned, after more than forty years in the Senate and on the Court combating the concept of judicial review of the policy of legislation, the suggestion that somehow this could be done under the Ninth Amendment was "shocking doctrine."

But while the bizarre Connecticut statute received what may perhaps be described as somewhat remarkable doctrinal treatment by the Supreme Court, the basic result remains. In the main area of its consequences, substantive due process has been at least dormant for thirty years, and this must be regarded as a major work of the New Deal and of Justice Black.

Commerce and Economic Regulation

Mr. Dooley, in commenting on Theodore Roosevelt's report of Spanish-American War military action, observed that it might well be called "Alone in Cuba." That error of overfocus must be avoided for Black; he was not "Alone on the Supreme Court" for long.

Yet he was "alone" for a time. It is the custom of historians to speak of a First New Deal and a Second New Deal. The First New Deal is the period of 1933 and 1934, the beginning of which was described earlier. This early program was blocked by some fourteen adverse Supreme Court decisions between 1934 and 1936. The response to these decisions, in the form of such new legislation as the National Labor Relations Act, has been called the Second New Deal.[43]

Justice Black, too, had his First and Second New Deals. The First comprised his first two years on the Court—the 1937 and 1938 terms or October 1937, to June 1939. After this initial two years, there were other New Dealers in force on the Court. By 1940, apart from the other newcomers, there were Black, Douglas, and Murphy making an unshakeable trio until Murphy's death in 1949. By 1942, the turnover was almost total; only Roberts and Stone of the pre-Black Court were still on the bench. By the time Mr. Roosevelt's "Dr. New Deal" had been replaced by his "Dr. Win-the-War," Dr. New Deal's prescriptions had passed their constitutional tests.

The resultant shift in Black's own role is numerically demonstrable. In the 1937 and 1938 terms, the Court decided 126 constitutional cases. Black dissented in thirteen of them and concurred specially in seventeen. Thus, in twenty-four percent of the constitutional cases in his first two years, Black disagreed with the majority either as to its result or as to its reasoning. On the other hand, in the 1939 term, Black dissented only twice and concurred specially only once.[44]

The largest single doctrinal victory of the Court's New Deal phalanx was the total overthrow of the commerce power restrictions, and the establishment of that power as the foundation stone of congressional power to govern. The commerce power war was over so quickly and conclusively that what was once the greatest constitutional issue before the country is now quite dead. The story is a familiar one. In 1936, before the election and before the Court fight, the Court held that Congress under the commerce power could not reach and regulate the conditions of the bituminous coal industry, the poultry sales industry, or agriculture.[45] In 1937, after the Court plan was before the Court, and before Black's appointment, the Court found that under the same power the Congress could regulate labor relations in the steel industry.[46] Within five years, the 1936 cases were meaningless. Because of its general effect on commerce, Congress could even regulate the transfer and use of wheat from a farmer's field to his barn.[47]

Though Black wrote none of the important Commerce Clause opinions from 1937 to 1942, his was the majority opinion in the 1944 *Southeastern Underwriters*[48] case which upheld the extension of national regulatory power to the insurance industry by determining that the antitrust laws applied to that industry. The striking effect of the decision on the powerful insurance industry, coupled with the fact that it was a four to three opinion due to two disqualifications, led to a greater controversy than any of the other Commerce Clause cases and resulted in a modification of the effect of the decision by an Act of Congress.[49] The effect of all of these decisions was to put aside the restrictions on the national power over business and industry developed between 1890 and 1936—to return the commerce power to the broad charter of federal government which John Marshall had conceived in the country's beginnings.[50]

Two of the "new" commerce cases involved bills Black had very materially helped to pass. The Fair Labor Standards Act, actually adopted after Black was on the Court, passed the Senate on July 31, 1937.[51] Black had been floor leader for the bill, then known as the Black-Connery Bill, in the debate from July 27th to the 31st. It was, without doubt, the most important legislation Black ever personally saw through the Senate and its handling reflects an experienced dexterity.[52]

The dates tell the constitutional story. The Black-Connery Bill moved through the Senate when the Court plan had just been tabled but was not assuredly dead; the wage-hour bill passed only a few days before Black was to be appointed. Black seemed to lean over backward to keep his legislation from being mingled with the Court bill. The opponents of the Court bill were also restrained—the wage-hour bill was popular, had been a major plank in the 1936 Democratic platform, had clearly been vindicated in the preceding election, and clearly was going to pass in some form. Court plan opponents also could not afford to get into the constitutional issue for if they opposed the wage-hour bill on constitutional grounds they might very well be aiding the Court bill.

The Court plan factions took their positions in different ways. The bill covered wages and hours and prohibited child labor, and the child labor portion of the bill could not be valid unless the earlier decision of *Hammer v. Dagenhart*[53] was overruled. Black discreetly stayed away from this subject. His position was that the act regulated those businesses "which engage in the transportation of their goods in interstate commerce"; and his position was that "the doctrine of the *Shreveport* decision[54]—with which, I am sure, every lawyer in this body is familiar—would authorize action in connection with those businesses and industries that are seriously competing with and having a substantial effect upon the flow of interstate commerce."[55]

Senators Wheeler of Montana and Johnson of Colorado, on the other hand, had opposed the Court plan, but they were for the abolition of child labor and thus opposed *Hammer v. Dagenhart*. They had therefore devised an amendment to the Black bill as their own plan which, as Senator Wheeler put it, "would for all practical purposes put an end to child labor."[56]

The validity of the act came before the Supreme Court in 1941, with Black then four years on the bench. In a unanimous opinion by Justice Stone, the act was upheld and *Hammer v. Dagenhart* was expressly overruled. The Court rested its decision both on the relatively narrow ground and authorities offered by Senators Wheeler and Johnson and, expressly, on the broader ground offered by Senator Black. A New Deal senatorial argument thus became contemporary constitutional law.

The second major case arising from Black's handiwork as a Senator involved the Public Utility Holding Company Act of 1935. This statute sought to abolish or limit the network of holding companies by which operating utilities were gathered together under layers of management and ownership concerns which added to the cost of electric power in the United States with no perceptible benefits in efficiency or service. Black was against the holding company system for all areas of the economy. He told the Senate:

> I am against the holding company system, whether in power, railroads, telephones, aviation, shipping, or any other business where there is given to those who manipulate the holding company the power to execute a device to defraud their stockholders, to impose upon the public, to extract exorbitant profits from the consumers, and under the name of salaries and bonuses to press down a burden upon the operating business of this country which if not prevented will sooner or later destroy it.[57]

As noted earlier, Black's prime function in the passage of the Public Utility Holding Company Act was his investigation of the means used to oppose it. It was this which caused Ray Clapper, Washington columnist of that era, to write, "if the death sentence finally goes into the utilities bill, it will be another notch in the gun of Senator Hugo Black."[58]

But Black had a second duty. Much of the debate on the bill was on its constitutionality and a considerable share of the argument in behalf of it fell to Senator Wheeler, its sponsor, and to Black. On May 27, 1935, the National Industrial Recovery Act was declared unconstitutional by the Supreme Court on the ground (among others) that it regulated "production" and therefore was beyond the reach of the commerce power.[59] A principal constitutional debate on the holding company act came before the Senate just a week later, on June 4, 1935. The point in time is important—the Supreme Court was just beginning its role as the detonator of the New Deal. At this point, no one had any idea of solving New Deal problems by a frontal attack on the Court itself. The N.R.A. decision was something to be lived with and worked around. In the debate in which Senator Hastings of Delaware, home state of the holding companies, attacked the bill and Senators Wheeler and Black defended it, Black's constitutional position, synthesized from his statements on the Senate floor on that day, was this:

> . . . in order to require registration, the person must either sell, transport, transmit, distribute, or own or operate some of these things for the transmission of electric energy or gas in the interstate commerce. . . . I think it would be immaterial whether the person was actually causing the transmission in interstate commerce. If he were in partnership or in agreement with someone else and they were working together to act in interstate commerce, then, it would be a joint undertaking. . . .

> . . . if the plant is used for the purpose of producing electricity which is immediately to be transmitted in interstate commerce, there is every presumption that the operation of the plant, so closely connected with the transmission of the electricity, would come within numerous decisions as to burdening or directly affecting interstate commerce.[60]

It was not Black's contention that the plant itself would be in interstate commerce, but that its activities would be:

Let us suppose, for instance, that a plant is producing electricity in such a way that it unnecessarily directly raises the price up to ten times what it should be, right on the verge of transmitting the electricity across a State line. There we have the question of an unnecessary, wasteful, unfair, exorbitant burden upon interstate commerce.[61]

Senator Hastings had read at length from the decision of John Marshall in *Gibbons v. Ogden*. Black said:

The Senator a few minutes ago read from the case of Gibbons against Ogden a quotation, with which I fully agree, to the effect that the authority of the Federal Government over interstate commerce is just as sovereign as the authority of the State over intrastate commerce. Admitting that, I believe the Senator certainly will agree that the Federal Government is not helpless, insofar as interstate commerce is concerned, to protect itself from a method of production which might be a burden to, or injure or destroy, interstate commerce.[62]

To Black this meant that the Federal Government could deny the entry into interstate commerce of any article produced even under intrastate regulation if its "entrance into interstate commerce would destroy interstate commerce, or would unduly fetter and burden interstate commerce."[63] With reference to the recent decision of the Supreme Court to the effect that production was an intrastate matter, Black said:

conceding that unquestionably to be the law the Senator also read from a case in which it was held that, so far as interstate commerce is concerned, as I caught it, this country is as though there were no State lines.

. . . That means that the Federal Government has complete, unrestricted power to regulate interstate commerce . . . unless there is something in the Constitution itself which directly stands in the way of that regulation of interstate commerce."[64]

In Black's view, it was immaterial whether the interstate commerce was "legitimate" or "illegitimate," whether the item under control was "deleterious" or whether it was not. In his view of the commerce power, "if electricity were produced in such a way as to fetter and burden interstate commerce, the Federal Government would have a right to remove the burden from interstate commerce in any way it saw fit to do so."[65]

Eleven years later Justice Murphy wrote the unanimous opinion of the Supreme Court upholding the constitutionality of the Public Utility Holding Company Act.[66] I do not know and do not mean to suggest that Justice Murphy read the Congressional debate of June 4, 1935, but if he did not, it is but further evidence that the Black and Murphy minds ran in strikingly parallel channels. Murphy said that the commerce clause

> does not operate so as to render the nation powerless to defend itself against economic forces that Congress decrees inimical or destructive of the national economy.
>
> . . . Congress may impose relevant conditions and requirements on those who use the channels of interstate commerce in order that those channels will not become the means of promoting or spreading evil, whether of a physical, moral or economic nature. . . . This power permits Congress to attack an evil directly at its source, provided that the evil bears a substantial relationship to interstate commerce. . . . The fact that an evil may involve a corporation's financial practices, its business structure or its security portfolio does not detract from the power of Congress under the commerce clause to promulgate rules in order to destroy that evil. Once it is established that the evil concerns or affects commerce in more states than one, Congress may act.[67]

The constitutional attack is not only a stroke to the jugular, an attempt to kill particular legislation; it is a double blow, seeking simultaneously to emasculate legislative power in a particular area. Such strokes against New Deal legislation had all been fended off, so far as the commerce clause was concerned, early in Black's judicial career. But the next means of attack, always, is to render impotent statutory construction or to encourage lackadaisical enforcement. From the standpoint of the New Deal opponents, it was not essential, though it might be desirable, that the New Deal laws be terminated; it would be enough if they fell into desuetude. The interpretation and enforcement of statutes is a task which never stops.

To analyze Black on the interpretation and operation of the National Labor Relations Act, Black on the interpretation and enforcement of the Fair Labor Standards Act, Black on all the rest of the New Deal statutes would require the telling of an excessively long story, and yet it is very close to the heart of the present subject. The initial task was to establish the power of administrative agencies to do their jobs. In his first three years on the Court, the Court had twenty-six cases involving Federal administrative action and reversed administrative rulings five times. Black dissented in each of these five cases.[68] His position was consistently that the agencies must come to their own conclusions and that the courts should not substitute judicial for administrative judgment. A dramatic illustration was *NLRB v. Waterman S.S. Corp.*[69] Nowhere in the country was resistance to labor legislation more intransigent than in Black's native South. In *Waterman,* the National Labor Relations Board expressly petitioned the Supreme Court for review on the ground that the Fifth Circuit Court of Appeals was consistently failing to give effect to Board conclusions of fact.

Black was thus called upon to review the practice of his own circuit and his own region. The substantive charge was that Waterman was "guilty of a most flagrant mass discrimination against its employees," and the evidence as Black comprehensively analyzed it, showed, at a minimum, that there was a substantial basis for the Board's conclusion. The opinion concluded:

> The Court of Appeals' failure to enforce the Board's order resulted from the substitution of its judgment on disputed facts for the Board's judgment—and power to do that has been denied the courts by Congress. Whether the court would reach the same conclusion as the

Board from the conflicting evidence is immaterial and
the court's disagreement with the Board could not warrant the disregard of the statutory division of authority
set up by Congress.[70]

In all these administrative and statutory matters, proper
interest in an anniversary must not obscure the fact that
the Justice was by no means alone. All the Roosevelt appointees were more or less of a similar point of view, and
Justices Black, Douglas, and Murphy, later joined by Justice
Rutledge, became a solid wall in the 40's; the other Roosevelt
appointees—Reed, Frankfurter, and Jackson—were sometimes
in colorful disagreement with them. Justice Murphy tended
to make the Fair Labor Standards Act a province of his own.
As was perceptively observed in 1940, Black was no longer
"spectacularly playing a lone hand." The new appointments
"brought new ideas to the group's deliberations; there has
been interaction; and the result is then that the majority of
his associates now share with Black, or, from another viewpoint, Black shares with his associates, a new attitude."[71]
The new attitude is nowhere better illustrated than in the
antitrust cases.

A Jacksonian Approach to Antitrust

Black had opposed the National Recovery Act because he
felt it conflicted with antitrust principles in which he completely believed. That belief he carried to the Court, and
he has made an undeviating record of the strongest possible
enforcement of the Sherman, Clayton, and Robinson-Patman
Acts. Black's first opinion was a trade regulation case in which
a company purported to give away an encyclopedia and charge
the public only for the looseleaf service which kept it up.[72] In
fact, the price charged for the looseleaf service was such as to
cover both the book and the service. The Court of Appeals
had reversed a Commission order forbidding this practice on
the ground that the Court of Appeals could not "take too seriously the suggestion that a man who is buying a set of books
and a ten years 'extension service' will be fatuous enough to be
misled by the mere statement that the first is given away, and

that he is paying only the second."[73] The Black opinion in turn reversed the Court of Appeals, saying "laws are made to protect the trusting as well as the suspicious. . . . [T]o fail to prohibit such evil practices would be to elevate deception in business and to give to it the standing and dignity of truth."[74]

There have been and there are other "antitrust Justices"; Justices Douglas and Brennan are examples. Black has written his own major opinions in the field,[75] and early took a lead on the relation of patents to monopoly. Since a patent, as an exception to the antitrust laws, does give a monopoly to the inventor or his corporate employer, Black seeks to confine the patent privilege narrowly under the statutes and the Constitution; he has done so since his earliest days on the Court.[76] While Black has given close attention to the matters of patent practice, his central goal (shared by Justice Douglas) has been to raise the standard of invention so that a patent will be given only for a real advance in the art. In dissenting from an opinion upholding the validity of a patent for a leakproof dry cell for a flashlight battery, Black said:

> The practice of granting patents for microscopic structural or mechanical improvements inevitably must reduce the United States Patent Office to a mass production factory for unearned special privileges which serve no purpose except unfairly to harass the honest pursuit of business. If the patentee here has "discovered" anything, it is that the creamy substance in the dry cell will not leak through a steel jacket which covers and is securely fastened to the ends of the cell. For that alleged discovery, this patent is today upheld. I do not deny that someone, somewhere, sometime, made the discovery that liquids would not leak through leakproof solids. My trouble is that, despite findings to the contrary, I cannot agree that this patentee is that discoverer.[77]

A comparison of May 31, 1966, and January 8, 1930, illustrates the oneness of today, tomorrow, and yesterday in Black's antitrust thinking. In January of 1930, it appeared that the Attorney General was being pressured to relax an old antitrust consent decree obtained against the meat packers in 1922. The meat packers wanted to go into the grocery business as a counter to the grocery chains in the meat business. On January 8, 1930, Black took the floor of the Senate to call to his colleagues' attention this matter "of extreme importance" and to ask them to urge the Attorney General not to relax the decree. He said:

> Monopoly should be discouraged, not encouraged and approved by Governmental authorities. Chain groceries, chain dry goods stores, chain drugstores, chain clothing stores, here today and merge tomorrow, grow in size and power. Railroad mergers, giant power monopolies, bank mergers, steel mergers, all kinds of mergers, concentrate more and more power and wealth in the hands of the few. In the name of "efficiency," monopoly is the order of the day. The giant business enterprises spread over our Nation, extend their tentacles into our schools, politics, and business. We are rapidly becoming a Nation of a few business masters and many clerks and servants. The local business man and merchant is passing, and his community loses his contribution to local affairs as an independent thinker and executive.[78]

Black turned then to the matter, not of nationwide or regional mergers, but of mergers within towns. As he described the evil he saw, he said:

> I mean that the little chains are being absorbed by the bigger ones. One springs up in my home town of Birmingham to-day. To-morrow it is merged into a larger one. The next day it is merged into a still larger one, and they continue the merging and are gradually getting into one center.[79]

He foresaw the day when the local businessman would be simply a clerk, yielding to the instructions of a far distant employer—"it will be exactly the system that Andrew Jackson came into the Presidency to curtail and curb. I am not so sure, I will say, that it is not about time for some man of that kind again to curb the tendency toward control in the hands of a few which we find existing in the country today."[80]

In 1930, Black did not know what to do about this problem. In 1950, Section 7 of the Clayton Act was amended by the Celler-Kefauver anti-merger bill, which provided against mergers in any line of commerce in any section of the country where "the effect of such acquisition may be substantially to lessen competition, or to tend to create a monopoly."[81] In 1960, two grocery chains operating in Los Angeles merged, the lesser concern including thirty-six grocery stores in the Los Angeles area. The two chains were the third and sixth ranking chains in the Los Angeles area and their joint sales amounted to 7.5% of the total retail groceries sold in Los Angeles. The government appropriately challenged the merger under Section 7.

Black's opinion for the Court[82] holding the merger illegal, is the toughest anti-merger decision under the Clayton Act. The opinion tracks a close parallel to the 1930 speech and quotes Congressman Celler and Senator Kefauver in statements made by them in 1950 strikingly similar to the earlier observations of Black in 1930.

The Independent New Dealer

Black brought his New Deal philosophy and his New Deal enthusiasms and his New Deal constitutional law and his New Deal loyalties to the Supreme Court, but he also brought his independence. As a Senator, Black had been with the President most of the time, but not all of it. He had, to repeat, opposed the National Industrial Recovery Act. His could be regarded as a New Deal vote on the Court, but it was never in any administration's pocket.

Two illustrations of this independence arose in cases which happened to relate to the steel industry. In *United States v. Bethlehem Steel Corp.*,[83] the Bethlehem Company had made something over $24 million on $109 million worth of ships sold to the government in World War I. The government sought to avoid paying what remained of this amount to Bethlehem and to recover some of what had been allegedly wrongfully paid earlier. It argued that Bethlehem had obtained the contract by duress and had made unconscionable profits.

No Justice ever went to the Supreme Court with a more severe distaste for war profiteering than Black. Mingling both a soldier's resentment against those who get rich by staying home and a Populist hostility to ill-gotten gains, he regarded excessive profits as simply outrageous.[84] But it seemed to Black absurd to suggest that any private corporation, no matter how powerful, was more powerful than the government of the United States. Hence, there could be no duress. And while the profits were high, they were no worse than those everyone else made in World War I. So far as Black was concerned, such war profits were scandalous; by outlining what the government might have done in World War I, he also laid down a blueprint for what the government could do in World War II, which America had just entered. The government could simply have set the price, told Bethlehem to produce, and let Bethlehem sue if it felt that the price was too low; in the alternative, the government had "the power to commandeer Bethlehem's entire plant and facilities." Hence, he concluded, "If the Executive is in need of additional laws by which to protect the nation against war profiteering, the Constitution has given to Congress, not to this Court, the power to make them." Congress, given this judicial challenge and clear opportunity, promptly accepted it and adopted the Renegotiation Act to control the profits of World War II.

In the steel seizure case, Black even more dramatically conflicted with the Democratic Administration, this time of President Harry Truman. The President had sought to end a steel strike by seizing the steel industry. The prestige of the Truman Administration was very much at stake. There was no apparent Congressional authority for the seizure, and it basically had to rest upon a claim of inherent Presidential power. Black reiterated what he had said in *Bethlehem Steel*—Congress could undoubtedly authorize the taking of the plants if it wished to do so; but "the Founders of this Nation entrusted the law making power to the Congress alone in both good and bad times."[85] The President could not exercise it.

Another facet of Black's independence shows in his relations to the goals of organized labor. Black was in a real sense a labor Senator and he had labor's strong support in the Court appointment controversy. His intuitive biases are strongly in favor of working men and their organizations, and if it were possible to measure and compare opinions in terms of labor sympathy, Black's record would be almost as sympathetic to labor as any in the Court's history.

But his is not automatic approval. Labor, like Presidents, has no Black blank check. His consistent and higher loyalty is to the enforcement of the orderly processes of the law. The great, new labor weapon immediately prior to Black's appointment was the sit-down strike, a device of seizing and holding the employer's premises during negotiations. The Supreme Court held this practice warranted discharge, and that the National Labor Relations Board could not reinstate such strikers. Black, joining a dissent of Justice Reed, was unwilling to make the sit-downers outlaws to this extent; he felt that the Board's remedies should be evaluated case by case. But the dissenting opinion made very clear that sit-downs were not sanctioned as a permitted bargaining device; that violence in defiance of law would not be condoned; and that the power to compel "obedience to law still remains in the hands of the peace officers."[86]

The same attitude was reflected in the course of the miners' strike of 1946 when Black's old backer, labor leader John L. Lewis, disobeyed an injunction of a federal district court. Friend or no friend, Black and Douglas said: "We agree that the court had power summarily to coerce obedience to those orders and to subject defendants to such conditional sanctions as were necessary to compel obedience. . . . Courts could not administer justice if persons were left free pending adjudication to engage in conduct which would either immediately interrupt the judicial proceedings or so change the *status quo* of the subject matter of a controversy that no effective judgment could be rendered."[87] They referred to "the duty of testing the restraining order by orderly appeal instead of disobedience and open defiance."[88]

The sharpest collision of Black's sympathies and values came when a labor organization insisted on a right of free speech through picketing to induce an employer to commit an unlawful act. Once again, good, conventional law and order carried the day. The union picketed an ice wholesaler to induce it to refrain from selling ice to nonunion ice peddlers, a form of boycott which, if achieved, would have violated the Missouri restraint of trade laws. Black had supported the extension of free speech protections to picketing, though always with a careful restriction of the privilege to communication.[89] But this was different:

> [I]t has never been deemed an abridgment of freedom of speech or press to make a course of conduct illegal merely because the conduct was in part initiated, evidenced, or carried out by means of language, either spoken, written, or printed. . . . Appellants' power with that of their allies was irresistible. And it is clear that appellants were doing more than exercising a right of free speech or press. . . . They were exercising their economic power together with that of their allies to compel Empire to abide by union rather than by state regulation of trade. . . . The state has provided for enforcement of its statutory rule by imposing civil and criminal sanctions. The union has provided for enforcement of its rule by sanctions against union members who cross picket lines. . . . We hold that the state's power to govern in this field is paramount, and that nothing in the constitutional guaranties of speech or press compels a state to apply or not to apply its antitrade restraint laws to groups of workers, businessmen or others.[90]

Given his firm attitude that valid laws must be enforced in an orderly way (scarcely a novel position), Black's position on racial "sit-ins" has been predictable. So far as he is concerned, there are unquestionably times and places in which one is simply not entitled to express a point of view in any way he sees fit: "We have a system of property, which means that a man does not have a right to do anything he wants anywhere he wants to do it. . . . That is a wonderful aphorism about shouting 'fire' in a crowded theater. But you do not have to shout 'fire' to get arrested. If a person creates a disorder in a theater, they would get him there not because of *what* he hollered but because he *hollered*."[91]

As applied to a "stand-in" at a public library in which the "standers" had been refused no service and in which they were not discriminated against, Black for four dissenting Justices said:

> I do not believe that any provision of the United States Constitution forbids any one of the 50 States of the Union, including Louisiana, to make it unlawful to stage "sit-ins" or "stand-ups" in their public libraries for the purpose of advertising objections to the State's public policies. . . . And it should be remembered that if one group can take over libraries for one cause, other groups will assert the right to do it for causes which, while wholly legal, may not be so appealing to this Court. . . .[92]

The New Deal and the Means of Democracy

The depression of the 1930's was the prime target of the New Deal years, but the New Deal was not confined solely to man's material needs. Freedom from want was but one goal and guiding principle; it was accompanied co-equally by freedom of religion, freedom of speech, freedom from fear. Even with a primary focus on the material, there remained the problem of how these and other needs of men were to be met in a democratic way.

Hence, just as Black cannot be fully understood by exclusive reference to his libertarian views, so his approach to the New Deal cannot be understood without considering his role as an apostle of personal freedom. Black is not two halves; his is a completely integrated philosophy of government. He continues to have, as he says jokingly of his college days, "one idea," and that idea is of a living, functioning democracy:

1. A democracy in which the people have a total capacity to govern themselves, without any appointed official of government—and certainly without any judge—deciding what is best for them. His approach is fundamentally a Congressional approach; he is Congress' man. Congress has all the power it

needs for any national purpose. The final accountability for the government of the United States is on the Congress, where sit the directly elected representatives of the people. Within express constitutional limits, Black is prepared to enforce whatever conclusion of Congressional deliberations. A Justice has substantial power to fill in the gaps Congress necessarily leaves in legislation, and Black has repeatedly used such power. But this is a power within the Congressional framework.[93] Not even a President, powerful as he is, can rise superior to his Congressional power-sources.

2. A democracy in which state governments, too, have adequate powers to deal with their problems; in which they, like individuals, are not subject to a big brother on the Court who will tell them what is good for them. So long as states do not bring themselves into conflict with express constitutional provisions or an act of Congress, they may go their way. On the other hand, in case of conflict with either, the states must unquestionably yield. There is no stronger exponent of the supremacy of the federal power than Black.

3. A democracy in which the people are capable of governing. The people can govern themselves if, but only if, there is no restraint on their freedom to persuade each other to a given course of action. Black will sanction government all-powerful in its domain, but only in an atmosphere of total freedom for each citizen. Such freedom includes complete freedom of speech and belief, a constitutionally prescribed and precise criminal procedure for the citizen who is crosswise with his government, complete equality for every citizen, and a free press—"a constitutionally chosen means for keeping officials elected by the people responsible to all the people whom they were selected to serve."[94] Individual freedom is the constitutional condition on the political power of the New Deal from Franklin Roosevelt to Lyndon Johnson.

4. A democracy in which power and freedom, the power to govern and the freedom to aspire to direct government, are together conditional upon a third value—order. Maintenance of an order in which the powerful government of free men can function is the first duty of any government. America, in

Black's view, can maintain that order without sacrifice of individual liberties.

These elements of Black's democracy—the proper role of government including the Supreme Court, the rightful place of the individual as man and citizen, and the essential values to which both man and government must cling as distinct from possibly temporary forms and means which themselves must not be worshipped—were reflected in some informal remarks he made in 1966 just before the twenty-ninth anniversary of his appointment to the Court. The setting for those remarks was a dinner party given in his honor in his old home of Birmingham where, because of his unequivocal opposition to segregation laws, in many quarters in recent years he has been completely unwelcome. He talked about something—the Court's active role in the development of the law—that had precipitated such hostility, yet his remarks were not altogether directed towards his fellow townsmen. Indeed, those remarks were largely introspective. He said:

> I am not afraid of change if the people will it, even change of the Court if the Constitution's method of amendment is preserved. When I first came to the Court, I had grave doubts about judicial review. Grave doubts. But I am now convinced that if we are to have the form of free government and free society which the Constitution intends, the Court must function as it has.

With great gravity, he concluded: "The American dream calls for a society in which every individual shall live as a free man."[95]

For Hugo Black, the old New Dealer, men can truly live as free men not only when their freedom to think and speak is absolutely guaranteed, but also only when their convictions and preferences can be translated into governmental policy through democratic procedures of representation; when their health and welfare are not subordinated to a falsely sanctified system of corporate business rights; when alternative opportunities for individual economic advancement are retained outside the powerful system of impersonal, efficiency-oriented industrial giants; and when participation in the several realms of the great American experiment—political, educational, and economic—is not denied to any for reasons of class, color, or belief. In short, for Black, men live as free men when, within the limitations of fate, they have maximum opportunity to be and to make of life what they will.

When Martin Van Buren appointed Peter V. Daniel to the United States Supreme Court in 1841, he wrote to his predecessor, Andrew Jackson, that he had made that choice because he wanted to choose a Democrat *"ab ovo"*—from the egg. When Franklin D. Roosevelt made his first appointment to the Supreme Court, he wanted to choose a New Dealer *ab ovo*. He did. What Senator Black told his colleagues during the Court fight, about the appointment of any Justice, perfectly applied to F.D.R.'s first selection a few months later:

"After he goes on the bench he will still be the same man he was before he went there."

CHAPTER THREE

The Persistent Race Issue

DANIEL M. BERMAN

HUGO Black left the South to go to Washington more than forty years ago. Yet the region where he was born and reared still exercises a potent influence on his life and thought, and the race issue that has so long been identified with that region continues to pursue him.

Black's soft Southern accent, totally unaffected by four decades in "the North," reveals his origins at once. That he takes pride in those origins is suggested by his passion for Southern history; that he feels a particular attachment to his home state is confirmed by his usual selection each year of at least one of his law clerks from Alabama.

The Southern heritage of Justice Black affects him in more substantial ways as well. It has left him with vivid memories of what hard-core poverty really is like, and his ears still ring with the local orators' heady prescriptions for radical reforms that he had heard from latter-day Populist orators in Alabama. It was, in fact, to a considerable extent because he was a Southerner that Black, then a Senator from Alabama, reacted so warmly to Franklin D. Roosevelt and his program for helping the "one third of the nation" that was "ill-fed, ill-clothed, and ill-housed." Black's Southern background is also relevant to the development of his philosophy of libertarianism and individual freedom, for Black was brought up in a kind of frontier country, where individualism was the hallmark.[1]

Notes appear at pages 288-291.

But the same South which made some of its sons economic egalitarians and civil libertarians also infected the minds of others with the myth of Negro inferiority. Black emerged from his prolonged exposure to the myth with fewer scars than might have been anticipated. True, a certain race-consciousness remains with him; he can still speak casually of "Anglo-Saxon courage" or "the characteristics of the Jewish race," unaware that he is using highly unscientific terminology. Social contact with Negroes is almost completely absent from his life. Yet there is not a shred of racism in his intellectual makeup. Indeed, what is noteworthy is not the obvious fact that he was at one time exposed to the mania of white supremacy, but rather the overwhelming proof that he has been able to shake off the burden of this aspect of Southern history.

And yet Black has never been allowed to forget the race issue. It has confronted him, in one or another of its aspects, throughout his public life. He was reminded of it dramatically at the time he was appointed to the Supreme Court. It was with him again when the Court had to decide whether segregated public schools were unconstitutional. And now it is facing him for the third time in his public career, as the Court grapples with the still-exploding consequences of its school segregation decision.

The Judge, the Negro, and the Klan

As a public official, Black's first contact with Negroes came in 1911 when, at age twenty-five, he was appointed to the bench of the Birmingham police court. Negroes constituted forty percent of Birmingham's population and—because of both the greater incidence of poverty among them and discriminatory police practices—an even larger proportion of those accused of petty crime. Black does not seem to have been a lenient judge, but his verdicts were rendered without bias of color. On one occasion, he took the somewhat unusual step of acquitting eleven Negroes charged with disorderly conduct, although a white officer had testified against them.[2] And, when a Negro furnace worker was tried on the charge of having assaulted a white installment collector, Black suppressed what might have become a "swearing contest" in which the word of the white man probably would have prevailed, and attempted instead to reconstruct the setting in which the alleged attack had taken place. The collector, it turned out, had insisted on repossessing the Negro's furniture, disregarding the man's plea that his wife was ill and should not be disturbed. Black dismissed the case.[3]

It was an aspect of the race issue—the treatment of Negroes accused of minor offenses—that helped Black win his second public office, that of solicitor, or prosecutor of Jefferson County. The solicitorship was an elective position, and Black had to campaign hard against the incumbent, Harrington Heflin, brother of United States Senator Tom Heflin. In his campaign speeches, Black sharply criticized the arrangement whereby the state paid a per diem fee to jailors and sheriffs for each person in their custody; the arrangement, in effect, invited efforts to get trials postponed, since longer periods of detention for the prisoners meant increased income for the jailors and sheriffs. Black promised to abolish the "fee system." The people, he said, were "tired of having hundreds of Negroes arrested for shooting craps on payday and crowding the jail with these petty offenders."

The election campaign that he waged on this and other issues was successful, and Black took office as solicitor of Jefferson County in December 1914. One of his first official acts was to release 500 prisoners who had been held for undue periods because of the practice he had attacked.[4]

The abolishment of the fee system was by no means the most spectacular action Solicitor Black took during his two and one-half years in office. Early in his term, Black began to wonder why the neighboring town of Bessemer was producing an inordinate number of confessions, especially from Negroes. An investigation revealed that police were using the most brutal third degree methods, including merciless nighttime beatings. Because there was some question about Black's jurisdiction over the Bessemer police, the new solicitor decided to present the facts he had uncovered to a grand jury. Upon hearing the evidence, its members were as horrified as Black had been. They proceeded to adopt a report, written by Black, in which the charge was made that prisoners had been beaten until "they were red with their own blood, in an effort to obtain confessions [and that] a leather strap with a buckle on one end was invented for the purpose of assisting the officers in this heinous practice. . . ." The report branded such methods "dishonorable, tyrannical, and despotic. . . ." Fundamental rights, it said, should "not be surrendered to any officer or set of officers. . . ."[5] The document containing these strong words was submitted to the judges of the criminal court, with the ultimate result that the barbarity uncovered by Black was eliminated.[6]

Despite these aspects of his early career, young Black was no zealous apostle of racial equality. Had he been able to transcend completely the cultural, social, and political environment of the Alabama of that era, it is highly unlikely that he would have chosen to join the Ku Klux Klan. But join he did, becoming a member of the Robert E. Lee Klan No. 1 of Birmingham, on September 11, 1923. He remained in the Klan for only two years, and during that time he attended three or four meetings. There is no evidence of the role he played at these meetings, though in all likelihood his participation was consistent with the sentiments he expressed in an address to a state convention of the Klan in 1926, more than a year after his friendly resignation from the organization. In that speech, he made the point that what he liked about the Klan was "not the burning of crosses, . . . not attempting to regulate anybody," but rather the effort that he thought the Klan was making to keep the door of hope open "to the boy that comes up on the humble hillside, or in the lowly valley."[7]

Why had Black become a member of the Klan? The main answer appears to be that joining the Klan was "the thing to do" for any aspiring Alabama politician, since winning public office, though not impossible without Klan support, was very difficult with active Klan opposition. During the period of Black's membership, there were as many as 85,000 Klan members in Alabama, and Klansmen filled state, county, and city offices.[8] The Grand Dragon of the Klan was the Assistant Attorney General of the State.[9] It was therefore not surprising that, for this reason alone, those who were interested in advancing Black's political career urged him to join the Klan. Some of those who knew him offered additional reasons for his joining. Herman Beck, a leading Jewish merchant in Birmingham, encouraged his young friend Black to become a Klansman so that he could help contain the trouble-making element just coming to the fore of the organization in Alabama.

Black resisted the idea for a while. He was already a member of a great many organizations[10] and this, rather than any ideological disagreement, seems to have been the most important factor in his reluctance. In fact, he found certain elements of the Klan's program attractive, for the Klan, like later Fascist movements, affected a kind of pseudo-radicalism on nonracial issues. It argued, for example, that wages could be raised by cutting off the influx of cheap immigrant labor. Such an approach had considerable appeal to a young progressive, and Black was too much a product of his region to be repelled by the racism that went with it.[11] There was racism in the Alabama Klan,[12] of course, although at the time there was probably less of it than in some other Southern states.[13]

After remaining in the organization for almost two years, Black resigned on July 9, 1925, the day before he announced that he would be a candidate for a seat in the United States Senate. In spite of his resignation, the Klan in Alabama seems to have favored his election to the Senate, though the national organization preferred another candidate.[14] Largely by dint of indefatigable campaigning, Black won the election, and in 1927 he took his seat in the United States Senate.

As a Senator, Black embraced certain positions that were no doubt pleasing to the Klan: he led a battle in the Senate against Federal anti-lynching legislation, assuring his colleagues that Negroes and whites lived in peace and harmony in Alabama;[15] and he went so far as to indicate doubt about whether Negroes should be allowed to vote.[16] Yet he was eloquent in his denunciation of violence against Negroes, and the Klan, now rapidly degenerating into a band of racist terrorists, started to reappraise its former member. Klansmen viewed as alarming errors his support of Al Smith, a Catholic, in 1928; his opposition to Senator Tom Heflin, a Klan protégé, in 1930; and his fight to safeguard the Negro's position in Federal legislation on fair labor standards.[17] By 1937, when Black was nominated to the Supreme Court, he had become so obnoxious to the Klan that the organization decided to destroy

his career. The result was the most painful crisis Black had
faced in his public life.

The Appointment, the Exposé, and the Reaction

The method the Ku Klux Klan chose to ruin Hugo Black
may have set a new record in political cynicism: disclosure of
Black's former membership in the Klan by the organization
itself. Accordingly, internal documents proving that Black
had been in the Klan were turned over to a conservative newspaper, the *Pittsburgh Post Gazette*.

Fortunately for Black, it was not until after the Senate had
already confirmed his nomination as an Associate Justice of
the Supreme Court that the Pittsburgh newspaper published
its exposé of his Klan past. On September 13, 1937, the *Post
Gazette* began publication of a six-part series on Black which
was to win its author, Ray Sprigle, a Pulitzer Prize. Sprigle
charged that Black had not only been a member of the Klan
in the past but that he still belonged to the organization. The
reporter spared no adjectives. His first article began:

> Hugo L. Black, Associate Justice of the United States
> Supreme Court, is a member of the hooded brotherhood
> that for ten long, blood-drenched years ruled the South-
> land with lash and noose and torch, the Invisible Em-
> pire, Knights of the Ku Klux Klan. He holds his mem-
> bership in the masked and oath-bound legion as he holds
> his office on the nation's supreme tribunal—for life.[18]

The "proof" that the Justice still belonged to the Klan was
a "Grand Passport" that Black had been given after his 1926
primary victory. Though the document said nothing about
life membership, Sprigle professed to find significance in the
fact that no expiration date was given. Since Black appeared
in person at a "klorero" (state meeting) to accept the passport
more than a year after his resignation, Sprigle concluded that
the resignation had been spurious. Credence was lent to this
charge by Black's letter of resignation, which had been signed,
"Yours, I. T. S. U. B., Hugo L. Black." The initials meant,
"In The Sacred and Unfailing Bond." Though there was no

evidence of his having had any further connection with the Klan in the eleven years preceding the Court appointment, Sprigle charged that Black's use of the formula in 1925 implied his continuing allegiance to the organization. The reporter also attached significance to the address Black had given at the Klan meeting where he was presented with the "life membership," for in it Black was quoted as having uttered the following words: "I realize that I was elected by men who believe in the principles that I have sought to advocate and which are the principles of this organization."[19]

Sprigle's revelations were page-one news in every newspaper in the country. Black was vacationing in Europe at the time and declined to comment until he returned home. Once back in the United States, he asked for radio time so that he could speak directly to the American people without risking distortion of his words by a hostile press. The request for time was granted, and on the night of October 1, 1937, about 50 million listeners—the largest audience in radio history except for that which had listened to the abdication address of King Edward VIII[20]—heard Black make his first and last public comment on his association with the Klan. He admitted that he had been a member, but denied that he had remained one after his letter of resignation was submitted in 1925. His denial was categorical:

> I never rejoined. What appeared then or what appears now on the records of the organization, I do not know. I have never considered and I do not now consider the unsolicited card given to me shortly after my nomination to the Senate as a membership of any kind in the Ku Klux Klan. I never used it. I did not even keep it. . . . Before becoming a Senator I dropped the Klan. I have had nothing to do with it since that time. I abandoned it. I completely discontinued my association with the organization. I have never resumed it and I never expect to do so.[21]

But Black's admission of past membership in the Klan was the big news in the press. The religious, as well as racial, bigotry of the organization's tenets were played up. On balance the radio address only added to the furor. Few people seemed persuaded by Black's allegation that a "planned and concerted" campaign had been launched against him, and that the inevitable result would be "the projection of religious beliefs into a position of prime importance in political campaigns and to reinfect our social and business life with the poison of religious bigotry. . . ."[22]

The *New York World-Telegram* said that the speech was "clever . . . 'too damned clever.' "[23] David Lawrence called Black ". . . an insult to the millions of Catholics, Protestants, Jews, white and colored citizens."[24] The *New York Times* declared that the cause of liberalism had been betrayed.[25] The *New York Herald Tribune* labeled Black a "coward"[26] and the *American Mercury* summed him up as "a vulgar dog."[27] The *Washington Post* said: "By this confession, extracted from Mr. Black only when he was unable to continue his attitude of concealment, the reputation of the American Judiciary is permanently smirched."[28]

The Sprigle articles not only inflamed much of the rest of the press but confirmed the suspicions of already hostile segments of the political community as well. Raymond Moley had warned earlier that Black was a ". . . product of that dark political hour in the twenties when fiery crosses flared on thousands of hillsides."[29] Senator Royal S. Copeland of New York, an anti-Roosevelt Democrat who had opposed Black's nomination, sought to capitalize on the issue in his race for mayor of New York.[30] Norman Thomas assailed Black[31] and the National Association for the Advancement of Colored People pressed the new Justice to resign.[32]

Within a few weeks, however, the storm had died down sufficiently that Black could assure his niece that the "conspiracy to ruin me has not worked," and that there was no need to "worry about the press and their fight." He expressed surprise that the articles in the *Post Gazette* had been treated as though they contained something new. Actually, he wrote, "there was nothing new in the articles . . . except the venom and the false implications." He explained:

All of the statements [in the newspaper series] have been thrashed out in Alabama campaigns. Governor [Thomas

E.] Kilby supplied the "gold card" memorandum from his campaign files. It was widely published in Alabama in 1932 and all the leading newspapers throughout the nation as well as the magazines have repeatedly published the fact that I was formerly a member of the Klan. Of course, these papers knew it and were aware that everybody else knew it who had kept up with politics in the country.[33]

In the same letter, Black said that he had "never missed one single minute's sleep over the incident,"[34] for he felt that his conscience was clear. Yet clearly he was paying a heavy price for his Southern past. The public confession he had been compelled to make could not have been easy. And it would be some time before the suspicion would die, especially among Negroes, that he had indulged in self-serving rhetoric when he said in his radio address, "I have among my friends many members of the colored race. I have watched the progress of its members with sympathy and admiration. Certainly they are entitled to the full measure of protection accorded to the citizenship of our country by the Constitution and our laws."[35]

A Champion Emerges, A Prophet Is Disowned

Those who had forecast in 1937 that Black's judicial actions would reflect his past Klan association were soon proved wrong. In a 1940 case involving the use of third degree methods against Negro suspects, Black spoke out with an indignation reminiscent of his days as county solicitor. The case concerned four Negroes whose death sentences had been affirmed by Florida's Supreme Court in spite of the fact that they rested on confessions extracted only after six days of almost continuous questioning. Black called the documents that the Negroes had signed "sunrise confessions,"[36] and he looked upon the case as a classic in police brutality. In it, he noted, one could observe

the dragnet methods of arrest on suspicion without warrant, and the protracted questioning and cross-questioning of . . . ignorant young colored tenant farmers by state officers and other white citizens, in a fourth floor jail room, where as prisoners they were without friends, advisers or counsellors under circumstances calculated to break the strongest nerves and the stoutest resistance.[37]

To him such procedures were typical of tyrannical governments, which had "immemorially utilized dictatorial criminal procedure and punishment to make scapegoats of the weak, or of helpless political, religious, or racial minorities and those who differed, who would not conform and who resisted tyranny."[38] Appropriately, Black read his opinion on Lincoln's birthday. The following day, President Roosevelt, who had placed Black on the Supreme Court three years earlier, suggested at a press conference that the newspapers owed the Justice an apology for the slurs they had cast on him in 1937 because of his former affiliation with the Klan.[39]

Black's opinion in the Florida case presaged the unfolding of a basic philosophy. In the years that followed, the Alabamian made himself the champion of the individual and of disadvantaged minorities and, thus, of the Negro. His conviction that equality before the law embraces everyone was spelled out in cases challenging racial exclusion on grand and petit juries,[40] as well as in those challenging segregation in transportation facilities,[41] in voting,[42] and in education.

It was, of course, in the field of education that the Supreme Court, in 1954, made its most far-reaching decision with respect to racial segregation. The Court had been leading up to that decision at least as long as Black had been a member of it. In 1938, Black had been with the majority of seven whose decision, announced by Chief Justice Charles Evans Hughes, forbade the exclusion of Negroes in Missouri from a state law school; Missouri's plan for paying the expenses of its Negro citizens who went outside the state to get their law training was held by the Court to be an unacceptable substitute for "equal protection of the law" in education.[43] Ten years later a unanimous Court had re-emphasized that conclusion in an Oklahoma case of similar circumstances.[44] And in 1950, the Court, again with Black's active participation and consent, had advanced the cause of equality for Negroes in education two steps further. In one decision,[45] it barred racial segregation of classrooms, libraries, and other facilities *within* institutions; in another,[46] the Court indicated that it would no longer uncritically accept and thus tacitly reinforce the old "separate but equal" doctrine, which had been established in a transportation case in 1896[47] but had later been assumed to apply as well to other public facilities, including schools. These decisions specifically affected higher education, but they also sparked activity on the part of those who were concerned about the effects on Negro children of segregated public schools in Southern and Border states.

During the course of its term beginning in October 1952, the Court first heard arguments in a group of cases challenging segregation in elementary and high schools in Kansas, South Carolina, Virginia, and Delaware. They were considered at the same time by virtue of the common issue, and took the name of the Kansas case, *Brown v. Board of Educ.*[48] The complexities of the cases and, more particularly, the potential ramifications of their resolution, caused the Court to re-schedule them for further argument for the next October term. That argument took place in December 1953, with a new Chief Justice, Earl Warren, presiding.

From the outset, Black favored reviewing the cases challenging the constitutionality of segregated public schools, and behind the scenes he played an important part in helping the Chief Justice to marshal a unanimous Court. When the 9-0 decision striking down public school segregation was announced on May 17, 1954,[49] the vote cast by Black infuriated white Southerners, who felt he had betrayed them.

The attack on him that followed was shrill and mean. Of the spate of letters he received following the decision, most were from the South and of those the great majority were hostile. Frequently they were ugly. A number of letters were also written to and published in the daily newspapers in Alabama. One suggested that the State Legislature "pass a resolution asking Justice Hugo Black to no longer consider himself a citizen of Alabama";[50] in fact, similar resolutions were seriously discussed in the state capital, Montgomery. The Andalusia *Star-News* editorially asked and then answered a jibing question that typified the Southern reaction: "If the

Ku Klux Klan is revived in the South, where will this put Hizzoner Hugo Black, Alabama's contribution to the Supreme Court? When a monument is erected to Hugo Black as a great man, it will have to depict him atop a fence, jumping from one side to the other."[51]

One week after the *Brown* decision, Senator James Eastland of Mississippi launched a broadside attack on the entire membership of the Supreme Court. Charging that the Court had been "indoctrinated and brainwashed by leftwing pressure groups," he implied that some of the brainwashing was coming from members of the Court itself. Black was one of five justices he singled out for special abuse, for Black, he pointed out, had been given an award by the Southern Conference for Human Welfare, "a notorious Communist front organization."[52]

Indeed, as the Court moved to apply the principle of the school desegregation cases to other fields in the months and years that immediately followed, and as Black continued to support this development, the sentiment against him grew in volume and intensity. The castigation to which he was subjected in the South troubled Black as the attacks against him over his Ku Klux Klan membership never had. Shunned by many of his old friends, he began to visit his beloved Alabama less frequently; then, for a time, he stopped returning altogether. The ostracism to which he was subjected extended to members of his family, too. The only one of his children who still made his home there, Hugo L. Black, Jr., decided to give up his law practice in Birmingham and move to Florida.

Yet Black did not condemn those Southerners who found it impossible to adjust to the near-revolutionary changes that the Supreme Court had ordained. Nor, despite the attacks on him, did he become embittered, for he is the rare kind of person who genuinely respects the opinions of others—however intemperately expressed.

Meanwhile, the same actions by Justice Black that aroused such intense anger in much of the white South endeared him to the Negro leaders who had anathematized him at the time his membership in the Klan was brought to national attention. Ironically, Black now came to be lionized by some of the very same people who had previously condemned him.

The Issue Persists

The irony may not end here. Since 1954, the most pressing constitutional issues have changed radically in character; indeed, the pendulum may be swinging again, with Justice Black once more a target of criticism by the most politically conscious elements in the Negro community and of other staunch civil rights advocates.

The issue on which Black differs with the civil rights movement relates to the use of two tactics: protest demonstrations and civil disobedience. There is irony here, too, for it is probable that neither the protest demonstrations nor the civil disobedience would have come about—at least until later— had not Negro expectations been raised by the very Supreme Court decisions to which Black contributed so much. When these hopes—for equal opportunity and "freedom now"—were thwarted by a recalcitrant South and a lackadaisical North, Negroes more and more often took to the streets and resorted to direct action. They were undeterred when their demonstrations ran afoul of local and state laws, for the Supreme Court decisions had spurred a belief that the federal Constitution and federal law were both on their side, and they had no doubt that right and justice were, too. Thus began the marches and the freedom rides, the sit-ins, swim-ins, pray-ins, stall-ins, and lie-ins. And thus began, also, the disenchantment of Hugo Black.

Black's critical attitude toward civil rights demonstrations began to manifest itself in 1964, when the Supreme Court, reversing the Maryland Court of Appeals upset the trespass convictions of Negro students for their participation in a sit-in at a restaurant in Baltimore. Writing for the majority, Justice William J. Brennan, Jr., chose to stand on highly technical ground, pointing out that the Court of Appeals had affirmed the convictions prior to the enactment by the state of Maryland and the city of Baltimore of "public accommodations laws." In view of the new laws, said Brennan, the state Court of Appeals should be given an opportunity to determine whether the Negro students should be punished for having engaged in conduct that was now clearly legal.[53] Chief Justice Warren and Justices William O. Douglas and

Arthur Goldberg agreed with Brennan that the convictions could not be allowed to stand, but they saw no justification for avoiding the constitutional question. They said they would have preferred a holding that the Fourteenth Amendment precludes outright the exclusion of Negroes from places of public accommodation whether or not they are governmentally owned or operated.

In a sharp dissent, Black agreed that the Court should have dealt with the central constitutional issue, but his interpretation of the Fourteenth Amendment bore no resemblance to that endorsed by Warren, Douglas, and Goldberg. Black pointed out that the Amendment was directed only against state action; state action, he said, does not exist merely because, as had happened in the present instance, a property-owner calls on the police to help him exclude Negroes from an enterprise that he owns. As Black saw it, any other interpretation of the Fourteenth Amendment would "severely handicap a state's efforts to maintain a peaceful and orderly society." This was his reasoning:

> Our society has put its trust in a system of criminal laws to punish lawless conduct. To avert personal feuds and violent brawls it has led its people to believe and expect that wrongs against them will be vindicated in the courts. Instead of attempting to take the law into their own hands, people have been taught to call for police protection to protect their rights wherever possible. It would betray our whole plan for a tranquil and orderly society to say that a citizen, because of his personal prejudices, habits, attitudes, or beliefs, is cast outside the law's protection and cannot call for the aid of officers sworn to uphold the law and preserve the peace. The worst citizen no less than the best is entitled to equal protection of the laws of his state and of his nation.[54]

Thus, as far as Black was concerned, the Fourteenth Amendment did not *of its own force* prohibit owners of establishments serving the public from refusing service to Negroes or "compel either a black man or a white man running his own private business to trade with anyone else against his will."[55]

Since Black for many years had been the most vigilant defender on the Court of First Amendment rights, the lawyers for the Negroes in the Maryland case had hoped that he might be attracted by their argument that, in conducting their sit-in demonstration, the Negroes were merely exercising the freedom of expression guaranteed them by the First Amendment. But Black could see in this case no legitimate infringement of rights under the First Amendment. In his opinion, an individual's right to express his views applies only in places where he has an unquestioned legal right to be present. "The right to freedom of expression," he said pointedly, "is a right to express views—not a right to force other people to supply a platform or a pulpit."[56]

Only two of the most conservative Justices on the Court, John Marshall Harlan and Byron White, joined Black in his dissent. The Justices who were usually his staunchest allies—Warren, Douglas, Goldberg, and Brennan—were all on the other side. In another 1964 case, somewhat similar to the one from Maryland, only three conservative Justices—Harlan, Stewart, and White—wrote dissents along with Black; Tom Clark, usually considered a conservative, joined Warren, Brennan, Douglas, and Goldberg to make up the five-member majority. As in the earlier case, the underlying question in this case involving South Carolina was whether a new public accommodations statute should be construed as abating prior trespass convictions of sit-in demonstrators. The principal difference was that in this case the new statute was a federal enactment—Title II of the Civil Rights Act of 1964.[57]

The majority, speaking through Justice Clark, held that the convictions had, indeed, been abated. Black disagreed on two counts. First, he rejected the argument that especially because of the 1964 statute "persons who are unlawfully refused service [have] a 'right' to take the law into their own hands by sitting down and occupying the premises for as long as they choose to stay." As he read the statute, it was designed "to take such disputes out of the streets and restaurants and into the courts, which Congress has granted power to provide an adequate and orderly judicial remedy."[58] His second objection to the decision reached by the Court related to the holding on retroactivity. His own research into the legislative history made him feel sure that Congress had not intended to abate existing prosecutions. One could not find in the statute, he said, "one paragraph, one sentence, one clause, or one word . . . on which the most strained efforts of the most fertile imagination could support such a conclusion."[59]

When Congress enacts legislation under its constitutional authority, an entirely different situation is created for Black than when the Court is asked to use judicial construction to achieve the same result. Not long after dissenting in the Maryland case, he voted to sustain the constitutionality of the public accommodations title in the Civil Rights Act of 1964 as a valid exercise of the congressional power to regulate commerce. He denied being guilty of inconsistency. His earlier dissent, he explained:

> . . . stated only that the Fourteenth Amendment in and of itself, without implementation by a law passed by Congress, does not bar racial discrimination in privately owned places of business in the absence of state action. The opinion did not discuss the power of Congress under the Commerce and Necessary and Proper Clauses or under section 5 of the Fourteenth Amendment to pass a law forbidding such discrimination. . . . Because the Civil Rights Act of 1964 as applied here is wholly valid under the Commerce clause and the Necessary and Proper clause, there is no need to consider whether this Act is also constitutionally supportable under section 5 of the Fourteenth Amendment. . . .[60]

Black's approach to this problem is entirely in character. He inclines to take an expansive view of congressional power and a restrictive view of the power of judges. In an age when the courts have come to be much admired for their defense of individual rights, he for one is not ready to abandon a traditional democratic notion that judges, who are exempt from retribution at the polls, may be tempted to usurp power and perform tyrannical actions, while Congress is restrained to some extent by its responsibility and accountability to the electorate.

Yet even when Congress has acted, Black can be sternly disapproving if he feels that constitutional corners have been cut in order to promote racial equality. While concurring in the Court's decision upholding the most important provisions of the Voting Rights Act of 1965,[61] he could not bring himself to approve one section of that law. The provision to which he objected—Title 5 of the law—prohibited states that had been using literacy tests as devices for maintaining racial disfranchisement from amending their constitutions or laws relating to voting without receiving approval in advance from either the United States District Court for the District of Columbia or the Attorney General of the United States. Black could discern no constitutional authorization for the kind of power that Title 5 purported to bestow on the District Court for the District of Columbia. That court, he said, was in effect being empowered to render advisory opinions without having any case or controversy before it. But he had an even more basic objection to the procedure provided for by the Act:

> Section 5, by providing that some of the states cannot pass state laws or adopt state constitutional amendments without first being compelled to beg Federal authorities to approve their policies, so distorts our constitutional structure of government as to render any distinction drawn in the Constitution between state and Federal power almost meaningless. . . . Certainly if all the provisions of our Constitution which limit the power of the Federal government and reserve other power to the states are to mean anything, they mean at least that the states have power to pass laws and amend their constitutions without first sending their officials hundreds of miles away to beg Federal authorities to approve them.[62]

Efforts to tear down barriers against Negro voting were also involved in another Supreme Court case[63] in which Black found himself in the minority. This case concerned the use of the poll tax by Virginia in state elections. The Twenty-fourth Amendment had banned the tax only in Federal elections,[64] and Congress had declined to extend this ban in the Voting Rights Act of 1965. Instead, it had instructed the Attorney General to bring a case before the Court to determine whether state poll tax laws did in reality violate the Constitution. The Attorney General acted as he had been instructed to do, and brought suit to outlaw the tax in Virginia. When the case came before the Supreme Court, the decision was to strike down the Virginia poll tax as a violation of the equal protection clause of the Fourteenth Amendment. The reason given was that since the qualifications of voters "have no relation to wealth nor to paying or not paying this or any other tax," the State had made an invidious distinction between those citizens who could afford to pay the tax and those who could not.

Black dissented from this decision, in the belief that the Court had made an essentially legislative determination, using the equal protection clause "to write into the Constitution its notions of what it thinks is good governmental policy." In the absence of any evidence that the poll tax in Virginia had been used for racially discriminatory purposes, he said, the Court had no warrant to act; it was only Congress that had the power to legislate the poll tax out of existence, under Section 5 of the Fourteenth Amendment.[65]

In the cases just discussed, Black found himself in a dissenting minority. But twice he was with the majority in civil rights cases during the October 1965 term, and in both these instances his vote was decisive. In one case, the National Association for the Advancement of Colored People was held liable for damages because members of one of its chapters had engaged in picketing a grocery store illegally;[66] in the other, the Court rejected the arguments of arrested civil rights demonstrators who wanted to have their cases removed from a state court to a Federal court on the ground that otherwise they would be denied a fair trial on account of their race.[67]

It is "unlawful" civil rights demonstrations that offend Black the most. On one occasion, the question before the Court was whether to affirm the breach of the peace convictions of five Negro youths who had conducted the most placid sort of demonstration in favor of their right to use the facilities of a public library in Louisiana. Justice Abe Fortas, who spoke for the majority in reversing the conviction, noted that there had been no noise and no disturbance in the course of the demonstration. The Negroes, he said, were "neither loud, boisterous, obstreperous, indecorous nor impolite. . . . They sat and stood in the room, quietly, as monuments of protest against the segregation of the library."[68] Black agreed that the Negroes had "never talked in unusually loud voices and used no bad language," but he was indignant at the reversals and deeply apprehensive about what the consequences would be. He said:

> I am deeply troubled with the fear that powerful private groups throughout the nation will read the Court's action as I do—that is, as granting them a license to invade the tranquility and beauty of our libraries whenever they have quarrel with some state policy which may or may not exist. It is an unhappy circumstance in my judgment that the group, which more than any other has need of a government of equal laws and equal justice, is now encouraged to believe that the best way for it to advance its cause, which is a worthy one, is by taking the law into its own hands from place to place and from time to time. Governments like ours were formed to substitute the rule of law for the rule of force. . . . The holding in this case today makes it more necessary than ever that we stop and look more closely at where we are going.[69]

In a case handed down on November 14, 1966,[70] it was made apparent that, after several years of sometimes lonely protest, Hugo Black had finally gotten a majority of the Court to "stop and look more closely" at the question of public protests. Justice Black was allowed to speak for the five-man majority and he was careful to draw distinctions between the particular demonstration at issue—protesters massing on "that part of the jail grounds reserved for jail uses"[71]—and other public protest demonstrations in public places which the Court had previously allowed. He distinguished, for example, between the Florida law in question which prevented trespassing "upon the property of another, committed with a malicious or mischievous intent . . ." and the vague "breach of peace" statutes which had been used by state and local governments in other situations to break up peaceful demonstrations which constituted no threat to public order or to the functioning of any governmental process. But beyond proscribing mass demon-

strations from essential access routes to public jails, Black
again challenged what he saw as the "major unarticulated
premise" of such civil rights demonstrators "that people who
want to propagandize protests or views have a constitutional
right to do so whenever and however and wherever they
please."[72] He said:

> The State, no less than a private owner of property,
> has power to preserve the property under its control for
> the use to which it is lawfully dedicated. For this reason
> there is no merit to the petitioners' argument that they
> had a constitutional right to stay on the property, over
> the jail custodian's objections, because this "area chosen
> for peaceful civil rights demonstration was not only 'rea-
> sonable' but particularly appropriate. . . ." The United
> States Constitution does not forbid a State to control use
> of its own property for its own lawful non-discrimina-
> tory purpose.[73]

Now it was another, Mr. Justice Douglas, who was in bitter
dissent. Joined by the Chief Justice and Justices Brennan and
Fortas, he charged that the majority had wrought a "tragic
consequence" in allowing a trespass law to be "used to bludgeon those who peacefully exercise a First Amendment right to
protest to government against one of the most grievous of all
modern oppressions which some of our States are inflicting on
our citizens."[74] Twitting Justice Black on his position by
quoting from certain of Black's previous opinions and from
Black's friend, Edmund Cahn, Douglas warned that Black and
the majority were only serving to "increase the forces of frustration which the conditions of second-class citizenship are
generating amongst us."[75]

The press reported the case in a variety of terms. *The Washington Post* highlighted the fact that "for the first time in the
civil rights revolution of the 1960's, the Supreme Court upheld
the conviction of civil rights demonstrators."[76] The *Post* then
immediately noted that Justice Black had achieved "a majority
that has eluded him for the last two years."[77] *Newsweek* suggested that whether or not "the Court followed 'th' iliction returns,' the Tallassee case looked like a straw in the prevailing

wind—a wind no longer blowing the Negro demonstrators' way."[78] The *St. Louis Globe-Democrat* succinctly headlined its story: "High Court Decision Blow to Civil Rights Groups."[79]

Of all the opinions by Black in a somewhat similar vein,[80] the opinion in the Louisiana library case was perhaps his major effort to warn the Negro community that it stands to lose a great deal if it relies only on "self-help" and ignores the processes of law. He was clearly trying to say that while the ends sought by the civil rights movement are ones he thoroughly applauds, the means employed in the Louisiana library sit-in and similar situations are ill-calculated to achieve those ends.

In condemning certain tactics of direct action on the ground that they are self-defeating, Black may be wrong, but there is no reason to doubt the sincerity of his statement that he considers the cause of the civil rights movement "a worthy one." To refuse to take the statement at face value and to conclude that he no longer believes in the cause of civil rights —that is, the cause of full equality for all citizens—is to make a serious misjudgment. One must consider the special vantage point of Black's more than fifty years in public life, during which he has seen other worthy goals doomed by the very means employed to achieve them. He does not want such a fate to befall the precious cause of civil rights.

Thus, those who—like the author of this chapter—do not share Black's antipathy for the techniques of direct action should keep that fact in mind. The issues Black has raised deserve critical, objective consideration. They must not be obscured by another round of name-calling. For that would be a disservice to the cause of civil rights and would, as well, compound the injustice—and the irony of that injustice—done to Hugo Black over the race issue of thirty years ago.

CHAPTER FOUR

The Individual and the Bill of Absolute Rights

IRVING DILLIARD

WHEN Senator Black became Justice Black, Charles Evans Hughes was Chief Justice. Since then, there have been three other Chief Justices—Harlan Fiske Stone, Frederick Moore Vinson, and Earl Warren—and twenty-four Associate Justices, one of whom (Stone) advanced to Chief Justice. Thus Black has had twenty-seven colleagues in his thirty years of service. That impressive number is even more striking when it is put into historical perspective: it means that Black has served with almost one-third of all the Justices who have sat on the Court in its 178-year history. Moreover, Black has already served longer than all but eight of his ninety-plus predecessors.[1]

But Mr. Justice Black's unquestioned place in history stands on far more solid substance than three decades of Supreme Court service with almost as many colleagues in the span as years. His importance is secured in accomplishment, not in mere endurance. He has left his own clear impress on many vital aspects of our law and life, and has made significant contributions in still other areas. Most important of all has been his contribution to that area of Supreme Court jurisdiction which itself may be said to be most important—the realm of human liberty. Indeed, without depreciating any other areas of its adjudication, it is not too much to say that the Supreme

Notes appear at pages 292-297.

Court's active involvement in the protections of our basic freedoms as guaranteed by the Constitution has come to be its preeminent role.[2]

The Court is, of course, the indispensable referee in federal-state relationships when those relationships sharpen into intergovernmental disputes which require settlement. Also, the Court must occasionally settle problems between or among states. This necessary umpire function, assigned by the Constitution, has been practiced by the Court since its earliest days. Similarly, its interpretation of the commerce powers and the laws passed under them—sometimes involving delicate questions of governmental regulation of business and industry in a society dedicated to the proposition of free and unfettered private enterprise—has not only been a traditional but a consistent activity. Yet only in the present century, notably since World War I and more frequently since World War II, has the Supreme Court, by force of rising issues and circumstances, become the foremost guardian of individual rights.

The period of greatest intensification of this newer mission, from World War II on, has paralleled the period of Black's extended tenure. Since necessity has a way of producing its own men, it would seem no accident that these historical and personal periods have coincided. Throughout this era, totalitarian concepts and practices have stifled individual freedom in vast expanses of the foreign world; and sadly, in one form or another and on too many occasions, similar dictatorial forces have also threatened human liberty in these United States. Fortunately for the American people, Hugo Black has all the while been stationed at a key position in the crucial defenses. While most of us have had our sights lowered to minor personal concerns of no enduring importance even to ourselves, he has been engaged in a major struggle: to make secure for all of us the Freedoms that the Constitution so plainly guarantees but that others, judges as well as lawmakers, would allow to atrophy in unconcern or actively help to "balance" away.

The position of Justice Black on individual liberty and the Bill of Rights can be simply and quickly stated. He believes that the Constitution says what it means about our civil liberties and our civil rights and, equally important, that it means what it says. Black has stated repeatedly his conviction that the Bill of Rights must be in practice what it is in language—a bill of *absolute* rights. With Justice Douglas he has said:

> First Amendment rights are beyond abridgment either by legislation that directly restrains their exercise or by suppression or impairment through harassment, humiliation, or exposure by government. One of those rights, freedom of assembly, includes of course freedom of association; and it is entitled to no less protection than any other First Amendment right. . . . These are principles applicable to all people under our Constitution irrespective of their race, color, politics, or religion.[3]

Black reasons from a thorough examination of the historical record and from the fact that such principles are not vaguely phrased but are models of simple clarity. He finds the specifications of the Founding Fathers, who framed the First Amendment almost simultaneously with the ratification of the Constitution, to be deliberate choices. Consequently, to read the Bill of Rights as a collection of admonitions which may or may not be taken seriously is to do the Bill of Rights and ourselves a dangerous, if not in the end an irreparable, disservice.

Black has said:

> [I believe] that the First Amendment grants an absolute right to believe in any governmental system, [to] discuss all governmental affairs, and [to] argue for desired changes in the existing order. This freedom is too dangerous for bad, tyrannical governments to permit. But those who wrote and adopted our First Amendment weighed those dangers against the dangers of censorship and deliberately chose the First Amendment's unequivocal command that freedom of assembly, petition, speech and press shall not be abridged. I happen to believe this was a wise choice and that our free way of life enlists such respect and love that our Nation cannot be imperiled by mere talk.[4]

In taking such a position, Justice Black does not shut his eyes to the needs of organized society through the instruments of government. As a Senator for ten critical years, he learned the problem from the viewpoint of the lawmaker as well. He is fully aware of the "balancing" argument: the right of an individual citizen may be abridged on any occasion when its exercise would cause so much injury to the public that this injury would outweigh the injury to the individual who is deprived of the right. For the most part, such balancing has been in response to seemingly urgent pressures; but those pressures, which may well deserve attention and even understanding, should not be erected into constitutional principles.

Black is equally aware of the related argument that the guarantees in the Bill of Rights must "compete" for survival against general powers expressly granted to Congress: that the right of the individual must, if necessary, compete with government's power to conduct affairs in the public interest, and that the courts must decide, according to their momentary lights, who wins the given competition. He finds these restricting ideas about individual liberties and freedoms stemming from the premise that there are no "absolute" prohibitions in the Constitution and that "all constitutional problems are questions of reasonableness, proximity and degree."

Justice Black could not be more emphatic in rejecting such a set of views. In delivering the first James Madison Lecture at the New York University School of Law,[5] he said:

> I cannot accept this approach to the Bill of Rights. It is my belief that there *are* "absolutes" in our Bill of Rights, and they were put there on purpose by men who knew what words meant, and meant their prohibitions to be "absolutes." The whole history and background of the Constitution and the Bill of Rights, as I understand it, belies the assumption or conclusion that our ultimate constitutional freedoms are no more than our English ancestors had when they came to this new land to get new freedoms. The historical and practical purposes of a Bill of Rights, the very use of a written constitution, indigenous to America, the language the Framers used, the kind of three-department government they took pains to set up, all point to the creation of a government which was denied all power to do some

things under any and all circumstances, and all power
to do other things except precisely in the manner prescribed.[6]

So it is that Black reads our basic charter as a virtually im-
penetrable protection of the individual, his rights, and his
role in society. Such protection, embracing all citizens, thus
may be claimed by the lone dissident or the minority group,
in disagreeing with policies of, or even in defying restrictions
imposed by, any unit of government. The situation must be
most exceptional to move the Senior Justice from his solid
position.

The Unfolding of a Conviction

Justice Black was not long on the Supreme Court before
he began speaking out on Bill of Rights cases. Then as now,
these, of course, were not the only type of cases he grappled with
which had significant implications for constitutional law. Many
subjects required his attention and thought in the first years.
Indeed, for a freshman member, the former Senator from
Alabama was relatively busy in his first term. Because of ill-
ness, Justice Cardozo was unable to hear many of the arguments. Justice Reed, who came on the Court some months
after Black, also participated only in part of the work of the
term. With the Supreme Court short-handed to this extent,
the first of F.D.R.'s appointees wrote an average of one opinion
a week. Many of the opinions for the Court he considered
"easy,"[7] and so it was on his dissents that he worked hardest.
Several of his early opinions were impressive pieces of work
for a beginner on the bench. In his one-man dissent to the
per curiam decision in *McCart v. Indianapolis Water Co.*,[8]
Black boldly and painstakingly defended the right of the state
of Indiana to regulate the price of water in Indianapolis "free
from interference by Federal courts." He was equally bold
in opposing Justice Stone's majority opinion in *Connecticut
Life Ins. Co. v. Johnson*,[9] with a dissent that in effect charged
the courts with having originated and continued a distortion
of the original meaning of the Fourteenth Amendment by

allowing corporations to be considered as "persons" under the
Due Process and Equal Protection Clauses.

Beginning with these earliest opinions, Black wrote his statements of facts and conclusions so plainly and clearly that laymen as well as lawyers could easily understand situations and
reasoning that in many other hands would have been obscured.
In *Federal Trade Comm'n v. Standard Educ. Soc'y*[10] the defendant company had attempted to evade the law with the contention that its advertising was so manifestly untrue that no one
would be foolish enough to believe it. In this case speaking for
a unanimous Court, Black demolished this brazen argument
in sentences of compelling clarity. "Laws are made to protect
the trusting as well as the suspicious. . . . There is no duty
resting upon the citizen to suspect the honesty of those with
whom he does business."[11]

Although the issues in *Connecticut* and *Standard Educ.* did
not directly involve individual rights, Black's own concern
with the individual as the focus of American constitutional
democracy began to be revealed. Even questions of government regulation of business, and of what constituted fair trade
practices in the competitive commercial marketplace, would
be considered in terms of the individual—whenever his rights
would be impaired or his place in society diminished by not
considering such terms.

No opinion of Black's first term was more important than
his decision for the Supreme Court's majority in *Johnson v.
Zerbst,*[12] which involved vital protections of accused persons.
Two penniless men of little education and no friends were
arrested in Charleston, S.C., and charged with the federal crime
of counterfeiting. The record of their prosecution and conviction showed no respect whatever for the right to writs of habeas
corpus and little more for the Sixth Amendment's guarantee of
the right to the assistance of legal counsel. They were convicted without the benefit of any legal advice and were denied
the opportunity of having the government show cause before a
judge why they should be detained. The Supreme Court reversed the Federal District Court and sent the case back to it to
determine whether in fact, they had been denied the right to
counsel in the trial. This was a beginning that told much
about the way the new Justice would apply the Bill of Rights

in cases arising from failure to enforce the Constitution's plainly worded protections of those accused of crime.

At one point, the Black opinion in *Johnson v. Zerbst* looked straight ahead twenty-five years to *Gideon v. Wainright*.[13] Recalling Justice Sutherland's landmark opinion in *Powell v. Alabama*,[14] the Scottsboro right-to-counsel case, the new Justice said:

> The Sixth Amendment . . . embodies a realistic recognition of the obvious truth that the average defendant does not have the professional legal skill to protect himself when brought before a tribunal with power to take his life or liberty, wherein the prosecution is presented by experienced and learned Counsel. That which is simple, orderly and necessary to the lawyer—to the untrained layman—may appear intricate, complex and mysterious.[15]

A quarter century would pass before the Supreme Court would say finally that the Sixth Amendment, like the First, was made applicable to the states by the Fourteenth. And when the Supreme Court would say it in 1963,[16] the opinion would be by the Justice who read the 1938 decision in *Johnson v. Zerbst*.

In the next three terms, Justice Black wrote important decisions in a series of cases dealing with fair trial procedures. The high point of the series was the unanimous decision in *Chambers v. Florida*,[17] dealing with involuntary confessions. This opinion, Black's strongest up to that time, is still regarded as one of his major works. In it he vigorously attacked all extra-legal procedures for securing confessions—and especially such brutal ones as had been employed in this case—as the work of totalitarian governments and the shame of democratic systems like ours. And he saw such practices, here employed on poor, ignorant Negro farmers accused of criminal offense, as easily extending to political or religious areas.

As term followed on term, Justice Black continued to speak out frequently for fair hearings and fairness in trial procedures. Sometimes his opinion was given for the Court, sometimes it was in dissent. A historic dissenting opinion came in *Betts v.*

Brady[18] where the petitioner was an uneducated, jobless farm hand, on relief in Maryland, who contended that his Bill of Rights protections were ignored when his request for the assistance of legal counsel was rejected by the trial court. Speaking also for Justices Douglas and Murphy, Black hit hard at the injustice of a criminal proceeding that refused an indigent defendant's pleas for counsel, allowed him to attempt to conduct his own defense against a robbery charge, and then sentenced him to eight years in prison when he was not skilled enough to prove the innocence he claimed. Said Justice Black:

> If this case had come to us from a federal court, it is clear we should have had to reverse it, because the Sixth Amendment makes the right to counsel in criminal cases inviolable by the Federal Government. I believe that the Fourteenth Amendment made the Sixth applicable to the states. But this view, although often urged in dissents, has never been accepted by a majority of this Court and it is not accepted today. . . . This Court has just declared that due process of law is denied if a trial is conducted in such a manner that it is "shocking to the universal sense of justice" or "offensive to the common and fundamental ideas of fairness and right. . . ."
>
> A practice cannot be reconciled with "common and fundamental ideas of fairness and right" which subjects innocent men to increased dangers of conviction merely because of their poverty. Whether a man is innocent cannot be determined from a trial in which, as here, denial of counsel has made it impossible to conclude, with any satisfactory degree of certainty, that the defendant's case was adequately presented. . . . Most of the states have shown their agreement by constitutional provisions, statutes, or established practice judicially approved, which assure that no man shall be deprived of counsel merely because of his poverty. Any other practice seems to me to defeat the promise of our democratic society to provide equal justice under the law.[19]

How deeply Justice Black felt on this basic issue can be told from the exchange between him and Justice Frankfurter, who gave the five-four majority opinion in *Foster v. Illinois* in 1947.[20] Rejecting a right-to-counsel plea, Justice Frankfurter said:

> After all, due process, "itself a historical product," is not to be turned into a destructive dogma in the administration of systems of criminal justice under which the states have lived not only before the Fourteenth Amendment but for the eighty years since its adoption. It does not militate against respect for the deeply rooted systems of criminal justice in the states that such an abrupt innovation as recognition of the constitutional claim here made implies, would furnish opportunities hitherto uncontemplated for opening wide the prison doors of the land.[21]

Replying directly for the four dissenters, Justice Black used words that still burn with indignation after two decades:

> This decision is another example of the consequences which can be produced by the substitution of this Court's day-to-day opinion of what kind of trial is fair and decent for the kind of trial which the Bill of Rights guarantees. This time it is the right of counsel. We cannot know what Bill of Rights provision will next be attenuated by the Court. . . . The Court's decision relies heavily on *Betts v. Brady.* . . . That case is precedent for this one. But it is the kind of precedent that I had hoped this Court would not perpetuate.

> One thing more. The Court seems to fear that protecting these defendants' right to counsel to the full extent defined in the Bill of Rights would furnish "opportunities hitherto uncontemplated for opening wide the prison doors of the land," because, presumably, there are many people like Betts, Foster and Payne behind those doors after trials without having had the benefit of counsel. I do not believe that such a reason is even

relevant to a determination that we should decline to
enforce the Bill of Rights.[22]

In his first several terms, Black's interest in the Bill of Rights
often seemed to center on the assurance of fair procedures
in trials of those accused of crime. He wrote opinions for the
Court in cases dealing with the exclusion of Negroes from
juries, the use of deception to obtain guilty pleas, and involuntary confessions. And from the record of such cases from the
early days to the present, it is fair to say that in those cases
accepted by the Court for argument and decision Black is
often on the side of the petitioner who invokes a freedom
or protection declared in the Constitution.

To be sure, there is not always a clear demarcation between
procedural rights and substantive rights, and it must not be
inferred that Black, in the early years of his Court service,
cared more for the former than the latter. Indeed, to repeat,
though the *Chambers* case concerned the trial rights of persons accused of violent crime, it is clear that Black, as he wrote
the opinion, was thinking also of those who might be accused
of political nonconformity.

The Fourth Amendment: Further Procedural Questions

Determining the rights of the individual in the area of
search and seizure has been a difficult job for the Court. It
has been difficult for Black as well. But though his record in
this area is less straightforward or at least not so clear as in
others, it is one that has now largely been resolved. It did
so in *Mapp v. Ohio*[23] which established belated order after
a tangle of confusing and at times conflicting decisions. The
confusion stemmed not so much from the effort to determine
what was "reasonable" search and seizure and what evidence
could properly be admitted in federal cases, though that has
been difficult enough; the greater confusion arose over the
question of what standards of admissibility should be applied
to state trials, where the Supreme Court generally has considered the only guide to be the Due Process Clause of the
Fourteenth Amendment.

En route to the long-delayed showdown in *Mapp* were a number of difficult cases which often saw the Court closely and sharply divided. Justice Black wrote opinions in such cases as *Wolf v. Colorado*,[24] *United States v. Rabinowitz*,[25] *Rochin v. California*,[26] and *Irvine v. California*.[27]

In the 1949 *Wolf* case, Black agreed with the majority that because evidence had been obtained by "unreasonable search and seizure" (in which case it would have been automatically excluded from a federal trial because of a federal rule on the subject, the *Weeks* Rule) it did not automatically follow that such evidence could not be considered in a state trial. Yet in the 1950 *Rabinowitz* case, Black seemed to be on the other side. In that case he objected, in dissent, to the majority's upholding the admission of evidence secured without benefit of a search warrant. But his chief objection to the majority's position was that it overturned a federal rule (the *Trupiano* Rule) previously promulgated by the Supreme Court in its role as overseer of the federal court system. Justice Minton, for the majority, indicated that the Court must retain for itself the right to decide in all cases what is and what is not reasonable, thus inviting in search and seizure cases the kind of judging by "evanescent standards of the majority's philosophy"[28] for which Black has always expressed intense dislike. Once a "reasonable" guideline was established for helping to measure reasonableness, Black would strongly prefer to maintain it, for, as *Rabinowitz* illustrates, he believes that clarity and consistency are aids to justice.

Irvine v. California is surely one of the sorriest decisions in the long history of the Supreme Court and just as surely one or more of those Justices who made its five-member majority possible must have wished later that they could have expunged it from the record. In order to establish a case of horse-racing bookmaking, California police officers entered the home of petitioner Irvine during his absence and hid a microphone in his bedroom. They strung wires to a neighbor's garage and set up a long eavesdropping operation. When they did not get the evidence they wanted, the police re-entered, again in Irvine's absence, and shifted the listening device to a more advantageous spot. Eventually they used evidence thus obtained in Irvine's trial and it helped to produce his conviction.

The Supreme Court majority in 1954 upheld the conviction and, in effect, the admission of the evidence obtained through illegal entry and stealth. However, Justice Jackson who announced the judgment and Chief Justice Warren who joined in the Jackson opinion said additionally that they believed that a copy of the record should be forwarded to the United States Attorney General for a determination of whether a federal crime had been committed by the trespassing police.[29]

Justice Black's dissent, in which Justice Douglas joined, centered on the fact that the state prosecution relied on documentary evidence of the defendant's compliance with the federal law providing for a tax on wagering. The Black objection to that head-on conflict could not be plainer. Said the dissent:

> So far as this case is concerned it is enough for me that Irvine was convicted in a state court on a confession coerced by the Federal Government. I believe this frustrates a basic purpose of the Fifth Amendment—to free Americans from fear that federal power could be used to compel them to confess conduct or belief in order to take away their life, liberty or property. For this reason I would reverse Irvine's conviction.[30]

In a final paragraph of dissent Justice Black addressed himself to the highly unusual proposal of the Chief Justice and Justice Jackson:

> It has been suggested that the Court should call on the Attorney General to investigate this record in order to start criminal prosecutions against certain California officers. I would strongly object to any such action by this Court. It is inconsistent with my own view of the judicial function in our Government. Prosecution, or anything approaching it, should, I think, be left to the government officers whose duty it is.[31]

In the 1961 *Mapp* case, a six-man majority finally and positively overturned the *Wolf* rule. One of the reasons they did so was that it had in effect allowed evidence obtained by federal authorities to be turned over to state courts, into which the federal exclusionary rules could not reach. As Justice Douglas pointed out, this arrangement "reduced the guarantees against unreasonable search and seizures to a 'dead letter.' "[32] Black agreed with the majority, and in a concurring opinion he spelled out his own finally clarified view (previously generally suggested in his *Rochin* and *Irvine* opinions) of the inadmissibility of certain evidence in state courts; following *Boyd v. United States*,[33] he would rule that if the evidence is secured by unreasonable search and seizure and is of such personal nature that its introduction amounts to self-incrimination, it must be excluded.[34] In short, the Fourth and Fifth Amendments must be applied together and together they provide the rule. Thus whether based on a new and broadened interpretation of the Due Process Clause preferred by the majority, or a re-inforced linking of the Fourth and Fifth Amendments as insisted upon by Black, the individual's right to be protected against unreasonable searches or seizures has now been solidly reinforced.

A Conviction Expands

The vagaries written into the Fourth Amendment are not to be found in the other Amendments of the Bill of Rights which constitute guaranties of personal freedom and protection. Yet the kind of questionable tactics forbidden under federal rules as violating other protections of the Bill continued to be employed by zealous prosecutors in state courts who were interested in convicting the accused above all else; and examples of this double standard of justice continued to come before the Supreme Court. An example of such a practice was presented in *Adamson v. California*[35] in 1947. Under question there as to constitutional propriety was the conduct of a state prosecutor who had specially called to a jury's attention the fact that the defendant had not taken the witness stand in his own behalf. The obvious intent was to suggest that silence meant guilt. Also obvious was the fact that such a tactic would have been forbidden in a federal court under rules made pursuant to the Fifth Amendment's protection against self-incrimination.

Black thought the procedure to be outrageous and said so. But he went further than the abuse at hand. Probably prompted as much by the history of such cases as by the single disturbing practice in the present instance, Black had made an intensive study of the Fourteenth Amendment, which he appended to his dissenting opinion,[36] dealing with the circumstances of its drafting, its adoption in Congress, and its ratification by the states. That study led to his conclusion that the first eight Amendments were applicable to the states in their entirety and were not merely to be selectively employed according to Court-made precedent or current judicial opinions as to which of the guaranties of the Bill constituted such basic traditional rights that their abridgment by states violated due process of law. He has adhered to this conviction ever since.

The First Amendment's High Preferred Place

Meantime Justice Black had begun to be directly concerned with the First Amendment's protection of free speech and to take his stands accordingly. In his fourth term he wrote a dissent for himself and Justice Douglas in *Milk Wagon Drivers Union v. Meadowmoor Dairies*[37] that found an injunction against peaceful picketing to be an invasion of free speech. Unable to discover a single thing in the record of the labor dispute to show "such imminent, clear and present danger as to justify an abridgment of the rights of freedom of speech," he opposed the majority position as one that "seriously infringes upon constitutional rights." Only four years after he took his seat, he was writing thoughts like these into the literature of the law:

> In determining whether the injunction does deprive petitioners of their constitutional liberties, we cannot and should not lose sight of the nature and importance of the particular liberties that are at stake. And in reaching my conclusion I view the guaranties of the First Amendment as the foundation upon which our governmental structure rests and without which it could not

continue to endure as conceived and planned. Freedom
to speak and write about public questions is as important to the life of our government as is the heart of
the human body. In fact, this privilege is the heart of
our government. If that heart be weakened, the result is
debilitation; if it be stilled, the result is death.[38]

His steadfast conviction about the absolute right of free
speech, evidenced not only in early cases in this specific category but mirrored in a wide variety of others from the
time of his first term, seemed to reach special fervor during
the 1950's when the McCarthy era was at its zenith. Perhaps
it was just that the cause of free speech was unpopular in the
context in which he sought to insure it. Or perhaps convictions
are always more eloquently expressed in dissent. In any event,
Black's opinions of that decade seem especially to attest to the
vigor and persistence of his full faith in liberty.

The *Dennis*[39] case in 1951 confirmed, in Supreme Court
annals, a sad period's arrival. Admitted Communist leaders
were convicted of violating the Smith Act on the basis of their
membership in the Communist Party and the doctrines and
goals of the Party. Simultaneously, the constitutionality of the
Act was upheld. Only two Justices, Black and Douglas, dissented. Black realized that the decision was influenced by
the immediate atmosphere; and appealing to what Chief
Justice Hughes once called "the brooding spirit of the law, to
the intelligence of a future day," he expressed the hope that
"in calmer times, when present pressures, passions, and fears
subside, this or some later Court will restore the First Amendment liberties to the high preferred place where they belong
in a free society."[40]

In *American Communications Workers Ass'n v. Douds*[41]
the year before, Black's dissent gave even more pointed description of the temper of the times. The Court majority
voted to uphold a federal law requiring union officials to file
affidavit evidence of non-affiliation with the Communist party.
Said Black:

The Court assures us that today's encroachment on
liberty is just a small one, that this particular statutory

provision "touches only a relative handful of persons, leaving the great majority of persons of the identified affiliations and beliefs completely free from restraint." But not the least of the virtues of the First Amendment is its protection of each member of the smallest and most unorthodox minority. Centuries of experience testify that laws aimed at one political or religious group, however rational these laws may be in their beginnings, generate hatreds and prejudices which rapidly spread beyond control. Fears of alien ideologies have frequently agitated the nation and inspired legislation aimed at suppressing advocacy of those ideologies. At such times the fog of public excitement obscures the ancient landmarks set up in our Bill of Rights. Yet then, of all times, should this Court adhere most closely to the course they mark.[42]

He continued to urge a return to full appreciation of the meaning of freedom of speech and association the next year when, it seemed to some, fear of suspected but unseen foes was bringing the country to a climate of near-hysteria. In a concurring opinion, he said:

In this day when prejudice, hate and fear are constantly invoked to justify irresponsible smears and persecution of persons even faintly suspected of entertaining unpopular views, it may be futile to suggest that the cause of internal security would be fostered, not hurt, by faithful adherence to our constitutional guarantees of individual liberty. Nevertheless, since prejudice manifests itself in much the same way in every age and country and since what has happened before can happen again, it surely should not be amiss to call attention to what has occurred when dominant governmental groups have been left free to give uncontrolled rein to their prejudices against unorthodox minorities. As specific illustration, I am adding as an appendix Macaulay's account of a parliamentary proscription which took place when popular prejudice was high; this is only one of many similar instances that readily can be found. Memories of such events were fresh in the minds of the Founders when they forbade the use of the bill of attainder.[43]

But suspicions were to give rise to even more restrictions before they both subsided. And state government agencies as well as those of the federal government were to be involved. In *Adler v. Board of Educ. of the City of New York*,[44] opposing a state law under which a teacher was disqualified as subversive because of political beliefs and not because of overt acts, Black pressed his dissent.

> This is another of those rapidly multiplying legislative enactments which make it dangerous—this time for school teachers—to think or say anything except what a transient majority happen to approve at the moment. Basically these laws rest on the belief that government should supervise and limit the flow of ideas into the minds of men. The tendency of such governmental policy is to mold people in a common intellectual pattern. Quite a different governmental policy rests on the belief that government should leave the mind and spirit of man absolutely free. Such a governmental policy encourages varied intellectual outlooks in the belief that the best views will prevail. This policy of freedom is in my judgment embodied in the First Amendment and made applicable to the states by the Fourteenth. Because of this policy public officials cannot be constitutionally vested with powers to select the ideas people can think about, censor the public views they can express, or choose the persons or groups people can associate with. Public officials with such powers are not public servants; they are public masters. I dissent from the Court's judgment sustaining this law which effectively penalizes school teachers for their thoughts and their associates.[45]

It was to be six years after the *Dennis* case that the fervent hope Black expressed there came to be realized at least in part. In 1957 the Court, with some changes in personnel and a lessening of "pressures, passions, and fears," decided the cases of the California second-string Communists, also indicted under the Smith Act. Depending on who the analyst is, the new decision, *Yates v. United States*,[46] substantially weakened *Dennis* if it did not make it impotent. For in *Yates* the Court distinguished between teaching and advocacy on the one hand and overt acts of force and violence designed to overthrow the Government on the other. The decision dismissed the charges against most of the petitioners and called for new trials for the others—new trials that Justice Department officials had not asked for. Concurring in part and dissenting in part, Justice Black, joined by Justice Douglas, declared himself in words that no one could mistake: "I would reverse every one of these convictions and direct that all the defendants be acquitted."[47] He based his conclusion in one of the clearest of libertarian appeals in the long history of man's striving toward freedom. He said:

> In essence, petitioners were tried upon the charge that they believe in and want to foist upon this country a different and to us despicable form of authoritarian government in which voices criticizing the existing order are summarily silenced. I fear that the present type of prosecutions are more in line with the philosophy of authoritarian government than with that expressed by our First Amendment.
>
> Doubtlessly, dictators have to stamp out causes and beliefs which they deem subversive to their evil regimes. But governmental suppression of causes and beliefs seems to be the very antithesis of what our Constitution stands for. The choice expressed in the First Amendment in favor of free expression was made against a turbulent background by men such as Jefferson, Madison and Mason—men who believed that loyalty to the provisions of this Amendment was the best way to assure a long life for this new nation and its Government. Unless there is complete freedom for expression of all ideas, whether we like them or not, concerning the way government should be run and who shall run it, I doubt if any views in the long run can be secured against the censor. The First Amendment provides the only kind of

security system that can preserve a free government—
one that leaves the way wide open for people to favor,
discuss, advocate, or incite causes and doctrines however obnoxious and antagonistic such views may be to
the rest of us.[48]

For many students of Justice Black's defense of the First
Amendment freedoms, one of his greatest services came in his
third decade with his dissent in the 1959 case of *Barenblatt v.
United States*.[49] A college teacher was convicted of contempt
because he would not answer questions put by a House Un-
American Activities Subcommittee. In one of his longest, most
carefully prepared, most impressive opinions, Justice Black
answered the five-man majority point by point. After a recital
of historical precedents of repressive acts against nonconform-
ists in England, he concluded:

The memory of one of these, John Lilburne—banished
and disgraced by a parliamentary committee on penalty
of death if he returned to his country—was particularly
vivid when our Constitution was written. His attack on
trials by such committees and his warning that "what is
done unto anyone, may be done unto everyone" were
part of the history of the times which moved those who
wrote our Constitution to determine that no such arbitrary punishments should ever occur here. It is the protection from arbitrary punishments through the right to
a judicial trial with all these safeguards which over the
years has distinguished America from lands where drum-
head courts and other similar "tribunals" deprive the
weak and the unorthodox of life, liberty and property
without due process of law. It is the same right which
is denied Barenblatt, because the Court today fails to
see what is here for all to see—that exposure and punishment is the aim of this Committee and the reason
for its existence. To deny this is to ignore the Committee's own claims and the reports it has issued ever since
it was established. I cannot believe that the nature of
our judicial office requires us to be so blind, and must
conclude that the Un-American Activities Committee's

"identification" and "exposure" of Communists and suspected Communists, like the activities of the Committee in *Kilbourn v. Thompson*, amount to an encroachment on the judiciary which bodes ill for the liberties of the people of this land.

Ultimately all the questions in this case really boil down to one—whether we as a people will try fearfully and futilely to preserve democracy by adopting totalitarian methods, or whether in accordance with our traditions and our Constitution we will have the confidence and courage to be free.[50]

The McCarthy era at last whimpered to an end. Yet its traces are still to be found; or at least, the types of accusatory techniques or restrictions on freedom of action by government which typified that era still exist. Where they do, Black would root them out in the name of liberty. He has, for example, consistently opposed some of the tactics of the House Un-American Activities Committee that have continued to come before the Court for review from time to time. Indeed, given the fact that Black more willingly draws the line on freedom of legislative action when the rights of individuals are involved, and given the history of HUAC, it is not surprising that he was opposing the Committee in certain of its endeavors as far back as 1946. Then, in *United States v. Lovett*,[51] in that year, Black spoke for the Court in invalidating a congressional action that sought to deny salaries to three Government employees whose loyalty was challenged by the Committee. To Black and the Court, this was tantamount to inflicting punishment without judicial trial; they denied that the Committee had any such authority. His *Barenblatt* opinion indicated a heightened concern about such procedures, and his concurring opinion in the 1966 case of *Gojack v. United States*[52] reiterated his objections succinctly. In *Gojack*, Justice Fortas' opinion for the Court held that the Committee had violated its own rules by not specifying the subject of the inquiry and by not lawfully delegating to its subcommittee necessary authority to conduct the investigation. Black agreed with the result, but said he "would prefer to reverse the judgment by holding the House Un-American Activities Committee's inquiries here amounted to an unconstitutional encroachment on the judicial power. . . ."[53]

His is not, of course, merely an argument with a Congressional committee. Black believes that the establishment of a network of special, elaborate laws and machinery for the purpose of identifying and preventing "subversion"—by abridging free speech and association—is not worthy of a free society. His dissenting opinion in a case involving the Subversive Activities Control Board spells out his convictions in cogent terms:

> I think that among other things the [Subversive Activities Control] Act is a bill of attainder; that it imposes cruel, unusual and savage punishment for thought, speech, writing, petition and assembly; that it stigmatizes people for their beliefs, associations and views about politics, law and government. The Act has borrowed the worst features of old laws intended to put shackles on the minds and bodies of men, to make them confess to crime, to make them miserable while in this country, and to make it a crime even to attempt to get out of it. It is difficult to find laws more thought-stifling than this even in countries considered the most benighted. Previous efforts to have this Court pass on the constitutionality of the various provisions of this freedom-crushing law have met with frustration on one excuse or another. I protest against following this course again. My vote is to hear the case now and hold the law to be what I think it is—a wholesale denial of what I believe to be the constitutional heritage of every freedom-loving American.[54]

And if the particular definitions and broad purposes of such laws are repressive to Black, the administrative arrangements, whereby, for example, Congress has turned over to the State Department full authority for drawing up and implementing travel restrictions on citizens whose loyalty is questioned or who are otherwise suspect, bother him even more. The 1965 case of *Zemel v. Rusk*[55] found him raising additional objections to such use of travel restrictions as "punishment without trial" beyond those of his concurring opinion in *Aptheker v. Secretary of State*[56] of the previous year. In *Zemel*, the Court majority upheld a State Department ruling and simultaneously the Congressional-Executive arrangement, and denied a citizen's request to have his passport validated for travel to Cuba for the purpose of satisfying his own desire to learn firsthand about conditions in that country. Said Black:

> Our Constitution has ordained that laws restricting the liberty of our people can be enacted by Congress and by the Congress only. I do not think our Constitution intended that this vital legislative function could be farmed out in large blocks to any governmental official, whoever he might be, or to any governmental department or bureau, whatever administrative expertise it might be thought to have. The Congress was created on the assumption that enactment of this free country's laws could be safely entrusted to the representatives of the people in Congress, and to no other official or government agency. The people who are called upon to obey laws have a constitutional right to have them passed only in this constitutional way. This right becomes all the more essential when as here the person called upon to obey may be punished by five years' imprisonment and a $5,000 fine if he dares to travel without the consent of the Secretary [of State] or one of his subordinates. It is irksome enough for one who wishes to travel to be told by the Congress, the constitutional lawmaker with power to legislate in this field, that he cannot go where he wishes. . . . I think the 1926 Act gives the lawmaking power of Congress to the Secretary and the President and that it therefore violates the constitutional command that "All" legislative power be vested in the Congress. . . .[57]

The Essentiality of a Free Press

To isolate representative opinions of Justice Black in the fields of free speech, free assembly, free press, and censorship is, in a way, to pull apart a fabric whose threads are carefully interwoven. The categories are not naturally distinct. Inevitably they overlap. For example, the Black dissent in the *Dennis*[58] case was concerned not only with free speech and free assembly but also with freedom of the press, although a surprisingly large number of newspaper editors did not seem to realize it. Perhaps for this very reason, Justice Black's continuing stanch defense of a free press deserves special emphasis, in view of press freedom's essential relationship with free speech and the other First Amendment freedoms.

Four years after he joined the Court Justice Black spoke for it in *Bridges v. California*[59] where a very influential newspaper, the *Los Angeles Times,* had improperly sought to influence the course of the trial of longshoreman leader Harry Bridges. The *Times* had likened Bridges and his colleagues to "gorillas" and had editorially urged the trial judge to convict them and so make examples of them. The issue was whether, for that reason, the *Times* should be held in contempt of court. The Black opinion upheld the newspaper's position (especially since it did not involve a situation of "clear and present danger") thus showing the extent to which he would defend freedom of the press.

The Black position extends to a protection of the press against libel suits which are aimed, as he sees it, at stifling frank reporting and free judgment about those in public affairs. In the 1964 *New York Times*[60] case, in which the Court reversed a half-million dollar libel suit against the newspaper, Black felt the need to write a separate concurring opinion to spell out his strong feelings on the subject:

> We would, I think, more faithfully interpret the First Amendment by holding that at the very least it leaves the people and the press free to criticize officials and discuss public affairs with impunity. . . . To punish the exercise of this right to discuss public affairs or to penalize it through libel judgments is to abridge or shut off discussion of the very kind most needed. This nation, I suspect, can live in peace without libel suits based on public discussions of public affairs and public officials. But I doubt that a country can live in freedom where its people can be made to suffer physically or

financially for criticizing their government, its actions, or its officials. . . . An unconditional right to say what one pleases about public affairs is what I consider to be the minimum guarantee of the First Amendment. I regret that the Court has stopped short of holding this indispensable to preserve our free press from destruction.[61]

In 1966 he spoke for eight members of the Court in invalidating Alabama's law which forbade newspapers from editorially soliciting votes on election day, saying: "We hold that no test of reasonableness can save a state law from invalidation as a violation of the First Amendment when that law makes it a crime for a newspaper editor to do nothing more than urge people to vote one way or another in a publicly held election."[62]

And Black's position can be said to be mirrored also in his dissenting positions in two of the most spectacular cases of our age. One involved newspaper coverage and the other television coverage of the two original trials—those of Billie Sol Estes[63] and Dr. Samuel H. Sheppard.[64] In the *Sheppard* case, the plea the Court considered was that the defendant had been denied a fair and objective trial because of sensational newspaper coverage of the crime and the trial. Estes's lawyers claimed that the broadcasting and televising of their client's trial magnified and dramatized the notoriety of earlier aspects of the case to such an extent that the resulting atmosphere prevented a fair trial and violated due process of law. In this day, it seems logical to include radio and television in the category of public news media and Black would definitely guarantee them the same freedom that is specifically reserved to the press by the Constitution. Thus in both cases, when the Court majority upheld the appeals of the accused and thereby suggested an application of restrictions to full and open reporting of such major events, Black felt constrained to dissent. The dissent in the otherwise unanimous *Sheppard* case was lodged without an opinion.[65] In the *Estes* case, a five to four decision, Black joined Justice Stewart's dissenting opinion[66] which denied that the televising of a trial per se violated a person's constitutional rights.

That Black includes radio and television as latter-day categories of the "press" is made clear in a 1964 case wherein the major issue was a labor dispute.[67] In that regard Black agreed with the Court's decision upholding peaceful picketing at a secondary site as not an unfair labor practice. But being sensitive to all kinds and degrees of First Amendment right curtailments, he found the statute in question to contain an unconstitutional curb on freedom of speech and press:

> I cannot accept my Brother Harlan's view that the abridgment of speech and press here does not violate the First Amendment because other methods of communication are left open. This reason for abridgment strikes me as being on a par with the holding that governmental suppression of a newspaper in a city would not violate the First Amendment because there continue to be radio and television stations. First Amendment freedoms can no more validly be taken away by degrees than by one fell swoop.[68]

The First Amendment's "high, preferred place" for Black is similarly reflected in his approach to censorship. At least from the time of his *Beauharnais*[69] dissent in 1952, where once more he would have upheld the right to public espousal of a cause which was personally offensive to him, he has made censorship of thought and speech a major target. This, of course, was merely a part of his attack on all forms of suppression of utterance, his assertion of the absolute impropriety of governmental interference with ideas, however unpleasant, irrational, or even hateful. Then in his twenty-ninth term came a trio of decisions that attracted widespread attention— the "pornography" cases decided in the spring term of 1966.[70] One of them was that of *Eros* publisher Ralph Ginzburg[71] who had been sentenced to jail for violating the federal obscenity statute. How strongly the five-to-four decision in the *Ginzburg* case went against Justice Black's deepest beliefs can be told from the opening words of his dissent:

> Only one stark fact emerges with clarity out of the confusing welter of opinions and thousands of words written in this and the two other cases today. That fact

is that Ginzburg, petitioner here, is now finally and authoritatively condemned to serve five years in prison for distributing printed matter about sex which neither Ginzburg nor anyone else could possibly have known to be criminal. . . . As I have said many times, I believe that the Federal Government is without any power whatever under the Constitution to put any type of burden on speech and expression of ideas of any kind (as distinguished from conduct). . . . I agree with my Brother Harlan that the Court has in effect rewritten the federal obscenity statute and thereby imposed on Ginzburg standards and criteria that Congress never thought about, or if it did think about them certainly did not adopt them. Consequently Ginzburg is, as I see it, having his conviction and sentence affirmed upon the basis of a statute amended by this Court for violation of which amended statute he was not charged in the courts below. Such an affirmance we have said violates due process. . . .[72]

(As a further note on censorship, Justice Black and Justice Douglas would agree that the protections of the First Amendment extend to motion pictures.)[73]

New Questions About an Old Belief

It is both right and natural that Hugo Black should have been thought of, through the years, as a friend of the Negro citizen. His record on the Supreme Court since the *Chambers*[74] case, as well as his fairness to Negroes as a police court judge in Birmingham, give meaning to that ideal. Indeed, he has actively participated—and written many opinions for the Court—in decisions that have helped Negroes stake out new advances in claiming old residual rights in constitutional territory.

Now Black's friendship is apparently being called into question in some quarters. The questions are centered on his objections to certain civil disobedience type tactics, which objections have been expressed in various dissenting opinions in the last several years and particularly in his opinion for the Court in *Adderley v. Florida* during the October 1966 term.[75]

Yet it may be asked how discrete dissents in civil rights cases can so overshadow the positive record that Black has continued to compile. After all, Justice Black concurred with the Court majority in *Bates v. Little Rock*[76] in holding that the Constitution's guarantee of freedom of assembly includes freedom of association regardless of race or color. That decision helped knock down a last local artificial barrier to school desegregation. It was Black who, in 1963, issued the order that ended the legal merry-go-round being used to deny a qualified Negro student, James Meredith, admission to the University of Mississippi.[77] He also spoke for a unanimous Court in the 1964 Virginia school desegregation case of *Griffin v. Prince Edward County*.[78] There the Supreme Court upheld the power of the Federal District Court to enjoin county officials from awarding tuition grants out of county funds or giving tax exemptions, by which practice the county circumvented a court order to desegregate public schools. The *Griffin* decision forced the re-opening of the public schools.

In other areas, Black spoke for a unanimous Court in a case which reversed a state court dismissal of a complaint by a Negro who had applied for, and been denied, a job as a pilot with an interstate airline,[79] and concurred separately in a Florida case wherein the Court denied the right of the State to require members of the NAACP to reveal the names of their alleged Communist associates.[80] And in two 1965 cases,[81] Black announced decisions that upheld procedures designed to assist Negro applicants to become registered voters. In one of these, the Court invalidated Louisiana's so-called "interpretation" test under which voting applicants were required to "interpret" any section of the state or federal constitution that was read to them by a voting registrar. This obstacle to voting was seen as a violation of the Fourteenth and Fifteenth Amendments.[82]

But apart from this record of particular indications of support for the Negro, it may be wondered if those who now begin to doubt Black's support for minority groups have not all along misunderstood its basis. In the *Florida-NAACP* case referred to above, that support is put into full perspective:

> In my view the constitutional right of association in-
> cludes the privilege of *any person* [emphasis added] to
> associate with Communists or anti-Communists, Social-
> ists or anti-Socialists, or, for that matter, with people of
> all kinds of beliefs, popular or unpopular. . . . Since, as
> I believe, the National Association for the Advancement
> of Colored People and its members have a constitutional
> right to choose their own associates, I cannot understand
> by what constitutional authority Florida can compel
> answers to questions which abridge that right. Accord-
> ingly I would reverse here on the ground that there has
> been a direct abridgment of the right of association of
> the National Association for the Advancement of Col-
> ored People and its members.[83]

Thus strengthened is the suggestion made several years ago
by someone close to Black that the Justice should not be
thought of as "the champion of the Negro or of any other
minority group as such."[84] He further explained:

> His concern is not with the defense of constitutional
> rights of members of specific groups, but rather with the
> defense of the rights of people as people. He is aware
> that our legal and constitutional safeguards are not se-
> lective: they must protect everybody—regardless of race,
> creed or political belief—or they will not long protect
> anybody.[85]

The Later Years

The rounding out of twenty-five years on the Supreme Court
in the early 1960's came in a set of circumstances that led
Justice Black to speak out with increasing force for Bill of
Rights provisions. New appointments to the highest bench
resulted in a relatively large number of five-to-four decisions
in controversial civil liberties cases. It was not uncommon
in this period to find Black dissenting most vigorously in
such cases in the company of Chief Justice Warren and Justices Douglas and Brennan. This was the period of the
decisions in the cases of *Willard Uphaus,*[86] *Carl Braden,*[87]

Frank Wilkinson,[88] *Junius Scales,*[89] *George Anastaplo,*[90] and others that involved freedom of speech and governmental authority, and thus invited the kind of "balancing" and weighing of "competing interests" which Black had always opposed. In his dissents in these and similar cases,[91] Hugo Black put all the strength of protest that he believed proper to register.

And as a new quarter century opened up for the senior Associate Justice, an old constitutional cycle seemed to begin anew: among Bill of Rights cases, many involved procedural rights of the accused. If some of the First Amendment cases brought Black grave disappointment, some involving rights under the Fourth, Fifth, and Sixth Amendments must have given him profound satisfaction. In the *Gideon* case, already noted in connection with *Johnson v. Zerbst* and *Betts v. Brady,* Justice Black expressed the views of seven members of the Court and Justices Clark and Harlan concurred in the result. It had taken twenty-one years to reverse *Betts,* but when it was done there was no dissent. Perhaps the thinking of the country had changed like that of the Court. Justice Black pointed out in his opinion[92] that while Florida and two other states asked that the *Betts* decision be left intact, "twenty-two states, as friends of the Court, argue that *Betts* 'was an anachronism when handed down' and that it should now be overruled." Concluded Justice Black: "We agree. The judgment is reversed. . . ."[93] So ended, after a generation, what to many laymen will always be an inexplicable precedent under which countless men remained in prison notwithstanding the command of the Constitution that defendants in criminal cases have the right to be represented by counsel.

The decision in *Malloy v. Hogan*[94] in 1964 must have given Black almost as much satisfaction as *Gideon* although he wrote no opinion in it. For his vote was one of the five that made Justice Brennan's majority opinion possible. Further, *Malloy* reversed *Adamson v. California*[95] just as *Gideon* had reversed *Betts.* Said the majority:

> We hold today that the Fifth Amendment's exception from compulsory self-incrimination is also protected by the Fourteenth Amendment against abridgment by the States. Decisions of the Court since *Twining* and

Adamson have departed from the contrary view expressed in those cases. . . . The Fourteenth Amendment
secures against state invasion the same privilege that the
Fifth Amendment guarantees against federal infringement—the right of a person to remain silent unless he
chooses to speak in the unfettered exercise of his own
will, and to suffer no penalty. . . .[96]

In *United States v. Behrens*,[97] Justice Black spoke for eight
members of the Court in a decision holding that a prisoner
was entitled to be present at the final imposition of a sentence. Noting that "it is only then that the judge's final words
are spoken and the defendant's punishment fixed," Black
pointed out that "it is then that the right of the defendant
to be afforded an opportunity to make a statement to the judge
in his own behalf is of most importance."[98] He underscored
that right by calling it ancient in the law. Black also spoke
for seven members of the Court in *Pointer v. Texas*[99] in 1965,
holding that the Sixth Amendment's protection of an accused
person's right to confront the witness against him was made
obligatory on the states by the Fourteenth Amendment. And
in *Brookhart v. Janis*,[100] Justice Black expressed the views of
an eight-member majority to the effect that the petitioner
neither directly waived his constitutional right to confront and
cross-examine nor waived it through acquiescence in an attempted waiver by his lawyer.

But there were dissents as well, as in *Linkletter v. Walker*[101]
in 1965 in which the Court held that the rule in *Mapp v.
Ohio*[102] did not operate retroactively upon cases that were
decided before *Mapp*. This limiting of *Mapp* led Justice Black,
joined by Justice Douglas, to say in protest:

> The plain facts here are that the Court's opinion cuts
> off many defendants who are now in jail from any hope
> of relief from unconstitutional convictions. The opin-
> ion today also beats a timid retreat from the wholesome
> and refreshing principle announced in *Noia*.[103] No
> state should be considered to have a vested interest in
> keeping prisoners in jail who were convicted because
> of lawless conduct by the State's officials. Careful analy-

sis of the Court's opinion shows that it rests on the premise that the State's assumed interest in the old, repudiated rule outweighs the interests of the States and of the people convicted in having wrongful convictions set aside. It certainly offends my sense of justice to say that a State holding in jail people who were convicted by unconstitutional methods has a vested interest in keeping them there that outweighs the right of persons adjudged guilty of crime to challenge their convictions at any time.[104]

Justice Black dissented also in *Namet v. United States*,[105] again with Justice Douglas. The facts showed that a prosecutor interrogated two witnesses although he knew they would invoke their constitutional privilege against incriminating themselves. The dissenters took the position that the trial court erred when it allowed the prosecuting attorney in the jury's presence to ask questions that he knew the witnesses would refuse to answer on constitutional grounds.[106] The same two Justices dissented in *Tehan v. United States ex rel. Shott*[107] wherein the prosecutor commented at length on the respondent's failure to testify in defense of himself against charges brought under the Ohio Securities Act. The position of Justices Black and Douglas was that although a declaration of unconstitutionality is not enunciated judicially until after conviction, persons who are still held in prison under conditions that are unconstitutional should have those convictions set aside.[108]

The five-to-four decision in *Schmerber v. California*,[109] upholding a compulsory blood test for drivers as not violating a defendant's constitutional rights, led Justice Black to strong dissent. Said the Black opinion, joined by Justice Douglas:

The Court today departs from the teachings of *Boyd*.[110] Petitioner Schmerber has undoubtedly been compelled to give his blood "to furnish evidence against himself," yet the Court holds that this is not forbidden by the Fifth Amendment. With all deference I must say that the Court here gives the Bill of Rights' safeguard against compulsory self-incrimination a construction that would generally be considered too narrow and too technical even in the interpretation of an ordinary commercial contract. . . .

The refined, subtle reasoning and balancing procedures used here to narrow the scope of the Bill of Rights' safeguard against self-incrimination provides a handy instrument for further narrowing of that constitutional protection, as well as others, in the future. Believing with the Framers that these constitutional safeguards broadly construed by independent tribunals of justice provide our best hope for keeping our people free from governmental oppression, I deeply regret the Court's holding.[111]

Justice Black was happy to find himself with the majority which made possible the decisions in two other important recent cases relating to fair criminal procedure, *Harris v. United States*[112] and *Miranda v. Arizona*.[113] In the *Harris* case the Court reversed its ruling in *Brown v. United States*.[114] The effect of the new ruling was to require official notice and a hearing before a "balky witness" could be declared guilty of contempt of court. In the *Miranda* case, the question was the admissibility of statements obtained from an individual subjected to custodial police interrogation, and the need for procedures that protect the privilege against self-incrimination.

Freedom and the Individual

In the diversity of recent cases involving the Bill of Rights, there runs through the Black position and opinions the same consistent thread: protect the individual and his freedoms. The consistency is seen in such cases as those where he participated in the decision that an addressee's right of free speech is violated if he is required by federal statute to request in writing the delivery of nonsealed mail from abroad containing Communist propaganda;[115] helped make up the five-man majority by which an Arizona statute requiring a loyalty oath of state employees, including teachers, was held unconstitutional because it infringed unnecessarily on freedom of associa-

tion;[116] concurred with Justices Stewart and Douglas in calling
for reversal of the conviction of a husband and wife for receiving through the mails films of each other posing in the nude,
"not because [the conviction] violates the policy of the Justice
Department, but because it violates the Constitution."[117]   In
the area of religion, Black reads both the religious freedom
clause and the "Establishment Clause" of the First Amendment
as liberating the individual to do whatever he wishes, and
believe whatever he wants to believe, with respect to religion.
Whatever problems the Establishment Clause may give
Black,[118] the thread that ties all his "religious" opinions together—from the second *Flag Salute* case[119] in 1943, through
Torasco v. Watkins[120] in 1961, to *Engel v. Vitale*[121] in 1962, and
the conscientious objector case[122] of a more recent term—is,
once more, the obvious effort to protect still another sphere,
specified by the Constitution, of individual freedom.

The reason that Black attaches such high importance to the
rights of the individual, and thus is so zealous in his protection
and extension of the Bill of Rights, is simply because he
attaches preeminent importance to the individual. Indeed,
Black believes not only that the focus of democracy should be
kept on the individual but that the Constitution as a whole
is designed to keep it there. It is for this reason that, in the
early days of his Court service, even in his opinions dealing
with such things as interpretations of the Commerce Clause
and the laws passed under it, he always kept one eye on the
effects of statutes and situations on the individual. It is for
this reason that, in particular, he continues to be suspicious
of corporate mergers—because they move us still further from
the days when more individuals had a better chance to control
or at least affect the economic enterprises they were involved in,
into an era where more individuals are more likely *to be* controlled by the highly mechanized-computerized, smoothly oiled
economic enterprises in which they find themselves. Big, powerful government, of the kind implicit in the causes of the New
Deal and the Great Society, is accepted insofar as it helps to
liberate man from social and economic pitfalls, but is attacked
when it too becomes an agent of restriction.

Black's belief that our whole system of government is designed to enhance man as an individual, equal to and as free

as other individuals, is exemplified also in his work in the area of legislative apportionment, completely outside of the Bill of Rights. More than twenty years ago he advanced the belief, in a dissenting opinion in *Colegrove v. Green*,[123] that proper government depended on equitable representation in legislative assemblies, and that courts, as protectors of the constitutional rights of citizens, had the right to help insure it. Justice Frankfurter led the plurality of four to its conclusion that, on the contrary, the judiciary should stay out of the "political thicket" of redrawing congressional districts and reapportioning state legislatures. In the decade and a half that followed, the disparities among sizes of legislative constituencies grew increasingly greater as "rotten borough" members of state legislatures ignored appeals from voters for fair reapportionment and chose instead to hold on to their grossly underpopulated districts.

By the start of the 1960's protest cases had arisen from voters in many states. The Supreme Court now decided to reconsider its previous stance and consider possible violations of the Constitution. In *Baker v. Carr*,[124] those Tennessee citizens bringing the suit charged that because of malapportionment, they were being denied equal protection of the laws by virtue of the debasement of their votes. The suit grew out of the fact that there had been no reapportionment of the State Legislature in sixty years, despite a requirement of the Tennessee Constitution that such reapportionment be effected every ten years; as a result, urban citizens found themselves seriously underrepresented, their votes worth only a fraction of their rural neighbors' in terms of representation. The Supreme Court majority, including Justice Black, opened the door to correction of that situation by agreeing that those who brought the suit and the thousands of their fellow Tennesseans similarly situated were indeed being denied equal protection of the laws. Two years later, in 1964, the Court extended relief to those residing in overpopulated Congressional districts. Justice Black spoke for the Court in *Wesberry v. Sanders*.[125] In a detailed history of the Constitutional Convention and, in particular, of the drafting of Article 1 as a part of the Great Compromise, he dramatized the belief of the majority of the Framers, and the ultimate consensus achieved by the Convention, that representation in the House of Representatives was to be on the basis of generally equal numbers of persons in each district. Drawing largely on Madison, Black quoted his description of who the electors of the federal representatives would be:

> Not the rich more than the poor; not the learned more than the ignorant; not the haughty heirs of distinguished names, more than the humble sons of obscure and unpropitious fortune. The electors are to be the great body of people of the United States. . . .[126]

That assessment of the equal importance of persons of every walk of life, added to other statements of the Founders calling for "equal elections," could be taken, said Black, to mean "one person, one vote."[127] He concluded:

> While it may not be possible to draw congressional districts with mathematical precision, that is no excuse for ignoring our Constitution's plain objective of making equal representation for equal numbers of people the fundamental goal for the House of Representatives. That is the high standard of justice and common sense which the Founders set for us.[128]

From that case, the Court moved ahead to insure equal representation in state legislatures, by requiring that both houses of state legislatures be apportioned on the basis of population.[129] The majority included Justice Black, and their opinion was by Chief Justice Warren. Their rationale was: "Simply stated, an individual's right to vote for state legislators is unconstitutionally impaired when its weight is in substantial fashion diluted when compared with the votes of citizens living in other parts of the state."[130]

These decisions met with violent objections in many political quarters, but they were welcomed by the people as a whole and in large part by the press. The Reynolds case stirred Senator Everett McKinley Dirksen to try for a constitutional amendment that would enable a state to set aside the Court ruling with respect to one branch of its legislature if its citizens chose by referendum to do so. But like his anti-Supreme Court "prayer amendment," this proposal failed to achieve the necessary two-thirds vote in the Senate in 1966.

It has been said that the reapportionment decisions have provoked a peaceful revolution in the American political process, that they have properly readjusted the balance of power between urban and rural populations, and that they have made it possible to turn the tide of problems sweeping in over city life. Perhaps these descriptions are all true. But what is certainly equally true is that, apart from terms of competing populations and urban blight and rotten boroughs, the decisions have also contributed to the elevation of the individual and his place in the democratic process. And it is no doubt this which has especially prompted Black's active role in providing the possibility of such political reform.

It is the great good fortune of the American people that during the sometimes frightening, sometimes exhilarating, always crucial years from 1937 to the present, Hugo Lafayette Black's conscience and concern and his fearless conviction have been at the service of the individual and his preeminent place in our democratic society. Following the plain command of the Bill of Absolute Rights, he has been on guard for our personal liberties wherever or whenever they might otherwise be bartered or balanced away. But he has done even more. In word and deed he has challenged us as individuals and as a nation to decide the ultimate question: "whether in accordance with our traditions and our Constitution we will have the confidence and the courage to be free."

CHAPTER FIVE

The Living Constitution and the Court's Role

CHARLES A. REICH

LONG service on the Supreme Court has given Mr. Justice Black an opportunity to write many volumes of opinions on major issues, and to stamp the institution with his strong personality. But his main impact stems from deeper sources. A distinct philosophy concerning constitutional law runs through all of his work. It is a highly controversial philosophy, and it has been often misstated by critics and by friends as well. But for better or worse it has indelibly marked the Court and the law. It represents Justice Black's unique contribution, for while other Justices have shared his views on many issues, none have produced such a comprehensive and individual philosophy.

Why has Black's philosophy often been misstated? The Justice has described himself as "a rather backward country fellow."[1] This is an unduly modest description. But it is true that while he has set down much of his philosophy with clarity and eloquence, there is also much that he has not articulated and many questions he has not answered.

The main problem is that Justice Black has not explained how his philosophy operates—the various jobs that it performs in resolving constitutional questions. Moreover, superficially

Notes appear at pages 298-301.

understood, it appears to contain contradictions or paradoxes. For example, is it possible to be literal in interpreting the Constitution—to avoid weighing values—and still give its provisions changing applications as society changes? Is Black's search for justice in each case before him reconcilable with his rejection of natural law? Does his fear of too much power in the hands of judges square with the greatly elevated role he would give the Court? Finally, what is the nature of the Constitution that Black's philosophy would create?

It is my purpose here to advance a theory to answer these questions. It may not be Justice Black's own theory, nor would he necessarily agree with it. It is offered in the spirit of exploration.

The Bill of Rights: Contemporary Challenges and the Court's Response

Because Mr. Justice Black's philosophy has so largely appeared in dissents, it may be appropriate to begin with some observations about the trend of decisions of the Court. It is worth recalling that the original Constitution did not even include a bill of rights. In *The Federalist,* Hamilton argued that none was necessary: the people retained all powers not expressly granted. "For why declare that things shall not be done which there is no power to do?" he asked. "Why, for instance, should it be said that the liberty of the press shall not be restrained, when no power is given by which restrictions may be imposed?"[2] While many people of the time did not share his complacence, it seems clear that the Bill of Rights as adopted was not intended to be the primary protection against the growth of centralized governmental power. The grant of only enumerated powers, their careful separation, the checks and balances, and the federal system all were insurance against the national government getting out of hand. And even greater insurance lay in the individualistic nature of society with its system of private property that put so much power wholly beyond the reach of any government.

Today these first-line safeguards have largely vanished. The powers granted by the Constitution have expanded so prodigiously, and have been used successfully to achieve so many objects unrelated to their original purposes, that the doctrine of enumerated powers imposes virtually no limitation upon the national government. Powers as diverse as the commerce power, the defense power, and the power to establish post offices have been held to include power to regulate speech and press.[3] And government's direct powers are supplemented by far-reaching indirect power deriving from taxing, spending, public ownership, and public employment. The separation of powers and the checks and balances remain to permit Congress and the President to harass each other, but they have not significantly slowed the assumption of power by both. The sovereign states, with certain proud exceptions, have been reduced to penury and puniness. Even private property is no longer a wall against government; government today has vast powers to regulate private property in the interest of the nation or the local community. The very structure of society, based as it is on organization, encourages the growth of central power just as frontier isolation once restrained it.

Today virtually nothing in the Constitution effectively limits the massive advance of government power except the Bill of Rights. It is the final barrier, all others having been overwhelmed. Even this wall extends only a limited distance; the surge of power in many areas is constitutionally unimpeded. But the Bill of Rights does set off a protected area for each individual; and it also restricts the manner in which government may proceed against individuals in the exercise of any of its powers, great as they may be. It is in this role and setting that the Bill of Rights must be viewed today.

How has the Court responded to these changes? In a word, it has failed to make the protections of the Bill of Rights grow to the same extent as the constitutional grants of power. The power to regulate commerce among the states now reaches the food a farmer grows to feed his animals or himself;[4] at the same time, it extends to jet travel and the television-radio spectrum. The prohibition against bills of attainder, on the other hand, is an Eighteenth Century relic with little or no application to the contemporary world.[5]

Speaking generally, in the areas where powers and rights come into conflict the Court has sanctioned new governmental methods of coercing individuals but has not always subjected these methods to Bill of Rights' safeguards. It has permitted the Government to accomplish by indirect means ends which the Bill of Rights forbids it to reach directly. It has permitted the government to exert pressure to induce people to give up their rights "voluntarily." And, in balancing constitutional powers against rights, it has added modern developments to the government side of the scale but not to the other side. These tendencies of the Court, most of which overlap, are best described by way of illustrations.

One of the clearest examples of the Court's disparate treatment of rights and powers was its 1959 ruling on double jeopardy.[6] On the theory that the United States and each state are separate sovereignties, the Court upheld Illinois' conviction of a man for a robbery for which he had previously been tried and acquitted in federal court. The Court ruled that this was not double jeopardy in the constitutional sense despite these facts: (a) federal power to punish bank robbery is a recent development which the Framers of the Constitution could hardly have foreseen, since it is derived from federal insurance of bank deposits; (b) the evidence used by state prosecutors was gathered by federal authorities and turned over to state officials after failure of the federal prosecution; this was pursuant to a general pattern of federal-state cooperation in the enforcement of criminal laws, a pattern similarly unforeseeable in 1789; (c) the federal authorities actually instigated the prosecution in state court and gathered additional evidence after the defendant had been acquitted in federal court; and the federal court itself cooperated by postponing sentencing of the defendant's accomplices (who had been convicted) until they testified against him at his second trial.[7] The dual sovereignty limitation upon double jeopardy might well have been accepted when there was little important overlapping between federal and state criminal jurisdiction and therefore no substantial danger of dual prosecutions. But where the Court rendered decisions which greatly widened federal criminal jurisdiction, sweeping in such local matters as illegal production of alcohol, extortion, obscenity, and bank robbery, to that extent it made the dual sovereignty concept inappropriate with respect to the protection against double jeopardy. Under this decision, there are many crimes for which a person might be tried twice.

The same inconsistent treatment of powers and rights is found in the Court's decisions on the problem of self-incrimination in two sovereignties. The issue here was whether a person could refuse to give testimony in a federal proceeding on the ground that it might subject him to criminal prosecution by a state, or vice versa. The Court restricted the protection against self-incrimination to prosecution by the same sovereignty, despite the rapid growth of parallel federal and state criminal jurisdiction,[8] and cooperation between the prosecuting authorities.[9] Indeed, the Court sanctioned federal legislation expressly designed to force individuals to supply information which would subject them to state criminal prosecution.[10] With state and federal jurisdiction so largely overlapping, the practical result is that the constitutional protection against compulsory self-incrimination does not prevent the national government from compelling people to give information that is incriminating in the states, and the states have comparable power.

Another illustration of the Court's contrasting attitudes toward powers and rights is its treatment of government action against the reputations of individuals. Recently various agencies of government have begun to exercise the power to punish people by means of publicity. It has proven possible to destroy people's reputations and opportunities for earning money by listing them on an official blacklist;[11] by "exposing" them by forcing public admission of "guilt" before a congressional committee;[12] or, in the case of government employees, by publicly denouncing them as disloyal or dangerous to the United States.[13] Such actions rest on implied government powers which have a newly acquired potency because of the greatly increased importance and indelible nature of reputation in highly organized modern society. Today publicity carries with it the capacity to injure permanently an individual's status and ability to earn. The Court, having allowed these implied powers of punishment to grow, has been asked to surround them with constitutional safeguards such as the opportunity to confront adverse witnesses, and to apply the constitutional prohibition against punishment by agencies other than courts.[14] It has not responded.

Still another area in which the processes of punishment have been permitted to outstrip the safeguards is represented by the growth of federal and state investigatory power. Various types of "civil" or "preliminary" investigations can be used, and commonly are used, to obtain evidence to be introduced later in criminal prosecutions. Investigations thus become an integral part of the criminal trial itself. The Court has steadily approved the proliferating investigatory powers of various federal and state authorities. Yet the Court has not extended to those summoned as witnesses such elementary Bill of Rights' safeguards as the right to counsel, or the right to have the proceeding open to the public.[15] Government is thus invited to use investigations in place of trials.

One of the most striking illustrations of the Court's failure to counterweight rights against powers is found in the many instances in which the Court has permitted government to use its expanded power to induce or force people to abandon constitutional rights. As an initial proposition, it might seem strange indeed that government, a creature of the Constitution, should have any power at all to ask or demand the relinquishment of rights given by the Constitution. But the Court has allowed government to insist that millions of public employees, in order to keep their jobs, must give up First Amendment rights[16] and "voluntarily" abandon their privilege against self-incrimination.[17] In so ruling, the Court has given little or no consideration to how much greater a segment of the nation is dependent upon public employment today than ever before. Further, the Court has allowed government's enormously magnified power to regulate occupations and professions to be used to induce people to give up First[18] and Fifth Amendment[19] rights. It has permitted similar use of the power to certify unions as collective bargaining agents,[20] and it has allowed states to demand that as a condition of public employment people waive even the statutory immunity from prosecution that other state laws require them to accept in lieu of the privilege against self-incrimination.[21] Under the Court's rulings, if the point is ever reached where everyone works for the government or at a job licensed by the government, everyone could be forced to renounce various constitutional rights.

One final illustration shows the inequality of the Court's treatment of rights and powers in a somewhat different setting. In certain types of First Amendment cases the Court has undertaken to balance the "competing interests at stake."[22] But while it has viewed the "government interest" in the most contemporary terms, emphasizing international threats to democracy, the "first amendment interest" has not been similarly weighed in terms of modern needs. In a mass society, with access to information about what is happening in government increasingly difficult to obtain, with increasing monopolization of all the media of communication, and with heavy pressure for conformity from the large-scale organizations for which most people work, freedom of expression and political association are easily reduced to impotence. If it is true that they are indispensable to the functioning of a free society, could it not be argued that the need for maintaining maximum legal protection of these rights has been greatly increased by modern developments? The Court has weighed Eighteenth Century needs for rights against Twentieth Century demands for power.

Black's Approach: Original Purpose as a Guide to Current Meaning

Justice Black dissented from the reasoning used in all the decisions just discussed. He called repeatedly for more "faithful adherence" to the Bill of Rights. How would his philosophy have functioned if it had been adopted by the Court?

By "faithful adherence" Black has demanded adherence to the spirit and objectives of the Bill of Rights, rather than to any particular interpretation of its provisions. His approach is functional in nature. He asks what a given provision of the Bill of Rights was designed to accomplish—what evils it was intended to prevent. Then he seeks to give the provision a meaning which will, in a contemporary setting, accomplish the same general purposes and prevent the same kinds of evils. Thus he interprets the Bill of Rights in the same way in which the Court has often interpreted the enumerated powers in the Constitution.[23]

If in modern times the national and state governments have concurrent criminal jurisdiction, Black insists that the guarantees against double jeopardy and self-incrimination be given an interpretation broad enough to take account of this fact, so that the Constitution continues to protect against the evils to which that provision of the Bill of Rights was originally directed.[24] If conditions in the nation have made official injury to reputation a severe and lasting form of punishment, and government agencies use it for this purpose, Black would hold such actions to be unlawful because they are criminal proceedings within the exclusive province of the judiciary and because they lack essential judicial safeguards.[25] If contemporary criminal trials are in effect fragmented, so that crucial evidence is obtained at "investigatory hearings," then Black insists that a witness be given counsel at any such hearing.[26] The safeguard comes into play whenever the danger it was designed to prevent is present:

> I also firmly believe that the Due Process Clause requires that a person interrogated be allowed to use legal counsel whenever he is compelled to give testimony to law-enforcement officers which may be instrumental in his prosecution and conviction for a criminal offense.[27]

If public employment has become a major and indispensable element in American life, rather than a minor reward for a few office-seekers, Black rejects any unlimited power of government to require the abandonment of the citizen's right to participate in politics, or to demand "loyalty" of the public employee.[28] And the same principle forbids government to demand "loyalty" as the price of a professional or occupational license.[29] In short, his concept of "faithful adherence" keeps the Bill of Rights alive and capable of growth along with the rest of the Constitution.

Black has not fully articulated this approach, but he has suggested it often enough. In objecting to summary trials for contempt of court, he explicitly stated that the law should be re-examined because of the growth of the contempt power in ways the Framers could not have foreseen and would not have countenanced,[30] and he referred to one decision of the Court as "another ominous step in the incredible transformation and growth of the contempt power and in the consequent erosion of constitutional safeguards. . . ."[31] In cases where the legislature or executive has acted in punitive fashion against individuals or members of particular groups Black has repeatedly contended that such actions are modern equivalents of bills of attainder, and should be condemned as such.[32] Several times he has suggested that sedition and espionage laws punish modern equivalents of treason, and should thus be subject to constitutional requirements for treason trials.[33]

Black's Bill of Rights, composed as it is of provisions designed to cut down power, is like a buzz saw. This is well illustrated by the First Amendment. As government power spreads and reaches out, his First Amendment relentlessly cuts it down whenever and however it advances into the forbidden area of speech and association. Regardless of whether pressure against these freedoms comes from government investigatory power, power over government employment, power to license occupations, power to compel membership in organizations, or any other source, old or new, the reach of the First Amendment is the same. It chops off every extension of government, every tendril and every growth that intrudes on the protected zone as that zone is defined in terms compelled by modern society. The Court's First Amendment has sometimes been an inert thing that can be surmounted or undermined; Black's Amendment is a living guardian that shears off every attack, no matter how stealthy or indirect.

Constancy and Change in Constitutional Interpretation

If this is how Black's philosophy operates, why has he always talked primarily in terms of the literal language and history of the Bill of Rights? How can a dynamic conception of a constitution be squared with a literal one? The answer is that in a dynamic society the Bill of Rights must keep changing in its application or lose even its original meaning. There is no such thing as a constitutional provision with a static meaning. If it stays the same while other provisions of the Constitution change and society itself changes, the provision will atrophy. That, indeed, is what has happened to some of the safeguards of the Bill of Rights. A constitutional provision can maintain its integrity only by moving in the same direction and at the same rate as the rest of society. In constitutions, constancy requires change.

The constitutional problems discussed above all illustrate this principle. If the protections against self-incrimination and double jeopardy are kept applicable to only one sovereignty despite the growth of overlapping criminal jurisdiction and federal-state cooperation, these safeguards become formalisms which fail in practice to prevent much compelled self-incrimination and many double trials. If the criminal safeguards are not extended to investigations, they cease to be effective declarations that no person can be tried or punished except according to procedures they prescribe. If government can use economic pressure to induce people to waive constitutional rights, it has to that extent gained the power to do things constitutional limitations say it shall not do. If only Eighteenth Century rights of free speech are protected today, speech will not have the meaning or impact in the Twentieth Century that it had when the First Amendment was written.

Thus it is paradoxical but true that Justice Black's constitutional philosophy, although it embodies motion and change, is in a large sense devoted to maintaining the Bill of Rights in its original significance. What he has really sought in the language and history of the Bill of Rights is its spirit and purpose, and these he has tried to keep constant. Moving almost by instinct, he has developed a functional doctrine of an unchanging Bill of Rights. If it lacks articulation, that is perhaps because it was not drawn from established legal or political philosophy. It came, in the case of this "backward country fellow," from within.

"Absolutes" and the Process of Judging

Mr. Justice Black's Bill of Rights is, then, a functional one which changes and grows. Yet Black would deny judges the power to weigh values in order to arrive at a contemporary interpretation of the Constitution.[34] How can these two aspects of his philosophy be reconciled? How can judges find a contemporary meaning for the Constitution except by a weighing process? The answers to these questions require an examination of Justice Black's most controversial concept—the doctrine of "absolutes."

Justice Black uses the term "absolutes" to describe particular provisions of the Constitution; for example, he says that the First Amendment's language is "absolute." But to use the term in this way, and to say no more, has caused much confusion. "Absolutes" is not merely a description of constitutional language; it is also concerned with the process of judging. "Absolutes" is the way Black refers to that part of his philosophy which denies to judges the power to weigh competing values. And "absolutes" is the outgrowth of a dissenting position. Only when seen as a judicial process, and contrasted with a different judicial process, can the seeming contradictions of "absolutes" be resolved.

During Justice Black's years on the Court its majority has been dominated by a philosophy of constitutional adjudication based upon the weighing of conflicting values. According to this philosophy, most constitutional issues which reach the Court essentially present conflicts in policies and values. The task of judges is to resolve these conflicts by the exercise of judgment.[35]

The basic criticisms of this approach are three. First, it makes constitutional law a series of individual adjudications, and therefore does not permit the establishment of general principles. Second, the balancing actually undertaken by the Court has been inadequate, and this is inevitable, because judges are not equipped to do an adequate job. Third, the balancing is done without reference to any objective scale or standard. These criticisms require some general comment.

The development of law through case-to-case adjudication is no stranger to the English or American lawyer; on the contrary, it is the characteristic method of the common law. But the method of common-law adjudication is not necessarily well-adapted to interpretation of the Bill of Rights. The common law builds its own architecture as it grows; it has no definite starting point, but represents by its very nature a continuing process of adjustment. Constitutional law, on the other hand, exists within a structure, and its object is to maintain the structure. By its nature it would seem to require a higher plane of generality than the common law.

But when the Supreme Court's decisions on the Bill of Rights are examined, they appear to offer very little generality indeed—in fact, a considerably lower plane of generality than the common law. Under the Due Process Clause of the Fourteenth Amendment, the Court has held that incriminating evidence may not be obtained by physical[36] or psychological[37] pressure, or by a scientific device designed to produce vomiting of tangible evidence.[38] On the other hand, the Court has decided that the following do not violate due process: using evidence disclosed under compulsion of law in another jurisdiction;[39] requiring an individual to give incriminating testimony on pain of loss of his profession[40] or the opportunity for public employment;[41] using evidence obtained by a microphone concealed in the suspect's bedroom;[42] extracting tangible evidence (blood) with a needle from an unconscious suspect.[43]

Of course, these cases do not all raise the same issues. But has the Supreme Court explained what the differences are, or attempted to fit the cases into a pattern from which any principles emerge? Even the common law seeks to reconcile its precedents and build an ascertainable standard such as "legal cause" or "reasonable care." The Supreme Court rarely reconciles anything; its due process decisions are each a unique balance of special circumstances, taking little from the past and offering less for the future; each is a law unto itself.

In deciding cases on obscenity the Supreme Court has also adopted a case-to-case approach, examining each photograph, picture, or book, and rendering an individual decision that is rarely explained in terms of any previous decision. This process led Justice Black to comment:

> We are told that the only way we can decide whether a State or municipality can constitutionally bar movies is for this Court to view and appraise each movie on a case-by-case basis. Under these circumstances, every member of the Court must exercise his own judgment as to how bad a picture is, a judgment that is ultimately

based at least in large part on his own standard of what is immoral. The end result of such decisions seems to me to be a purely personal determination of individual Justices as to whether a particular picture viewed is too bad to allow it to be seen by the public. Such an individualized determination cannot be guided by reasonably fixed and certain standards. Accordingly, neither States nor moving picture makers can possibly know in advance, with any fair degree of certainty, what can or cannot be done in the field of movie making and exhibiting. This uncertainty cannot easily be reconciled with the rule of law which our Constitution envisages.[44]

But the differences between common-law adjudication and constitutional adjudication are even greater than has been suggested up to now. Constitutional adjudication, as undertaken by the Supreme Court, has come to be characterized by a form of balancing of values which raises special difficulties of its own, as an illustration will show.

Legislative investigations which expose to a hostile public the political or organizational affiliations of individuals tend to deter freedom of association and political activity. The Court has undertaken to determine the constitutionality of such investigations by weighing the "individual" interest in privacy against the "governmental" interest in obtaining the information. When Alabama sought the membership lists of the NAACP to determine whether that organization was subject to the state's business regulation statutes, the Court said it could not perceive how this information had a "substantial" bearing on what Alabama needed to know; therefore, Alabama had not shown a "controlling justification" for invading First Amendment rights.[45] When the House Committee on Un-American Activities asked a college teacher whether he was a member of the Communist Party, the Court said that the investigation was for a valid legislative purpose (investigating the danger of overthrow of the government); that information concerning the Party was related to the danger of overthrow; and that it was relevant to the Committee's purpose to ask a witness from the field of education whether he was a Communist.

Therefore, the "state interest" outweighed the "individual's interest."[46]

These two cases offer some explanation of why the case-to-case process, whether or not it is workable in the common law, poses tremendous problems in constitutional adjudication. In the first place, the balancing that was undertaken in the above cases seems hopelessly inadequate. Constitutional cases involve vast issues. The Court would have had to know far more about why the information was needed in each case, whether it could be obtained from other sources, and what it added to information already known. Thus, there is nothing at all to show why the House Committee needed to know whether a particular teacher was a Communist. In addition, the Court would have had to know far more about the consequences to the individual and to the democratic process of such enforced disclosure. There is nothing to show it had any knowledge concerning either. Many other essential inquiries for the Court could be suggested, but this would require a study in itself; here we can only note how unsatisfactory the Court's process was.

The complexity of the inquiry which constitutional balancing requires raises a second question: Is this a task which judges are qualified to undertake? Courts have no sources of information other than the records before them, and judges have no special knowledge to assist them in evaluating information of a social and political nature if they were able to obtain it. Black has made this point for years; he restated it in pungent form when the Court said it would attempt to evaluate alleged obscenity according to contemporary community standards:

> So far as I know, judges possess no special expertise providing exceptional competency to set standards and supervise the private morals of the Nation. In addition, the Justices of this Court seem especially unsuited to make the kind of value judgments—as to what movies are good or bad for local communities—which the concurring opinions appear to require.[47]

But the problem is, perhaps, even deeper than Black has suggested. Is case-to-case constitutional balancing an undertaking which is capable of being performed by anyone, however expert? How does anyone "balance" a given likelihood of interference with freedom of association against a particular need for information? How can one even be certain that the same standard is being applied to both sides of the scales? In the case of the teacher, was not a *general* need for information about possible overthrow of the government balanced against the *particular* refusal to answer? If such disparate measures are used, the result may well be predetermined.

What has just been said about disparate standards raises a still larger question. To what standard does the entire case-to-case method of constitutional adjudication have reference? This problem can be illustrated by the contrasting judicial approaches to the question of court-martial jurisdiction. Several recent cases presented the question whether Congress could provide for the military trial of certain civilians who committed crimes overseas. Under Black's approach, the question for determination was the civilians' status: whether the civilians were "in" the armed forces and therefore within the constitutional provisions for cases arising in the land or naval forces.[48] On the other hand, Mr. Justice Harlan rejected a literal approach:

> Decision is easy if one adopts the constricting view that these constitutional guarantees do or do not "apply" overseas. But, for me, the question is *which* guarantees of the Constitution *should* apply in view of the particular circumstances, the practical necessities, and the possible alternatives that Congress had before it. The question is one of judgment, not of compulsion. And so I agree with my brother Frankfurter that, in view of *Ross* and the *Insular* cases, we have before us a question analogous, ultimately, to issues of due process; one may say, in fact, that the question of which specific safeguards of the Constitution are appropriately to be applied in a particular context overseas can be reduced to the issue of what process is "due" a defendant in the particular circumstances of a particular case.[49]

Black's literal approach leaves judges with the task of determining which persons are "in" the land and naval forces. That may prove to be a very difficult question. But at least it is a question that can be answered by the application of reason based upon the meaning of words, their historic significance and purpose, and the facts as to the status of the civilians in question. It asks judges to reason from the general to the particular, to extrapolate from an old policy to new circumstances. But what is the process demanded by the contrasting view, which asks *"which* guarantees of the Constitution *should* apply?"

The question Mr. Justice Harlan asks—what requirements *should* apply—might be an appropriate question for a common-law judge to ask in another context. But Harlan asks the question without reference to any constitutional standard for finding an answer. To what norm does the question have reference? The word "should" puts the Court out to sea; nothing in Harlan's statement suggests that there is any chart for navigating.

This problem—the lack of an objective standard for a constitutional judgment—lies at the heart of Black's criticism of the Court's due process decisions and obscenity and legislative investigation decisions under the First Amendment. And, as we shall now see, it is the key to the concept of "absolutes," for it is the fundamental deficiency which "absolutes" seeks to cure.

The Ultimate Meaning of Absolutes

The doctrine of absolutes calls upon judges to render their decisions concerning the Bill of Rights not by using an *ad hoc* balance but by reference to an underlying balance established by the Constitution. The Constitution is, in John Marshall's noble words, "intended to endure for ages to come, and consequently, to be adapted to the various crises of human affairs."[50] It is not a detailed code, but a structure, a fundamental charter for a society that in 1789 could hardly be envisioned. One of the chief concerns of the Constitution was to strike a lasting balance between the individual and the community, one that would ensure the existence of a nation that was both strong and free. Such a balance might be composed of very different elements at different times. It was and is a matter of proportion. The infant nation could grow to be a giant, but its organic balance must remain.

Justice Black's approach says that it is the duty of judges to maintain that structure. The ultimate test of a constitutional decision is whether it retains, rather than alters, the grand design. Of course no contemporary decision can be reached by looking to the past and stopping there, and Mr. Justice Black, like every other judge, has had to decide issues composed of contemporary facts and problems. But the question he asks is always a question that has reference to the standards of the Constitution, even though the answers must be given in contemporary terms. It might be said that, in looking at present day issues, Black uses the Framers' scales and seeks to approximate the Framers' balance.

Each of the provisions of the Bill of Rights represents a marker on the boundary drawn by the Framers between the individual and the state. By using the literal language of a provision as a starting point, and its underlying purpose as a guide, Black can voyage outwards but not lose sight of the Framers' lines; that is all that "absolutes" can hope to promise.

By contrast, each "balancing decision" by the Court's majority, because it strikes an *ad hoc* balance, creates a new, *ad hoc* constitution. When the Court asks which guarantees should apply or under what circumstances freedom of association should be protected, it is asking questions that the Framers of a constitution might well ask. This is why the Court's balancing process seems so difficult, so unsatisfactory. Whatever momentary balance results, it will not necessarily be the same relationship between the community and the individual that the Constitution ordained. The scales are those of the members of the Court. There is nothing in the Court's process that is designed to ensure that the original constitutional proportions between individual and state will be maintained.

Moreover, the Court's *ad hoc* balances are on a "slippery slope." Each is likely to reflect present day needs and views. Each has for a standard its predecessor, and by degrees what is thought shocking to the conscience or necessary to the maintenance of democratic society may become far different from what was first conceived. The urgencies of the day, like gravity, pull the Court along; there is no counterweight in its formula to maintain a constant level.

"Absolutes" certainly do not offer a simple solution to every Bill of Rights problem that comes before the Court. Problems of definition, of application, and of conflicting policies remain as difficult as before. "Absolutes" do require that judges ask a question significantly different from what the Court has been asking. They do demand a far higher plane of generality than the balancing formula demands. They do provide a psychological hindrance for judges who might otherwise unwittingly descend the "slippery slope." And they do refer ultimately to "an outside frame of reference, called, for convenience, 'the law.' "[51]

In part, the concept of "absolutes" is a search for the rule of law. Nobody, including Justice Black, supposes that the ideal can fully be achieved. "[W]e know full well that law must be administered by men, and that human judgment is an inevitable element in the application of law."[52] Commentators often plead for constant striving on the part of judges for intellectual detachment and disinterestedness. Black adds a practical man's proposal: if judges are to be guided by "an outside frame of reference" that frame of reference should be the words of the Constitution itself, and the basic proportions that the words imply.

The notion of "absolutes" can best be seen, then, as an answer to a process of judging which Black believes to be out of keeping with the Constitution. It developed as a dissenting position. It represents a plea for constitutional adjudication with definite standards. But it is in no way inconsistent with the application of the Constitution to contemporary problems. It is simply a different process for approaching such problems. It is another aspect of Black's attempt to make the Constitution a living organism that nevertheless maintains its fundamental structure and purpose.

In its simplicity, the concept of "absolutes" is, perhaps, an unsophisticated one that once more recalls the image of a "backward country fellow." Bracton's phrase, "Not under man but under God and the Law" is also an unsophisticated concept, and an over-simplification. But, like "absolutes," it expresses a high ideal.

The Role of Courts in a Dynamic Society

Justice Black's basic substantive philosophy concerning the Constitution functions is, as we have seen, to endow the Bill of Rights with the power of growth and at the same time to preserve the basic structure and balance it represents, by restricting the power of judges to reweigh the factors behind it. Black's philosophy of courts demands that they take an active, positive, forceful part, and says that they need not always follow precedent or defer to other branches of government. Do these two philosophies fit together? Here again, perspective is needed to supply an answer.

Justice Black has always insisted that the power to interpret the Constitution and to invalidate acts of Congress and the executive carries with it special responsibilities. Courts, he has said, have the primary obligation of giving force and effect to constitutional limitations and liberties. They are, in Madison's words, the "guardians" of the Constitution; Black sees this duty as a "sacred trust."[53]

The course of the nation's development since the Constitution was adopted has added much weight to the responsibilities the Supreme Court assumed when it first undertook to review the constitutionality of legislative enactments. At that time, many people believed that the three branches of government could share responsibility for interpreting and enforcing the Constitution, and that the ultimate safeguard lay with the people themselves, through the political process. Today, however, neither the legislative nor the executive branch takes any significant responsibility with respect to the Constitution. Congress is under great and increasing pressure to solve problems by passing laws; there is little popularity in self-restraint.[54] Action is even more urgently demanded of the executive; Presidents find themselves pushed to the outer limits of their powers.

Moreover, Congress and the executive have developed institutional characteristics which further disable them from being satisfactory custodians of the Constitution. The problem of unequal apportionment has demonstrated how vested interests in a particular system can bar an effort to conform to constitutional requirements. And bureaucracy, a predominant underlying force in the executive branch, is characterized by its need steadily to increase its own powers; it seems intrinsically incapable of imposing limits, constitutional or otherwise, on itself. Thus it is that law enforcement agencies find the pressure to tap wires stronger than the duty to obey an act of Congress.

The public itself is under additional disabilities. In a highly specialized society the public can take no continuing interest in constitutional developments. The press and television, by their failure to inform and by actually misinforming, make independent thinking about constitutional issues increasingly difficult. Organized conformity in society makes it ever more unlikely that people will act on such individual beliefs as they may be able to acquire. And it is difficult for even the best informed citizens to make themselves heard if they do have a point of view and the desire to make it known.

What has been said above suggests some general reasons for courts to assume primary responsibility for the enforcement of the Constitution. But these reasons do not sufficiently justify a forceful role in uprooting precedents, reinterpreting safeguards, and reshaping society. The explanation for this must be sought by considering the constitutional responsibilities of a court in a dynamic society.

The basic point about constitutional law in a changing society is that no constitutional rule, however sound, can be left untended. All rules and decisions are bottomed on factual assumptions which may become invalid at a later date. The rule permitting the State Department to issue or deny a passport in its sole discretion originated in the days when a passport was merely an application by the United States for safe conduct for the passport holder.[55] But when passports became a necessity without which foreign travel was impossible, State Department discretion cut far deeper into the zone of liberty protected by the Constitution, and hence the rule required re-examination.[56] Similarly, changed circumstances explain why the two-sovereignty rule with respect to self-incrimination and double jeopardy has been so vigorously questioned. Changed knowledge explains in part the Court's rejection of the "separate but equal" doctrine under the Fourteenth Amendment. Changed circumstances also account for

the increasingly close constitutional supervision of congressional investigations, as the emphasis of some investigations has
shifted from fact-finding to the discovery of wrongdoing and
the exposure of the beliefs and associations of individuals. In
these situations, adherence to the old precedents would not
result in maintenance of the constitutional *status quo;* the
Court might find itself actually in motion—moving backwards
relative to the other forces in society.

Frequently the Supreme Court is faced not merely by familiar problems in new factual settings but by largely new problems, often beyond the contemplation of the Framers. The
growth of hearing-type investigations of wrongdoing, which
fragmentize criminal trials, is an illustration. What happens
if a court restricts its thinking to old precedents? If it does
no more than this in the case of investigations, it is actually
holding that the criminal safeguards of the Constitution do
not apply to all situations in which government moves against
individuals, but only those situations (criminal trials) which
were familiar in 1789. This "passive" attitude of the Court
therefore permits active changes in the scope of constitutional
guarantees: the fact that the changes are effected not by the
Court, but by the use of new methods to accomplish old results
does not diminish the Court's responsibility.

Investigations are not the only new practice capable of
changing the meaning of a provision of the Constitution.
Another is the increasing use of "registration" statutes to
compel persons to submit to onerous regulations, and to admit
to incriminating facts, without actually being subject to
"criminal" sanctions. A third is the use of contempt of court
as a method of trying people for the "crime" of violation of
regulatory orders. A fourth is the use of the largess of government—benefits, contracts, and subsidies—to impose controls
on the behavior of individuals and businesses. If a "passive"
Court allows these new methods to enjoy a freedom from
constitutional safeguards applicable to older methods of accomplishing the same ends, how can the Court be said to be
meeting its responsibility to preserve the Constitution intact?

Black's Philosophy and the Active Court

In light of what has just been said concerning the responsibilities of courts in a dynamic society, it is possible to examine how Black's philosophy of courts functions. In brief, it works to enable and to urge courts to meet their responsibilities. It accomplishes this in three ways: by allowing and, indeed, requiring courts to act when action is needed, by permitting doctrine to keep pace with the times, and by making judicial action effective.

If courts must constantly re-examine constitutional doctrine, their duty forbids them to withhold action too long. By limiting use of the various discretionary methods for avoiding the decision of constitutional issues, Black's philosophy works to confront the Court regularly with its task of revision.

Inaction can easily permit new practices of undetermined constitutionality to become embedded beyond the Court's ability to excise them. The Court, for example, has for many years avoided decision of the underlying issues presented by the government's loyalty-security-personnel programs.[57] But its failure to decide has had lasting consequences just as a decision would have had. For at least fifteen years government employees and their families have been severely inhibited in their political activities and associations; the public has come to accept the desirability and assumed legality of the system, with its attendant characteristics of conformity and informing; the government has been deprived of the services and thinking of those who cannot "pass" the security tests; the practices introduced by government have spread to private businesses and institutions where they are largely beyond the power of courts to eradicate; and countless individual lives have been irreparably damaged.[58] It is, perhaps, true that if the Court had decided the constitutionality of security procedures it might have upheld them, particularly during their early years. But the program went forward as if it had been approved, and the Court's inaction sanctioned the growth of a major influence in national life.

Black's underlying thesis—that the original meaning and objectives of the Constitution must constantly be applied to changing conditions—is made possible of achievement by his willingness on occasion to bypass precedents. By limiting the force of precedents, his philosophy asks courts always to return to the principles of the document itself. This does not mean, however, that judges are invited to indulge their own personal interpretations of the Constitution in place of those settled by former decision. Rather, judges are urged toward their responsibility of keeping the meaning of the Constitution constant, no matter how circumstances (and, therefore, particular applications of rules) may change. Black does not ask that judges say, "We are . . . prepared to deem ourselves wiser or more sensitive to human rights than our predecessors. . . ."[59] He asks that they be, in their own times, at least as sensitive as their predecessors. His view on precedents operates to relieve judges of any obligation toward mistaken or obsolete rulings of the past, and to compel them to see their duty in terms of the Constitution itself.

The principle that limits deference to legislative judgments in cases involving Bill of Rights questions operates in much the same way. Legislatures respond to changing circumstances and changing needs, and as they do so they are as likely as not to get further and further away from the original spirit and purposes of the Constitution. A court that owes its duty to the Constitution is not solely concerned with the immediate needs of society, and therefore cannot defer unduly to legislative judgments.

Black's reluctance to defer to legislatures has sometimes been compared to the attitude of the pre-1937 Court which struck down so much economic and social legislation. But the resemblance is a very limited one. The old Court in many of its cases dealt with the powers of Congress, rather than with the Bill of Rights. It is far more appropriate to look to the judgment of Congress in determining the extent and appropriate applications of a power granted to Congress than it is to accept that body's view concerning a *limitation* on Congress. Moreover, whether they dealt with powers or limitations, the Justices of the old Court paid far less attention to the spirit and purpose of the Constitution than Black has paid. Unlike Black, they failed to give effect to it as a living structure, and allowed outworn interpretations to strangle the nation's growth. And they frequently indulged in the very *ad hoc* weighing of values that Black has insisted is not the province of judges. For all of these reasons, the old Court had less justification for upsetting legislative judgment in a given case than would a court following Black's philosophy with respect to the Bill of Rights. Despite these differences, some similarity remains between Black's concept of the judicial function and that of the old Court. Both agree that courts are the guardians of the Constitution and should not hesitate to act vigorously in defense of the Constitution as they understand it.

Needs of the Law: Clarity, Certainty and Generality

The duty of courts as guardians of the Constitution does not end with constant reinterpretation and vigorous action. They must also attempt to make their action effective. Here "absolutes" play a second important role.

The responsibility to be effective is not adequately met by case-to-case adjudications that produce uncertain, unpredictable rules. The present interpretation of the due process clause of the Fourteenth Amendment reveals the weakness of indefinite constitutional rules. The Court's concept of due process confers many rights on individuals. But they cannot be certain when or to what extent these rights will be available. Even with the help of counsel, citizens cannot be sure of their rights. Consequently, many such rights doubtless remain unexercised because few persons care to risk the penalties of an incorrect guess. Law enforcement officials face similar dilemmas in deciding what methods of investigation and prosecution to employ; a mistake can mean loss of a case. Even the federal district courts and courts of appeals are unable to offer certainty. A case-to-case method of interpreting the Constitution really means that the Supreme Court has to settle everything itself. In practice, this means that the Court's declarations will have little impact. It can decide only a handful of cases; the vast majority, no matter how "wrong," must be left unreviewed. Constitutional rights that are neither recognized nor vindicated unless decided by the Supreme Court have little meaning for the people and, therefore, little vitality. Hence one consequence of the Court's duty to enforce the

Constitution is that the rules it hands down must be of a kind that can be understood and applied by the people.

Rules that are comparatively definite and general fill this need. Justice Black has always sought to have the Court promulgate such rules—for the states under the Due Process Clause, and for the nation under the Bill of Rights. Surely an effective Constitution has been one of the goals of his literalism and his "absolutes." They represent a practical concept of judicial administration recognizing that some degree of certainty is essential if constitutional rights are to be a meaningful and enforceable part of the life of the nation.

For much the same reason, Black's philosophy also tells the Court that on occasion it should lay down principles beyond the case at hand. This permits the Court to fulfill its responsibility as interpreter of the Constitution by acting as an educator, so that the Constitution continues to be understood by the lower courts, the bar, and the people. Opinions written with simplicity and broadness help to perform this function. For example, in the 1962 case concerning public school prayers,[60] decision of the precise issue before the Court could have been accomplished with an opinion written on very narrow grounds. Justice Black, however, used the opportunity to state what he deemed to be the broad underlying principle, in a phrase that could be widely understood. He said, "in this country it is no part of the business of government to compose official prayers for any group of the American people to recite as part of a religious program carried on by government."[61] In Black's view if the Court had said less it would have failed in its responsibilities. His philosophy operates to require leadership and teaching by the keeper of the Constitution.

The active court is the indispensable means for the preservation of a vital Constitution capable of adapting to the changes in society. Its activeness is not opposed to law. Indeed, no other kind of court can maintain the law's meaning. The active court is the keystone of Black's philosophy, for it and only it makes the constitutional ideal of liberty and justice a living reality.

Justice and Liberty Under Rule of Law

The years since the Black appointment have seen a revolution in the role of the Supreme Court. It has become an institution largely concerned with problems of individual liberty. And it has become a prime mover in influencing the direction of American society. In both of these trends Black's spirit is manifest.

The Court's preoccupation with liberty is basically a historical development—the result of the rise of government power, which naturally clashes more and more frequently with the limitations in the Constitution. But the Court's concern for liberty also owes much to Justice Black. He was one of the first to see the Bill of Rights issues of his time, and he was a pioneer in demanding that the Court deal with them.

Some of Black's views, first stated in dissent, have now been accepted by the majority and become law. A much larger part of his views have not been adopted literally, but have prevailed in a more general, modified form. Another large part of his views have been rejected, but even here they had a persistent, prodding effect, and some may yet be reconsidered and eventually prevail. And his impact is not the mere sum of the views to which the Court has responded. It is found in the totality of the Court's awareness of the Bill of Rights, and its sensitivity to issues involving liberty and equality.

Black's influence is also of the greatest importance in the Court's view of the judicial function. In the area of equal protection of the laws, the Court has undertaken the responsibility of reinterpreting the law and assuming active leadership to give force to the Constitution. The Court was long out in front in dealing with racial segregation, far ahead of Congress and the executive. Another Court-led revolution may follow the *Reapportionment Case,* which offers a promise of political equality for the urban voter, a matter of profound significance which made no progress in the other branches of government. That case represented a sweeping victory for Black's philosophy concerning the proper function of courts. One has only to read volume 302 of the *United States Reports,* that of the first year of Black's service, to realize how completely the role of the Court has changed in a quarter century. In that 1937-38 volume, *Baker v. Carr*[62] or, for that matter, *Brown v. Board of Educ.*,[63] would have been unthinkable.

In many other areas the Court has undertaken an affirmative and powerful role. It has exercised authority to review investigations conducted by Congress and by state legislatures, at a time when such investigations are becoming a steadily more important part of the activity of legislative bodies. It has exercised ever closer supervision of criminal procedures in state courts; in 1963, for example, the Court reversed its previous stand and ruled that defendants must be provided with counsel in all state criminal prosecutions.[64] It has actively entered the rising controversy concerning the relationship between religion and government. Its decisions increasingly influence state and federal employee security programs, the treatment of aliens, and the conduct of military trials.

Indeed, the judicial philosophy which Justice Black stands for is acquiring a life of its own. Other Justices shared his views over the years, and many of the victories of Justice Black's philosophy are marked by the opinions of other members of the Court. The new generation of Justices appointed by recent Presidents includes men schooled in an era in which Black's views on the Bill of Rights and the duty of the Court were already a part of the lawyer's education. The presence of such men on the Court makes it possible that much of his philosophy will persist and even grow long after his service is ended. Very few judges have made their mark so deep.

Granting that Justice Black's influence has been great, has he played the part of a judge? Sometimes it is said that he has been too strong in his views to be "judicial"—that his position is too readily predictable. But the record of his service on the Court is not a record of obstinate rigidity. It is, on the contrary, a record of extraordinary growth and change, of humility, searching, and constant re-examination. It is doubtful that any judge in the history of the Court ever showed a greater willingness to change—and Black is still changing and searching today.

Does Black's concept of a dynamic Constitution square with the accepted notion of law? It can well be answered that no other concept is capable of maintaining the rule of law. When judges act as the self-restrained embodiments of "received traditions" they attempt to follow the rule of law; but instead of ruling, the law eventually withers. In a dynamic society the law passively handed down becomes a relic the words of which no longer mean what they used to mean; the Constitution may then be left "a magnificent structure, indeed, to look at, but totally unfit for use."[65] "Our form of government may remain notwithstanding legislation or decision, but, as long ago observed, it is with governments, as with religions, the form may survive the substance of the faith."[66]

To obey the law, to preserve it in any true sense, surely can mean nothing less than to keep its spirit functioning— to see that it continues to achieve the objectives for which it was originally designed. This takes more than a passive Court. It requires a Court that sees, understands, and creates—and then actively enforces the law in its current setting so that it becomes a reality for the people. Only when given life by such a Court can the law "rule."

The qualities that are required of a judge of constitutional law are rare indeed. He must have not only much learning and skill in the law, but also a profound ability to see the issues of his day in the tangled facts of the cases before him. And he must have the courage to act on the basis of what he sees, no matter how unpopular such action may be. These are the indispensable qualities of a judge which Black brought to the Court.

And he brought even more. He brought an exalted vision of democratic society that rose above the challenges of depression and economic change within, and totalitarianism without. And he brought a passion for justice—a love for justice that was part of a love for man.

Ultimately, Justice Black's own devotion to the rule of law is revealed by the fact that so much of his service on the Court has been concerned with preserving and fostering an ideal embodied in law. The trend of America today is away from its traditions. The trend is toward strong central government, economic collectivism, and a society that stresses organization and not the individual. This trend has been sanctioned and furthered by many Supreme Court decisions from which Black has dissented. These decisions have held that the "interests of government" are increasingly more important than those of the individual. They have placed ever less value on individualism, nonconformity, and dissent as significant elements in society. They have magnified, rather than feared, the primacy of the state. Judged by the original objectives of the Constitution, these decisions are truly radical.

It is, perhaps, ironic that Justice Black, who has been called a liberal, an activist, a creative judge, should be at heart a conservative. But that has been his role. He never sought to return to earlier days, nor has he objected to things because they were new. Rather, he has sought to preserve the lasting values of the nation—values that transcend any particular time or form of society. He is a modern man who accepts today's world, its forms of government and economic and social organization. But as a judge he has become like a figure from the Old Testament, who never ceases to warn and to affirm that all governments are instituted among men to secure to individuals their inalienable rights to life, liberty, and the pursuit of happiness.

Is his effort hopeless? Is the Eighteenth Century concept of individual liberty irreconcilable with the Twentieth Century? Certainly the Bill of Rights alone cannot preserve liberty. The social and economic structure of a country, its political processes, and the knowledge and concern of its people all are forces that profoundly affect liberty. Black knows this, but it has not lessened his faith in the Bill of Rights. He would answer that it deals with evils that are deep in human nature and thus age-old. It deals, above all, with the dangers of too much power in the hands of men. Such power magnifies the faults of human nature, and has produced much of the misery that has afflicted mankind. Justice Black has said many times that no government, old or new, can ever be tyrannical if it is restricted by safeguards such as those found in the Bill of Rights. In this way, the Bill of Rights is a modern concept as well as an old one. No matter what form government takes, so long as it is composed of men, it will be subject to the same evils. And if the evils of government transcend any particular form so do the ultimate goals. No government exists for its own sake. The ideal of individual liberty belongs as much to the 1960's as it did to any previous age.

The America which produced Hugo LaFayette Black and his philosophy—a country of small farms and businesses, of local government and stubborn individuals—will not return. Time, storms, and the coming of a new, glittering society have left him a lonely sentinel—but one whose vigil looks not merely to the past but forward. During times of fear and upheaval that threaten the very existence of the Constitution, Black's true greatness is measured by how much he has done, through intelligence, boldness, courage, and passion, to maintain its living spirit. For he has stood—"against any winds that blow" —to preserve for future generations that ancient vision of a land "where the mind and spirit of man would be free."

CHAPTER SIX

Federal Taxation: Questions of
Power and Propriety

RANDOLPH E. PAUL

AS Hugo Black came to the Supreme Court in 1937, restless spirits were busy disturbing the academic peace of the economists. Arguments to the Supreme Court in favor of experimental legislation designed to relieve an extraordinary emergency were beginning to depart from established doctrines of *laissez-faire* and to put unprecedented emphasis upon the promotion of the general welfare. Moreover, an English economist named Keynes, who had acquired great wealth and was later to acquire a title, joined intellectual forces with an American banker named Eccles, who was also being unfaithful to his wealthy class, to preach startling doctrines of a compensatory economy. To these prophets of a new economic deal, and to many who followed in their rapidly moving footsteps, debts were the other side of investment and not in themselves sinful. Nor was saving an unadulterated virtue. In their opinion the forces of supply and demand would not, as the classical economists thought, necessarily keep the economy at the full employment level. The interest rate was not a perfect mechanism which assured that demand for investment goods would always be forthcoming in an amount sufficient to utilize all resources not being used for meeting consumer demand. Investment sometimes needed the encouragement of governmental action; government was an indispensable partner of

Notes appear at pages 302-312.

business rather than its patron. Perhaps worst of all in the eyes of some, this new fiscal philosophy called for a tax system which would counteract tendencies toward disproportionate saving, and promote tendencies to enlarge consumption to keep it in step with rises in productive capacity.

This was a persuasive and an ominous rationalization of a progressive tax system which would impose a heavier burden upon high bracket incomes, which are largely saved, than upon low bracket incomes, which are largely spent. It is hardly surprising that the higher income groups did not feel like taking these new heresies lying down. The opposition of many became almost religious in its intensity; a national deficit became in protesting minds a criminal act; and even the ravages of depression were thought by some to be preferable to profligate government spending. But there was ultimate victory in modified form for many of the Keynesian doctrines, and an ultimate demonstration of the truth of Keynes' observation that "the power of vested interests is vastly exaggerated compared with the gradual encroachment of ideas. . . . [I]t is ideas, not vested interests, which are dangerous for good or evil,"[1] and rule the world. For Keynes commanded the future from his study more than Napoleon had from his throne. Many of his ideas triumphed in the ideological battles that began in the mid-thirties, and have by now been translated into practices that would have been unthinkable in the golden twenties.

Taxes in a Great Depression

Even Roosevelt's worst enemies would hardly have disagreed with his assertion that the mid-thirties were "changing times." By the middle of 1937, change, with its long arm, its disturbing touch, its decree of things not yet manifest, was making what was left of wealth sorrowful and afraid. Newness had suddenly acquired a new prevalence and scope and acceleration, so that the years of the lives of men then in high places began to measure not some small growth or rearrangement or moderation of what they had learned in childhood, but a great upheaval. Depression and gloom gripped a formerly ecstatic economy. New and suspicious brands of taxation were finding

favor on Capitol Hill. In 1936 Congress had stunned the business and financial world by passing an undistributed profits
tax suggested by a heretical President. The bill enacted was
not the Administration proposal, and even the Senate version
of the bill was not to the liking of Senators Black and LaFollette of the Finance Committee, who suggested substantial
amendment. Their substitute bill would have collected $600
million annually from the "privileged" higher income group
which was avoiding the higher individual income taxes.[2]
Joined by Senator Norris, Senators Black and LaFollette fought
for the Administration bill on the floor of the Senate. They
fought in vain, and the bill that did pass came to a sad and
quick end in 1939[3] in response to a vigorous campaign of objection throughout the short period of its existence.

The undistributed profits tax was not the only villain of
the troubled times that brought Hugo Black to the Supreme
Court. In 1935 President Roosevelt had suggested a tax upon
inheritances which "bless neither those who bequeath nor
those who receive,"[4] and the Congress of which Black was a
member had responded with increased estate tax rates.[5]

The most dramatic events were taking place in June and
July of 1937, just before Black's appointment to the Supreme
Court. A revived Treasury, no longer reconciled to tax avoidance *de luxe*, was presenting to a joint congressional committee a lurid and unbelievable story of tax avoidance.[6] Witnesses
at public hearings before the Joint Committee on Tax Evasion
and Avoidance described schemes and mentioned names. The
"red herring" investigation, as it was called, filled newspapers
with scandalous detail. A hot summer was cooler than many
tempers. Though it provided "juicy copy," to use a term
coined by *Time Magazine*, the press was not happy with the
investigation. The *New York Times* conceded that the government should not tolerate evasion or fraud, but wondered
if the Administration itself had set an example of scrupulous
fairness. The *New York Herald Tribune* accused the "master
drawer of herrings" of trying to give the impression that the
failure of the rich to pay their income taxes, rather than
some failures of the Administration, was responsible for the
deficit. Senator Vandenberg used the investigation as a spring-
board for another reference to his favorite subject. "I wish,"

he said, "there was as much enthusiasm about stopping loop-holes in expenditures. If we took all income of tax-dodgers, we would still be sunk in a tragic deficit."

In the Revenue Act of 1937,[7] Congress responded with some stern measures to curb tax avoidance of the bold sort revealed in the hearings. The act became law on August 26, 1937, just after Justice Black's confirmation. As he later discovered, it fell far short of making the tax structure avoidance-proof, but it closed for good a number of the loopholes the President had called to the attention of Congress. It did not attempt to deal with community property, family partnerships, pension trusts, and percentage depletion—subjects which had been mentioned by the President. But tax avoidance was never again to be the simple matter it had been previously; it was destined to develop into a finer and subtler art, requiring more skillful devices, greater imagination, and a closer attention to detail.

Tax Law at a Crossroads

A consciousness of the inadequacy of many accepted no-tions of law had come to lawyers perhaps even before dissatis-faction with their established creeds began to plague some of the more open-minded of the economists. "In the brief space of about seventy years," said Justice Stone, "our law has been called upon to accommodate itself to changes of conditions, social and economic, more marked and extensive in their creation of new interests requiring legal protection and con-trol than occurred in the three centuries which followed the discovery of America."[8] This description of the developments creating new necessities for law in the period prior to 1937 would be a vast understatement of the tumbling stream of events that followed Justice Black's appointment to the Su-preme Court. Franklin D. Roosevelt made his famous, pro-phetic quarantine speech in 1937. In September 1939, German troops marched into Poland, and—in the vivid metaphor of a Chinese statesman—the sky was suddenly "black with the wings of chickens coming home to roost." The inevitable quickly followed. Early on a Sunday morning in December 1941, a Japanese air squadron descended from the blue of the

Hawaiian skies to cripple the American Navy. Just as suddenly the law had to face the problems of World War II. In a short time it was being forced to carry a heavy load associated with price and wage control, rationing, credit control, foreign funds control, renegotiation, and a burden of additional tax controversy incident to war rates of taxation. The complications of a scarce labor market and military procurement added to the responsibilities put upon law in this riotous period.

World War II also changed the pace and scale of fiscal development. Experience taught an incredulous people that an internal debt of $275 billion does not wreck a prosperous nation. In one year the federal budget rose to more than twice the amount of the national income of the depression year 1929. Unemployment all but disappeared. The anemic purchasing power of the thirties suddenly became an eager giant ready to devour much more than the country's busy industrial plants could produce. Goods, not buyers, were lacking; a sellers' market replaced a buyers' market of more than a decade. A country grown weary of deflation had more inflation than it wanted. The new objective was to find means of production to win the war and at the same time supply goods for the constantly increasing civilian spending power created by war activities. War had brought too much prosperity.[9]

World War II and the years that followed also brought new meanings and values and magnitudes to taxation. It was out of all question to pay completely for the war as we went. That would have wrecked the production effort, so essential to winning the war. The home front problem was inflation, with danger potentials almost as great and evil as war itself. Taxation was used not only to help finance the war effort but, in partnership with direct controls and assisted by an unexpected pattern of savings, to control inflation. There was some inflation, but military victory in the war abroad finally came to a country unravaged by inflation at home. Something else came, too—a realization by many people that a nation can thrive under a staggering burden of taxation, and that taxation is one of the most valuable instruments of economic control the world has ever known. No longer would taxes be merely the exactions of a greedy government that spends and spends and spends, or even a government that fails to spend enough.

No longer would taxes be for revenue only; thenceforth, the power to tax, in association with other governmental powers, would be exercised in the light of a new sense of federal responsibility for the welfare of the economy.[10] It would be a power to fulfill a better destiny for the American people.

Qualifications for the Supreme Court

Of such were the times in which Hugo Black assumed the responsibilities of a Justice of the Supreme Court. From the perspective of today it is startling to consider how myopic was the discussion, in the late thirties, of his qualifications for the role he has performed so well. Few talked at the time about the Senator's capacity to deal with the legal aspects of the problems many new tax and fiscal urgencies would bring to the Supreme Court. Indeed, the problems themselves were only dimly visible on a distant horizon. There was, however, a widespread belief that Black was not sufficiently learned in the intricacies of the law to serve competently on the highest Court of the land. In May of 1938 Marquis Childs reported that Black was causing his colleagues on the Court "acute discomfort and embarrassment" because he was "unable to carry his share of the heavy burden of work that falls on the Court."[11] In the light of the Justice's performance this was puzzling comment even at the time it was made. The fact was that few men have come to the Court better equipped.

Black's training in law was not so elaborate as that of some other appointees.[12] But it was more extensive than John Marshall's[13] and at least equalled that of other Supreme Court Justices.[14] From an obscure beginning Black had risen to eminence in the practice of law; much of this practice had been in the appellate courts.[15] He had had eighteen months' experience as a police court judge. He had seen considerable service as a prosecuting attorney. A Democrat, he had been selected by Republican Attorney General Stone to represent the Department of Justice in some important Prohibition cases. He had been elected to the Senate in 1926 and by 1937 had served in that body for almost two terms.[16] During this service he learned from Senator LaFollette "much of the technical aspects of tax law."[17] He was a vigorous fifty-one years old when he was nominated.

Black had supplemented his schooling by reading on a broad scale. The first book he read after his election to the Senate was Adam Smith's *Wealth of Nations*. John Draper's *History of the Intellectual Development of Europe* led him on to much historical reading, including the writings of Franklin, Hamilton, and John Adams, and all of Jefferson's voluminous writings; the records of the Federal Constitutional Convention and of the state ratifying conventions; numerous biographies of Revolutionary and Nineteenth Century American political leaders; Warren's and Myers' Supreme Court histories; most of the writings of Charles Beard; and numerous other historical works. His reading in Greek, Roman, and European history, though less comprehensive, was extensive, and included translations of Herodotus, Thucydides, Plutarch, Suetonius, Seneca, and Cicero.

Black's reading in other fields was far more than a sampling, and gave him "a comfortable acquaintance with the social sciences and the humanities."[18] He read Shakespeare frequently, and Milton, and the romantic English poets of the Nineteenth Century. He read Nineteenth Century American writers such as Hawthorne, Thoreau, and Twain. In government and economics he read, among others, Montesquieu, Rousseau, Locke, Bryce, Mill, Marx, and Spencer. He particularly cherished Veblen. In philosophy he read Aristotle, Spinoza, and some of St. Thomas Aquinas and St. Augustine. His thorough reading of William James and John Dewey awaited a summer after his appointment to the Court which he devoted to modern legal philosophy and the American philosophers in whom that legal philosophy originates.

Those who criticized Black for lack of learning in the intricacies of the law made out a weak case for their point. True, he had never been a professor,[19] and his judicial experience had been a limited one on a police court.[20] Unlike Brandeis and Cardozo he had never published any scholarly books. But he had been phenomenally successful in practice, and had had considerable experience in public life. He had applied himself diligently to the lessons of experience. He had had more experience in practice than Holmes or Cardozo. He had had

more experience in public service than Pierce Butler or the
later appointed Felix Frankfurter. Indeed, his qualifications for
the Court compared favorably with those of many eminent
previous appointees, including John Marshall, Louis Brandeis,
and Charles Evans Hughes.[21] Altogether, the impression is
unavoidable that the criticism based upon an alleged deficiency
in legal learning camouflaged objections to other qualities
brought to light by Black's public record and particularly by
his work in his second Senate term.

There is, moreover, an odd irrelevance in the stress, in much
of the discussion about any Supreme Court appointment, on
the appointee's learning in the law. For one thing, learning
in the law is a vague, immeasurable abstraction that defies
definition. Possibly the central theme of the concept is a
knowledge of past law in the sense of many precedents and
the principles that have accumulated throughout the centuries.
But this kind of knowledge, whatever it may be, can be gained
from many sources. A complete formal education in the arts
and the law is hardly a guarantee that it has been acquired.

Even more important, it must be remembered that most
of the major questions presented to the Supreme Court cannot
be answered out of the books that record the thousands of
answers to questions previously presented.[22] The questions
that must be decided by the Court are often difficult and
delicate questions of fact[23] that strict logic and a judicious
selection among rival precedents can answer in favor of either
side of a controversy.[24] A resourceful judge can give almost
any conclusion a logical form.[25] But as a basis for decision,
logic must yield first place to experience, and in the Supreme
Court "the felt necessities of the time, the prevalent moral
and political theories, intuitions of public policy, avowed
or unconscious," have "a good deal more to do than the syl-
logism in determining the rules by which men should be
governed."[26] There is in the equation of most important decisions of the Supreme Court a clash of policy, an element of
imponderable conflict between competing social and economic
philosophies or forces in our society. And as Justices Holmes
and Stone have intimated, the prejudices that a judge shares
with his fellow men and the individual predilections of each
Justice toward the problem before the Court may affect his

decision.[27] "Traditional beliefs, acquired convictions, an outlook on life, and a conception of social ends" are some of the
deep forces that tug at judges.[28]

It is, in sum, a myth that the Supreme Court is either an
impersonal or a· nonpolitical body. It makes many political
decisions,[29] especially in constitutional matters,[30] not in the
"sense of partisanship but in the sense of policy-making."[31]
This political role of the Court has been too obscure to laymen, and even to many lawyers. Constitutional interpretation,
and to a large extent statutory interpretation, compel the
translation of policy into judgment. In this process of interpretation the Justices of the Court gather meaning not only
from reading the Constitution and the statutes, but also from
reading life.[32]

These are some of the considerations which influence Presidents in their selection of Supremè Court Justices. Of course
Presidents look to an appointee's legal learning and equipment, his experience at the bar, his reputation among his colleagues and the judges before whom he has appeared, the
character of his clientele, and many other items that add up
to the total of the technical ability he can bring to a judicial
job. But even though the Supreme Court is an institution, an
appointing President knows that individuals, with all their
diversities of endowment, experience and outlook, determine
its actions.[33] He therefore wisely looks far beyond the horizon
of strictly legal capacity. He knows, with Chesterton, that
the most important thing about a man is his philosophy. The
determining factor is, and should be, the appointee's approach
to, and attitude toward, the social and economic questions of
the day.

Presidential Choice and Rationale

Some Presidents have candidly revealed the considerations
that guided them in selecting members of the Supreme Court.
Lincoln once gave his reasons for appointing Chase as Chief
Justice. One was Chase's large place in the public mind.
Another was that "we wish for a Chief Justice who will sustain
what has been done in regard to emancipation and the legal

tenders. We cannot ask a man what he will do, and if we should, and he should answer us we should despise him for it. Therefore, we must take a man whose opinions are known."[34] In a letter to Senator Lodge, Theodore Roosevelt gave the reasons why he was in favor of Justice Holmes. "The ablest lawyers and the greatest judges," he said, were men whose past "has naturally brought them into close relationship with the wealthiest and the most powerful clients," and Roosevelt was glad when he could find a judge like Holmes "who has been able to preserve his aloofness of mind so as to keep his broad humanity of feeling and his sympathy for the class from which he has not drawn his clients."[35] Roosevelt went on to add that a judge of the Supreme Court should be neither "partisan" nor "politician" in the "ordinary and low sense" which we attach to these words. But "in the higher sense, in the proper sense," he should be "a party man, a constructive statesman, constantly keeping in mind his adherence to the principles and policies under which this nation has been built up and in accordance with which it must go on."[36] And Roosevelt wanted to know that Judge Holmes was "in entire sympathy with our views, that is, with your views and mine," before he would feel justified in appointing him.[37]

It was not wholly accidental that Wilson had an opportunity to appoint only three Justices in his eight years of presidency whereas Taft in his four years had appointed six members to the Court. In a candid newspaper conference held at the time he turned over the White House to Wilson in 1913, Taft said that he had told his appointees: "Damn you, if any of you die I'll disown you."[38] Obviously, most of Taft's appointees took his threat to heart. Later, in the 1920 campaign, Taft urged the election of Mr. Harding on the ground that four of the incumbent Justices of the Supreme Court were beyond the retiring age of seventy, so that the next President would probably be called upon to appoint their successors. He urged that the election of Harding would help to insure the maintenance of the Supreme Court "as the bulwark to enforce the guaranty that no man shall be deprived of his property without due process of law."[39] Later, while serving on the Court himself, Taft likewise saw the Court as a check on President Hoover, whom he suspected of liberal intervals. He once confessed that though he was "older and slower and less acute and more confused," he must stay on the Court as long as things continued as they were and he was able to answer in his place, "to prevent the Bolsheviki from getting control."[40]

Political considerations of this kind are particularly relevant to appointments made during a period like the mid-thirties, and President Roosevelt might well have looked less to legal learning than to his version of wisdom in making the selections he made. Much of the legal learning of the past had crumbled before his eyes while he was in office. The education of most eligibles for the Court at that time had been acquired in large part in a past that was gone forever. It had been reversed by a powerful march of events that had swept away its foundations. It was dated. A new learning had to be assembled in a dazzling process of trial and error. At such a time a vested interest in obsolete legal learning might be a handicap to a new Justice on the Supreme Court.[41] What was needed more than scholarship in any pedestrian sense of that term, and over and above strictly legal learning, was adaptability of attitude, a capacity for rapid assimilation of the lessons that violent experience was forcing upon puzzled minds, and a mature acceptance of life in a chaotic new world that had replaced the world in which most existing legal learning had developed.

Stare Decisis in a Brave New World

Justice Black's concurring opinion in *Helvering v. Gerhardt*,[42] decided shortly after he joined the Court, was truly what Chief Justice Hughes in speaking of dissents had called "an appeal to the brooding spirit of the law, to the intelligence of a future day."[43] It gave early proof that Justice Black was not the kind of judge "to deny the reality of change" or to "conceal the truth of adaptation behind a verbal disguise of fixity and universality."[44] Rather he would, in the democratic tradition, choose the principle of blunt, open, and direct disclosure.[45] Black's *Gerhardt* opinion furnished as well an indication of his attitude toward stare decisis (let the decision stand), the doctrine of following the rules or principles laid down in previous cases.

The *Gerhardt* case involved the constitutional power of the federal government to impose income tax upon salaries received by employees of the Port of New York Authority, a bi-state corporation created by compact between New York and New Jersey to operate transportation facilities between the two states. The taxpayers relied principally upon *McCulloch v. Maryland*[46] and *Collector v. Day*.[47] In the former case Chief Justice Marshall's 1819 opinion invalidated a state tax upon national banks. In the latter the Court held, in 1871, that the salary of a state probate judge was immune from the federal income tax.

Justice Stone, as spokesman for the Court in upholding the challenged tax, composed the cautious, compromise type of opinion that would satisfy some other Justices by hiding innovation "behind a formal distinction."[48] He proved himself equal to the dexterous task of sustaining the tax without over-ruling *Collector v. Day*. He accomplished this objective by distinguishing and limiting that case, giving it lip service but confining its message to its particular facts.[49] *Collector v. Day* had involved a tax upon the salary of an officer "engaged in the performance of an indispensable function of the state which cannot be delegated to private individuals."[50] But the tax challenged in the *Gerhardt* case neither precluded nor threatened "unreasonably to obstruct any function essential to the continued existence of the state government."[51] So much of the burden of the tax laid upon the taxpayer's salary as might reach the state was "but a necessary incident to the co-existence within the same organized government of the two taxing sovereigns," and hence was a burden contemplated by the Constitution.[52]

While Justice Black agreed that the payment of a nondiscriminatory federal income tax on their salaries by employees of the Port of New York Authority would not impair or defeat the governmental operations of the state of New York, he was unable to reconcile the majority opinion with the principle announced in *Collector v. Day* and later opinions applying that principle. To him the rule established by the majority opinion made the tax status of every state employee uncertain until the Supreme Court passed upon the classification of his particular employment, and created a "confusion in the field of inter-

governmental tax immunity" which the new Justice believed
could be "clarified by complete review of the subject."[53] The
uncertainty and inequality of treatment created by the test was
manifest: there might be a tax upon the income of an officer
of a state-operated transportation system but none upon the
income of the manager of a municipal water works system.

In Black's view the *Gerhardt* case afforded an appropriate
occasion for a thorough re-examination of the rule of *Collector
v. Day*. His opinion ended with these two paragraphs:

> There is not, and there cannot be, any unchanging
> line of demarcation between essential and nonessential
> governmental functions. Many governmental functions
> of today have at some time in the past been non-govern-
> mental. The genius of our government provides that,
> within the sphere of constitutional action, the people
> —acting not through the courts but through their
> elected legislative representatives—have the power to
> determine as conditions demand, what services and
> functions the public welfare requires.

> Surely, the Constitution contains no imperative man-
> date that public employees—or others—drawing equal
> salaries (income) should be divided into taxpaying and
> non-taxpaying groups. Ordinarily such a result is dis-
> crimination. Uniform taxation upon those equally able
> to bear their fair shares of the burdens of government
> is the objective of every just government. The language
> of the Sixteenth Amendment empowering Congress to
> "collect taxes on incomes, from whatever source de-
> rived"—given its most obvious meaning—is broad
> enough to accomplish this purpose.[54]

Further re-examination of the doctrine of *Collector v. Day*
came more promptly than Justice Black could have anticipated.
Within two years the case was explicitly overruled insofar as
it recognized "an implied constitutional immunity from income taxation of the salaries of officers or employees of a
national or a state government or their instrumentalities."[55]

Black's concurring opinion in the *Gerhardt* case illustrated
at an early date a basic attitude of Roosevelt's first appointee

to the Court. It was incumbent upon the Court, in his view, to face constitutional issues squarely. Obsolete doctrines should be abandoned "openly and avowedly."[56] The interpretation of the Constitution should move forward with changing times.[57] Its dynamic march should not be obstructed by an unwillingness to overrule precedents simply because they were hallowed with age. The Court must bow "to the lessons of experience and the force of better reasoning, recognizing that the process of trial and error, so fruitful in the physical sciences, is appropriate also in the judicial function."[58]

The rule of stare decisis has "only a limited application in the field of constitutional law."[59] It has more potency in cases where correction can be achieved through legislation than in those involving the Constitution, where correction is only possible through the laborious process of amendment.[60] But "legislative correction of judicial errors is often difficult to effect,"[61] and the courts must occasionally take a hand in dispelling error that they have themselves produced. So in *Commissioner v. Estate of Church*[62] in 1949 Justice Black spoke for a majority of the Court in stating that the policy of stare decisis and "an alleged interest in stability and certainty"[63] should not prevent the Court from overruling its decision in *May v. Heiner*,[64] handed down eighteen years previously and reaffirmed in three per curiam decisions joined in by Chief Justice Hughes and Justices Holmes, Brandeis, and Stone.[65]

The *Church* case involved the interpretation of that part of the 1939 Internal Revenue Code which required the inclusion in a decedent's gross estate of the value of all property the decedent had transferred to a trust "intended to take effect in possession or enjoyment at or after his death."[66]

The question was whether property in a trust was includible in the taxable estate of its grantor because of a clause reserving its income to the grantor for life. Against the strong trend of previous authority, the Supreme Court had held in *May v. Heiner* that the property was not to be included. After the reaffirmation of this astonishing ruling in the per curiam decisions referred to,[67] Congress had promptly responded with a joint resolution[68] providing for the inclusion of the property of such a trust in the grantor's estate, and this joint resolution had been incorporated in the 1932 Act,[69] at least as to trusts created after the passage of the resolution.[70] The trust in the *Church* case had been set up before the resolution; and so the vitality of *May v. Heiner* was still in question. Justice Black's majority opinion held that *May v. Heiner* should no longer be accepted as a controlling interpretation of the "possession or enjoyment" clause because *Helvering v. Hallock*[71] "directly and unequivocally rejected the only support that could possibly suffice" for what the Court held in *May v. Heiner*.[72] Speaking of a transfer in trust with a reservation of a life interest, he wrote:

> How is it possible to call this trust transfer "complete" except by invoking a fiction? Church was sole owner of the stocks before the transfer. Probably their greatest property value to Church was his continuing right to get their income. . . . That property right did not pass to the trust beneficiaries when the trust was executed; it remained in Church until he died. He made no "complete" gift effective before that date, unless we view the trust transfer as a "complete" gift to the trustees. But Church gave the trustees nothing, either partially or completely. He transferred no right to them to get and spend the stock income. And under the teaching of the *Hallock Case*, quite in contrast to that of *May v. Heiner*, passage of the mere technical legal title to a trustee is not necessarily crucial in determining whether and when a gift becomes "complete" for estate tax purposes. Looking to substance and not merely to form, as we must unless we depart from the teaching of *Hallock*, the inescapable fact is that Church retained for himself until death a most valuable property right in these stocks—the right to get and to spend their income. Thus Church did far more than attach a "string" to a remotely possible reversionary interest in the property, a sufficient reservation under the *Hallock* rule to make the value of the corpus subject to an estate tax. Church did not even risk attaching an unbreakable cable to the most valuable property attribute of the stocks, their income. He simply retained this valuable property, the right to the income, for himself until death, when for the first

time the stock with all its property attributes "passed" from Church to the trust beneficiaries. Even if the interest of Church was merely "obliterated," in *May v. Heiner* language, it is beyond all doubt that simultaneously with his death, Church no longer owned the right to the income; the beneficiaries did. It had then "passed." It never had before. For the first time, the gift had become "complete."[73]

Justice Frankfurter, who had written the *Hallock* majority opinion, disagreed sharply with Justice Black's majority opinion in the *Church* case. He thought that it reflected an inappropriate attitude toward a series of long standing unanimous decisions of the Court, and too little respect for the expressed intention of Congress. To him, also, stare decisis was not "a universal, inexorable command," but neither was it "a doctrine of the dead hand."[74] It made a difference to him, as it did not to Justice Black, that the Court was not dealing in the *Church* case with "a ruling which cramps the power of Government," or with "a constitutional adjudication which time and experience have proved a parochial instead of a spacious view of the Constitution and which thus calls for self-correction by the Court without waiting for the leaden-footed process of constitutional amendment"; that the Court was dealing, rather, with an exercise of the Court's "duty to construe what Congress has enacted with ample powers on its part quickly and completely to correct misconstruction."[75]

It required about 55,000 words to express the divergent views of the various members of the Supreme Court in the *Church* case and its companion, the *Spiegel* case.[76] Despite this "outbreak of . . . explanation," the blood pressure of the tax bar rose to a new high if for no other reason, Adrian DeWind has explained,[77] than the short shrift the decision gave to the doctrine of stare decisis as a protection for entrenched interest in error. The Treasury, discreetly feeling that it had won too much for its own comfort, decided that the early error of the Supreme Court was too deeply embedded in tax law to be fully corrected immediately. Accordingly, the Treasury partially reinstated the earlier overruled doctrine of the Supreme Court, by a regulation that made the new correct doctrine inapplicable to the estates of decedents dying before January 17, 1949,[78] the date of the *Church* decision. An even more generous Congress quickly granted further relief. In the Technical Changes Act of 1949[79] it extended to January 1, 1950, the immunity granted by the Treasury in its amended regulation (and, as well, expressed disapproval of the Court decision in the *Spiegel* case). The theory was that some months would be needed to relinquish or assign the life estates which condemned entire estates to the impact of the estate tax.[80] Under this provision the new rule established by the *Church* case would apply only to decedents dying after December 31, 1949. In addition, the statute allowed a further period in which to transfer or relinquish the tainted life interests. Transfers in 1949 and 1950 escaped gift tax; transfers in 1949 escaped the possibility of the charge that they were made in contemplation of death; and transfers in 1951 and later years were to be subject to the gift tax and the possibility of estate taxation if they were found to have been made in contemplation of death.

[In 1965, speaking for eight members of the Court, Justice Black held that accident insurance, like ordinary life insurance, was to be considered a taxable part of estates. The basis on which the Court of Appeals had decided otherwise was that the decedent had given the insurance policies in question to his wife before boarding an ill-fated plane, saying that from that moment they belonged to her. The wife subsequently claimed that the policies were not part of the estate actually left to her at her husband's death. But the Supreme Court could see "no distinction between 'policies on the life of the decedent' which must be paid in all events and those payable only if death comes in a certain way or within a certain time," and (pointing to the insured's legal right to designate a change of beneficiary at any point prior to death) held that "the estate tax liability . . . depends on a general, legal power to exercise ownership, without regard to the owner's ability to exercise it at a given moment."[81]

The case also has significance in that it demonstrates Black's unwillingness to use tax laws for other purposes than to collect revenues. Cases discussed below emphasize his strong distaste for using tax laws to enforce local laws. Here, Black would not thwart the obvious purpose of the estate tax in order to reduce its financial burden on a widow. In short, Black would not employ tax laws as a vehicle for the Court to establish public policy. *Editor's note.*]

Tax Avoidance in Later Manifestation

Tax law has its share of "seductive *clichés*"[82] and verbalistic distinctions. One of the most overworked distinctions in tax opinions and briefs contrasts the vague alternatives of "form" and "substance"—terms which Judge Learned Hand has called "anodynes for the pains of reasoning."[83] Though they are sometimes useful as terms of general contrast, these favorite "catch words and labels" are "subject to the dangers that lurk in metaphors and symbols, and must be watched with circumspection lest they put us off our guard."[84] One test of a judge is whether he succumbs to the dangers against which Justice Cardozo thus wisely warned us. And so the question may be asked whether Justice Black is a cliché thinker, who lets himself be led astray by these and other semanticisms of tax lawyers.

It is true that "form" and "substance" are words which appear with relative frequency in opinions written by Justice Black in the field of taxation. "The incidence of taxation depends," he has said, "upon the substance of a transaction."[85] "In the field of taxation, administrators of the laws, and the courts, are concerned with substance and realities, and formal written documents are not rigidly binding."[86] The question in tax cases is whether a gain is "real and substantial."[87] "The essence of a gift by trust is the abandonment of control over the property put in trust," and it is important to note that the grantor "has neither the form nor substance of control."[88] "Bookkeeping devices and paper contrivances should not be permitted to make two payments out of one," and the tax statutes do not compel the conclusion that Congress "intended to reward ingenuity in paper work by granting multiple tax reductions for a single money payment to discharge a single corporate obligation."[89] The Supreme Court "must not give effect to any contrivance which would defeat a tax Congress plainly intended to impose. The use of bookkeeping and accounting forms and devices cannot be permitted to devitalize valid tax laws."[90]

These quotations suggest the flavor of Justice Black's basic approach to tax law. It is to his credit, however, that he is never content to let his opinions rest upon sweeping generalizations. Fully aware that "general propositions do not decide concrete cases,"[91] he puts general terms such as "form" and "substance" in the context of careful factual accounts of transactions. In the *Court Holding* case[92] the facts showed that the sale of corporation property by stockholders was, as the Tax Court had found, "in substance the sale of the corporation,"[93] and Justice Black held for the Court that it should be taxed as such. But it did not follow in Justice Black's mind that there could be no escape from corporate tax if there was a genuine liquidation and distribution and the stockholders were more than mere conduits through which to pass title. The *Cumberland* case[94] brought to the Court a transaction in which the lower court had found that there had been a genuine liquidation. In this case the Cumberland Company stockholders offered to sell all their stock to a competing cooperative. The cooperative refused to buy the stock, but countered with an offer to buy the transmission and distribution equipment of the Cumberland Company. At the same time the Cumberland shareholders, desiring to escape payment of the corporate capital gains tax, offered to acquire the equipment and sell it to the cooperative. The cooperative accepted; the corporation transferred the equipment to its shareholders in partial liquidation; after a sale of remaining assets the corporation was dissolved. The shareholders then executed the previously contemplated sale to the cooperative. To the government this looked like another *Court Holding* case. But not to Justice Black. A corporation cannot be taxed "when the sale has been made by its stockholders following a genuine liquidation and dissolution," even though "a major motive of the shareholders was to reduce taxes"; the motive of the shareholders was relevant in determining whether the transaction was "real or a sham," but sales of physical property following a genuine liquidation distribution cannot "be attributed to the corporation for tax purposes."[95]

In working his way to this conclusion, the Justice was perfectly aware of the shadowy and artificial character of the distinction between sales by a corporation and shareholder sales after a distribution in kind. But Congress had chosen to recognize the distinction, and the Court was bound to follow the mandate of Congress that different tax consequences should "flow from different methods by which the shareholders of a closely held corporation may dispose of corporate property."[96]

The *Cumberland* opinion of Justice Black, like many other tax opinions of the Supreme Court, had a legislative sequel.[97] In the new and much publicized *1954 Code,* Congress made a valiant attempt to eliminate the oddities of tax consequences and emerge from different ways of selling the assets of liquidating corporations.[98]

[In a 1965 case,[99] Black and the Chief Justice joined Justice Goldberg in disagreeing with a majority of their brethren about whether the transaction in question was "real or sham," and therefore whether the taxes in dispute should have been paid on ordinary income or on income from capital gains. There a company had been sold by a small, family-dominated group of stockholders to a nonprofit research institute; the bulk of the money paid the stockholders came from their company's lease and rental property, and the company president was retained as manager of a successor enterprise operated for the research institute. Said Goldberg, speaking for the three:

> In effect the Institute sold the respondents the use of its tax exemption . . . [It] was used by the Institute as a part of the arrangement that allowed it to buy a business that in fact cost it nothing . . . I believe the sellers retained an economic interest in the business. . . .[100]

Yet the Court majority held here, as Black had held in *Cumberland,* that the original sales transaction was genuine and that therefore, regardless of the motives of the sellers, they were entitled under the law to pay tax at the capital gains rate rather than at the much higher rate required for ordinary income. *Editor's note.*]

The *Court Holding* and *Cumberland* cases edge into the controversial field of tax avoidance. One of the principal devices of the thirties and later years for the minimization of family tax liability was the family partnership.[101] It is customary for taxpayers to rely in tax avoidance cases upon the shopworn principle that they have a "legal right" to avoid taxes by means which the law permits.[102] But tax avoidance is one part of tax law that has brought home to many taxpayers the grim lesson that general abstract propositions do not decide particular cases. This was the first lesson to be learned from two of Justice Black's opinions dealing with family partnerships—the *Tower*[103] and *Lusthaus*[104] cases. The next decision, in the *Culbertson* case[105] should have taught the Treasury the equally important lesson that it is dangerous to overplay victory, for the Treasury was less successful in its second round in the Supreme Court on the family partnership problem.

The *Tower* and *Lusthaus* cases involved a family partnership device that created an acute problem for the tax collector in that era. The facts of the *Tower* case sufficiently illustrate the conventional pattern of the device. For nearly thirty years the taxpayer had done a manufacturing business in Michigan. From 1933 to 1937, the business was operated as a corporation. The taxpayer was president of the corporation and owned almost all of the outstanding shares of stock; his wife was vice-president and owned a few shares. The wife was on the board of three directors, along with her husband and a bookkeeper who also owned a few shares. The husband managed the corporate affairs; the wife performed no business services.

In 1937, when substantial profits pointed to increased taxes, the taxpayer's attorney and his tax accountant advised him that the dissolution of the corporation and the formation of a partnership would save taxes and eliminate the necessity of filing corporate returns. Acting upon this advice, the taxpayer transferred a block of stock to his wife on condition that she place the corporate assets represented by the transferred shares in a new partnership. This she did three days after the stock transfer. The husband paid a small gift tax on the transfer of the shares to the wife. The wife became a limited partner in the new partnership. A certificate of partnership was filed

as required by Michigan law. The formation of the partnership did not in any way alter the conduct of the business:[106] the
husband continued to have the controlling voice as to pur-
chases, sales, salaries, the time of distribution of income, and
all other essentials. The wife used her drawings from the
partnership to buy "what a husband usually buys for his wife
such as clothes and things for the family or to carry on activities ordinarily of interest to the family as a group."[107]

In Justice Black's majority opinion these facts were sufficient
to support the Tax Court's finding that for tax purposes
the wife was not a partner in the business. The validity of
the partnership under Michigan law did not make it "a real
partnership" under federal tax law. "The simple expedient
of drawing up papers" was not enough to divide "single tax
earnings" into "two tax units" for purposes of a tax law that
looks to command of the taxpayer over income and seeks to
tax income to the person who earns it.[108] The creation of
the partnership did not change the economic relation of the
husband and wife to the income of the business. "[T]he result
of the partnership was a mere paper reallocation of income
among the family members," and there was more than ample
evidence to support the Tax Court's finding that no genuine
union for partnership business purposes was ever intended,
and that the husband earned the income.[109]

The Court did not reject the principle that taxpayers have
a right to avoid taxes by legal means. That principle would
apply, Justice Black's majority opinion stated, in "a situation
where a member of a partnership, in order to keep from paying
future taxes on partnership profits and in order to get into a
lower income tax bracket sells his interest to a stranger,
relinquishing all control of the business."[110] The principle did
not apply where the taxpayer

> draws a paper purporting to sell his partnership interest
> even to a stranger, though actually he continues to con-
> trol the business to the extent he had before the "sale"
> and channels the income to his wife. Then a showing
> that the arrangement was made for the express purpose
> of reducing taxes simply lends further support to the
> inference that the husband still controls the income

from his partnership interest, that no partnership really exists, and that the earnings are really his and are therefore taxable to him and not to his wife. The arrangement we are here considering was of the type where proof of a motive to reduce income taxes lent further strength to the inference drawn by the Tax Court that the wife was not really a partner. . . . To rule otherwise would mean ordering the Tax Court to shut its eyes to the realities of tax avoidance schemes.[111]

In the *Culbertson* case[112] Chief Justice Vinson made a courageous, but unsuccessful, effort to clarify a difficult subject which Justice Black's opinions in the *Tower* and *Lusthaus*[113] cases had left in considerable obscurity. Culbertson for many years had operated a cattle business in partnership with a man named Coon. Coon, who was seventy-nine years old in 1939, wished to dissolve the partnership because of ill-health. The greater part of the partnership herd was sold, but Culbertson wished to keep about 1,500 Herefords, the brood or foundation herd. He offered to buy these cattle, and Coon agreed on condition that Culbertson would sell an undivided one-half interest in the herd to Culbertson's four sons at the same price. Coon's reasons for exacting this condition were his interest in maintaining the Hereford strain, his conviction that Culbertson was too old to carry on the work alone, and his personal interest in the Culbertson boys. The boys paid for their interests largely with notes and partly with the proceeds of a gift from Culbertson. The old partnership was dissolved. A new oral partnership continued the business.

The four Culbertson boys were young when the new partnership began business. The oldest boy, twenty-four years old, was married and lived on the ranch. A college graduate, he had been foreman for two years under the old partnership. He received $100 a month plus board and lodging for himself and his wife, both before and after the new partnership was organized, and until he entered the Army. The second boy was twenty-two years old and married. He finished college during the first year of the new partnership, and then went directly into the Army following graduation and rendered no services for the partnership. The two younger sons were eighteen and sixteen years old. They went to school during the winter and worked on the ranch during the summer.

The principal factual difference between the *Tower* and *Lusthaus* cases on the one hand and the *Culbertson* case on the other was that a tax avoidance motive reared its ugly head in the former cases and seems to have been absent from the latter.[114] Perhaps this is the "inarticulate major premise" of any retreat which may have been made by the Court in the later case.[115] It must be admitted in any event that the total interpretation furnished by the three cases left something to be desired. When taken in the aggregate, Justice Black's earlier opinions seemed to some lawyers and judges to make the tax validity of a family partnership depend upon either the contribution of original (not donated) capital or the performance of services by the wife. But in the *Culbertson* case the Court said that the use of these tests by the Tax Court was "at best, an error in emphasis."[116] The test is rather whether the partnership is "real," whether "the parties in good faith and acting with a business purpose intended to join together in the present conduct of the enterprise."[117] Thus the Court seemed to establish an "intention" test, making the validity of a family partnership depend upon subjective considerations.[118]

Congress with some justification thought that the *Tower*, *Lusthaus*, and *Culbertson* cases had produced "confusion."[119] Whether its remedy is worse than the disease is not certain. In any event, in the 1951 Act, Congress amended the *Code* to wipe out the "intention" criterion set up by the *Culbertson* opinion and the factual standards set up by the *Tower* and *Lusthaus* opinions.[120] Under the provisions incorporated in the *1954 Code*,[121] a partnership capital interest will be recognized even though it was acquired by purchase or gift from any other person, including a member of the family. Where a capital interest has been acquired by gift, the distributable share of the donee partner under the partnership agreement must be included in the donee's gross income "except to the extent that such share is determined without allowance of reasonable compensation for services rendered to the partnership by the donor, and except to the extent that the portion of such share attributable to the donated capital is proportionately greater than the share of the donor attributable to the donor's capital."[122] The distributive share of a partner in the earnings of a partnership cannot be diminished because of absence due to military service.

This legislative solution can hardly be regarded as ideal. Since the adoption of income-splitting for husband and wife in 1948, the problem has narrowed to one involving child partners, or partnerships with trustee members.[123] A partnership consisting of a father and a business acquaintance trustee for a minor son has been recognized.[124] A trust of which a father-partner is trustee may be a limited partner;[125] so may a third party trustee for a minor son of the settlor-partner.[126] But it has also been held that there is no valid partnership for tax purposes where the partner-trustee for a minor son was first a physician who had nothing to offer the business and later one of the other partners.[127] On the other hand, two men who placed their partnership interests in trust for a mother and wife respectively, and then ran the business as trustees, have been treated as partners.[128]

These attempted solutions in particular cases of the complex problem of family partnerships have in them a sardonic humor which suggests that subtleties have not been completely eliminated from the tax scene. Humor of a lighter character may also be admitted to the premises. In their income tax casebook Surrey and Warren tell of one case in which partnership agreements were prepared with the name of the new partner left blank "awaiting his expected birth so that sex and name could then be supplied."[129] They also call attention to the case of *Redd v. Commissioner*,[130] involving as partners a husband, a wife, and four children aged seven, five and two years, and three months. On the trial of this case the partner's wife testified as follows:

"Q. Now, do you participate in the management of the LaSalle Livestock Company?

"A. Well, I have been producing partners.

"Q. Beg pardon.

"A. I have been too busy producing partners, so far."[131] Similarly, tax lawyers are still busy producing family partnerships with infant members.

It might have been better if the courts and Congress had adopted a *Clifford*[132] approach to this elusive problem. In his *Tower* opinion Justice Black did mention the *Clifford* case for the point that the purpose of the tax statute to tax all income to the person who controlled its distribution could not be frustrated by family group arrangements, even though the arrangements were valid for state law purposes; and for the point that "transactions between husband and wife calculated to reduce family taxes should always be subjected to special scrutiny."[133] And in the *Culbertson* case Chief Justice Vinson cited the *Clifford* case for the point that income "must be taxed to him who earns it"; but he also stated that the "Clifford-Horst" principle does not follow "automatically upon a gift to a member of one's family, followed by its investment in the family partnership."[134] The Senate Report on the 1951 Act refers to cases "where the transferor retains so many of the incidents of ownership that he will continue to be recognized as a substantial owner of the interest which he purports to have given away. . . ."[135] This quotation suggests an approach to the problem to which the courts may have insufficiently resorted. What can be done to trusts can certainly be done to partnerships.

The Use of Federal Tax Statutes to Enforce Local Law

No discussion of Justice Black's attitude toward federal taxation would be complete without some reference to his vigorous dissent in *Rutkin v. United States* in 1952.[136] There a slim majority of the Supreme Court, despite its eight-to-one *Wilcox* decision[137] that embezzled funds do not constitute income, gave its blessing to the use of the federal income tax to punish the local crime of extortion. Justice Black protested that the federal government would never collect substantial amounts of money from extortioners, and that the purpose of the policy implicit in the prosecution of Rutkin was "to give Washington more and more power to punish purely local crimes." The majority decision, he thought, authorized "an expansion of Federal criminal jurisdiction into fields of law enforcement heretofore wholly left to states and local communities."[138]

The dissenting opinion of Justice Black went on to indicate the dangers of such a policy. Taking over enforcement of local criminal laws lowers "the prestige of the federal system of justice," and makes that system "top-heavy." "The United States cannot perform the monumental tasks which lie beyond state power if the time, energy, and funds of federal institutions are expended in the field of state criminal law enforcement."[139]

Justice Black, along with the three other dissenting Justices in the *Rutkin* case, was also concerned about the states. Local crimes—extortion, robbery, and embezzlement, for example—are matters of local concern. The precise elements of these crimes, as well as the problems underlying them, vary from state to state. As former United States Attorney General William D. Mitchell once pointed out, federal enforcement of local laws must of necessity tend to free the states from a sense of responsibility for their own local conditions.[140] And, Justice Black added:

> Even when states attempt to play their traditional role in the field of law enforcement, the overriding federal authority forces them to surrender control over the manner and policy of construing and applying their own laws. State courts not only lose control over the interpretation of their own laws, but also are deprived of the chance to use the discretion vested in them by state legislatures to impose sentences in accordance with local ideas. Moreover, state prosecutors are deprived of the all-important function of deciding what local offenders should be prosecuted. Final authority to make these important decisions becomes located in the distant city of Washington, D.C. Here, as elsewhere, too many cooks may spoil the broth.[141]

(The undue expansion of federal jurisdiction entails one more complicating factor. "Criminal rules of substance and of procedure vary widely among the jurisdictions. Punishment is frequently different. In fact, the same kind of conduct may be ignored as not worth criminal punishment by one jurisdiction while considered a serious criminal offense by another.")[142]

Justice Black's dissenting opinion in the *Rutkin* case also cited figures that showed in striking fashion that the federal government was using the federal tax statute to suppress local crime rather than to collect taxes—so that "it can hardly be said that Rutkin was tried for tax evasion."[143] A total of only thirteen pages in a voluminous record of 900 pages had any reference to taxes. The remaining 887 pages were devoted to inflammatory aspects of Rutkin's past life and associations, including his bootlegging activities in Prohibition days and various charges of swindling made by Rutkin and others against one Reinfeld. Subsequent events have certainly proved the truth of Justice Black's suggestion that "if we are going to depart from the *Wilcox* holding," the *Rutkin* case was "a poor case in which to do so."[144]

[What Black anticipated in *Rutkin* came to pass in 1961 in *James v. United States.*[145] Though split in several directions as to details of the proper meaning and consequences of its action, a majority of the Court agreed that *Wilcox* should be specifically overruled. Generally, their basis was that *Rutkin* had "devitalized" *Wilcox*: that the differences between embezzlement (producing income not taxable according to *Wilcox*) and extortion (producing taxable income according to *Rutkin*) were "attenuated subtleties." They accepted the Government's argument that *Wilcox* effectively meant that embezzled funds, alone among various kinds of unlawful income, illogically were exempted from taxation. Justice Black strongly objected on several grounds. First, he disagreed that embezzlement was not distinguishable from other types of unlawful income. "The whole basis of the *Wilcox* opinion was that an embezzlement is not in itself a 'gain' or 'income' to the embezzler within the tax sense, for the obvious reason that embezzled property still belongs, and is known to belong, to the rightful owner."[146] Further, despite being repeatedly asked to do so, Congress had refused to amend the Internal Revenue Code to counteract *Wilcox* so as to bring embezzlement within the scope of taxability. But his deepest objection was that:

... except for the possible adverse effect on the rightful owners, the only substantial result that one can foresee from today's holding is that the Federal Government will, under the guise of a tax evasion charge, prosecute people for a simple embezzlement. But the Constitution grants power to Congress to get revenue, not to prosecute local crimes. And if there is any offense which under our dual system of government is a purely local one which the States should handle, it is embezzlement or theft.[147]

Editor's note.]

The issues raised by Justice Black in this area remain important in connection with various attempts of the Internal Revenue Service to enforce federal and local public policy. From time to time the Commissioner and the Department of Justice[148] have seemed to proceed on the theory that the Internal Revenue Code was more an essay on morality, designed and enacted to encourage virtue and discourage sin, than an attempt to raise revenue to defray the cost of government.[149] Justice Black has strongly indicated his lack of sympathy with an extraneous use of a taxing statute to implement the public policy of the federal and state governments beyond the area of taxation.[150] Taxes can be, and should be, a powerful instrument of economic and social policy.[151] But, as the Supreme Court pointed out in its *Wilcox* opinion, "moral turpitude is not a touchstone of taxability."[152] If they are dedicated to the purpose of improving men's hearts,[153] tax laws should give plain notice of their commands.[154] "A statute which either forbids or requires the doing of an act in terms so vague that men of common intelligence must necessarily guess at its meaning and differ as to its application" violates "the first essential of due process of law."[155] It likewise violates a first principle of sound tax policy, for the Commissioner is hardly an expert on morality or on the meaning of the statutes and public policies of all of the states and the many nontax statutes passed by Congress.

Taxpayers are entitled to know, at least with a fair degree of certainty, the basis of claims against them.[156] Certainty is not altogether attainable; we cannot make tax statutes as

plain as the Ten Commandments.[157] But the Commissioner
can take the statute as he finds it, leaving to other authorities
the job of specifying sanctions for the enforcement of statutes
having nothing to do with taxes. For, in the incisive words
of an English jurist, public policy is "a very unruly horse,
and when once you get astride it, you never know where it
will carry you."[158] It sometimes carries the Treasury further
than it wants to go, and carries taxpayers to a point of financial
ruin on account of transactions involving less than clearly
proved technical guilt, and at most mere technical guilt, but
no moral turpitude whatever.

The Test of Responsibility

The measure of any man in public life, not excluding a
Justice of the Supreme Court, must be in terms of the problems presented by the times in which he serves. The Supreme
Court is not an ivory tower. True, its Justices are insulated
from partisan political activity. But they occupy key positions
near the center of the country's national life. They are on a
big stage. Their audience is a large one, and sometimes,
properly, a highly critical one.[159] They must supply their own
script. In the sense that they can deal only with cases and
controversies presented to the Court, their range of effective
action is a limited one; even in the decision of those cases
the writer of a majority opinion may have but a narrow scope
to express his ideas.[160] But most controversial issues usually
manage to find their way to the Court, and this means that
each Justice must take a position on one side or the other of
these issues. And in another sense the Justices have almost
boundless freedom in dealing with the questions which reach
them. The answers to many of these questions, which affect the
American people for better or for worse, cannot be found
among reported precedents. Nor can strict logic supply solutions to the complex riddles involved in the imponderable
problems of modern law in the United States. Answers must
come from a deeper source. They must depend in the last
analysis upon the feelings and intuitions and theories and sense
of policy of the individual Justices on the Court. Their collec-

tive will must be done on a large part of the earth, for the Court is a court of last resort.

This means that the Court has a grave and delicate responsibility. The responsibility may be greatest in the field of constitutional law where the process of constitutional amendment is long and slow.[161] If we would keep the Constitution in harmony with the activities of modern America, and the power of government "unrestrained by the social or economic theories one set of judges may entertain," the Constitution must not be an "ark of the covenant, too sacred to be touched."[162] It is therefore important that the Supreme Court be ever ready to re-examine its own doctrines. "Stare decisis embodies an important social policy. It represents an element of continuity in law, and is rooted in the psychologic need to satisfy reasonable expectations."[163] "It is a strong tie which the future has to the past."[164] But it is a principle of policy, and not a mechanical formula to be followed even in response to pleas to let Congress correct mistakes that the Court has made. For "legislative correction of judicial errors is often difficult to effect."[165]

The responsibilities of the Supreme Court have been especially heavy during Black's incumbency. He came to the Court at an anxious time. The disturbance then enveloping the Court was part of a crisis facing the whole country. Urgency has changed its character since 1937, but it has not abated. The problems of depression have become problems of prosperity. It is not a serene prosperity, but rather a nervous prosperity which feeds on war and rumors of war. And the problems that have been solved are few compared to the many that remain to be solved. This is especially true in the field of taxation, where the work of the Court involves the interpretation of some of the most complex statutes enacted by Congress. Words being what they are—or the little they are—it is not an easy task to discover the policy of these statutes. They involve a very difficult subject;[166] and they are too often hastily drafted. But they represent an attempt to deal with problems intimately associated with the development of the economy and with the welfare of the whole social fabric.

Against this background it can properly be said that Justice Black has served the Court well in matters of taxation. His most important work has not been in tax territory, but what he has done in that area has been highly useful. It has been in the same pattern as his other work. Evidently believing that confidence based upon understanding is more enduring than confidence based upon awe,[167] he has advocated full disclosure when a precedent was being overruled. He has been willing to correct judicial error even where correction might be effected by legislation. In the tricky area of tax avoidance, where questions of degree abound,[168] his attitude has been a balanced one. He has been unwilling to sanction tax avoidance schemes and contrivances that lacked reality, but he has not tried to be the keeper of the congressional conscience. He has bowed his head in obedience to legislative mandate where Congress has drawn a line and the taxpayer has been on the safe side of that line. He has respected the principle that different tax consequences may flow from different methods of accomplishing the same ultimate economic result, and that taxpayers are entitled to select the method that results in the lower liability.[169] And finally, though he has been called a "social reformer,"[170] the Justice has resisted the great temptation to which some judges succumb in tax cases. Knowing that the federal tax statute is a *federal* statute, and that its use to suppress *state* and *local* crime involves great dangers for our system of Government, he has protested against the use of a federal tax statute, directed to the raising of revenue and to the economic welfare of the nation as a whole, for the improvement of men's hearts and the accomplishment of moral reform.[171]

Hugo Black has responded with distinction to the needs of the times which brought him to the Supreme Court. His federal tax opinions have maintained the standards of his other work on the Court. And those are high standards, indeed.

CHAPTER SEVEN

The Development of Antitrust

W. WALLACE KIRKPATRICK

THERE has long been in this country a deep-seated opposition to strong and centralized economic power. This opposition, exemplified by the fall of the United States Bank in the 1830's, grew stronger in the 70's and 80's. As a result, the railroads and the "trusts" being built up in many consumer-goods industries were the objects of suspicion and hostility. In the words of a contemporary writer:

> Indeed the public mind has begun to assume a state of apprehension, almost amounting to alarm, regarding the evil economic and social tendencies of these organizations. The social atmosphere seems to be surcharged with an indefinite, but almost inexpressible fear of trusts.[1]

Against this background, the Congress in 1887 moved to exert some control over the railroads by enacting the first of the regulatory statutes—the Interstate Commerce Act.[2] Three years later, the Sherman Act was passed "to protect trade and commerce against unlawful restraints and monopolies."[3] The act condemns all unreasonable restraints of trade and, in the language of Chief Justice Hughes, provides "as a charter of freedom . . . a generality and adaptability comparable to that found to be desirable in constitutional provisions."[4]

Notes appear at pages 313-324.

The Sherman Act, in its few lines, encompasses practically all of antitrust and seeks to assure freedom for competition through two interrelated provisions of the act.[5] Section 1 forbids any kind of joint or concerted action that is in "restraint of trade." Not every action that hinders or lessens trade is in "restraint of trade" since some acts may in reality enhance competition. Mr. Justice Brandeis, in the 1918 *Chicago Board of Trade* case, expressed the problem:

> [T]he legality of an agreement or regulation cannot be determined by so simple a test as whether it restrains competition. Every agreement concerning trade, every regulation of trade, restrains. To bind, to restrain, is of their very essence. The true test of legality is whether the restraint is such as merely regulates and perhaps thereby promotes competition, or whether it is such as may suppress or even destroy competition.[6]

In two landmark cases in 1911,[7] Chief Justice White helped clarify the meaning of the antitrust enactment by reading into the act the so-called rule of reason: not all courses of conduct that run counter to a literal and strict interpretation of the statutory words are illegal, but only activities that "unreasonably" restrain trade.

Section 1 of the Sherman Act thus proscribes joint action that results in an unreasonable restraint of trade. The evil and illegality arise from the joining together of two or more enterprises to engage in an act that lessens competition; the same act if done by only one would not offend this section. The agreement among the group, inevitably taking from each member at least some of his freedom to act on the basis of his own economic self-interest, makes the regulatory force of competition less effective to police the market in the public interest.

Section 2 of the act condemns monopolizing and so can be violated by the actions of one enterprise. To fall within its purview, however, the individual business must have deliberately acquired sufficient power over a defined market to control prices or exclude others from that market.[8]

In 1914 the Clayton Act was passed to implement the Sherman Act by, among other things, permitting certain activities, shown by experience to have inherently trade-restraining effects, to be stopped in their incipiency.

Antitrust is thus designed to maintain a free market place, accessible to all who wish to compete and operating without artificial restrictions imposed for some private objective or for a private interpretation of activities in the public good. The public can depend on market forces, operating in conformance with economic theory, to allocate the nation's wealth and resources among conflicting demands. Interference with this delicate mechanism damages the public. Perhaps the nation will decide, as indeed it has in some areas, that public authority must to some extent interfere with the market's mechanics. Such special situations apart, public reliance is on the free market, maintained by antitrust's prohibitions of group action in unreasonable restraint of trade and of the anticompetitive effects of dominating power used to control the market and exclude competitors. Essentially, this is all antitrust means.[9]

Atrophy and Revival

Despite the continuing element of antitrust sentiment in national thought, and despite actual federal statutes embodying those sentiments, the antitrust laws were only irregularly meaningful in their early years. Indeed, at the time Hugo Black came to the Supreme Court three decades ago the antitrust laws were widely regarded as having failed to accomplish their objective, as having, at best, only slight economic and public significance. Their "failure" was blamed on a protracted period of nonenforcement during which the businessman and his lawyer ignored the laws' existence.

Since then, however, antitrust has experienced extensive development, real invigoration. The great changes in the impact of antitrust laws over the last thirty years have not resulted from substantial legislative action in the field,[10] but rather have resulted from more zealous enforcement activities by the Department of Justice and from the interpretations

given the law by the Supreme Court. In this development,
Mr. Justice Black has been very much involved.

Beginning in 1938, one year after Justice Black joined the
Supreme Court, the Department of Justice's Antitrust Division
began a vigorous enforcement policy under the leadership of
Thurman Arnold. The newly appointed assistant attorney
general appraised the situation and specified a key to its solution in direct terms:

> The antitrust laws are the traditional instruments to
> preserve a competitive economy. They have been on the
> books almost fifty years, during which they have made
> business less ruthless and more polite, but they have not
> stopped the concentration of economic power. The
> practical question before us is how far they are capable
> of accomplishing their ends in the future. In order to
> answer that question, we must diagnose why they have
> failed in the past.
>
> The answer to that question is far easier than most
> people imagine. The antitrust laws have not failed. It
> is the organization provided for their enforcement that
> has failed. The reason is the simple one that you can-
> not police a country of one hundred and thirty million
> people with a corporal's guard.[11]

The key was apparently the right one. Two years after the
Arnold appointment, an "outsider" wrote:

> During the past two years, the fifty-year-old Sherman Act
> has achieved a vitality unprecedented in its existence.
> Its invigoration is due to no amendment of its terms
> nor to sudden change in the economy in which it oper-
> ates. What has happened is that the personnel of the
> agency charged with the Act's enforcement, the Anti-
> trust Division of the United States Department of
> Justice, has been increased to approximately eight times
> the size which it had averaged during the preceding fif-
> teen years and the range of its activities has been ex-
> tended in like proportion.[12]

In a larger sense, however, the increasing impact which the antitrust laws were to have on our economy was made possible by the fact that these laws were not enacted as a specific and detailed code of permissible and proscribed economic conduct.[13] Today, the Sherman Act's unchanged language still embodies the Congressional pronouncement of basic antitrust principles.[14] To continue Chief Justice Hughes' description of the act's "generality and adaptability":

> It does not go into detailed definitions which might either work injury to legitimate enterprise or through particularization defeat its purpose by providing loopholes for escape. The restrictions the Act imposes are not mechanical or artificial. Its general phrases, interpreted to attain its fundamental objects, set up the essential standard of reasonableness.[15]

Since 1938, the enforcement of the antitrust laws generally has continued to be vigorous,[16] thus providing the Supreme Court with many opportunities to interpret this "charter of freedom." The Court, with Hugo Black's encouragement, has responded by amplifying the basic objectives set forth in the Sherman Act, thus giving substance to the general economic principles which underlie it.

Statistics and figures cannot tell the complete story of Justice Black's activity in this field, but they do give some indication both of his interest and of the opportunity he has had to make an impact on the law. Since his appointment thirty years ago, there have been something over 200 cases decided by the Court involving antitrust and related questions. Black has written opinions in almost fifty of these cases; of these, thirty opinions were written for a majority of the Court and less than half that number were dissents; the rest were concurring opinions. In these 200-odd cases, Black voted against the application of the antitrust laws only about twenty times.

Quite apart from this quantitative contribution, Black has made a series of significant substantive contributions to today's antitrust principles. Specifically, his opinions have on many occasions extended the application of the antitrust laws into new areas. He has repeatedly shown a readiness to apply antitrust concepts to new fact situations, even in the face of sincere and powerful exhortations of the inappropriateness or even the inequity of such applications.[17] Insurance, liquor, newspapers, and foreign commerce have each, in turn, become the focal point for new departures in antitrust application. In addition, Justice Black has written major opinions dealing with group boycotts, labor's relation to antitrust, mergers, and price-fixing, among other basic problems confronting the antitrust laws.[18]

The reason for his active participation in the development of antitrust is simple: he believes in the objectives Congress sought to achieve when it enacted the Sherman Act. A concise summary of this belief is found in an opinion he wrote for the Court in 1958:

> The Sherman Act was designed to be a comprehensive charter of economic liberty aimed at preserving free and unfettered competition as the rule of trade. It rests on the premise that the interaction of competitive forces will yield the best allocation of our economic resources, the lowest prices, the highest quality, and the greatest material progress, while at the same time providing an environment conducive to the preservation of our democratic political and social institutions. But even were that premise open to question, the policy unequivocally laid down by the Act is competition.[19]

The study which follows will attempt to detail Black's antitrust philosophy by examining the scope of the elusive term "competition" which Black feels is "unequivocally laid down by the Act," and how it comports with his view of "our democratic political and social institutions."

The Clear Mandate of the Sherman Act

In view of the history of the Sherman Act's spasmodic enforcement, it is not surprising that its applicability to many fields of activity had not been resolved when Justice Black joined the Court. As new cases presented the opportunity to bring into sharper focus the application of antitrust principles, Black demonstrated his proclivity to carry out the Sherman Act's command.

Black wrote the opinion in *United States v. Southeastern Underwriters Ass'n,*[20] in 1944 in which the Court applied the act for the first time to the insurance industry and in so doing overturned seventy-five years of precedent.[21] All members of the Court agreed that Congress had the power to regulate the insurance business under the commerce clause of the Constitution, but, by applying the Sherman Act to insurance, Black and the majority held that the Congress had exercised its power over that business when it legislated in 1890. In the absence of any basis for believing that Congress intended to limit the applicability of the Sherman Act, or to exempt insurance from its coverage, he held that antitrust was fully applicable to the insurance business.

Two separate dissenting opinions in this case[22] decried upsetting a long line of past cases which had held that insurance companies were subject to state regulation. The dissenters feared the unnecessary spawning of excessive litigation and the commercial dislocations that would flow from the Court's ruling. But Black argued that the prior case law had only involved the applicability of state regulation to insurance and in no way granted to that business immunity from the all inclusive language of the Sherman Act.[23]

Four years later in an opinion[24] that generated much comment and concern, Justice Black, again relying on the plain language of the Sherman Act, held that antitrust precedents were fully applicable to foreign commerce. An American manufacturer had organized affiliated or controlled concerns in Britain and France, and agreements were made between the three related corporations to fix prices and divide territories. These practices were found illegal by a majority of the Court without any extended consideration of the nature of the foreign commerce or the asserted need for such practices. The dissenters, however, explicitly objected on the grounds that the Court's conclusions rested on an insufficient analysis of the facts and circumstances and further criticized the majority's resort to "talismanic" words to "displace the rule of reason by which breaches of the Sherman Law are determined."[25]

The *Timken* decision has disturbed some persons who argue that foreign commerce cannot be subjected to the full sweep of the antitrust laws.[26] But Justice Black's opinion shared no such doubts.[27] He was perfectly willing to rest on the "provisions in the Sherman Act" with little concern for a detailed and painstaking analysis of the business practices involved or their reasonableness under all the circumstances.

In one of the first antitrust opinions he wrote,[28] Black condemned, in unequivocal and sweeping terms, group boycotts by apparel manufacturers directed at retailers who patronized style pirates. In *Fashion Originators' Guild v. FTC*,[29] the Justice found that the manufacturers' concerted refusal to deal contravened the policies of the Sherman Act which declared that "competition, not combination, should be the law of trade."[30] In so ruling, Black brushed aside the defendant's assertions that no antitrust violation occurred since there was no finding that prices were fixed, production limited, or quality affected.[31] He also rejected the argument that the defendants' business practices were necessary to protect against the "devastating evils" of design pirating.[32] Black highlighted the want of exceptions to the application of the Sherman Act by concluding that even if it were assumed that style pirating were clearly tortious, such a "situation would not justify petitioners in combining together to regulate and restrain interstate commerce in violation of federal law."[33]

For Black, the combination was

> . . . in reality an extra-governmental agency, which prescribes rules for the regulation and restraint of interstate commerce, and provides extra-judicial tribunals for determination and punishment of violation and thus "trenches upon the power of the national legislature and violates the statute."[34]

In the opinion, Black shunts aside the asserted business and economic justifications for the boycott, relying only on the "policy of the prohibitions" declared in the antitrust laws. Without statistical elaborations, without market study, without meticulous analysis of the challenged practices under all of the circumstances and in light of all of the alleged justifications, the Court nonetheless found a clear violation of the antitrust laws.[35] This approach is the hallmark of Black's antitrust philosophy.

The absence of any discussion of the reasonableness of the defendants' behavior is even more interesting in the light of lower court opinions. In *Millinery Creators' Guild, Inc. v. FTC*,[36] the Second Circuit Court of Appeals had upheld a Federal Trade Commission order condemning the boycott on the ground that such conduct was unreasonable under the circumstances and transcended the "permissible zone of conduct." *Fashion Originators' Guild*[37] reached the Second Circuit later, and the boycott was condemned with a per se approach.[38] *Fashion Originators' Guild* and *Millinery Creators' Guild* were before the Supreme Court as companion cases, but despite the very different approaches taken by the same Circuit Court of Appeals, Black avoided distinguishing the two cases in "per se" or "reasonable" terms.[39] He simply found the conduct in each instance offensive to antitrust principles and hence illegal.[40]

Antitrust and the Unions

Black's readiness to apply the words of the Sherman Act to effectuate its meaning and basic objectives under any circumstance which invokes its mandate is further highlighted by his opinions dealing with the interaction of antitrust and labor laws.[41]

As a prelude to these opinions, two earlier landmark cases in this area should be noted. The first major case involving a clash between labor law and antitrust, after the passage of the Norris-LaGuardia Act,[42] was *Apex Hosiery Co. v. Leader*,[43] which held that the antitrust laws were inapplicable to a sit-in strike accompanied by violence. The Court's basis was that antitrust was concerned with preserving competition and was not aimed at policing interstate commerce, *i.e.*, that the kind of price competition based on differences in varying labor standards was not the kind of price competition prohibited by the Sherman Act.[44] In *United States v. Hutcheson*,[45] the Court handed down a major opinion clarifying the relationship between the Sherman, Clayton, and Norris-LaGuardia Acts and emphasizing that where labor is acting alone, without combining with nonlabor groups, in pursuit of its goals it is immune from antitrust prosecution.[46]

Apex Hosiery of 1940 and *Hutcheson* of 1941 created many doubts as to whether the antitrust laws had any remaining applicability to labor unions or to their practices. Perhaps the Court was heading towards the conclusion that, in effect, Congress had written a complete exemption from antitrust for labor, and that the country should no longer look to the antitrust laws for protection of its free enterprise system where a union's activities were involved. But a few years later, the Court, speaking through Justice Black, dispelled some of these doubts and made it clear that labor had no general antitrust exemption.

In *Allen-Bradley Co. v. Local No. 3, IBEW*,[47] the defendant union, a New York electricians' local, sought higher wages, shorter hours, and greater employment opportunities. It had entered into closed shop contracts with local electrical equipment manufacturers and contractors. According to the terms of these contracts, the manufacturers would not sell to nonunion contractors, and union members would not work for contractors buying from outside manufacturers. Allen-Bradley was an outside manufacturer who could not contract with the union whose jurisdiction was limited to the New York area, and was accordingly closed out of the New York market. Black's view is made clear by the following passage from his opinion:

> It must be remembered that the exemptions granted the unions were special exemptions to a general legislative plan. The primary objective of all the antitrust legislation has been to preserve business competition and to proscribe business monopoly. It would be a surprising thing if Congress, in order to prevent a misapplication of that legislation to labor unions, had bestowed upon such unions complete and unreviewable authority to aid business groups to frustrate its primary objective.[48]

In two of the Court's recent decisions in this antitrust-labor area, Black's votes were consistent with his previous approach, although he wrote no opinion in either case. In 1965, in *United Mine Workers v. Pennington*,[49] Black joined in Justice Douglas' concurring opinion which relied very heavily on *Allen-Bradley*. Their argument was that one industry-wide collective bargaining agreement, setting a wage scale that exceeded the financial ability of some companies to pay, was prima facie evidence of a violation of the Sherman Act if the agreement was made for the purpose of forcing those employers out of business. The Court indicated that the union could be liable under the antitrust laws since it had, by agreement with employers, imposed restraints on the product market. In another case[50] decided the same day Black joined a dissent written by Douglas urging that a union was liable under the antitrust laws because it was, in fact, acting in conspiracy with employers rather than acting alone, and hence had forfeited any exemption from the antitrust laws.[51]

The Extent of Antitrust Protection

Justice Black has pointed out that the Sherman Act was designed to preserve "free and unfettered competition" as the rule of trade. Certain of his opinions cast additional light on what he considers to be included within the ambit of that competition which is to be preserved free and unfettered.

In *United States v. Frankfort Distillers*,[52] Justice Black, writing for a majority of six Justices in a brief opinion, reversed the court below and affirmed a judgment of conviction. The government had charged that producers, wholesalers, and retailers had combined to maintain the price structure of liquor in Colorado by persuading producers to fair-trade all their brands and by boycotting producers who refused to enter into such fair-trade price-fixing agreements. A criminal conviction was reversed by the Court of Appeals on the ground that no restraint on interstate commerce had been charged. But Black held that although the conspiracy's ultimate objective was to set local retail prices, such conduct was not immunized from prosecution under the Sherman Act since the

means used to implement the agreement extended beyond
Colorado. He ruled that even though state law prohibited
Colorado retailers from buying from out-of-state producers,
the retailers' coercion, exercised through Colorado wholesalers,
reached into other states, and that such infringement was well
within the reach of the Sherman Act. The defendants sought
to rely on the Colorado fair trade laws as a justification for
their conduct. Black rejected this defense because he believed
that their agreement was a "traditional" restraint of trade and
that Colorado's Fair Trade Law did not sanction any collu-
sive or concerted coercion by retailers to force producers to set
resale prices.[53]

Black's belief that the antitrust laws should be applied to
local restraints when they have interstate overtones is further
illustrated by his dissent from the Court's denial of certiorari
in *Willard Dairy v. National Dairy Products Corp.*[54] The defendant in that case was an interstate operator but the questioned transactions did not involve any shipments from the
defendant's out-of-state plants. Even so, Black believed that
the antitrust laws should be applied to the situation when an
interstate business uses the resources of its multi-state operations in order to destroy local competition through local price
cuts.[55]

His position in this regard is also detailed in his prior
opinion in *Klor's, Inc. v. Broadway-Hale Stores, Inc.*[56] In
that case, the Circuit Court of Appeals dismissed a private suit
alleging damage caused by defendants who agreed to sell their
products only to plaintiff's local competitor. The dismissal
was based on a finding that no public injury whatsoever had
been alleged, that competition among retailers of the defendants' products was vigorous and effective, and that there was
no restraint on commerce.[57] Justice Black's opinion for a
unanimous Court not only reversed the lower court but completely reoriented the Circuit Court's approach to the application of the antitrust laws under these circumstances. He
held that a group boycott or concerted refusal to deal was
unlawful per se; such activity was not saved from condemnation by the antitrust laws merely because only one dealer was
the object of the boycott and, hence, the public injury mini-
mal. As Black saw it, any such concerted refusal to deal was

likely to drive a dealer out of business, and as such, was monopolistic in tendency. The existence of such a tendency was held sufficient to infect the transaction for antitrust purposes even though the total flow of interstate commerce was not directly affected and even though the public suffered neither from increased prices nor from an unavailability of products.

In short, for Black, the antitrust laws protect the fullest range of competition. Since the Constitution permits Congress to legislate with regard to certain types of activity, he assumes that legislation designed to regulate such activity is, unless otherwise specified, intended to be comprehensive.

Clear Objective and Simple Application

Justice Black's approach to the application of the antitrust laws to a particular set of facts has always been direct and untortured. He has evidenced little need for any detailed economic analysis or involved study of the competitive structure of the industry concerned. Instead, his efforts have been directed toward ensuring that the elemental objectives of the antitrust laws are realized. To accomplish this end, he has attempted to apply the purpose and letter of the law clearly and directly in all cases which are within its intended scope.

In a 1958 case,[58] Justice Black took the opportunity to explain the summary nature of so many of his antitrust opinions and his marked disinclination to engage in detailed factual and statistical analyses:

> [T]here are certain agreements or practices which because of their pernicious effect on competition and lack of any redeeming virtue are conclusively presumed to be unreasonable and therefore illegal without elaborate inquiry as to the precise harm they have caused or the business excuse for their use. This principle of per se unreasonableness not only makes the type of restraints which are proscribed by the Sherman Act more certain to the benefit of everyone concerned, but it also avoids the necessity for an incredibly complicated and prolonged economic investigation into the

entire history of the industry involved, as well as related industries, in an effort to determine at large whether a particular restraint has been unreasonable—an inquiry so often wholly fruitless when undertaken.[59]

This search for a clear and simple approach to antitrust problems is well illustrated by Black's opinions in the merger field. In 1966, Black wrote the Court's opinions in two of its most significant merger cases,[60] for which he was accused of applying last century's economic philosophy to the realities of present day business.[61]

To appreciate Black's views on the applicability of the antitrust laws to mergers, it is useful to recall briefly the development of the law in this area. In 1950, Congress, concerned with the detrimental effect on competition of increasing aggregations of economic power through mergers and disappointed with the courts' limited and ineffectual interpretation of the statutes governing mergers,[62] enacted the Celler-Kefauver amendment to the Clayton Act.[63] It is under the provisions of this relatively new statute that the antitrust laws, in recent years, have had a most significant impact on mergers and acquisitions.

In due course, the Supreme Court has had occasion to amplify the meaning and application of the amendment.[64] The Court deliberately sought to provide guidance in this new area, and its opinions were carefully detailed. In *Brown Shoe Co. v. United States*,[65] in 1962, Chief Justice Warren's elaborate opinion, in which Black was one of six concurring Justices, considered, in great detail, the concept of the "relevant market" and the effect in that market of the challenged acquisition. This landmark case was, and still is, the basis for considering the application of the amended Clayton Act to a merger or acquisition. While Black had up to that point expressed no views of his own in the merger field, he had continually joined a majority of the Court, intent, in case after case, on steadily expanding the application of the antitrust laws to mergers.[66]

Against this background, Black wrote his first major merger opinion in 1966 in *United States v. Von's Grocery Co.*[67] There, the third and sixth largest retail grocery chains in the

Los Angeles market area merged; the combined chain became the second largest in that market, but with only 7.5% of the total business. Black's opinion for the Court noted these facts, remarked that both parties to the merger were successful and aggressive competitors, and stated that the market was characterized by an ever-decreasing number of independent grocers and an ever-increasing percentage of business for the chains. He then summarily stated that: "These facts alone are enough to cause us to conclude contrary to the District Court that the Von-Shopping Bag merger did violate Sec. 7."[68]

The dissenting Justices in this case—Justices Stewart and Harlan—complained at length that Black had disregarded all precedent which required an inquiry into the contemporary economic context of the industry. They accused the Court of using a per se approach by resting the decision merely on increasing concentration and decreasing competition without a more sophisticated consideration of the "real" competitive structure of the market, the size and power of the chains, and the effects of the merger on the consumers.[69] Black was charged with seeking to preserve outdated "Mom and Pop" groceries in an era when their inefficiency had been demonstrated, and with ignoring the benefits accruing to the public as a result of competition among supermarket chains.[70] Characteristically, Black saw the situation more simply:

What we have here . . . is simply the case of two already powerful companies merging in a way that makes them even more powerful than they were before. If ever such a merger would not violate Sec. 7, certainly it does when it takes place in a market characterized by a long and continuous trend towards fewer and fewer owner-competitors, which is exactly the sort of trend which Congress, with power to do so, declared must be arrested.[71]

Justice Black also wrote the Court's opinion in *United States v. Pabst Brewing Co.*[72] The decision was unanimous, but only three Justices joined Black in his opinion. The government had attacked the acquisition of Blatz, a predominantly Wisconsin brewery, by Pabst, a national firm. The evidence at trial indicated that the combine enjoyed about 24% of Wisconsin's beer sales, 12% of the sales in the tri-state area of Wisconsin, Michigan and Illinois, but accounted for only about 4½% of beer sales nationwide. The trial court dismissed the government's complaint on the ground that it had not proved what was the relevant economic and geographic market in which the effects of this merger should be weighed.

The Supreme Court, speaking through Justice Black, reversed:

> The language of this section [Sec. 7] requires merely that the Government prove the merger has a substantial anti-competitive effect somewhere in the United States. . . . Proof of the section of the country where the anti-competitive effect exists is entirely subsidiary to the crucial question in this and every Sec. 7 case which is whether a merger may substantially lessen competition anywhere in the United States.[73]

This opinion, too, emphasizes his distinctive, straightforward approach to the solution of an antitrust problem. Black considered the market figures in each of the three areas as recorded by the trial court and held that in each instance the market share of the combined brewery was such that the probable detrimental effect on competition was enough to satisfy Section 7's standards. In view of the decline in the number of competitors in the industry and the increasing concentration, he did not hesitate in condemning the merger: "We hold that a trend toward concentration in an industry, whatever its causes, is a highly relevant factor in deciding how substantial the anti-competitive effect of a merger may be."[74]

Specific guidelines having been spelled out in the merger field by the landmark opinions of the last few years, Black's opinions suggest that the time has now come for something more like a per se approach to the solution of antitrust problems, so that the courts can give effective meaning to the fundamental objectives Congress sought to secure when it enacted the antitrust laws.[75]

The Need for Effective Relief

Paralleling Black's views of the proper approach to the application of the antitrust laws are his strong beliefs that once a violation of the antitrust laws has been established, the remedy must be complete and effective. His 1945 dissent in *Hartford Empire Co. v. United States,*[76] is an early illustration of this view. In that case, all members of the Court were in agreement that the defendant's conduct, involving a massive patent pooling arrangement, amounted to a violation of the antitrust laws. However, the majority of the Court modified the decree entered by the trial judge. Black's dissenting opinion supported the lower court's decree which provided for the control of patent royalties through the use of receivers and for royalty-free licensing for all of the patents then held by the defendants, and which also prohibited the defendants from obtaining additional patents which would "fence in" and "block off" new arrangements.[77] Basically, Black wanted to deprive patent owners of the benefits of their lawful patents when such owners had violated the antitrust laws by the unlawful use of their patents.[78]

In both *Ford Motor Co. v. United States*[79] and *United States v. United States Gypsum Co.,*[80] Black re-emphasized these views. In *Ford,* the Court suspended that part of a consent decree, which, by varying from the sanctions imposed against a competitor under a similar set of facts, placed Ford at a competitive disadvantage. In dissent, Black urged that the consent decree be given full force and effect as to Ford and that the decree be viewed as a judicial determination and order made in the public interest, and not as a contract between the parties. In *United States Gypsum Co.,* the Justice, in a concurring opinion, advocated the rendition of a broader decree against the defendants than the majority was willing to grant. He wanted to place upon the defendants the burden of establishing the reasonableness of the royalties they exacted, and further urged that the defendant's licensees be permitted to attack any of the licensed patents.

In the Spring 1966 term Black joined the majority's opinion in *FTC v. Dean Foods Co.*[81] which held that the Federal Trade Commission had authority to obtain preliminary injunctions against proposed mergers while it considered the legality of such mergers[82]—a holding which certainly makes more effective and meaningful the remedies which are available to the Federal Trade Commission under the antitrust laws. The Court ruled that the Commission had the power to seek preliminary injunctions despite the apparent belief of the Commission itself and the Department of Justice that the Commission probably had no such authority, and despite the fact that legislation giving the Commission power to seek preliminary injunctions had been repeatedly requested.[83]

Black's insistence on effective relief is further manifested by the construction he has given both to the statutory authorization of the Federal Trade Commission to prohibit unfair methods of competition under Section 5 of its act,[84] and to the interrelation of that statute to the Sherman Act. In 1948 he wrote the Court's opinion in *FTC v. Cement Institute*,[85] the leading decision establishing the interrelation between the Sherman and the Federal Trade Commission Acts. It is not surprising that Black believed that each statute should be given the broadest interpretation possible in order to facilitate proscription of anticompetitive practices in the most effective way. He held that the same conduct might violate both statutes and that the government might proceed under both, using these as cumulative remedies against activity detrimental to competition. The various laws in the antitrust field, Black wrote, were not intended to be mutually exclusive, but rather were enacted to provide a variety of remedies for inhibiting conduct obnoxious to public policy.

In 1966 Justice Black reiterated these thoughts in *FTC v. Brown Shoe Co.*,[86] wherein the Court approved a Commission finding that it was an unfair method of competition for the second largest shoe manufacturer to give preferential treatment to dealers who agreed to deal primarily in its shoes and not to buy competing shoes. Though this conduct had not been shown to violate the Sherman or Clayton Acts, the Court held that it could nevertheless be prohibited by the Commission. Black is convinced that all the statutes in this field must be read together so as to secure the most effective available relief.[87]

The Justice has, on occasion, displayed considerable impatience with various technical concepts or interpretations which could be employed to obstruct or hamper the effectiveness of the relief granted.[88] In line with this impatience with roadblocks confronting the successful application of the antitrust laws is the restrictive or narrow interpretation given by him to statutes or policies which hinder the reach of antitrust. Black's position in this regard is well illustrated by some of his opinions involving the interrelationship between antitrust law and patent law.[89]

In the first year he was on the Court, Black in *General Talking Pictures Corp. v. Western Elec. Co.*,[90] wrote a lone dissent arguing against an anticompetitive use of patents: "The patent statute which permits a patentee to 'make, use and vend' confers no powers to fix and restrict the uses to which a merchantable commodity may be put after it has been bought in the open market from one who was granted authority to manufacture and sell it."[91] In the years that followed, Justice Black joined, without any separate expression of his views, with the majority of the Court in a series of great cases which made it clear that patents offered no protection to price-fixing schemes.[92] Likewise, he voted against attempts by patentees to enlarge the scope of their patents or to expand the patent monopoly to cover nonpatented articles.[93]

This view of the appropriate relationship between antitrust and patent law is further exemplified by several cases in which he joined in opinions written by Justice Douglas. In *Special Equip. Co. v. Coe*,[94] Douglas argued that the suppression of a patent should not be sanctioned since the Constitution authorizes the granting of patents for the "Progress of Science and Useful Art" and that it would be a perversion of the concept of patentable property rights to permit them to be used only to preserve the status quo. Again, in *United States v. Line Material Co.*,[95] Black joined Douglas' concurring opinion which argued that allowing price-fixing agreements as part of patent licenses protected the patentee and not the progress of science and thus really amounted to restricting trade in violation of the Sherman Act. And finally, in *Automatic Radio Mfg. Co. v. Hazeltine Research, Inc.*,[96] Douglas and Black contended that permitting royalties to be based on a percentage of the total sales of a licensee's products, regardless of whether patented products were included, amounted to permitting the patentee to "bludgeon his way into a partnership with this licensee, collecting royalties on unpatented as well as patented articles."[97]

In two recent opinions, Justice Black has had occasion to review the nature and purpose of the patent system and has pointed out its relationship to the preservation of competition. These two companion cases, *Sears, Roebuck & Co. v. Stiffel Co.*,[98] and *Compco Corp. v. Day-Brite Lighting, Inc.*,[99] involved an attempt to use a state statute forbidding unfair competition to prevent copying and selling of an unpatented article. Black, in holding that such a result infringed the federal patent system, reviewed the constitutional grant to Congress of the power to enact a patent law, noting that it was designed to encourage invention and, at the same time, to safeguard the public interest. He pointed out (1) that the prerequisites to obtaining a patent must be carefully observed; (2) that once issued, it is to be strictly construed and cannot be used to secure any monopoly beyond that contained in the patent; (3) that the patentee's control over the product, when it leaves his hands, is sharply limited; (4) that the patent monopoly may not be used in disregard of the antitrust laws; and (5) that when the patent monopoly expires the right to produce the article inures to the public. Black's conclusion is that "the patent system is one in which uniform federal standards are carefully used to promote invention while at the same time preserving free competition."[100]

Limitations on Antitrust's Applicability

While Justice Black believes that the objectives sought by the antitrust laws are of primary importance, he does not believe that their applicability is without limitation.

First, he does not believe that antitrust laws were designed to, or should, govern political activity. This position was made clear in *Eastern R.R. Presidents Conference v. Noerr Motor Freight, Inc.*,[101] where the entire Court joined in Black's opinion. The case involved a publicity campaign, jointly fi-

nanced by several railroads, which essentially sought to promote state legislation restricting the trucking industry. The
campaign succeeded, the railroads' desired legislation was enacted, and the truckers sued—alleging that the railroads' concerted action violated the Sherman Act. The Court agreed
that the defendants had combined for a commercial purpose
and were in pursuit of ultimate business objectives, and further
indicated a distaste for the lack of ethics involved, but they
could not agree that the antitrust laws had been violated. To
so find would have been to hold that industries had no right
to seek to persuade elected legislatures about proposed legislation, a legitimate political activity.

Hence Black's position—and the Court's—is that the antitrust laws do not cover conduct which is basically political
even though anticompetitive motivations exist and damage to
competitors results.

Second, organized labor, when acting alone and in pursuit
of its own self-interest, enjoys immunity from antitrust prosecution. However, when labor combines with other nonlabor
groups, its immunity is forfeited and its conduct becomes subject to scrutiny under antitrust standards.[102] Black capsulized
his position regarding the limitations of antitrust in this area
in *Hunt v. Crumboch*[103] in 1945.

The third area in which Black believes that the antitrust
laws are limited in their application is the area of personal
rights. An instance of Black's rare opposition to the government's position in the antitrust field was in *Hughes v. United
States*,[104] in 1952, when he wrote the Court's opinion on the
basis of this reservation. The Government sought to compel
divestiture, by Howard Hughes, of certain of his holdings after
it had previously consented to the entry of a decree which gave
Hughes a choice of remedies. Black and the Court held
that the government should not be allowed to switch signals
in such fashion, to the detriment of the individual. They
agreed that the trial court could and did retain jurisdiction
to modify its original decree, but believed it could do so only
after a fair hearing on the merits and then only in light of
normal antitrust principles.

In *Pittsburgh Plate Glass Co. v. United States*,[105] Black
joined Justices Brennan, Warren, and Douglas in dissent, while

the majority sustained a criminal conviction against attack on the ground that the defendant should have been given access to the grand jury testimony of the prosecution's principal witness. The Court ruled that the defendant had no right to such testimony and that the trial judge had discretion to deny a request to review such testimony when no "particularized" need was demonstrated. The dissenters claimed that the defendant showed a sufficient "particularized" need for access to the grand jury testimony when the conviction depended on the witness' testimony, when there were no special reasons for secrecy, and when the defendants asked only to review that portion of the grand jury testimony relating to the testimony given at the trial. The dissent argued that it was absurd to require the defendant to show inconsistency before examining the grand jury transcript.[106]

In still another case, *United States v. National Dairy Products Corp.,*[107] Justice Black wrote a dissenting opinion in which he argued that Section 3 of the Robinson-Patman Act was so vague that it was unconstitutional. The Court sustained the validity of this statute which makes it a criminal offense to discriminate against competitors of the purchaser, to sell in one area at prices lower than those charged elsewhere for the purpose of eliminating competition or a competitor, or to sell at unreasonably low prices for the same purpose. The majority ruled that the statute was to be tested in light of the conduct charged in the indictment, which in this particular case consisted of selling below cost for the purpose of destroying competition. Black, however, contended that it was up to Congress to replace the vague test in the statute by unambiguous standards and that the Court should not perform this function. In his view, the statute was so vague as to fail to meet constitutional standards, and any necessary repairs should be left to Congress.

Black's regard for personal rights is further reflected by his dissent in *United States v. Welden*[108] wherein the Court held that the antitrust immunity statute[109] did not apply to a hearing before a Congressional investigating committee. Black joined Douglas' dissent based on the argument that Congressional hearings were covered by the word "proceeding" used in the immunity statute. Black also wrote a separate dissent, in which Douglas joined, based on the legislative history of the immunity statute which illustrated his basic regard for an individual's rights even when in conflict with antitrust principles:

> I think that when the Government makes an obligation in broad terms on which individuals have a reasonable right to rely, it should not seek to have all doubts resolved in its own favor against the private citizens who have taken it at its word. Important as I believe the antitrust laws to be, I believe it is more important still that there should be no room for anyone to doubt that when the Government makes a promise, it keeps it.[110]

Judicial Success and Practical Effect

With the active assistance of the Supreme Court and sometimes by virtue of its special leadership, the antitrust laws have come to have much more significance for our society today, and more substantive impact upon it, than when Hugo Black first joined the Court. And Black himself can claim a large share of the credit for this. The contributions he has made to the development and strengthening of this body of law are outstanding.

That he should have approved and been involved in this effort is not surprising. In the first place, he is always willing to give full implementation to the laws enacted by Congress under its Constitutional authority. But at least of equal weight is Black's belief that the preservation of our economic system—called free enterprise in shorthand language—is of urgent importance, and that the antitrust laws are an essential bulwark of that system.

Hence he has not been fearful of the Sherman Act's broad language but has felt entirely comfortable with it because of a clear view of its ultimate objective. His position is thus distinguished from that of certain of his colleagues.

While Black does not seem to be bound by rigid or intractable rules, it is fair to say that he basically approaches antitrust's applicability in "per se" terms. For him, some business combinations in and of themselves restrain trade and reduce competition in a way that the law seeks to prevent. Further, he distrusts the reliability and long-range usefulness of complicated and elaborate economic investigation. To the extent that each antitrust question must depend on lengthy, sophisticated economic analysis of peculiar facts, the antitrust laws, he feels, become more uncertain and furnish less useful guidance to law-abiding business. In terms of court treatment of such cases, the self-decided necessity to produce elaborate data has in a number of cases led trial courts to a complete obfuscation of what began as relatively clear and simple issues; similarly, it has caused enormous waste of time and effort in attempts to overdefine and overstudy factors which, in the end, were irrelevant to the basic question of whether the law had been violated.

Although Black's approach has not infrequently generated criticism, it is clearly justified if the deterrent function of antitrust laws is appreciated. Antitrust's objectives could never be secured if reliance were placed solely on the government's ability to catch and punish every lawbreaker. Absent a sympathetic comprehension of the antitrust laws' commands and the general willingness of business to comply with those commands, this nation's whole reliance on legal safeguards for our free enterprise system would be imperiled.

Justice Black realizes that an understanding of antitrust laws by businessmen is made much more feasible when the guidelines are set forth clearly and distinctly. To be sure, simplicity is not to be substituted for reason. But as has been said elsewhere in this volume, clarity and consistency are aids to justice, and in the field of antitrust, they are aids to compliance as well.

Of course, not every agreement between competitors is or should be a violation of the antitrust laws. Something must be understood about the practice agreed upon before it is condemned as trade-restraining. But it would deprive the law of all real meaning if every example of every such practice had to be evaluated in its own peculiar setting and in every detail. Moreover, Black is right that there is no assurance that the completion of lengthy analyses will provide better, more dependable, or more accurate measures of the anticompetitive nature of specific business conduct. Certainly the cases that

have followed the latter approach have not led to more una-
nimity of opinion as to their correctness than those in which
such studies were not indulged.

In insisting that fundamental purposes not be obscured in
evanescent tangles, Black has helped the Court give antitrust
a full and effective application. Indeed, his has been a double
success: preserving, on the Court, adherence to a sound and
simple philosophy; and elevating, in the conscience of the
nation, still another body of law to a level of real and lively
meaning.

CHAPTER EIGHT

The Federal Civil Rules and the Pursuit of Justice

GEORGE KAUFMANN

THIS symposium on Mr. Justice Black's judicial contributions is understandably concerned primarily with his opinions on constitutional law. However, the business of the Supreme Court is not limited to the dramatic constitutional issues, and neither its performance nor that of any of its individual Justices can be judged without reference to their total product. Moreover, a judge's mind is not compartmentalized, and his views of the Constitution's commands will often influence his decisions in other areas of the law. Certainly this is true of Justice Black's opinions regarding the Federal Rules of Civil Procedure. And these opinions have a broader interest, for they also reflect Black's attitude toward the litigation process and demonstrate that he is willing to raise novel and fundamental questions outside the area of constitutional adjudication.

Of particular importance is Justice Black's view that rules of procedure should not be enforced to deprive parties of a trial on the merits. In furtherance of that objective he has urged that a party ought not be held in default because of procedural missteps by his attorney. His most important and provocative statement of that position is his dissenting opinion in *Link v. Wabash R.R.*[1] Because it has previously received

---

Notes appear at pages 325-335.

less attention than it deserves, we will concentrate on that opinion in this Chapter.

The Origins and Operation of the Federal Rules

In the exercise of its supervisory powers over the administration of justice in the federal judicial system, the Supreme Court has adopted codes of procedure for civil, criminal, and other cases. The first such code of procedure adopted by the Court was the Federal Rules of Civil Procedure, pursuant to authority granted by Congress in an Enabling Act passed in 1934.[2] The Rules were first promulgated shortly after Justice Black came on the Court. It appears that he approved of their adoption since only Justice Brandeis noted his disapproval.[3] More recently, however, Justice Black has repeatedly dissented from the adoption of new rules by the Court. In 1944 he dissented without opinion from the decision to promulgate Federal Rules of Criminal Procedure.[4] He objected in 1954 to the Court's adoption of its own revised rules. While he recognized some changes were necessary, he believed that: "It would be far better to make these changes simply by amending the old rules rather than by adopting a whole new set."[5] He explained:

> The old rules and our interpretations of them are familiar to the bar, and, according to my observation, work about as well as could be expected of any rules. The principal function of procedural rules should be to serve as useful guides to help, not hinder, persons who have a legal right to bring their problems before the courts. But new rules without settled meanings breed mistakes and controversies that frequently make the way of litigants unnecessarily perilous. Volumes of new Rules Decisions in recent years attest to this. Judicial statistics would show, I fear, an unfortunately large number of meritorious cases lost due to inadvertent failure of lawyers to conform to procedural prescriptions having little if any relevancy to substantial justice.[6]

In 1961, in objecting to Amendments to the Rules of Civil Procedure, he simply noted: "Mr. Justice Black does not join in approval of the Rules because he believes that it would be better for Congress to act directly by legislation on the matters treated by the Rules."[7] Then, in 1963 in a joint statement with Mr. Justice Douglas, he elaborated on these views, stating that he believed the Enabling Act to be unconstitutional because it violates the constitutional separation of powers between the Congress and the courts:

> Mr. Justice Black and Mr. Justice Douglas are opposed to the submission of these rules to the Congress under a statute which permits them to "take effect" and to repeal "all laws in conflict with such rules" without requiring any affirmative consideration, action, or approval of the rules by Congress or by the President. We believe that while some of the Rules of Civil Procedure are simply housekeeping details, many determine matters so substantially affecting the rights of litigants in lawsuits that in practical effect they are the equivalent of new legislation which, in our judgment, the Constitution requires to be initiated in and enacted by the Congress and approved by the President. The Constitution, as we read it, provides that all laws shall be enacted by the House, the Senate, and the President, not by the mere failure of Congress to reject proposals of an outside agency.[8]

These views were reaffirmed in February 1966, when the most recent amendments to the Rules of Civil Procedure were submitted to Congress.[9]

Yet the principle upon which Black and Douglas rely does not require a total disavowal by the Court of any power to prescribe rules of procedure. Indeed, ever since Chief Justice Marshall's opinion in *Wayman v. Southard*[10] in 1825 such power has been recognized. The Enabling Act expressly provides that the Court, "shall neither abridge, enlarge, nor modify the substantive rights of any litigant." Thus, the Act would seem not to be unconstitutional on its face; the difficulty is in its application, since the line between procedure and substance is one of the most elusive in the law and "shifts as the legal context changes."[11]

As the Supreme Court has said, "The fact that this Court promulgated the rules . . . does not foreclose consideration of their validity, meaning, or consistency."[12] In *Sibbach v. Wilson & Co.*,[13] for example, the Court considered the validity, under the Enabling Act, of Rules 35 and 37 which authorize the federal courts to require a party to submit to a physical examination or be subject to default. In that case, the defendant had obtained an order from the District Court requiring that the plaintiff be examined. The plaintiff contended that her right to be free from compulsory physical examination was a substantive right, denial of which was not authorized by the Enabling Act. In his opinion for the Court, Justice Roberts declared that the test under the Enabling Act is "whether a rule really regulates procedure—the judicial process for enforcing rights and duties recognized by substantive law and for justly administering remedy and redress for disregard or infraction of them."[14] He determined that the rules in question qualified under this test. Justice Frankfurter dissented in an opinion in which Justices Black, Douglas, and Murphy joined. Frankfurter asserted that the validity of the rule cannot depend on an "analytical determination whether the power of examination here claimed is a matter of procedure or a matter of substance."[15] Rather, he felt that the inviolability of the person was a fundamental principle of Anglo-American law, a departure from which "ought not to be inferred from a general authorization to formulate rules for the more uniform and effective dispatch of business on the civil side of the federal courts."[16]

Protecting Trial by Jury

Another limitation which the Enabling Act placed on the Court's authority to promulgate rules of civil procedure is that such rules may not infringe upon the right to trial by jury. Since probably no Justice in the history of the Supreme Court has been a more vigorous champion of the jury system than Justice Black,[17] it is not surprising that he has insisted that this limitation be scrupulously observed.

In *Galloway v. United States*,[18] Black contended that the practice of judges directing juries to enter particular verdicts is contrary to the Seventh Amendment. Subsequently he reaffirmed that position in objecting to an amendment to Rule 50(a). That amendment made the order of a judge granting a motion for a directed verdict effective without actually submitting the question to the jury. Justice Black, joined by Justice Douglas, took exception:

> Although the amendment here is not itself a momentous one, it gives formal sanction to the process by which the courts have been wresting from juries the power to render verdicts. Since we do not approve of this sapping of the Seventh Amendment's guarantee of a jury trial, we cannot join even this technical *coup de grace*.[19]

On the same occasion they objected to a proposed amendment to Rule 56(e), dealing with summary judgments. The amendment provided: "When a motion for summary judgment is made and supported as provided in this rule, an adverse party may not rest upon the mere allegations or denials of his pleading, but his response, by affidavits or as otherwise provided in this rule, must set forth specific facts showing that there is a genuine issue for trial. If he does not so respond, summary judgment, if appropriate, shall be entered against him."

Said Black and Douglas:

> The proposed amendment to Rule 56(e) imposes additional burdens upon litigants. . . . The summary judgment procedure, while justified in some cases, is made a handy instrument to let judges rather than juries try lawsuits and to let those judges try cases not on evidence of witnesses subjected to cross-examination but on ex parte affidavits obtained by parties. Most trial lawyers would agree, we think, that a litigant can frequently obtain in an actual trial favorable testimony which

could not have been secured by affidavits or even by depositions.[20]

Black and Douglas have also proposed that Rule 49, dealing with special verdicts, be repealed, on the ground that special verdicts and jury interrogatories impair the power of juries to reach a general verdict, which power they believe juries rightly have under the Constitution.[21]

In addition to the Enabling Act's provision that no Federal Rules of Civil Procedure may be promulgated which interfere with the right to trial by jury under the Seventh Amendment, this right is also expressly preserved by Rule 38(a) of the Federal Rules. And as could be expected, Mr. Justice Black has given hospitable scope to this admonition.[22]

The Link Case: The Rules and the Judicial Process

Link v. Wabash R.R.[23] arose out of a collision between petitioner Link's automobile and one of respondent's trains. The suit was originally brought in August, 1954. The District Court granted a motion by the railroad for judgment on the pleadings, dismissing the suit. However, the Court of Appeals reversed that decision and remanded the case for trial, the Supreme Court denying the railroad's petition for certiorari in February, 1957. Thereafter, the case was twice set for trial, once on motion of each of the parties. In the meantime, the defendant had been submitting, and the plaintiff after delays answering, interrogatories. Then on September 29, 1960, the District Court notified counsel for both parties of the schedule of a pretrial conference for 1:00 p.m. on October 12, 1960. The Supreme Court's opinion described what next occurred:

> . . . During the preceding morning, October 11, petitioner's counsel telephoned respondent's lawyer from Indianapolis, stating that "he was doing some work on some papers," that he expected to be at the pretrial conference, but that he might not attend the taking of a deposition of the plaintiff scheduled for the same day. At about 10:45 on the morning of October 12 peti-

tioner's counsel telephoned the Hammond courthouse from Indianapolis (about 160 miles away), and after asking for the judge, who then was on the bench, requested the judge's secretary to convey to him this message: "that he [counsel] was busy preparing papers to file with the [Indiana] Supreme Court," that "he wasn't actually engaged in argument and that he couldn't be here by 1:00 o'clock, but he would be here either Thursday afternoon [October 13] or any time Friday [October 14] if it [the pretrial conference] could be reset."

When petitioner's counsel did not appear at the pretrial conference the District Court, after reviewing the history of the case and finding that counsel had failed "to indicate . . . a reasonable reason" for his nonappearance, dismissed the action "for failure of the plaintiff's counsel to appear at the pretrial, for failure to prosecute this action." The court, acting two hours after the appointed hour for the conference, stated that the dismissal was in the "exercise [of] its inherent power."[24]

The Court of Appeals affirmed this action by a two-to-one vote,[25] and that decision was in turn upheld by a four-to-three vote of the Supreme Court. Justice Harlan, who wrote the Court's opinion, saw the case as presenting two questions: (1) whether the District Court had power to dismiss the case in the absence of a motion to dismiss by the defendant; and (2) whether in the circumstances of the case the dismissal was a proper exercise of the District Court's discretion.

Rule 41(b) of the Federal Rules of Civil Procedure expressly authorizes the district courts, *on motion of the defendant,* to dismiss an action "for failure of the plaintiff to prosecute or to comply with these rules or any one of court." The Court held that the inherent power of courts to dismiss on these grounds—even without such a motion—had been recognized for centuries and that this power was not impliedly withdrawn by Rule 41(b).[26] It understood the District Court to have dismissed the case because the plaintiff had failed to

prosecute his suit and decided that, on the basis of the facts
before it, the District Court did not abuse its discretion in
exercising that power. Mr. Justice Black dissented in an opinion in which the Chief Justice joined. (Mr. Justice Douglas
also dissented, but without opinion.) In his dissent Mr.
Justice Black did not expressly disagree with the Court's
holding that the power which the District Courts can exercise on a motion by defendant can also be exercised without
such motion. Rather, he based his dissent on three points:
(1) the case was not dismissed for want of prosecution, but as
a sanction imposed because of the lawyer's disobedience to
the order; (2) the record did not support dismissal for want
of prosecution; and (3) it was unjust to dismiss Link's suit
because of his attorney's delinquencies. While the first point
is of lesser importance to the main theme of our discussion,
it should be noted that there was considerable evidence supporting Black's view of the basis of the District Court's action.
Despite Justice Harlan's reading of that Court's opinion,[27]
it also appears to have been the Court of Appeals' assumption that dismissal had been a sanction against the lawyer's
disobedience.[28] At best the District Judge's statement was
ambiguous, and the Court might well have reversed the case
on the ground that unless the basis of the dismissal is clearly
spelled out, it should not be sustained on appeal. The importance of a clear statement of the Judge's reasons is all the
greater because the Court ruled only that the Judge had not
abused his discretion, and not that his decision was correct
or that the Supreme Court, if faced with the same situation,
would have dismissed the suit.[29] While the Court was clearly
right in treating the exercise of discretion as subject only to
limited review, it could have more properly exercised that
limited review had it been certain of the reasons on which
the exercise of discretion was based. In entirely analogous
circumstances, the Court has required administrative agencies
to state with clarity the basis on which they make judgments
committed to them.[30]

In any event, given the Supreme Court's assumption that
its review in such cases is limited to determining whether
the District Court has abused its discretion, its acceptance of
the determination in this case that the plaintiff, Link, had

failed to prosecute his suit seems reasonable. The failure of Link's counsel not only to appear for the pretrial conference, but even to make adequate explanation for not appearing, strongly suggested substantial disinterest in the lawsuit, particularly when viewed in light of previous delays caused by the plaintiff. As Justice Black correctly pointed out, many of the previous delays, including those due to the original erroneous dismissal of the complaint, were attributable to the defendant. But this circumstance was only of limited probative value in determining whether the plaintiff was actively pursuing his claim.

The nature of a lawsuit is that the plaintiff must provide the impetus; it is he, after all, who is asking the Court for relief. If nothing happens, the defendant wins. This is not to say, of course, that there are not occasions on which a defendant must take certain steps or suffer default. It does, however, mean that the defendant's delays do not negate evidence showing that the plaintiff is, in the words of Rule 41, "failing to prosecute" his claim.

Justice Black stated in his dissent that "Counsel for both parties apparently were doing the best they could to bring the case to a successful conclusion for their respective clients."[31] On the other hand, it seems equally clear that neither of them was anxious that such conclusion occur within the near future. If this is so, the trial judge would have been justified in determining that the defendant was prepared to let the case die and that the plaintiff was prepared to leave the case on the docket for its nuisance value in order to obtain some relief by settlement—which could mean "success" if the claim was without merit. Seen in this light, it is possible to conclude that the district court's action was not, in fact, a bar to a person's trying "his lawsuit on its merits before an impartial judicial tribunal,"[32] the supreme goal for Justice Black.

The main interest of the *Link* case is in Justice Black's view that even if the plaintiff had failed to prosecute his suit, the District Court should not have dismissed his complaint without notice to him *personally* that it planned to do so. Justice Black declared it ". . . to be contrary to the most fundamental ideas of fairness and justice to impose the punishment for the

lawyer's failure to prosecute upon the plaintiff who, so far
as this record shows, was simply trusting his lawyer to take
care of his case as clients generally do." He thereby posed
a fundamental challenge to a proposition which had long
been considered axiomatic—that failures to meet time deadlines and comply with similar procedural rules may be treated
by the courts as defaults by the party, rather than as laying the
predicate for disciplinary action against his attorney.[33] When
amendments to the Federal Rules of Civil Procedure were
next proposed in 1963, Justice Black proposed that Rule 41
be amended to require a trial judge to serve notice on the
plaintiff himself before "dismissing a plaintiff's action for
failure of his lawyer to prosecute."[34] These views were reiterated and expanded at the time of the most recent amendment of the Federal Rules of Civil Procedure, in 1966.[35]

The Purpose of Rules

Mr. Justice Black's position derives from his general philosophy respecting the function of rules of procedure in litigation, as is shown by his dissent from a denial of certiorari in
the 1966 *Beaufort Concrete Co.* case.[36] There he reiterated
what he had said for the Court in *Surowitz v. Hilton Hotels:*[37]
"The basic purpose of the Federal Rules is to administer justice
through fair trials, not through summary dismissals as necessary
as they may be on occasion."[38]

In *Surowitz* he had added:

> These rules were designed in large part to get away
> from some of the old procedural booby traps which
> common-law pleaders could set to prevent unsophisti-
> cated litigants from ever having their day in court. If
> rules of procedure work as they should in an honest
> and fair judicial system, they not only permit, but
> should as nearly as possible guarantee that bona fide
> complaints be carried to an adjudication on the merits.
> Rule 23(b), like the other civil rules, was written to
> further, not defeat the ends of justice.[39]

That rules of procedure should not be used to avoid the disposition of cases on their merits has been basic to Justice Black's judicial philosophy from the beginning. In his first term on the Court, and prior to the adoption of the Federal Rules, he said in *Maty v. Grasseli Chem. Co.*:[40] "Pleadings are intended to serve as a means of arriving at fair and just settlements of controversies between litigants. They should not raise barriers which prevent the achievement of that end."[41]

In *Maty* it was decided that a statute of limitations did not bar an amended complaint where original suit based on the same cause of action was filed within the prescribed period. This principle was embodied in Rule 15(c) of the Federal Rules.[42] The broader principle that amendments to pleadings should be freely allowed has also been adopted in the Federal Rules, and Mr. Justice Black has objected vigorously when he believed that this rule was ignored. In *Willard Dairy Corp. v. National Dairy Prods. Corp.*,[43] dissenting from a denial of certiorari, he said:

> The trial judge saw fit to ignore Rule 15(a), which says that leave to amend "shall be freely given when justice so requires." This and the other Federal Rules "reject the approach that pleading is a game of skill in which one misstep by counsel may be decisive to the outcome and accept the principle that the purpose of pleading is to facilitate a proper decision on the merits." *Conley v. Gibson*, 355 U.S. 41, 48 (1947). The Federal Rules were meant to prevent just the sort of technical and arbitrary action that took place below. The frustration of statutory rights by harsh and unjustifiable procedural rulings is wholly out of place in an enlightened system of jurisprudence.[44]

Conley v. Gibson is Mr. Justice Black's most important decision on pleading. He there pointed out that the availability of broad discovery provisions under the Federal Rules makes it unnecessary for pleadings to be elaborate expositions of the parties' positions.[45] Given the history of the hypertechnical rules of pleading which long haunted the common-law, the Federal Rules effected a welcome reform.[46] There is no doubt that the availability of rules of discovery have limited need for specificity in pleadings in cases where the differences between the parties are factual. Many cases, however, involve no factual dispute but only questions of law and are properly disposed of on the pleadings. In those cases, the often elaborate and expensive discovery procedures are inappropriate. In considering motions for judgments on the pleadings, those pleadings are properly read generously in favor of the party opposing the motion.[47] Thus ambiguities and generalities—which are sometimes deliberate rather than careless—may frustrate the desirable result of a judgment on the pleadings without the necessity of a lawsuit.[48]

In *Hormel v. Helvering*,[49] Justice Black carefully stated the reasons why "ordinarily an appellate court does not give consideration to issues not raised below."[50] But he then held that this rule ought not be undeviatingly applied: "Rules of practice and procedure are devised to promote the ends of justice, not to defeat them. A rigid and undeviating judicially declared practice under which courts of review would invariably and under all circumstances decline to consider all questions which had not previously been specifically urged would be out of harmony with this policy. Orderly rules of procedure do not require sacrifice of the rules of fundamental justice."[51]

Justice Black's position in *Link* questioned both the desirability of strict enforcement of procedural rules and the assumption that sanctions for noncompliance should be imposed against the litigant rather than his attorney. That there are occasions in which literal adherence to the rules should be waived is illustrated by three recent decisions in which the Supreme Court (with Justice Black's concurrence) relieved a party of the consequences of his failure to comply with deadlines for filing an appeal. In *Harris Truck Lines v. Cherry Meat Packers, Inc.*,[52] the District Court had entered judgment against the petitioner and had denied a motion for new trial. Its counsel requested the District Court to grant an extension of time within which to appeal beyond the thirty-day limit prescribed by Rule 73(a). The rule does allow the thirty-day limit to be waived on a showing of "excusable neglect based on a failure of a party to learn of the entry of a judgment," and such extension was granted, the District Court determining that a sufficient showing had been made. The Court of Appeals, holding that an extension was not warranted and that therefore the thirty-day limit had been improperly waived by the District Court, dismissed the appeal as untimely filed. The Supreme Court reversed the Court of Appeals saying, "In view of the obvious great hardship to a party who relies upon the trial judge's finding of 'excusable neglect' prior to the expiration of the 30-day period and then suffers reversal of the finding, it should be given great deference by the reviewing court."[53] Only Mr. Justice Harlan dissented. He cited, *inter alia,* the *Link* decision with specific reference to that portion of the opinion which holds that parties are properly held responsible for the procedural omissions of their counsel.[54]

In *Thompson v. Immigration & Naturalization Serv.,*[55] a bare majority of the Court followed *Harris* to reinstate an appeal under the following circumstances. The District Court entered a final order denying naturalization to the petitioner. Twelve days later, he served notice that he would appear two days thereafter with post-trial motions to amend certain findings of fact pursuant to Rule 52 and for a new trial pursuant to Rule 59. The government raised no objection to the timeliness of these motions, and the District Court, although denying them, declared that the motion for a new trial had been made "in ample time." Within sixty days of the denial of the post-trial motions, but not within sixty days of the original judgment, petitioner filed his notice of appeal. The Court of Appeals dismissed the appeal on the ground that the post-trial motions were untimely filed and therefore did not toll the sixty-day period prescribed by Rule 73(a). The Supreme Court reversed. The majority held that since the petitioner relied on the government's failure to object and the District Court's statement that the motion had been made in ample time, it was justified in failing to appeal within the original sixty-day period. Therefore, the Court held the appeal should have been considered on the merits. However, three Justices who had been in the majority in *Harris* now joined Justice Harlan in dissent. In an opinion by Justice Clark, they chose to read *Harris* narrowly and would have limited it to a holding that the finding of excusable neglect should not have been reversed. They emphasized that although in *Harris*, the District Judge had *power* to make a finding of excusable neglect, Rule 6(b) of the Federal Rules expressly denies power to the district courts to enlarge the period during which the motions under Rules 52(b) and 59(b) may be filed. The result, as Justice Clark said in an almost identical case at the next term, is to "give trial judges the *de facto* power to grant extensions of time directly *contra* to the definite requirements of Rules 52(b) and 59 and the command of Rule 6(b)."[56]

While there is much force to this criticism, all three decisions can be justified on the ground that the parties who had failed to make a timely appeal could have complied with the rules but for their reliance on actions of the District Court. It is when the rules become a trap for litigants that adherence to them is most unjust. Indeed, such applications may amount to a denial of due process, "using that term in its primary sense of an opportunity to be heard and to defend a substantive right,"[57] where a party's rights are forfeited because he justifiably relied on the action of the Court.

In *Lord v. Helmandollar*, the United States Court of Appeals for the District of Columbia properly understood these three cases—*Harris*, *Thompson* and *Wolfsohn*—as holding "that the losing party should not be deprived of an appeal because it relied on the erroneous district court action."[58] But since in the *Lord* case the tardy appellant had not been misled by any action of the District Court, the Court of Appeals' dismissal of his appeal was consistent with the Supreme Court's decisions. The Supreme Court refused to review this dismissal, Mr. Justice Black dissenting without opinion.[59] He apparently had based his vote in *Harris* and the cases following it on the broader principle that an appeal should not be dismissed merely because it was untimely filed. For soon thereafter, in dissenting from the dismissal of an appeal untimely filed with the Supreme Court, Justice Black said: "The conflict between the interest of court clerk in the timely filing of papers and the interest of the citizen in having his lawsuit tried should be resolved in favor of the citizen, not the court clerk."[60]

Plaintiff, Defendant, and Court Clerk

In suggesting that the majority decision was based on the premise that the only interest involved in the timely filing of papers was that of the court clerk, Justice Black was permitting himself a rhetorical exaggeration.[61] But it is an especially interesting one for it indicates that he has not forgotten his own difficulties with the clerk of the Supreme Court in the course of the only case he ever argued before the Court as a lawyer. As reported in the introduction to this volume, Black in 1924 sought to bring a case before the Court in *forma pauperis* on behalf of a poor, injured Negro client whom he was representing without fee.[62] The clerk balked at the request that Black and his partner be allowed to present the case without the ordinarily expected professionally printed briefs in multiple copies, and the other expensive trappings, saying that exceptions to these formalities were rarely allowed. After pressing the matter at some length, Black was allowed to appeal directly to one of the Justices, who in the end allowed the proceedings to be brought as Black had requested, in *forma pauperis*.

Black has always been solicitous of the right of the poor to their day in court.[63] But it is precisely because the financial burden on litigants will usually be less if filings are timely made, that such rules should not be lightly disregarded. Justice Black has on other occasions recognized the more important interests that are at stake. In *Clay v. Sun Ins. Office*[64] in 1960 he said: "Litigants have a right to have their lawsuits decided without unreasonable and unnecessary delay or expense."[65] Elsewhere he has written of "our national policy of reducing insofar as possible the burdensome cost of litigation."[66] Furthermore, "[A]t least since Magna Carta some people have thought that to delay justice may be to deny justice."[67]

If the failure of the plaintiff's counsel to appear for the court hearing in *Link* had been condoned, the defendant would have been put to the additional expense of its counsel's making an unnecessary court appearance of several hours, and the lawsuit itself would have been further delayed. Delay generally prejudices plaintiffs more than defendants, but this is not so in every case. For example, defense witnesses may become unavailable, and the mere pendency of a lawsuit may have an adverse effect on a party by impairing his credit rating. Whether delay in the *Link* case would have adversely affected the defendant railroad does not appear from the decision,[68] but the additional cost is obvious. It is doubtless these considerations which Justice Harlan had in mind when he said that ". . . keeping this suit alive merely because plaintiff should not be penalized for the omissions of his own attorney would be visiting the sins of plaintiff's lawyer upon the *defendant*."[69]

In some situations, failure to insist that a party comply with the rules would be severely prejudicial to his adversary. This is illustrated by the *Beaufort Concrete Co.* case.[70] There the District Court had granted a summary judgment in favor of the defendant, Atlantic States Construction Co., refusing to consider the affidavits Beaufort had presented to show the existence of "a genuine issue of material fact" because they were submitted out of time. Rule 56(c) provides that affidavits in opposition to a motion for summary judgment must be filed "prior to the day of hearing"; Beaufort presented its affidavits to the Court and to opposing Counsel at the hearing. The Court of Appeals affirmed the District Court's judgment, and the Supreme Court denied certiorari. In dissenting, Justice Black wrote in part: "I find it entirely at odds with a fair system of trying lawsuits to throw out a litigant's case because his lawyer for negligence or some other reason fails by less than 24 hours to satisfy one of many procedural time limits. From the beginning to the end of a lawsuit a lawyer must meet a host of time limits for filing papers. Surely a judge should not have discretion to enter final judgment at will every time a slight lapse occurs which may delay for half a day or so the service of one of a multitude of papers that must be served during the trial and appeal of a lawsuit."[71]

When Justice Black states his case in such strong terms as this, the impression is that he gives inadequate weight to the interests of the party which filed the motion for summary judgment, whose counsel had the right to prepare for the hearing on the motion in the expectation that the rule would be complied with. By submitting its affidavits at the hearing,

Beaufort deprived Atlantic's counsel of the opportunity to study them and to plan his argument accordingly. Beaufort's counsel thus confronted his adversary with a choice between going into the hearing unprepared (and thus giving Beaufort an undeserved tactical advantage) or requesting an adjournment. Such an adjournment not only would have cost time of counsel on both sides, but of the Court as well, thus affecting the rights of all the other litigants waiting to have their cases placed on the Court calendar. Indeed, if the affidavits had been filed in time, and counsel could determine that they were sufficient to defeat the motion for summary judgment, that motion might have been withdrawn so that the hearing could have been cancelled. Alternatively, counsel would have been alerted to the factual issues raised by the affidavits and could have argued that these were not "material," or could have made appropriate argument to aid the Court in specifying under Rule 56(d) which facts remained controverted. Beaufort's tardiness in filing the affidavits frustrated such efforts. The very existence of rules creates reliance on the part of counsel that they will be followed, which indeed is one of their objectives. The elimination of surprise is one of the chief reforms effectuated by the Federal Rules of Civil Procedure, and not only through the rules providing for pretrial discovery. Where one party is permitted to spring material on his adversary at the time of the hearing, this purpose of the rules is frustrated.

There is, moreover, a definite advantage to counsel as well as to the courts in the establishment of a fixed period in which procedural steps should be taken.[72] The existence of such periods eliminates uncertainties like those which caused the difficulty in *Harris Truck Lines,* discussed above. Random rulings excusing even short delays can either undermine certainty and thus create more serious problems for the great majority of counsel who attempt to file papers on time (and for their clients) or lead to chaos by making all time regulations unenforceable. The pressures of law practice are such that counsel often file papers at the last possible moment, and if short delays become excused as a matter of course, lawyers will come to rely on them. If such delays are granted only sporadically, on the other hand, the possibilities of discrimination are obvious and the effects on counsel and their clients more onerous in the long run than the strict enforcement of clear rules. And the absence of any sanction would make it almost impossible to conduct the business of the courts. The point has been well made by Chief Judge Biggs:

> We recognize that the Federal Rules of Civil Procedure must be construed liberally to bring about a just, speedy and inexpensive determination of every action. Any requirement of compliance with barren technical formalities is to be avoided. But it cannot be denied that certain formalities are indispensable if litigation is to be just, speedy and inexpensive. This fundamental and most important objective can be achieved only by adherence to rather than rejection of the rules.[73]

Still, acceptance of this view does not answer the second question raised by Justice Black's dissent in *Link*: "How should such procedural rules be enforced consistent with justice?"

Enforcement of Rules and Pursuit of Justice

Even where there is no justification for a failure to file a paper on time, the penalty of dismissal of the suit or of an appeal may be too harsh, particularly in criminal cases. Thus, for example, the action of the Supreme Court of North Carolina in refusing to consider an appeal from a death sentence because the statement on appeal was filed by hand on the sixty-first day, although the same appeal would have been timely if the statement had been mailed on the sixtieth day, was barbarous. Subsequently the United States Supreme Court treated this dismissal as an adequate reason for not considering the federal constitutional questions that were raised.[74] This action understandably drew a sharp dissent from Justice Black,[75] and would not be followed today in light of *Fay v. Noia*.[76]

On the whole, the Supreme Court has been lenient with respect to time deadlines in criminal cases.[77] The Court's

attitude perhaps reflects the differences in the interests involved. The sanction of a punishment for a criminal conviction is usually more serious than a default judgment in a
civil suit. Moreover, unlike litigants in a civil case who simply wish to win their case with as little cost as possible, in a
criminal prosecution the government is held to have the
broader objective that justice be done. Further, even in civil
cases the courts generally are lenient with counsel who fail
to comply with rules; for example, by opening defaults for
failures to answer. But in both criminal and civil cases, in
addition to the necessity for reasonable consistency, some
rules are jurisdictional and, at least in theory, may not be
waived by the courts.

There are some cases in which an alternative remedy to
a dismissal of a suit will vindicate the interests protected by
the rules. In a case such as *Link,* for example, an order directing the plaintiff to pay the attorney's fees of the defendant for the time that the attorney was at the conference
which the court had called and the plaintiff did not attend
would have protected defendant's interest. It would not, of
course, have compensated for the waste of judicial time. In
the circumstances of the *Link* case, moreover, one may well
wonder whether such a judgment would not have been more
harsh to the plaintiff than the dismissal of his suit. Perhaps
an order requiring a party to pay the other side's costs or
suffer default in his suit would be appropriate in some cases.

However, even this does not meet Mr. Justice Black's
contention that the litigant is being punished for the sins
of his attorney. For Mr. Justice Black recommended in
Link that if the Court felt compelled to impose sanctions to
keep the rules inviolate, such sanctions should be designed
to discipline counsel for infractions rather than to take action against the client by dismissing his lawsuit. Mr. Justice
Harlan, speaking for the Court, could not accept this argument:

> There is certainly no merit to the contention that
> dismissal of petitioner's claim because of his counsel's
> unexcused conduct imposes an unjust penalty on the
> client. Petitioner voluntarily chose this attorney as

his representative in the action, and he cannot now avoid the consequences of the acts or omissions of this freely selected agent. Any other notion would be wholly inconsistent with our system of representative litigation, in which each party is deemed bound by the acts of his lawyer-agent and is considered to have "notice of all facts, notice of which can be charged upon the attorney." *Smith v. Ayer,* 101 U.S. 320, 326.[78]

To this Mr. Justice Black replied as follows:

One may readily accept the statement that there are circumstances under which a client is responsible for the acts or omissions of his attorney. But it stretches this generalized statement too far to say that he must always do that. This case is a good illustration of the deplorable kind of injustice that can come from the acceptance of any such mechanical rule. . . .

There surely can be no doubt that if the plaintiff's lawyer had gone into court without authority and asked the court to dismiss the case so as to bar any future suit from being filed, this Court would repudiate such conduct and give the plaintiff a remedy for the wrong so perpetrated against him. Or had the trial judge here, instead of putting an end to plaintiff's substantial cause of action, simply imposed a fine of several thousand dollars upon the plaintiff because of his lawyer's neglect, I cannot doubt that this Court would unanimously reverse such an unjust penalty. The result actually reached here, however, is that this Court condones a situation no different in fact from either of those described above. The plaintiff's cause of action is valuable property within the generally accepted sense of that word, and, as such, it is entitled to the protections of the Constitution. Due process requires that property shall not be taken away without notice and hearing. I do not see how the result here can be squared with that fundamental constitutional requirement.

Moreover, to say that the sins or faults or delinquencies of a lawyer must always be visited upon his client so as to impose tremendous financial penalties upon him, as here, is to ignore the practicalities and realities of the lawyer-client relationship. Lawyers everywhere in this country are granted licenses presumably because of their skill, their integrity, their learning in the law and their dependability. While there may be some clients sophisticated enough in the affairs of the world to be able to select the good from the bad among this mass of lawyers throughout the country, this unfortunately cannot always be the case. The average individual called upon, perhaps for the first time in his life, to select a lawyer to try a lawsuit may happen to choose the best lawyer or he may happen to choose one of the worst. He has a right to rely at least to some extent upon the fact that a lawyer has a license. From this he is also entitled to believe that the lawyer has the ability to look out for his case and that he should leave the lawyer free from constraint in doing so. Surely it cannot be said that there was a duty resting upon Link, a layman plaintiff, to try to supervise the daily professional services of the lawyer he had chosen to represent him. How could he know, even assuming that it is true, that his lawyer was a careless man or that he would have an adverse effect upon the trial judge by failing to appear when ordered? How could he know or why should he be presumed to know that it was his duty to see that the many steps a lawyer needs to take to bring his case to trial had been taken by his lawyer? Why should a client be awakened to his lawyer's incapacity for the first time by a sudden brutal pronouncement of the court: "Your lawyer has failed to perform his duty in prosecuting your case and we are therefore throwing you out of court on your heels"? So far as this record shows, the plaintiff never received one iota of information of any kind, character or type that should have put him on notice as an ordinary layman that his lawyer was not doing his duty.

Any general rule that clients must always suffer for the mistakes of their lawyers simply ignores all these problems. If a general rule is to be adopted, I think it would be far better in the interest of the administration of justice, and far more realistic in the light of what the relationship between a lawyer and his client actually is, to adopt the rule that no client is ever to be penalized, as this plaintiff has been, because of the conduct of his lawyer unless notice is given to the client himself that such a threat hangs over his head. Such a rule would do nothing more than incorporate basic constitutional requirements of fairness into the administration of justice in this country.[79]

Justice Black's argument that the District Court's action deprived Link of valuable property without due process has at least a rhetorical appeal. But there is another dimension, another element of justice that must be considered. It is, of course, true that a cause of action is property, but it is so only in a very special sense. Its value depends on the outcome of litigation and such litigation is subject to certain prescribed procedures.[80] To state that a property interest which is contingent on following certain procedures is denied by their enforcement, thus seems to beg the difficult but essential question as to what those procedures should be and how they should be enforced. Moreover, Justice Black may have exaggerated the question of personal notice to the plaintiff. Litigation could not be practicably conducted except under the rule that notice to the attorney is notice to the client; and since the rule is well established, easily understood, and universally observed, it is hard to see how it could be considered intrinsically unjust. Further, it may be questioned whether notice to the client would be of material benefit to him. If Link had been given notice personally that the District Judge was going to treat his counsel's failure to appear for the hearing as a failure to prosecute, he might, indeed, have said that he wished to continue his lawsuit; but such mere desire is not the test under Rule 41(b).[81] The more genuine issue is not one of notice of the intention to exercise the power to dismiss, but rather whether that power should be exercised at all.

The objection in principle to Justice Black's position is that it fails to take adequate account of the representative nature of litigation. It is true that in the course of legal action there are frequent junctures at which missteps by an attorney can have an adverse effect on his client.[82] But cases cannot be continually retried until there is a perfect trial in the sense that no party has made a material miscalculation or misstep. It is an unalterable, though sometimes harsh, fact that litigation cannot be conducted under conditions of an experiment in a scientific laboratory. The broad objective of achieving the truth is the same, but the methods necessarily vary.

There are also practical objections to laying penalties on lawyers for procedural errors. For one thing, as the *Beaufort* case shows, the disciplinary action against the attorney would certainly not help the adversary who was disadvantaged by the procedural misstep.

Secondly, if attorneys were personally penalized by judges as a means of coercing strict adherence to the rules, the practice would have a demoralizing influence on the bar and an adverse effect on relations between bench and bar. Unfortunately, the great power that federal judges have over the bar has not always been used temperately or wisely, as Justice Black himself has recognized. Just one week before the *Link* decision, he wrote an opinion for the Court, reversing a contempt conviction against an attorney whom the trial judge had deemed to have been too vigorous in the representation of his client; declaring that "an independent judiciary and an independent bar are both indispensable parts of our system of justice," he held that the contempt powers were inappropriate for disciplining counsel except "to prevent obstruction of justice."[83]

In any event, there is merit in Justice Black's objection to foisting upon the client—especially by throwing his case out of court—the procedural errors of his attorney who is licensed by the state and on whose ability he had a right and reason to rely. Of course, despite such reliance, it is not always true that the client is "innocent."[84] In some situations the delay is due to his own inaction—for example, in failing to decide whether to proceed further. In others, counsel's failure to follow a procedural rule is part of deliberate strategy to obtain some advantage or to keep a non-meritorious suit alive to retain its nuisance value for as long as possible. Nevertheless, there are unquestionably some instances where the failure to comply with the rules is due simply to the attorney's negligence. In those cases, it would seem preferable for the court to take appropriate action in the lawsuit instead of either dismissing it, or following Justice Black's alternative of exacting "a pound of flesh" from the attorney.[85]

It has been suggested elsewhere in this volume that Mr. Justice Black recognizes the fact that "clarity and consistency are aids to justice."[86] But at least two caveats must be entered when this is applied to his treatment of the Federal Rules of Civil Procedure. One is that even though he might concede that they assist, over the long run, in the attainment of justice, he sometimes finds it painfully difficult to apply them when he is convinced that their application will not result in justice, as he sees it, in a particular case.[87]

But while Justice Black's position in the *Link* case cannot be fully embraced, that position is, characteristically, a valuable contribution to the law. For it dramatizes the responsibility of the courts to assure that their rules be administered temperately and justly and that they do not become ends in themselves. Justice Black's special concern in *Link* and in his procedural opinions generally has been to protect the individual against being dealt with unfairly by government. It is this same concern which, as has been developed throughout this symposium, solidly underlies his constitutional philosophy.

CHAPTER NINE

Black on Balance

STEPHEN PARKS STRICKLAND

LITTLE wonder is aroused that Mr. Justice Black is well known as a liberal, an absolutist, a judicial activist, a libertarian, and, less flatteringly, a radical. Even his friends and admirers characterize him in the former four terms while his adversaries and more reactionary critics equate "radical" with all the others.

Eleanor Roosevelt affirmed the first label—the one most consistently applied—back in 1945. "I know that all of us," she said, "are deeply conscious of the service which Justice Black has rendered to the liberal cause."[1] Twenty years later a popular periodical (in answering questions for those who "want the facts" and "want to learn the truth about popular personalities") assured its millions of readers that Justice Black was a liberal interpreter of the law.[2] Professor Edmund Cahn thought of Black as a "libertarian jurist"[3] and Charles A. Madison would push that characterization further, calling Black a "passionate libertarian."[4] Journalist James E. Clayton, whose book on the Supreme Court appeared in 1964, constantly refers to Black as a judicial activist and is also among those who classify Black as an absolutist.[5] That Irving Dilliard would apply the same term is made manifestly evident by the fact that he devotes all 483 pages of his book on Black to an emphasis of the Justice's "absolutist views."[6] In still another characterization, two Harvard law students described Black (favorably, they thought), two years after he was appointed to

---

the High Court in 1937, as "the extremist on what appears to be a revolutionary court."[7] Carl Swisher, in this volume, suggests that at least in his early days on the Court Black's role was that of a "crusading innovator."[8]

The character of the ascriptions is itself revealing. For one thing, although the terms used most frequently—liberal, libertarian, judicial activist, and absolutist—seem to be used simultaneously if not interchangeably to describe Black, they do not necessarily sum up to the same thing. Indeed, they may indicate sharp contrast.

Next, it is significant that of the only three scholarly books which have treated of Black up to the present time,[9] only the Dilliard work seeks to place Black's libertarianism-absolutism on a preeminent level, and Dilliard admits from the outset his belief that all other constitutional issues coming before the Supreme Court are "far less significant than Bill of Rights issues."[10] The studies of Charlotte Williams and John P. Frank, covering the gamut of Black's opinions, do not carry such emphases.

At the present juncture, Justice Black "has lived to see the 'Warren Court,' as it is known out of respect for its Chief Justice, more accurately called the 'Black Court' after its chief philosopher."[11] As we review the work and philosophy of the man as judge, it seems especially important to re-examine cautiously those word-garbs so often pinned on him: to see if they fit, and if they do, to determine whether, in fact, they correctly summarize him.

The Bill of Rights: Absolutely Absolute?

In his now famous address on "The Bill of Rights,"[12] which in 1960 inaugurated the New York University Law School's James Madison Lectures, Justice Black focused his attention on three major points. They were that, in his view:

(1) The Constitution, with its Bill of Rights, is the best hope for the aspirations of freedom of Americans and men everywhere.

(2) The First Amendment, with its guarantees of freedom of religion, speech, press, peaceable assembly, and petition is the heart of the Bill of Rights.

(3) The freedoms and protections enumerated in the First and the other nine Amendments of the Bill of Rights are absolute in nature: the Government is absolutely prohibited from infringing upon them.

Two years later, in the course of an American Jewish Congress at a banquet in his honor, Justice Black was publicly queried about his Bill of Rights speech by Professor Edmund Cahn of the New York University Law School.[13] In replying, Black placed heavy emphasis on the absolutism of the phrase: "Congress shall pass no law." For him, he said, the crux of the matter lay in that one phrase. He pointed out that others have from time to time—and from bench, bar, and book—suggested that the rights of the Bill must be balanced with the Due Process Clause and other clauses of the Constitution; balanced, that is, according to the wisdom of the legislative branch of government and/or the Court.

A classic example of Black's absolutist position, vis-à-vis "balancing," is to be found in the case of *American Communications Ass'n v. Douds,* decided by the Supreme Court in 1950.[14] In that decision, Chief Justice Fred Vinson held, for the majority, that the portion of the Taft-Hartley law which in effect denied the right of Communist Party members to hold union office was not unconstitutional. Specifically, the Court, giving "deference due the Congressional judgment concerning the need for regulation of conduct affecting interstate commerce and the effect of that statute upon the rights of speech, assembly, and belief," concluded that the Act's paragraph 9(h) "does not unduly infringe freedoms protected by the First Amendment."[15]

This was exactly the kind of balancing to which Black specifically reiterated his objections twelve years later in the interview with Professor Cahn. In his dissent in the *Douds* case, he had said:

Crucial to the Court's . . . holding is the premise that congressional power to regulate trade and traffic in-

cludes power to proscribe "beliefs and political affiliations." No case cited by the Court provides the least
vestige of support for thus holding that the Commerce
Clause restricts the right to think. On the contrary, the
First Amendment was added after adoption of the Constitution for the express purpose of barring Congress
from using previously granted powers to abridge belief
or its expression. Freedom to think is inevitably
abridged when beliefs are penalized by imposition of
civil disabilities. . . .

The Court finds comfort in its assurance that we need
not fear too much legislative restriction of political
belief or association "while this Court sits." That expression, while felicitous, has no validity in this particular constitutional field. For it springs from the
assumption that individual mental freedom can be constitutionally abridged whenever any majority of this
Court finds a satisfactory legislative reason. . . .[16]

When in the *Dennis*[17] case decided the next year, 1951, the
Court upheld the Smith Act, and consequently the convictions
under it of certain Communists, Black again strongly dissented, finding the section of the law in question "a virulent
form of prior censorship of speech and press, which I believe
the First Amendment forbids."[18] He went on to say:

Public opinion being what it now is, few will protest
the conviction of these Communist petitioners. There
is hope, however, that in calmer times, when pressures,
passions and fears subside, this or some later Court will
restore the First Amendment liberties to the high preferred place where they belong in a free society.[19]

In 1950 and the next few years, the significance of Communists within our country was, at best, less than absolutely
certain. Though a few zealots considered the "internal Communist conspiracy" only a few steps away from the vital
machinery of government, the more rational probability was
that, on the contrary, the Communist movement, though

highly disciplined, was microscopic in size, philosophically impotent to convert many Americans to the cause, and organizationally incapable of doing severe damage either to the economy or the processes of government. Meanwhile, the North Korean and Chinese Communists were this country's adversaries in the Far East, and the conviction was that the Soviets were foursquare behind them. In any event, Americans had, since the late forties, been nervous about the Communist threat, internally as well as internationally. This is evidenced in the fact that Congress passed laws containing sections aimed at control of Communists in 1946 (Smith Act) and 1947 (Taft-Hartley). And the fact of a national nervousness over Communism was shortly to be dramatized by the hysterics of Senator Joseph McCarthy.

For Justice Black, such an uncertain danger was not to be met by abridging the Bill of Rights. His was a perspective shared by too few leaders during that period, and it is largely for that perspective that his absolutism has been singled out for praise or attack.

But consider another era, another danger, and another posture struck by Black. In 1941, following the Japanese attack on Pearl Harbor, the federal government began frantically organizing itself for war, and its efforts included both those of defense and offense. One adjunct of the defense effort was an act of Congress of March 21, 1942, which allowed the President, by Executive Order, to permit the establishment in this country of military areas or zones wherever they were deemed essential to the war effort, and to have excluded from them any undesirable persons. On the West Coast, thousands of Japanese-Americans were so excluded—in fact were evacuated indiscriminately, with some being detained in "assembly or relocation centers." Such practices brought a wave of court cases charging violations of the rights of individuals under the Constitution; and several of those cases reached the Supreme Court. The nation watched with perhaps more than ordinary interest to see how these cases would be resolved by the Court.

Justice Black wrote the decision in *Korematsu v. United States*,[20] in 1944, which specifically brought into question the validity of the exclusion orders used solely to deal with persons of Japanese descent. Warning that should such exclusion be based purely on racial grounds it *might* be unconstitutional, he reasoned that, in view of the possibility of a Japanese invasion of the West Coast (which possibility he conceded), the judgment of the military authorities and the Congress that there were disloyal members of the Japanese-American population, "whose number and strength could not be precisely and quickly ascertained," under such extreme circumstances must be accepted.[21]

> Compulsory exclusion of large groups of citizens from their homes, except under circumstances of direct emergency and peril, is inconsistent with our basic governmental institutions. But when under conditions of modern warfare our shores are threatened by hostile forces, the power to protect must be commensurate with the threatened danger.[22]

Whatever else might be said about this decision and the conditions under which it was written, it is obvious that there is a balance—not an absolutism—here. It appears that Justice Black, though unalterably opposed to the balancing of the Bill of Rights with the Commerce Clause or the Due Process Clause, in this particular instance balanced the Bill of Rights with the War Powers of the Government.

One of Black's former law clerks offers an important clue to the distinction Black would probably make between the balance he reached in *Korematsu* and the balancing he so stringently opposed in the *Douds* and *Dennis* cases: "While he shares the deep patriotism of Mr. Justice Holmes, Black does not think that the Nation is imperiled by words, and would go much further in permitting free speech than Holmes did in his famous opinions."[23]

Charlotte Williams says it this way: "When national safety is at stake he is willing to sacrifice personal liberties."[24] That is putting it too strongly, especially in view of Black's other wartime decisions,[25] but it makes the point.

It has long been accepted that the Fourteenth Amendment to the Constitution makes applicable to the states the guaranteed rights of the First Amendment. Justice Black would apply those guarantees with equal vigor to strike down such breaches as he saw in: (1) an Illinois law which made it a criminal offense to (among other things) distribute materials and publications which were "productive of breaches of the peace";[26] (2) an Oklahoma law requiring a loyalty oath of all its state officers and employees;[27] (3) a local ordinance in California imposing criminal liabilities for possession of any books which might be described as obscene.[28]

But are there no boundaries under the First Amendment, for Black, between the rights of individuals to do as they please, on the one hand, and the prerogatives of state and local governments, on the other, to regulate for the public welfare and order?

In the *Thornhill*[29] case of 1940, the Supreme Court overthrew an Alabama statute which severely restricted picketing. Black was with the majority whose decision, delivered by Justice Murphy, was hailed not only as a guarantee of the First Amendment right of peaceful assembly, but also as an extention of freedom of expression to include picketing. Black reiterated his position in his dissent in the 1941 case of *Milk Wagon Drivers Union, Local 753 v. Meadowmoor Dairies, Inc.*,[30] when the majority felt that, in this instance, the picketing might possibly incite violence.

However, in the *Giboney*[31] case eight years later, it was Justice Black who delivered the opinion of the Court in upholding a lower court injunction against picketing in a Missouri case where state law forbade "combinations" from joining together to restrain trade. Black's opinion meant the upholding of the state law; and he found ludicrous the union contention that the statute could be applied to combinations of businessmen but not to combinations of union members such as this situation involved. In this case, said Black, picketing was but a part of a connected and unlawful effort to restrain trade.

But Black had not shifted his position. As he emphasized in his *Giboney* decision, even in *Thornhill* "the Court was careful to point out that it was within the province of states 'to set limits of permissible contest open to industrial combatants.' "[32] And in *Milk Wagon Drivers Union*, though he would have upheld the picketing in question, he was even more emphatic about where the dividing line lay, and to what extent authority could be exercised on the state government's side of that line:

> When clear and present danger of riot, disorder, inter- ference with traffic upon the public streets, or other immediate threat to public safety, peace, or order ap- pears, the power of the Illinois courts to prevent or punish is obvious . . . because the preservation of peace and order is one of the first duties of the government.[33]

It may be premature and possibly otherwise unfair to sug- gest at this point that Justice Black, in the case of states, would balance the Bill of Rights with the police power. In any case, it is important to note how his reasoning carries over from the cases in the forties involving the "liberal" cause of union picketing to the cases of the present day, described be- low, involving the "liberal" cause of racial picketing.

Meanwhile, if within these further suggested limitations Black is still to be regarded as an absolutist, consider what happens, in his view, when the absolute guarantee of free speech of the First Amendment collides with the positive guarantee of protection of property by due process of law under the Fifth Amendment. In the course of the interview with Professor Cahn in 1962, Black provided hints as to how he would decide a case containing such elements:

> Nobody has ever said that the First Amendment gives people a right to go anywhere in the world they want to go or say anything in the world they want to say. . . . Buying the theater tickets did not buy the opportunity to make a speech there. We have a system of property in this country which is also protected by the Constitu- tion. . . . I realize the freedom of people to make a speech against the Supreme Court, but I do not want [them] to make it in my house.[34]

Problems of "Establishment"

It is in religious cases that other problems develop in the concept of absolutism. "No law" may well mean *no law;* but what does "establishment" mean?

Justice Black surely recognizes the dilemma, for he has had trouble with it himself. Originally he and Justice Douglas (and all the other members of the Court save Justice Stone) did not think, for example, that "free exercise" of religion prohibited a state from requiring all public school children to salute the United States flag, even though the Jehovah's Witnesses who brought the relevant court case believed that such a salute constituted paying homage to an earthly symbol, in violation of their religious beliefs.[35] But soon the two changed their views and concluded that sincere religious convictions should be honored rather than embarrassed. In *West Virginia Board of Educ. v. Barnette*,[36] Black wrote for himself and his colleague a concurring opinion in order to admit the change of approach.

From then on his problems with the Establishment and Free Exercise clauses became somewhat simpler—but not much. In *Everson v. Board of Educ.*,[37] in 1947, Justice Black delivered the opinion of the Court in a case which had as its crux the question of whether a state could authorize and finance from public funds transportation for all school children, including Catholic children who went to parochial schools. (Parents were reimbursed, by the township school board, for the cost of bus fares.) Since the state of New Jersey did not contribute money to the schools, nor otherwise support them, but merely provided "a general program to help parents get their children, regardless of their religion, safely and expeditiously to and from accredited schools,"[38] Black ruled, with four other Justices agreeing and four dissenting, that New Jersey had not violated what Thomas Jefferson saw as the Constitution's requirement of "separation of church and state." He said:

The First Amendment has erected a wall between church and state. That wall must be kept high and impregnable. We could not approve the slightest breach. New Jersey has not breached it here.[39]

The high, impregnable wall remains intact for Black, but even he would admit that it sometimes seems to be made of invisible steel.

Since the *Everson* case, Justice Black has been considered one of the Court's authorities on First Amendment cases relating to religion. Thus it came as no surprise when he gave the decision in 1961 which ruled unconstitutional New York's state-composed prayer, the recitation of which each morning in state schools was state-ordered. Though the prayer was denominationally discreet, not to say innocuous, and though any child who wished to be excused from the exercise could be, the Court held that the practice, under the direct sponsorship of the state, was in violation of the Establishment Clause.[40]

Viewed in the terms used here, similar to the terms of the case identified by the Court, the decision was an obvious one. For the state had been directly involved in a religious exercise from start to finish. And after the initial shrieks of alarm and anguish from various quarters around the country, it was broadly conceded that the Court's ruling in this case was eminently sound.[41] The more prolonged concern had to do with "how far the Court would go" in subsequent decisions.

Black felt constrained to add a footnote to his opinion in the New York case. It may have been added to ward off some of the anticipated criticism by those "conservatives" who consistently suspect the Court of trying to undermine God and the Constitution, or to assuage the genuine concern of those who merely wondered how far the Court would go; or it may have been added as a warning to the antireligious forces or to any "stricter absolutists" that there was a limit beyond which the Court would not go. The footnote said:

There is of course nothing in the decision reached here that is inconsistent with the fact . . . that there are many manifestations in our public life of belief in God. Such patriotic or ceremonial occasions bear no true resemblance to the unquestioned religious exercise that the State of New York has sponsored in this instance.[42]

One stricter absolutist seemed to be sitting right on the Court. Justice Douglas, whose 1952 decision for the Court in *Zorach v. Clauson*[43] (from which Black dissented) allowed New York to set aside free school periods for the purpose of allowing public school children to leave school property to receive religious instruction, now seemed to go all the way in the other direction. Naturally he concurred in the Court's present decision, but now he would reverse the *Everson* decision of 1947 because:

> The Everson Case seems in retrospect to be out of line with the First Amendment. Its result is appealing, as it allows aid to be given to needy children. Yet by the same token, public funds could be used to satisfy other needs of children in parochial schools—lunches, books, and tuition being obvious examples.[44]

In contrast with Douglas' latest position, Black's approach seems to include a practical element. For example, the *Everson* decision, with which he still holds, seems to have been affected by pragmatic as well as literal constitutional considerations; Justice Black has mentioned in private conversation the Court's taking into account the fact that many cities throughout the country had long subsidized local transit systems to enable them to offer school children—including those attending sectarian schools—reduced fares. The New Jersey system seemed but a logical extension of this practice. Still, Black's position has been consistent. There is an obvious difference in the providing for purely religious exercises and activities under the auspices of local governmental (school) authorities, which he has opposed,[45] and the providing of general public services which may include advantages for those of particular religious commitments, which he has upheld.[46]

Meanwhile, whatever the motivation behind Black's *Engel* footnote, it seems to contain two messages: One is that, for him, there is an important boundary inside of which freedom of or from religion must be clearly and positively preserved, but beyond which tradition—even with its religious overtones—has its proper and rightful place. The second message is that common sense, not antireligious zeal or rigid constitutional absolutism, should decide that boundary as the need arises.

The Uncertain Fourteenth

It is not actually Black's concept of the Bill of Rights as containing absolute restrictions against the federal government that has produced the greatest controversy, nor, similarly, his belief that the First Amendment guarantees are carried over to the states, absolutely, by the Fourteenth Amendment. Coupled with these beliefs is his fervent conviction that the Fourteenth Amendment makes the *entire* Bill of Rights applicable to the states, and it is this proposition that has produced the fiercer clash both on the Court and outside of it.

Black's position in this regard is one that he has taken at least since 1947 when, in his dissent in *Adamson v. California*,[47] he argued the point, in effect, on two grounds. First, as usual, he argued from a historical viewpoint. Appended to his opinion was a resumé, of some thirty pages, of the history of the Fourteenth Amendment, and that history, thought Black, conclusively showed that the drafters of the Amendment, those who voted for it in the Congress, and those who voted for it in the states all believed that one of its purposes was to guarantee state recognition of and deference to the specifics of the Bill of Rights. Justice Frankfurter met Black head-on on the historical grounds and, indeed, in his own best tradition felt the need of adding a concurring opinion[48] in order to do so. But that concurring opinion merely gave Black more ammunition for the second thrust of his attack. The alternative to the across-the-board application of the Bill's guarantees to the states, he said, is an interminable series of court opinions wherein judges would decide, case by case, according to their personal lights, just what "due process of law" meant. He was appalled at the vague contours of "reasonableness" which Justice Frankfurter said would guide judges in such cases: "civilized decency," "fundamental liberty and justice," "canons of decency and fairness," "expressions of justice of English-speaking peoples." Black pounded away at this line of reasoning, saying:

[Today] the Court concludes that although comment upon testimony in a federal court would violate the Fifth Amendment, identical comment in a state court does not violate today's fashion in civilized decency and fundamentals and is therefore not prohibited by the Federal Constitution as amended. . . . I would follow what I believe was the original purpose of the Fourteenth Amendment—to extend to all the people of the nation the complete protection of the Bill of Rights. To hold that this Court can determine what, if any, provisions of the Bill of Rights will be enforced, and if so to what degree, is to frustrate the great design of a written Constitution. . . .

Courts can strike down legislative enactments which violate the Constitution. This process, of course, involves interpretation, and since words can have many meanings, interpretation may obviously result in contraction or extension of the original purpose of a constitutional provision, thereby affecting policy. But to pass upon the constitutionality of statutes by looking to particular standards enumerated in the Bill of Rights and other parts of the Constitution is one thing: to invalidate statutes because of application of "natural law" deemed to be above and undefined by the Constitution is another. In one instance, courts proceeding within clearly marked constitutional boundaries seek to execute policies written into the Constitution; in the other, they roam at will in the limitless area of their own beliefs as to reasonableness and actually select policies, a responsibility which the Constitution entrusts to the legislative representatives of the people.[49]

The two countervailing arguments are still going on, though there has been some shifting in attitude on the Court since that time. While some Justices have been sympathetic, a majority of the Court has never accepted Black's history of the Fourteenth Amendment. For example, it is said that Justice Warren holds that the history of the Amendment is incomplete at best. It is true that, as Justice Douglas points out, ten

Justices who have sat on the Court in the last twenty-five years have agreed with Black and him on the total applicability question; but the problem is that no five of them have sat at the same time.[50]

Meanwhile, piecemeal or not, the Court has been rapidly accepting the equation of Bill of Rights specifics with "due process of law" in state criminal proceedings. In *Gideon v. Wainwright,* Justice Black had the pleasure of announcing the decision of the Court.[51] His opinion was but a forceful rephrasing of his dissent in *Betts v. Brady*[52] of 1942, in which he had argued that the right to counsel in state criminal trials (applying the Sixth Amendment) was essential to due process.

Giving Black exclusive credit for this development, *Time* magazine summed up the situation thus:

> . . . For the first time since 1791, virtually all the most important provisions of the Bill of Rights have become the state as well as the federal process due all Americans. Now demanded of the states are the entire First Amendment; the Fourth's guarantees against unreasonable searches and seizures; the Fifth's privilege against self-incrimination; the Sixth's right to counsel, jury trial, and confrontation with witnesses; the Eighth's guarantee against cruel and unusual punishment.[53]

It has occasionally been asked why Black has seemed to be less rigorous in the position he takes on the Fourth Amendment—regarding searches, seizures, and warrants—than he takes on the rest of the Amendments of the Bill of Rights. Black himself provided the answer in his concurring opinion in *Rochin v. California:*

> Some constitutional provisions are stated in absolute and unqualified language such, for illustration, as the First Amendment stating that no law shall be passed prohibiting the free exercise of religion or abridging the freedom of speech or press. Other constitutional provisions do require courts to choose between competing policies, such as the Fourth Amendment which, by its terms, necessitates a judicial decision as to what is an "unreasonable" search or seizure.[54]

In any event, the *effects* of Black's position on the Bill of
Rights have become law without a full-fledged acceptance of
the per se applicability of all of the Amendments to the states.
Several of the Justices who recently joined majority opinions in
such cases specifically demurred on the matter of wholesale
applicability. In short, though Black's reasoning on the basis
of history has not gained acceptance, his philosophy of what
due process is has become, to use Senator Sam J. Ervin's phrase,
"the best guide to what the law is."

Absolutism and Judicial Restraint

This issue—of absolutism and applicability—has been
dwelt upon because it illuminates, better than any other
subject area, any attempt to find the essence of Justice Black's
philosophy. There were, in fact, three markedly distinctive
positions taken by members of the Court in the *Adamson* case,
and these three positions help us locate, by comparison, the
Constitutional and philosophical positions of the three men
who espoused them:

(1) Justice Frankfurter (with the majority) conservatively
could not accept the offered line of history which would compel the application of the first eight Amendments to the states;
but, beyond that, he argued that:

> [The] relevant question is whether the . . . conviction
> deprived the accused of the due process of law to which
> the United States Constitution entitled him. Judicial
> review of that guaranty of the Fourteenth Amendment
> inescapably imposes upon this Court an exercise of judg-
> ment [but our] application of the Due Process Clause
> [does not] imply that judges are wholly at large. The
> judicial judgment . . . must move within . . . accepted
> notions of justice. . . .[55]

(2) Justice Black (joined by Justice Douglas) wrote:

> I fear to see the consequences of the Court's practice
> of substituting its own concepts of decency and funda-

mental justice for the language of the Bill of Rights as its point of departure in interpreting and enforcing that Bill of Rights.[56]

(3) And Justice Murphy (joined by Justice Rutledge) wrote:

> I agree that the specific guarantees of the Bill of Rights should be carried over intact into the first section of the Fourteenth Amendment. But I am not prepared to say that the latter is entirely and necessarily limited by the Bill of Rights. Occasions may arise where a proceeding falls so far short of conforming to fundamental standards of procedure as to warrant constitutional condemnation in terms of a lack of due process despite the absence of a specific provision in the Bill of Rights.[57]

Certainly Justice Black is the absolutist here: he would simply apply the Bill of Rights to guarantee due process of law. Justice Murphy is just as obviously the liberal: he would apply the Constitution as far as it goes but feels he should reserve the right to add a little wisdom of his own, if need be, in order to be quite certain that justice in due process of law is done. Justice Frankfurter is clearly the conservative insofar as his reaction to a new doctrine is concerned; and feeling that the constitutional provisions in question stop at all state lines, he would himself have to determine, relying on historical precedents and a general ethic, what due process is each time the question is raised.

Apart from the question of the history of the Fourteenth Amendment, one may speculate on the effect of each of these philosophies. Both the "conservative" and "liberal" philosophies incline to produce "judicial activism": one because it *has* to, the other because it *ought* to, keep the Court involved in continuously defining the meaning of "due process of law." The unfortunate element here, according to the Black view, is that the more often the Court is involved in such cases, the more interpretations are likely to be passed along as "law," and the more evanescent this one particular standard of just procedure might become.

On the other hand, the "absolutist" position, while not claiming to eliminate the need for judicial interpretation, might well reduce it by staking out clearer and more positive boundaries, based squarely on the Constitution's Bill of Rights. If so, then there might well also result, in this area of constitutional issues, a situation of "judicial restraint."

The case of *Griswold v. Connecticut*,[58] decided on June 7, 1965, would seem to bear out these possibilities. In a six-to-two decision, the majority agreed that the Connecticut law forbidding the use of contraceptive devices among married couples was unconstitutional by virtue of intruding upon "a relationship lying within the zone of privacy created by several fundamental constitutional guarantees,"[59] in the words of Justice Douglas' opinion for the Court. Three other "liberals" of the Court, the Chief Justice, Justice Brennan, and Justice Goldberg, in a concurring opinion written by the latter, admitted explicitly to the view that the constitutional protection of liberty

is not confined to the specific terms of the Bill of Rights, [because] "the Ninth Amendment shows a belief of the Constitution's authors that fundamental rights exist that are not expressly enumerated in the first eight amendments and an intent that the list of rights included there not be deemed exhaustive."[60]

The conservative Justice Harlan joined in the majority decision, and would rest the decision squarely on the Due Process Clause of the Fourteenth Amendment. However, due process, he insisted, should be determined not merely by scanning the universal conscience as Goldberg had suggested, but by

continual insistence upon respect for the teachings of history, solid recognition of the basic values that underlie our society, and wise appreciation of the great roles that the doctrines of federalism and separation of powers have played in establishing and preserving American freedoms.[61]

Meanwhile, the absolutist Justice Black (with Justice Stewart) found the law as personally offensive as did the opposing brethren, but not unconstitutional. Black declared:

> . . . I get nowhere in this case by talk about a constitutional "right of privacy" as an emanation of one or more constitutional provisions. I like my privacy as well as the next one, but I am nevertheless compelled to admit that government has a right to invade it unless prohibited by some specific constitutional provision. For these reasons I cannot agree with the Court's judgment and the reasons it gives for holding this Connecticut law unconstitutional.[62]

Black singled out the separate concurring opinions as being especially objectionable to him, for he saw the philosophy spelled out in them as a disguise for substituting judicial wisdom for particular constitutional provisions or, more specifically, the lack of them, and for infringing on the legislative prerogative. He said:

> I think that if properly construed neither the Due Process Clause nor the Ninth Amendment, nor both together, could under any circumstances be a proper basis for invalidating the Connecticut law. I discuss the due process and Ninth Amendment arguments together because on analysis they turn out to be the same thing—merely using different words to claim for this Court and the federal judiciary power to invalidate any legislative act which the judges find irrational, unreasonable or offensive.[63]

In short, Black argues that the "absolutism" of the Bill of Rights means, in cases of this nature, judicial restraint.

The Larger Black Versus the Smaller Labels

So far, the distinctions that have been made between various appellations often used interchangeably to describe Black suggest that such terms may be too rigid to provide true description. Further, some of the situations examined provide evidence that Black has made himself out to be more of an absolutist than he actually is.

But even if Black is accepted as a "modified absolutist" with regard to the Bill of Rights, there is a larger question, and several pertinent component inquiries, which need exploring.

That larger question is whether there is, in Black, such a preoccupation with the Bill of Rights and its absolutes that other constitutional considerations go begging. A first reaction would be to answer the question in the affirmative. For somehow, the attention that has been given to that one area of Black's judicial philosophy—by politicians, pundits, and scholars alike—has almost obscured, by a distortion of emphasis, the broader and more balanced meaning of the whole of his philosophy. There is no accusation here that the distortion of emphasis has been capricious. On the contrary, it may well be but the natural result of a needling preoccupation, over the last quarter of a century, with the problem of man's place as an individual in an ever-growing, ever more complex society in a geographically shrinking world.

In any case, the real answer to the question posed is "No," and one does not have to pick into the dark and tiny crevices of the record to gather crumbs for that response.

Part of that answer may be found by looking at one of the more difficult constitutional questions that has recurred throughout our history as a nation, dating at least from *Gibbons v. Ogden*[64] in 1824 and *Brown v. Maryland*[65] in 1827: How far may states go in regulating and taxing commerce within their boundaries in face of the constitutional assignment to Congress of the power to regulate interstate commerce? The early cases (especially *Cooley v. Port Wardens*,[66] 1851) produced two rules of thumb on the matter: where the commerce in question admits only of national and uniform regulation, the states are precluded from action; and where Congress exercises its authority under the Commerce Clause, it preempts the field.

Beginning with the years immediately postdating the Civil War, the Supreme Court, with a special eye for the health of business and industry, increasingly—albeit irregularly—narrowed the areas wherein the states might tax or regulate commerce. This attitude of preclusion has, as John Frank points out, dominated the Court's thinking for at least a hundred years, to the frustration of the states. Describing Black's approach to the problem, Frank states:

> In these cases Black sets himself squarely against the majority. He returns to principles similar to those held a century ago by Chief Justice Taney, and says shortly that unless the states directly discriminate against interstate commerce, they have a complete right to regulate in the absence of congressional direction to the contrary.[67]

In 1939 Mr. Justice Black was the lone dissenter in the *Gwin, White*[68] case, where the decision invalidated a Washington gross income tax of 1½ percent because it had been imposed on a local fruit marketing company which made many of its sales in other states. Black found the tax nondiscriminatory, found the question of state taxation of such enterprises ignored by Congress, and thus believed the state tax to be constitutional. What was unconstitutional, he implied clearly, was the usurpation of the regulatory power of states which the Court had indulged in here and in other recent decisions.

> Since the Constitution grants sole and exclusive power to Congress to regulate commerce among the States, repeated assumption of this power by the courts—even over a long period of years—could not make this assumption of power constitutional.[69]

In 1945 Black was still found to be dissenting in such cases, and now he was joined by Justice Douglas. In *Southern Pac. Co. v. Arizona ex rel. Sullivan*[70] the Court (six to two) invalidated a 1912 Arizona law that prohibited the operation of a railroad train of more than fourteen passenger cars or seventy freight cars because, as Justice Harlan Stone's opinion for the Court said, the statute violated the Commerce Clause by placing an undue burden on interstate commerce. Black's objections were strenuous and direct:

[The] determination of whether it is in the interest of society for the length of trains to be governmentally regulated is a matter of public policy. Someone must fix that policy—either the Congress, or the state, or the courts. A century and a half of constitutional history and government admonishes this Court to leave that choice to the elected legislative representatives of the people themselves, where it properly belongs on both democratic principles and by the requirements of efficient government.[71]

Black's concern and activity in this area has caused his astute biographer and interpreter, Mr. Frank, to say that:

Black is the strongest supporter of the power of the states of the union to regulate the economic affairs of men and concerns within their borders that the Court has had in more than a hundred years. Indeed, fair argument can be made that he is the most complete and consistent supporter of state power of all the Justices in the history of the Court.[72]

In addition to his support of state authority in the area of taxation and regulation of commerce, Black has lent strength to the states in the exercise of authority in other areas. For instance, going back to the Fourth Amendment, Black has felt at liberty, under the "reasonableness" criterion written into that one Article, to uphold certain state procedures in criminal proceedings which others, also called liberals, would not accept. He concurred in the decision of the Court in *Wolf v. Colorado*[73] in 1949, the result of which was that the Fourteenth Amendment did not bar use of evidence obtained in "unreasonable searches and seizure" in criminal proceedings. In interesting contrast, Justices Murphy, Douglas, and Rutledge strongly dissented.[74]

Black returned again to this position in a concurring opinion on April 29, 1965, in the case of *One 1958 Plymouth Sedan v. Pennsylvania*.[75] His point was that:

The language of the Fourth Amendment forbids "unreasonable searches and seizure" but it does not expressly or by implication provide that evidence secured in such a way cannot be used in a prosecution against the accused.[76]

And in the matter of the exercise of local authority to regulate for order and the public welfare, Black's position would seem to be as clear and simple as the theme of Justice Douglas' opinion, which Black announced and concurred in, in *Saia v. New York:*[77]

> Courts must balance the various community interests in passing on the constitutionality of local regulations. . . . But in that process they should be mindful to keep the freedoms of the First Amendment in a preferred position.[78]

(The decision invalidated a penal ordinance of the City of Lockport, forbidding the use of sound amplification devices except by prior permission of the Chief of Police.)

A point previously made is pertinent here: the Justice recognizes a distinction between simple speech and expression, which poses no peril, and freedom of activity, which might. Indeed, in a 1966 opinion he specifically made such a distinction, saying, "I believe that the Federal Government is without any power whatever under the Constitution to put any type burden on speech and expression of ideas of any kind (as distinguished from conduct). . . ."[79] Further, in this regard, Justice Black has already been quoted on the authority and duty of state and local governments to maintain order. It is with his eyes on both of these elements that he would strike the balance—though without calling it that.

In January of 1965 Black dissented in a civil rights decision[80] because, he felt, the Court had not struck the proper balance. Indeed, he believed that, in the name of "civil rights," the majority had forgotten two other ingredients indispensable to justice: the sanctity of judicial proceedings from pressure and the authority of local governments to protect that sanctity. Some expressed surprise that Black—the civil rights advocate, the liberal, the absolutist—should now turn his back on those Negroes demonstrating for "freedom." In reality, he did not turn his back; nor did he turn his mind in a new and different direction. He merely applied the same philosophy which had prompted his *Giboney* opinion in 1949 and which had been spelled out in *Saia* the year before that: he balanced.

> I would sustain the conviction of appellant for violation of Louisiana's [statute] which makes it an offense for anyone, under any conditions, to picket or parade near a courthouse, residence or other building used by a judge, juror, witness, or court officer, "with the intent of influencing" any of them. Certainly the record shows beyond all doubt that the purpose of the 2,000 or more people who stood right across the street from the court-house and jail was to protest the arrest of members of their group who were then in jail. . . .
>
> The very purpose of a court system is to adjudicate controversies, both criminal and civil, in the calmness and solemnity of the courtroom according to legal procedures. Justice cannot be rightly administered . . . where throngs of people clamor against the processes of justice right outside the courthouse or jailhouse doors. The streets are not now and never have been the proper place to administer justice. . . .
>
> Minority groups in particular need always to bear in mind that the Constitution, while it requires States to treat all citizens equally and protect them in the exercise of rights granted by the Federal Constitution and laws, does not take away the State's power, indeed its duty, to keep order and to do justice according to law.[81]

It is Black's reasoning and philosophy as manifested in these separate areas involving the authority and rights of state and local governments[82] that led two writers—one a constitutional law scholar, the other a professor of law—to describe Black and Douglas as being, in one sense, "states' righters."

> They believe that where the states may constitutionally act and where they possess the resources to act, they should be allowed to act. But they mean (a) *state* action,

not action of private groups that appeal to specious and sentimental arguments for state sovereignty, and (b) state action in the economic and social, not in the civil liberties, realm. The national government should be allowed to exercise sufficient powers to do what only it can do and what it is constitutionally authorized to do. But those powers should not be excessive, nor claimed when they are not needed. If they are, then not only the reserved powers of the states but also the retained rights of the people are clearly invaded.[83]

In the same article, Black is by implication included in the group of "Supreme Court liberals, New Deal Democrats and Keynesian economists" whose "new doctrines . . . were evolving and becoming enshrined even as old ones were fading into oblivion."[84] Given current clichés it is difficult to see how Black can be both a liberal and a states' righter. But is it impossible?

In the 1930's and '40's there were several characteristics which marked the "liberals," by their own standards and in the eyes of others. One of these characteristics was support for government regulation of the economy and another was support for the laboring man and his unions. Black qualified on both counts. Indeed, his appointment to the Court in 1937 signaled the transition into a new era: from that time on, the High Court upheld New Deal legislation, especially that regulating the economy and guaranteeing better wages, hours, and working conditions for members of the labor force.

Of course, one of the first cases which seemed to embody these two major elements of the liberalism of the new era was decided in April 1937, before the President had the opportunity to inject into the Court, by the appointment of new Justices, an antidote for what he saw as the essential negativism of "nine old men." The case was that of the *National Labor Relations Board v. Jones & Laughlin Steel Corp.*,[85] decided in 1937. Upholding the National Labor Relations Act as properly within the assigned sphere of Congressional regulation, the Court, in its five-man majority decision announced by Chief Justice Charles Evans Hughes, indicated that it was returning to an old standard of measuring constitutionality which in the immediately preceding years had fallen into disuse. In language that seemed to be self-directed, it said:

> . . . the cardinal principle of statutory construction is to save and not to destroy: we have repeatedly held that as between two possible interpretations of a statute, by one of which it would be unconstitutional and by the other valid, our plain duty is to adopt that which will save the act.[86]

Black came on the Court after that decision, though in the same year, and he thoroughly agreed with its philosophy. In fact, he has never equivocated in giving the broadest possible interpretation to the constitutional power of Congress to regulate interstate commerce for any purpose, except such purposes as collide (as in the previously discussed section of the Taft-Hartley Act) with the Bill of Rights.

As some of the cases cited indicate,[87] Black has consistently upheld not only the right of laboring men to join unions, in order to bargain more successfully for a better position in life economically, but also the subsequent right to put their case, especially through picketing, before the public. But "in instances where organized labor has seemed to him to be manifestly working to the disadvantage of the public he has not hesitated to speak and vote against it."[88] Once more, there is a balance.

Having consistently upheld federal regulatory activity under laws enacted by Congress pursuant to the commerce power, Justice Black gave no surprise by voting with the majority of the Court to uphold the Civil Rights Act of 1964 which, by principal reliance on the Commerce Clause, forbade segregation in places of public accommodation which serve interstate travelers or that are otherwise heavily involved in interstate commerce.

But some professed astonishment when, in *Hamm v. City of Rock Hill*,[89] Justice Clark, a "conservative," announced the decision of the Court to vacate certain local "sit-in" convictions on the basis of the Civil Rights Act which was enacted subsequent to those convictions, while Justice Black, the famous "liberal," sharply dissented and charged that the Court was legislating.[90]

It was at this point in his long career on the Court that, suddenly, friends began to frown and critics became converts. A professional conservative like James J. Kilpatrick expressed delight, in one of his syndicated newspaper articles, that Black was becoming more conservative, and supposed he was merely following the example of the once-radical Felix Frankfurter and simply mellowing with increasing age.[91] A *Wall Street Journal* article also suggested that Black was following Frankfurter, but in an intellectual rather than physiological way:

> With the 1962 retirement of Justice Frankfurter, the Supreme Court lost its most eloquent and persuasive advocate of restraint. Succeeding appointments have served to accentuate, or at least not impede, the activist trend. So much so that Justice Black, intellectual leader that he is, has taken it upon himself to raise the cautionary hand.[92]

Meanwhile, the liberal newspaper, the *Washington Post,* worried editorially about Black's Connecticut birth-control opinion, saying that the Senior Associate Justice "in this rare instance . . . ignored . . . the Court's obligation as a sentinel of freedom," and found in his dissent "judicial restraint carried to the point of abdication."[93]

The Ultimate Balance

Miss Williams believes that the "most persistent question that has stalked the Supreme Court throughout its history" is that of a proper balance in the relationship between the federal government and its constituent states:[94]

> Older than the Supreme Court and coeval with the Union itself, the problem has survived the vicissitudes of war and the mutations of time and seems destined to demand attention so long as the government remains federal or the states retain any element of sovereignty.[95]

She goes on to suggest that those liberal conceptualists who viewed Justices as good or bad according to which side they would take in this on-going struggle were pleased with the appointment of Hugo Black to the Court because they thought that:

> [Being] a loyal supporter of the New Deal, [he] could be counted on to exert his influence to increase the power of the national government at the expense of the states.[96]

But these liberal hopefuls were wrong, for

> more consistently than any member of the Court he undertook to uphold the authority of the several states to levy taxes according to their chosen methods, to control business within their borders as their respective legislatures saw fit, and to regulate the rates and practices of their public service corporations with a minimum of interference from the Federal government.[97]

Did this mean, then, that he would pursue a course of restricting activities of the federal government? Those who so feared were wrong again for, "on the contrary, he uniformly tends to favor liberal construction when federal authority is challenged."[98]

There is a riddle suggested here, but it is the kind of riddle that mainly bothers startled conceptualists who suddenly realize that their expectations have not been fulfilled, and they cannot fathom why. Thus the riddle of Mr. Justice Black is now confronting, alike, his conceptualist friends and admirers who saw in him only the champion of their pet causes, and his conceptualist enemies and detractors who were sure they recognized in him the cynical overturner of their cherished positions.

But Black is not to be captured in any quick conceptualistic term, any rigid label or easy description so far advanced.

However, recognizing that, for some, a riddle does exist in Justice Black, let us offer a key to its solution. That key is a fact which is not only recognized in every semi-serious discussion of the Senior Associate Justice from Alabama, but one which he confesses—or rather, proudly *professes*. The key is simply that Black is a Madisonian.

Somehow, Black's being a Madisonian is so obvious that people forget what that means. But as his numerous particular reliances on Madison for his speeches and opinions suggest,[99] and as the comprehensive record of his judicial career clearly shows, Justice Black has not forgotten. For Madison's chief fame is not as the promoter of the Bill of Rights;[100] he was, as Black has specifically acknowledged, the Father of the Constitution.[101] He was, further, the chief explainer and defender of every part of that Constitution by virtue of being the author of the majority of the Federalist papers.

It would be ludicrous to suggest, in the face of that evidence—in the face of Madison's cogent arguments in support of every governmental arrangement proposed in the Constitution—that the Bill of Rights was so important to him that he placed on a secondary level such provisions as those relating to the separation of powers, the legislative authority of Congress, the role of the Supreme Court, or the delineation of authority between the federal and state governments. Quite obviously, he did not. And neither, according to the *whole* record, does his devoted follower, Justice Black.

Black may consider that the Bill of Rights lies at the heart of the Constitution, just as he considers that the First Amendment *is* the heart of the Bill of Rights. But even if this is so, he would also assert that there are other vital organs. Key words in his 1960 Madison lecture at New York University Law School were: "I believe that *our Constitution, with* its absolute guarantee of individual rights, is the best hope for the aspirations of freedom which men share everywhere."[102]

Thus Black can be an "absolutist," albeit "modified," in applying the Bill of Rights; a "states' righter" in supporting the regulatory powers of the states; a "liberal" as regards construction of the Congressional commerce power; and a "libertarian" in applying the law in defense of free speech, free exercise of religion, and free exercise of belief.

Chief Justice Earl Warren said of Hugo Black in 1962:

Of the 97 justices who have been appointed to this Court, only 16 have served as long as has Mr. Justice Black and none with greater fidelity or singleness of

purpose. His unflagging devotion has been to the Constitution of the United States.[103]

Therein lies the solution to the riddle of Mr. Justice Black.
And therein lies his ultimate conservatism.

Notes

CHAPTER ONE

History's Panorama and Justice Black's Career

——*Carl Brent Swisher*——

[1] Massachusetts v. Mellon, 262 U.S. 447, 67 L. Ed. 1078, 43 Sup. Ct. 597 (1923).

[2] See CORWIN, THE TWILIGHT OF THE SUPREME COURT (1935).

[3] 83 CONG. REC. 2830 (1937).

[4] Ashwander v. Tennessee Valley Authority, 297 U.S. 288, 80 L. Ed. 688, 56 Sup. Ct. 466 (1936).

[5] William Howard Taft, *Mr. Wilson and the Campaign*, 10 YALE REV. (n.s.) 1, 19-20 (1921).

[6] 83 CONG. REC. 1294 (1937).

[7] WILLIAMS, HUGO L. BLACK: A STUDY IN THE JUDICIAL PROCESS 68 (1950). See John Frank's citation of Black's dissents in constitutional cases in the first three terms in Chapter Two of this volume on page 57.

[8] McCart v. Indianapolis Water Co., 302 U.S. 419, 423, 82 L. Ed. 336, 58 Sup. Ct. 324 (1938) (dissenting opinion).

[9] New York Life Ins. Co. v. Gamer, 303 U.S. 161, 172, 82 L. Ed. 726, 58 Sup. Ct. 500 (1938) (dissenting opinion).

[10] Erie R.R. v. Tompkins, 304 U.S. 64, 82 L. Ed. 1188, 58 Sup. Ct. 817 (1938).

[11] MASON, HARLAN FISKE STONE: PILLAR OF THE LAW 467-77 (1956).

[12] Connecticut Gen. Life Ins. Co. v. Johnson, 303 U.S. 77, 83, 82 L. Ed. 673, 58 Sup. Ct. 436 (1938) (dissenting opinion).

[13] Massachusetts v. Mellon, 262 U.S. 447, 67 L. Ed. 1078, 43 Sup. Ct. 597 (1923).

[14] See NLRB v. Jones & Laughlin Steel Corp., 301 U.S. 1, 81 L. Ed. 893, 57 Sup. Ct. 615 (1937).

[15] United States v. Butler, 297 U.S. 1, 87, 80 L. Ed. 477, 56 Sup. Ct. 312 (1936).

[16] See ROBERT H. JACKSON, THE STRUGGLE FOR JUDICIARY SUPREMACY (1941).

[17] United States v. Bethlehem Steel Corp., 315 U.S. 289, 86 L. Ed. 855, 62 Sup. Ct. 581 (1942).

[18] Lichter v. United States, 334 U.S. 742, 92 L. Ed. 1694, 68 Sup. Ct. 1294 (1948).

19 Bowles v. Willingham, 321 U.S. 503, 537, 88 L. Ed. 892, 64 Sup. Ct. 641 (1944) (dissenting opinion).

20 See Opp Cotton Mills, Inc. v. Administrator, 312 U.S. 126, 85 L. Ed. 624, 61 Sup. Ct. 524 (1941).

21 See United States v. Pink, 315 U.S. 203, 86 L. Ed. 796, 62 Sup. Ct. 552 (1942).

22 Youngstown Sheet & Tube Co. v. Sawyer, 343 U.S. 579, 96 L. Ed. 1153, 72 Sup. Ct. 863, 26 A.L.R.2d 1378 (1952).

23 See Ex parte Quirin, 317 U.S. 1, 87 L. Ed. 3, 63 Sup. Ct. 1, 2 (1942); MASON, HARLAN FISKE STONE: PILLAR OF THE LAW 653-65 (1956).

24 Hirabayashi v. United States, 320 U.S. 81, 87 L. Ed. 1774, 63 Sup. Ct. 1375 (1941).

25 Korematsu v. United States, 323 U.S. 214, 219, 89 L. Ed. 194, 65 Sup. Ct. 193 (1944).

26 Id. at 244-45 (dissenting opinion).

27 Id. at 225 (concurring opinion).

28 Ex parte Endo, 323 U.S. 283, 89 L. Ed. 243, 65 Sup. Ct. 208 (1944).

29 Cramer v. United States, 325 U.S. 1, 89 L. Ed. 1441, 65 Sup. Ct. 918 (1945). See also Haupt v. United States, 330 U.S. 631, 91 L. Ed. 1145, 67 Sup. Ct. 874 (1947).

30 Kahanamoku v. United States, 327 U.S. 304, 322-23, 90 L. Ed. 688, 66 Sup. Ct. 606 (1946).

31 Yamashita v. Styer, 327 U.S. 1, 90 L. Ed. 499, 66 Sup. Ct. 340 (1946).

32 Johnson v. Eisentrager, 339 U.S. 763, 94 L. Ed. 1255, 70 Sup. Ct. 936 (1950).

33 Earl Warren, The Bill of Rights and the Military, 37 N.Y.U.L. REV. 181, 192-93 (1962).

34 Warren, supra note 33, at 191.

35 Schenck v. United States, 249 U.S. 47, 63 L. Ed. 470, 39 Sup. Ct. 247 (1919).

36 Bridges v. California, 314 U.S. 252, 263, 86 L. Ed. 192, 62 Sup. Ct. 190 (1941).

37 ONE MAN'S STAND FOR FREEDOM: MR. JUSTICE BLACK AND THE BILL OF RIGHTS 479 (Dilliard ed. 1963).

38 Dennis v. United States, 341 U.S. 494, 508, 95 L. Ed. 1137, 71 Sup. Ct. 857 (1951).

39 Id. at 581 (dissenting opinion).

40 Id. at 580 (dissenting opinion).

41 Ludecke v. Watkins, 335 U.S. 160, 183, 92 L. Ed. 1881, 68 Sup. Ct. 1429 (1948) (dissenting opinion).

42 American Communications Ass'n v. Douds, 339 U.S. 382, 453, 94 L. Ed. 925, 70 Sup. Ct. 674 (1956) (dissenting opinion).

43 See Joint Anti-Fascist Refugee Comm. v. McGrath, 341 U.S. 123, 95 L. Ed. 817, 71 Sup. Ct. 624 (1951).

44 Watkins v. United States, 354 U.S. 178, 200, 1 L. Ed. 2d 1273, 77 Sup. Ct. 1173 (1957).

45 Id. at 217 (dissenting opinion).

46 Barenblatt v. United States, 360 U.S. 109, 132, 3 L. Ed. 2d 1115, 79 Sup. Ct. 1081 (1959).

47 Id. at 134.

48 Id. at 144 (dissenting opinion).

49 Barenblatt v. United States, 360 U.S. 109, 146, 3 L. Ed. 2d 1115,

79 Sup. Ct. 1081 (1959).

[50] See his position as taken in Adamson v. California, 332 U.S. 46, 68, 91 L. Ed. 1903, 67 Sup. Ct. 1672 (1947) (dissenting opinion).

[51] Barron v. Baltimore, 32 U.S. (7 Pet.) 243, 8 L. Ed. 672 (1833).

[52] 372 U.S. 335, 9 L. Ed. 2d 799, 83 Sup. Ct. 792, 93 A.L.R.2d 733 (1963), *overruling* Betts v. Brady, 316 U.S. 455, 86 L. Ed. 1595, 62 Sup. Ct. 1252 (1942).

[53] For a dramatic account of the case and its background see LEWIS, GIDEON'S TRUMPET (1964).

[54] 378 U.S. 478, 12 L. Ed. 2d 977, 84 Sup. Ct. 1758 (1964).

[55] 384 U.S. 436, 86 Sup. Ct. 1602 (1966).

[56] *Id.* at 504 (dissenting opinion).

[57] *Id.* at 545 (dissenting opinion).

[58] *Id.* at 441-42.

[59] Sherbert v. Verner, 374 U.S. 398, 10 L. Ed. 2d 965, 83 Sup. Ct. 1790 (1963).

[60] McGowan v. Maryland, 366 U.S. 420, 6 L. Ed. 2d 393, 81 Sup. Ct. 1101 (1961); Two Guys from Harrison-Allentown, Inc. v. McGinley, 366 U.S. 582, 6 L. Ed. 2d 551, 81 Sup. Ct. 1135 (1961).

[61] Everson v. Board of Educ., 330 U.S. 1, 91 L. Ed. 711, 67 Sup. Ct. 504 (1947).

[62] Engel v. Vitale, 370 U.S. 421, 429-30, 8 L. Ed. 2d 601, 82 Sup. Ct. 1261, 86 A.L.R.2d 1285 (1962). For the outlawing of Bible reading as a religious exercise in public schools see Abingdon School Dist. v. Schempp, 374 U.S. 203, 10 L. Ed. 2d 844, 83 Sup. Ct. 1560 (1963).

[63] Sweatt v. Painter, 339 U.S. 629, 94 L. Ed. 1114, 70 Sup. Ct. 848 (1950). For the Supreme Court's initial statement of the separate-but-equal doctrine see Plessy v. Ferguson, 163 U.S. 537, 41 L. Ed. 256, 16 Sup. Ct. 1138 (1896).

[64] Brown v. Board of Educ., 347 U.S. 483, 495, 98 L. Ed. 873, 74 Sup. Ct. 686, 38 A.L.R.2d 1180 (1954).

[65] Bolling v. Sharpe, 347 U.S. 497, 499, 98 L. Ed. 884, 74 Sup. Ct. 693 (1954).

[66] For discussion and citation of per curiam cases see WECHSLER, PRINCIPLES, POLITICS AND FUNDAMENTAL LAW 31 (1961).

[67] Dilliard, *op. cit. supra* note 37, at 477.

[68] Bell v. Maryland, 378 U.S. 226, 325, 12 L. Ed. 2d 822, 84 Sup. Ct. 1814 (1964) (dissenting opinion).

[69] Atlanta Motel v. United States, 379 U.S. 241, 268, 13 L. Ed. 2d 258, 85 Sup. Ct. 348 (1964) (concurring opinion).

[70] Katzenbach v. McClung, 379 U.S. 294, 298, 13 L. Ed. 2d 290, 85 Sup. Ct. 377 (1964) (concurring opinion in *Atlanta Motel* also applies to *Katzenbach v. McClung*).

[71] Baker v. Carr, 369 U.S. 186, 7 L. Ed. 2d 663, 82 Sup. Ct. 691 (1962).

[72] Colegrove v. Green, 328 U.S. 549, 90 L. Ed. 1432, 66 Sup. Ct. 1198 (1946).

[73] Reynolds v. Sims, 377 U.S. 533, 568, 12 L. Ed. 2d 506, 84 Sup. Ct. 1362 (1964).

[74] Colegrove v. Green, 328 U.S. 549, 566, 90 L. Ed. 1432, 66 Sup. Ct. 1198 (1946).

[75] Kelly, *Clio and the Court: An Illicit Love Affair,* in THE SUPREME COURT REVIEW 119, 135 (Kurland ed. 1965).

76 United States v. Philadelphia Nat'l Bank, 374 U.S. 321, 10 L. Ed. 2d 915, 83 Sup. Ct. 1715 (1963); United States v. First Nat'l Bank, 376 U.S. 665, 12 L. Ed. 2d 1, 84 Sup. Ct. 1033 (1964). The period of this intensification was apparently quite brief, if numbers of cases filed are proper indication. After climbing to a new peak in 1962, the number dropped back to earlier levels and even lower. See Wallace Kirkpatrick's table in note 16 to Chapter Seven, pp. 314, 315.

77 United States v. Von's Grocery Co., 384 U.S. 270, 86 Sup. Ct. 1480 (1966).

78 *Id.* at 274.

CHAPTER TWO

The New Court and the New Deal

————*John P. Frank*————

[1] Havighurst, *Mr. Justice Black,* 1 NATIONAL LAW. GUILD Q. 181 (1938).

[2] Weissman, *Mr. Justice Black at 70: The Man and His World,* 16 LAW. GUILD REV. 101 (1956).

[3] Gordon, *Justice Hugo Black: First Amendment Fundamentalist,* 20 LAW. GUILD REV. 1 (1960). This interest in the Justice as a civil libertarian is reflected endlessly. For example, Irving Dilliard's useful volume, ONE MAN'S STAND FOR FREEDOM: MR. JUSTICE BLACK AND THE BILL OF RIGHTS (1963), gives this focus in its title. Dilliard continues to emphasize this aspect of Black in Chapter Four of this volume. The leading analytical work on Black's jurisprudence, Reich, *Mr. Justice Black and the Living Constitution,* 76 HARV. L. REV. 673 (1963), covers all fields. However, in the section in which Professor Reich "explores" Black's "philosophy" (included in this volume as Chapter Five), every case cited is in the civil liberties area.

[4] Black, *Reminiscences,* 18 ALA. L. REV. 3, 8 (1965).

[5] I have given illustrations in my MR. JUSTICE BLACK, ch. 2 (1949); see also pp. 55-56.

[6] Johnson v. Zerbst, 304 U.S. 458, 82 L. Ed. 1461, 58 Sup. Ct. 1019 (1938); Chambers v. Florida, 309 U.S. 227, 84 L. Ed. 716, 60 Sup. Ct. 472 (1940); and the dissent in Betts v. Brady, 316 U.S. 455, 86 L. Ed. 1595, 62 Sup. Ct. 1252 (1942), a dissent which finally became the law almost twenty-five years later in Gideon v. Wainwright, 372 U.S. 335, 9 L. Ed. 2d 799, 83 Sup. Ct. 792 (1963). Dilliard, *op. cit. supra* note 3, quotes ten opinions in his collection of Black's civil rights work from the first six years; on the other hand, he had fourteen opinions from the last two years in his collection, 1961 to 1962.

[7] Philadelphia Record, Aug. 13, 1937, reprinted 81 CONG. REC. (App.) 2090-91 (1937).

[8] BROGAN, THE ERA OF FRANKLIN D. ROOSEVELT 360 (1950).

[9] SCHLESINGER, THE CRISIS OF THE OLD ORDER 425 (1957), gives the excerpt from the Commonwealth Club speech used here and comments on it.

[10] The list is taken from MORISON, THE OXFORD HISTORY OF THE AMERICAN PEOPLE 954 (1965).

[11] For an account of Black's role in the New Deal, see J. P. FRANK, *op. cit. supra* note 5, at ch. 4. One element of the early New Deal was wholly unacceptable to Black. Arthur Schlesinger, Jr. summarizes it:

The tenets of the First New Deal were that the technological
revolution had rendered bigness inevitable; that competition
could no longer be relied on to protect social interests; that
large units were an opportunity to be seized rather than a
danger to be fought; and that the formula for stability in the
new society must be combination and cooperation under enlarged
federal authority.

SCHLESINGER, THE COMING OF THE NEW DEAL 179 (1959). Black had
no problem in accepting the federal authority, but the theory that "competition could no longer be relied on to protect social interests" was the
one major element of the New Deal which was in total conflict with
earlier Populist-Progressive theory. The principal manifestation of this
attitude in the first Roosevelt administration was the National Industrial
Recovery Act, a system of business "codes" which Black voted against.

12 For discussion of the rise of the opposition, see SCHLESINGER,
op. cit. supra note 11, § VII.

13 Never, however, in a personal way. Black had been sized up by
his law school classmates in 1905 as one who would "use the devil himself with courtesy," Black, supra note 4, at 8. Black hit his share of hard
blows, particularly in the 1936 campaign, but always impersonally. A
striking feature of the 1937 confirmation controversy is the evident regard
of his fellow Senators for Black's courtesy in his dealings with them.
As I said in another place, "few spirits are so little rusted with rancor."
J. P. Frank, Mr. Justice Black: A Biographical Appreciation, 65 YALE L.J.
454, 462 (1956).

14 Beard, Introduction to J. P. FRANK, MR. JUSTICE BLACK, op. cit.
supra note 5, at viii.

15 United States v. Butler, 297 U.S. 1, 62, 80 L. Ed. 477, 56 Sup. Ct.
312 (1936).

16 81 CONG. REC. 2828 (1937).

17 Radio Address, Feb. 23, 1937, reprinted 81 CONG. REC. (App.) 306
(1937).

18 Id. at 307. The President's initial argument had been that judicial
efficiency required younger Justices, an argument which given the Court
of the period was so unpersuasive that the President largely abandoned
it. So far as judicial efficiency was concerned, Black was also dissatisfied
because he thought that the Court had proved itself unable to deal with
the personal injury cases which came before it. As an old tort lawyer,
just dealings with injured employees seemed to him as important as great
constitutional questions. When the friends of the Court said that it was
disposing of all "important" cases, Black strenuously disagreed; it was
not disposing of cases of injured railroad workers or seamen. In March
1937, he and three other Senators discussed in detail a particular injury
case which had arisen from California the same year before in which the
Court had denied certiorari. Five years later, it took a similar case and
reached a result opposite to that of the California Court five years earlier.
Meanwhile the California courts had treated the denial of the certiorari
as an adjudication of the legal point involved. So far as Black was
concerned, the argument that the denial of certiorari had not decided the
particular point, but merely left the law as it found it, was so much
flapdoodle; the bald fact remained that for five years persons in the
position of that employee in California had had no coverage. "It may

be true," he said, "that the case was not of great constitutional importance to all the people of the nation. It was a case of great importance to the individuals who lived in the State of California, and who were injured while in the employment of their masters." He argued that the employee injury cases with precedent value should have "the status of importance essential even under their own rules." To deal with all these cases, he thought that more Justices were needed. 81 CONG. REC. 2828-29 (1937). Black also gave other illustrations of his contention that the Court had too much to do; see *id.* at 2830, one example being that the court had not yet decided the validity of the Tennessee Valley Authority.

The employee injury cases did become "important" after Black went to the Court and in no area of the law has his personal influence been as strong as in the rejuvenation of the trial jury and in the development of new rules concerning employee injuries. See Leon Green, *Jury Trial and Mr. Justice Black,* 65 YALE L.J. 482 (1956). Leading Black opinions on employee injuries are Galloway v. United States, 319 U.S. 372, 396, 87 L. Ed. 1458, 63 Sup. Ct. 1077 (1943), a comprehensive dissent on jury trial, most of the practical principles of which are now largely accepted in practice; and Tiller v. Atlantic Coastline R.R., 318 U.S. 54, 87 L. Ed. 610, 63 Sup. Ct. 444, 143 A.L.R. 967 (1943), an opinion holding that Black's favorite *bête noir* of practice days, the doctrine of assumption of risk, had been totally obliterated in the railroad field by the Federal Employers' Liability Act.

19 81 CONG. REC. 2833 (1937).

20 81 CONG. REC. (App.) 307 (1937).

21 81 CONG. REC. (App.) 638 (1937).

22 *Id.* at 307.

23 *Ibid.*

24 J. P. FRANK, *op. cit. supra* note 5, at 65.

25 *Id.* at 93.

26 West Coast Hotel Co. v. Parrish, 300 U.S. 379, 81 L. Ed. 703, 57 Sup. Ct. 578 (1937) (minimum wages); NLRB v. Jones & Laughlin Steel Corp., 301 U.S. 1, 81 L. Ed. 893, 57 Sup. Ct. 615, 108 A.L.R. 1352 (1937) (National Labor Relations Act).

27 Meador, *Justice Black and His Law Clerks,* 15 ALA. L. REV. 57 (1962); and for a description of his method in the earlier years, see J. P. FRANK, *op. cit. supra* note 5, at 135-36. A "poem" enjoyed with some hilarity at a recent Black law clerk's affair was universally accepted as an accurate allusion to the clerk's place in the order of things. This literary work, written by someone with intimate knowledge of the process, in one quatrain describes the clerk's satisfaction when he gets a word in:

> The colons and the commas and
> The adjectives are right,
> And the sentence YOU inserted
> Stays in there nice and tight.

28 See material cited Barnett, *infra* note 44, at 21, n.2; for the most patronizing of the early attacks, see Marquis Childs, *The Supreme Court Today,* 176 HARPER'S MAGAZINE 581 (May 1938).

29 See note 6 *supra,* and accompanying text. Two of Black's more noteworthy errors, errors of plain inexperience or of insufficient oppor-

tunity in earlier life to study the subject matter, were in two civil rights cases. In the first flag salute case, he joined in the opinion of Justice Frankfurter, upholding the validity of the flag salute requirement, a conclusion on which he swiftly confessed error and reversed himself. See Minersville School Dist. v. Gobitis, 310 U.S. 586, 84 L. Ed. 1375, 60 Sup. Ct. 1010, 127 A.L.R. 1493 (1940) and the expression of opposite view of Jones v. Opelika, 316 U.S. 584, 86 L. Ed. 1691, 62 Sup. Ct. 1231, 141 A.L.R. 514 (1942), culminating in West Virginia State Bd. of Educ. v. Barnette, 319 U.S. 624, 87 L. Ed. 1628, 63 Sup. Ct. 1178, 147 A.L.R. 674 (1943). But the flag salute case involved only the application of an accepted principle to a particular fact situation; it involved no fundamental theory of the Constitution. A greater error of the early years was Black's joinder in Justice Cardozo's opinion in Palko v. Connecticut, 302 U.S. 319, 82 L. Ed. 288, 58 Sup. Ct. 149 (1937), in which Justice Cardozo laid down his theory of selective incorporation of the Bill of Rights into the Fourteenth Amendment. This theory of selective incorporation is in the teeth of Black's later, full-scale position that the entirety of the Bill of Rights is subsumed into the Fourteenth Amendment, one of the most important articles of the Justice's credo. For Black's comprehensive development of this position, see Adamson v. California, 332 U.S. 46, 91 L. Ed. 1903, 67 Sup. Ct. 1672, 171 A.L.R. 1223 (1947) (dissenting opinion). The Justice's *Adamson* statement, ten years after *Palko*, was the product of at least two years of very substantial work and thought, and *Palko* can only be regarded as a major matter on which the Justice had not yet studied the subject thoroughly enough to have made up his mind.

30 Baldwin v. Missouri, 281 U.S. 586, 595, 74 L. Ed. 1056, 50 Sup. Ct. 436, 72 A.L.R. 1303 (1930). For illustration of an instance in which Holmes found a violation of due process, see Pennsylvania Coal Co. v. Mahon, 260 U.S. 393, 67 L. Ed. 322, 43 Sup. Ct. 158, 28 A.L.R. 1321 (1923).

31 See for example, his speech of February 23, 1937, 81 CONG. REC. (App.) 306 (1937).

32 See note 21 *supra,* and accompanying text.

33 Connecticut Gen. Life Ins. Co. v. Johnson, 303 U.S. 77, 87, 82 L. Ed. 673, 58 Sup. Ct. 436 (1938).

34 Stone v. Farmers' Loan & Trust Co., 116 U.S. 307, 29 L. Ed. 636, 6 Sup. Ct. 334, 388, 1191 (1886).

35 Federal Power Comm'n v. Natural Gas Pipeline Co., 315 U.S. 575, 599, 600, 86 L. Ed. 1037, 62 Sup. Ct. 736 (1942); and for further development, see Justice Douglas's opinion of the Court in Federal Power Comm'n v. Hope Natural Gas Co., 320 U.S. 591, 88 L. Ed. 333, 64 Sup. Ct. 281 (1944). Perhaps the most colorful opinion of Black's first year was a lone dissent in McCart v. Indianapolis Water Co., 302 U.S. 419, 423, 82 L. Ed. 336, 58 Sup. Ct. 324 (1938). At issue was the so-called "reproduction new" method of calculating utility rates. The ultimate question was the proper rate structure for the water company in Indianapolis. This matter had been in litigation seven years by the time the Court wrote, and a majority sent it back for further proceedings. In *McCart,* Black, as a lone Justice, criticized any judicial participation in rate making (302 U.S. at 427-28), thus becoming the first voice on the Court since 1890 to attack the entire conception. But assuming there was to be judicial review, no one had laid such impious hands on the theory of valuation before. He analyzed

and demonstrated the "phantom concepts of property" and made the entire reproduction cost theory of valuation look preposterous. A devastating passage, analyzing a cost element attributed to possible, but wholly hypothetical claims of persons who would lose sailing rights as a result of the utilities operation, led to Black's conclusion of "an imaginary damage to these imaginary sailors" (302 U.S. 433). This was Black's first major dissent, and it attracted more general attention than any other opinion of his first year except the corporations and Fourteenth Amendment opinion, *supra* note 33. The doctrine of the *McCart* dissent is the law today. As for the practical result, it is my undocumented understanding that the Company took a voluntary reduction.

36 The subject has largely dropped out of the legal literature. For illustration, the leading authority, JAMES DANBRIGHT, in his PRINCIPLES OF PUBLIC UTILITY RATES (1961) has little or nothing on constitutional aspects.

37 305 U.S. 5, 83 L. Ed. 6, 59 Sup. Ct. 40 (1938).

38 Black quoted Powell v. Pennsylvania, 127 U.S. 678, 686, 32 L. Ed. 253, 8 Sup. Ct. 992, 1257 (1888):

> If all that can be said of this legislation is that it is unwise, or unnecessarily oppressive to those manufacturing or selling wholesome oleomargarine as an article of food, their appeal must be to the Legislature, or to the ballot box, not to the judiciary. The latter cannot interfere without usurping powers committed to another department of government.

39 See notably, Olsen v. Nebraska, 313 U.S. 236, 85 L. Ed. 1305, 61 Sup. Ct. 862, 133 A.L.R. 1500 (1941), a far-reaching opinion by Justice Douglas overruling Ribnik v. McBride, 277 U.S. 350, 72 L. Ed. 913, 48 Sup. Ct. 545, 56 A.L.R. 1327 (1928), a leading due process case which had held that a state might not regulate the compensation of employment agencies.

40 Lincoln Fed. Labor Union v. Northwestern Iron & Metal Co., 335 U.S. 525, 93 L. Ed. 212, 69 Sup. Ct. 251, 6 A.L.R.2d 473 (1949); Ferguson v. Skrupa, 372 U.S. 726, 10 L. Ed. 2d 93, 83 Sup. Ct. 1028, 95 A.L.R.2d 1347 (1963).

41 Quoted in a useful, concise note, LOCKHART, KAMISAR & CHOPER, CONSTITUTIONAL LAW (Casebook) 611 (1964).

42 381 U.S. 479, 14 L. Ed. 2d 510, 85 Sup. Ct. 1678 (1965), the Douglas opinion appearing at 480 for the Court; the Goldberg concurrence, which the Chief Justice and Justice Brennan joined at 486; the Harlan concurrence at 499; the White concurrence at 502; the Black dissent at 507; and the Stewart dissent at 527.

43 ERIKSSON, *New Deal,* in DICTIONARY OF AMERICAN HISTORY 95-96 (Adams ed. 1940).

44 Barnett, *Mr. Justice Black and the Supreme Court,* 8 U. CHI. L. REV. 20 (1940). This excellent article, valuable both for information and for insight, is the most indispensable writing on Black for the early Court years. Carl Swisher cites the dissents in the 1937-38 term for all types of cases in Chapter One of this volume on page 8.

45 Carter v. Carter Coal Co., 298 U.S. 238, 80 L. Ed. 1160, 56 Sup. Ct. 855 (1936); Schechter Poultry Corp. v. United States, 295 U.S. 495, 79 L. Ed. 1570, 55 Sup. Ct. 837, 97 A.L.R. 947 (1937); United States v. Butler, 297 U.S. 1, 62, 80 L. Ed. 477, 56 Sup. Ct. 312 (1937). The leading work on the development narrated in the text above is Stern, *The Commerce Clause and the National Economy, 1933-46,* 59 HARV. L. REV. 645 (1946); SELECTED ESSAYS ON CONSTITUTIONAL LAW 218 (1963).

46 NLRB v. Jones & Laughlin Steel Corp., 301 U.S. 1, 81 L. Ed. 893, 57 Sup. Ct. 615, 108 A.L.R. 1352 (1937) (National Labor Relations Act).

47 Wickard v. Filburn, 317 U.S. 111, 87 L. Ed. 122, 63 Sup. Ct. 82 (1942).

48 United States v. Southeastern Underwriters Ass'n, 322 U.S. 533, 88 L. Ed. 1440, 64 Sup. Ct. 1162 (1944). The opinion discarded the contrary decision of long standing, Paul v. Virginia, 75 U.S. (8 Wall.) 168, 19 L. Ed. 357 (1869).

49 The McCarran Act, 59 Stat. 33 (1945), 15 U.S.C. §§ 1011-15 [F.C.A. 15 §§ 1011-15].

50 I follow here the argument of Mr. Stern on the scope of the phrase "interstate commerce," 41 A.B.A.J. 823 (1955), SELECTED ESSAYS ON CONSTITUTIONAL LAW 298 (1963), though with some misgivings. It is true that the contemporary rule on the Commerce Clause is within the very broad language of Marshall in Gibbons v. Ogden, 22 U.S. (9 Wheat.) 1, 6 L. Ed. 23 (1824), but the entire concept of the use of the power in the mid-20th century is so utterly alien to anything Marshall could have conceived of that the analogy may be more verbal than real. On the other hand, for illustration of the effect of *Gibbons v. Ogden* on Black's thinking as a Senator, see text accompanying note 60.

51 The vote was 56 to 28; 81 CONG. REC. 7957 (1937), but many amendments were much closer.

52 Pearson and Allen, nationally syndicated column, Aug. 16, 1937, said of the Act: "[T]hat it emerged from the committee and later passed the Senate was due largely to his parliamentary skill and dogged perseverance. The feat is one of the outstanding personal triumphs of the session." The debate also reflects Black's tendency to use historical materials to buttress his arguments. He spoke to the Senate of the English experience in 1833 and 1845 including an eloquent quotation from Charles Dickens; as he made his concluding remarks a few moments before passage of the bill, he had in his hand a hundred year old "Speech of Mr. Noodle," a satire on legislators who "were usually for the principle, they were for the objective, but they were against the method. They were for the principle and for the objective, but they wanted to have a commission appointed. They told their constituents that they were for the principle and for the objective." 81 CONG. REC. 7945-46 (1937). The "Noodle" text by Sidney Smith, reprinted 27 HARV. CLASSICS 236, is still a Black favorite and was within his ready reach in 1966.

53 247 U.S. 251, 62 L. Ed. 1101, 38 Sup. Ct. 529, Ann. Cas. 1918E, 724, 3 A.L.R. 649 (1918).

54 The Shreveport Rate Case, 234 U.S. 342, 58 L. Ed. 1341, 34 Sup. Ct. 833 (1914).

55 81 CONG. REC. 7648 (1937).

56 See as illustrative of this discussion the statements of Senator Johnson and Senator Wheeler, *id.,* 7663-67. The chief reliance of these Senators for authority to circumvent *Hammer v. Dagenhart* was the prison labor case, Kentucky Whip & Collar Co. v. Illinois Cent. R.R., 299 U.S. 334, 81 L. Ed. 270, 57 Sup. Ct. 277 (1937).

57 79 Cong. Rec. 9045 (1935).

58 J. P. Frank, Mr. Justice Black 81 (1949).

59 Schechter Poultry Corp. v. United States, 295 U.S. 495, 79 L. Ed. 1570, 55 Sup. Ct. 837, 97 A.L.R. 947 (1935).

60 79 Cong. Rec. 8627-28 (1935).

61 *Id.* at 8628.

62 *Ibid.*

63 79 Cong. Rec. 8629 (1935).

64 *Ibid.*

65 The quotations are taken and put together from 79 Cong. Rec. 8627-29 (1935).

66 North American Co. v. SEC, 327 U.S. 686, 705-06, 90 L. Ed. 945, 66 Sup. Ct. 785 (1946).

67 The authority most heavily relied upon by Senator Hastings in his attack on the Public Utility Holding Company Act was *Paul v. Virginia,* holding that insurance was not commerce and not subject to regulation, 79 Cong. Rec. 8671 (1935). For discussion of the Black opinion overruling the *Paul* case, see note 48 *supra,* and accompanying text.

68 Barnett, *supra* note 44, at 34.

69 309 U.S. 206, 226, 84 L. Ed. 704, 60 Sup. Ct. 493 (1940).

70 *Id.* at 226.

71 Barnett, *supra* note 44, at 40.

72 Federal Trade Comm'n v. Standard Educ. Soc'y, 302 U.S. 112, 82 L. Ed. 141, 58 Sup. Ct. 113 (1937). For a detailed discussion of Black's antitrust approach, and an analysis of many of his opinions, see Chapter Seven of this volume by Wallace Kirkpatrick.

73 Federal Trade Comm'n v. Standard Educ. Soc'y, *supra* note 72, at 116.

74 *Ibid.*

75 See, *e.g.,* Associated Press v. United States, 326 U.S. 1, 89 L. Ed. 2013, 65 Sup. Ct. 1416 (1945).

76 See for illustrations of full perception of the monopolistic consequences of patents Crown Cork & Seal Co. v. Ferdinand Gutmann Co., 304 U.S. 159, 82 L. Ed. 1265, 58 Sup. Ct. 842 (1938) (dissenting opinion); General Talking Pictures Co. v. Western Elec. Co., 304 U.S. 175, 82 L. Ed. 1273, 58 Sup. Ct. 849 (1938) (dissenting opinion).

77 Goodyear Tire & Rubber Co. v. Ray-O-Vac Co., 321 U.S. 275, 279-80, 88 L. Ed. 721, 64 Sup. Ct. 593 (1945). I have written a little about the war between the Supreme Court and the Patent Office in J. P. Frank, Marble Palace: The Supreme Court in American Life 24-27 (1958). As was there developed, this appears to be a battle which the Supreme Court cannot win. The Patent Office can grind out patents faster than the Supreme Court can do anything about them. However, the Court keeps trying; for the most recent effort to state a rule under which "obvious" advances would not be patentable, see Graham v. John Deere Co., 86 Sup. Ct. 684 (1966).

78 72 Cong. Rec. 1239-40 (1930).

79 *Id.* at 1241.

80 *Ibid.*

81 64 Stat. 1125 (1950), 15 U.S.C. § 18 [F.C.A. 15 § 18] (1952), amending 38 Stat. 731 (1914).

82 United States v. Von's Grocery Co., 384 U.S. 270, 16 L. Ed. 2d 555, 86 Sup. Ct. 1478 (1966). Mr. Justice Brennan, who was acquainted with the Black 1930 speech, sent Black a note at the time the grocery case was pending saying, "Hugo, you should sue Estes Kefauver's estate and Manny Celler for plagiarism; they certainly put your idea into Section 7."

83 315 U.S. 289, 86 L. Ed. 855, 62 Sup. Ct. 581 (1942).

84 Although Black grew up on the heels of the Populist era and clearly inherits many Populist ideas, this is not to suggest that he was ever associated with the Populist Party. Indeed, it had largely disappeared while he was still a boy. A recent southern visit produced an old-timer who recalled Black, even before he could speak clearly, as saying "I am a Democat," and he certainly was. As a boy, he did set type for local printers which included services as typesetter for the *Peoples Party Advocate.*

85 Youngstown Sheet & Tube Co. v. Sawyer, 343 U.S. 579, 589, 96 L. Ed. 1153, 72 Sup. Ct. 863, 26 A.L.R.2d 1378 (1952).

86 NLRB v. Fansteel Metal Co., 306 U.S. 240, 267, 83 L. Ed. 627, 59 Sup. Ct. 490, 123 A.L.R. 599 (1939).

87 United States v. UMW, 330 U.S. 258, 330-31, 91 L. Ed. 884, 67 Sup. Ct. 677 (1947).

88 Giboney v. Empire Storage & Ice Co., 336 U.S. 490, 502-04, 93 L. Ed. 834, 69 Sup. Ct. 684 (1949); United States v. UMW, *supra* note 87, at 334.

89 In a dissenting opinion in Carpenters & Joiners Union, Local 213 v. Ritter's Cafe, 315 U.S. 722, 729, 731, 86 L. Ed. 1143, 62 Sup. Ct. 807 (1942), Justice Black emphasized equally the power of the state "to regulate the use of its streets or the conduct of those rightfully upon them" in the interest of law and the right of "using the streets to convey information to the public." See similarly the concurrence of Justice Douglas in which Justice Black joined in Bakery & Pastry Drivers, Local 802 v. Wohl, 315 U.S. 769, 775, 776-77, 86 L. Ed. 1178, 62 Sup. Ct. 816 (1942).

90 Giboney v. Empire Storage & Ice Co., 336 U.S. 490, 502-04, 93 L. Ed. 834, 69 Sup. Ct. 684 (1949).

91 Cahn, *Justice Black and First Amendment "Absolutes": A Public Interview,* 37 N.Y.U.L. REV. 549, 558 (1962).

92 Brown v. Louisiana, 86 Sup. Ct. 719, at 729, 736-37 (1966).

93 This raises, of course, and does not answer the question of when the judge "merely" fills in and when he "legislates"; when he finds policy and when he makes it. Certainly Black has taken a broad policy approach to many questions; as I said in MR. JUSTICE BLACK at 139, "His significance as a Justice is that he knows what to do with the power thus given him." Each Justice will have his own outer limit in cutting a new direction. Recent illustrations of a Black broad view are his position that the First Amendment extends to obscenity, see, *e.g.,* Ginzburg v. United States, 383 U.S. 463, 16 L. Ed. 2d 31, 86 Sup. Ct. 942, 950 (1966), (dissenting opinion); or that the equal protection clause bars malapportioned Congressional districts, Wesberry v. Sanders, 376 U.S. 1, 11 L. Ed. 2d 481, 84 Sup. Ct. 526 (1964). For illustration of a narrower approach, see his conclusion that the

equal protection clause does not, at least without an act of Congress, bar a poll tax as a condition of voting, Harper v. Virginia State Bd. of Elections, 86 Sup. Ct. 1079, 1083 (1966); or Kotch v. Board of River Pilot Comm'rs, 330 U.S. 552, 91 L. Ed. 1093, 67 Sup. Ct. 910 (1947), holding valid a Louisiana system of restrictive entry into the harbor pilotage trade to members of a pilot's family, perhaps as hard a bit of deference to legislation as the Justice ever had to pay.

94 Mills v. Alabama, 86 Sup. Ct. 1434, 1437 (1966).

95 The Birmingham meeting is briefly reported on the editorial page of the Birmingham News, July 17, 1966, and the event has been elaborated for me privately by a member of the audience.

CHAPTER THREE

The Persistent Race Issue

——*Daniel Berman*——

[1] As one Southerner has put it:

> The devastation of the [Civil] War and the freeing of the slaves wiped out much of the relatively short distance the South had gone from the frontier, and lack of capital for business and industrial development tended to preserve its characteristics as a frontier for a long time. . . . The very lawlessness of the frontier tends to generate a respect for law. Its equalitarianism creates a demand that law be equally applied to all. . . . More important, the frontier is not hospitable to the "Organization Man." It is a society of individualists.

Durr, *Hugo Black, Southerner: The Southern Background,* 10 AM. U.L. REV. 32 (1961).

[2] J. P. FRANK, MR. JUSTICE BLACK: THE MAN AND HIS OPINIONS 18 (1949).

[3] Scholastic, Sept. 18, 1937, p. 14.

[4] FRANK, *op. cit. supra* note 2, at 22.

[5] Birmingham Age-Herald, Sept. 18, 1915, p. 5, cols. 3 & 4.

[6] FRANK, *op. cit. supra* note 2, at 27-30.

[7] The text of the speech appeared in the Pittsburgh Post-Gazette, Sept. 15, 1937, p. 2, col. 2.

[8] New York Times, Sept. 13, 1937, p. 3, col. 1.

[9] *Id.,* Nov. 26, 1926, p. 15, col. 3.

[10] He was Chancellor of Alabama's Knights of Pythias, an officer of a Masonic lodge, and a member of Civitan, Odd Fellows, Moose, Pretorians, and the American Legion.

[11] As one analyst put it, the Klan "combined a spurious radicalism with terrorism. Those who leaned toward the first were often able to shut their eyes to the second." Max Lerner, The Nation, Oct. 9, 1937, p. 367.

[12] The New York Times reported, on July 4, 1923, p. 1, col. 2, a parade of 1,000 Klansmen through Tuskegee in silent protest against the hiring of Negro personnel at the local Negro War Veterans' Hospital, and on April 11, 1925, p. 9, col. 1, the flogging of a hotel clerk who had talked about the Klan.

[13] Alabama was scarcely mentioned in the investigation of the Klan conducted in 1921 by a congressional committee. HOUSE COMM. ON RULES, 67TH CONG., 1ST SESS., THE KU KLUX KLAN (1921). The New York

World, which published a twenty-one part exposé of the Klan in 1921, seems not to have had much evidence against the Alabama organization. The series in the World began on Sept. 8, 1921, and concluded on Sept. 26, 1921.

[14] New York Times, Aug. 12, 1926, p. 1, col. 5.

[15] 79 CONG. REC. 6521 (1935).

[16] 69 CONG. REC. 8815 (1928).

[17] New Republic, Sept. 29, 1937, p. 200.

[18] Pittsburgh Post-Gazette, Sept. 13, 1937, p. 1, col. 7.

[19] Ibid.

[20] FRANK, op. cit. supra note 2, at 105.

[21] New York Times, Oct. 2, 1937, p. 3, col. 2.

[22] Id. at p. 1, col. 6.

[23] Oct. 2, 1937, p. 20, col. 1.

[24] The Digest (Review of Reviews), Oct. 16, 1937, p. 7.

[25] Oct. 2, 1937, p. 20, col. 2.

[26] Oct. 2, 1937, p. 14, col. 2.

[27] Oct. issue, 1937, pp. 229-33.

[28] Oct. 3, 1937, p. B-8, col. 2.

[29] Newsweek, Aug. 21, 1937, p. 40.

[30] New York Times, Sept. 17, 1937, p. 1, col. 8. Copeland, however, lost the Republican nomination to Fiorello LaGuardia and the Democratic nomination to Jeremiah T. Mahoney.

[31] Letter to Nation, Oct. 9, 1937, p. 387.

[32] Pittsburgh Post-Gazette, Oct. 2, 1937, p. 2, col. 7.

[33] Letter to Hazel Black Davis, Oct. 17, 1937, published in DAVIS, UNCLE HUGO: AN INTIMATE PORTRAIT OF MR. JUSTICE BLACK 31-32 (1965) (privately printed).

[34] Ibid. Even today he asserts, only half-jokingly, that the only organization he regrets joining is the American Bar Association.

[35] New York Times, Oct. 2, 1937, p. 3, col. 5.

[36] Chambers v. Florida, 309 U.S. 227, 235, 84 L. Ed. 716, 60 Sup. Ct. 472 (1940).

[37] Id. at 238-39.

[38] Id. at 236.

[39] New York Times, Feb. 14, 1940, p. 14, col. 4.

[40] See, for example, Eubanks v. Louisiana, 356 U.S. 584, 2 L. Ed. 2d 991, 78 Sup. Ct. 970 (1958); Reece v. Georgia, 350 U.S. 85, 100 L. Ed. 77, 76 Sup. Ct. 167 (1955); Brown v. Allen, 344 U.S. 443, 97 L. Ed. 469, 73 Sup. Ct. 397, 437 (1953) (dissenting opinion); Patton v. Mississippi, 332 U.S. 463, 92 L. Ed. 76, 68 Sup. Ct. 184, 1 A.L.R. 1286 (1947); Smith v. Texas, 311 U.S. 128, 85 L. Ed. 84, 61 Sup. Ct. 164 (1940); Pierre v. Louisiana, 306 U.S. 354, 83 L. Ed. 757, 59 Sup. Ct. 536 (1939).

[41] Morgan v. Virginia, 328 U.S. 373, 386, 90 L. Ed. 1317, 66 Sup. Ct. 1050, 165 A.L.R. 574 (1946) (concurring opinion); Mitchell v. United States, 313 U.S. 80, 85 L. Ed. 1201, 61 Sup. Ct. 873 (1941); Henderson v. United States, 339 U.S. 816, 94 L. Ed. 1302, 70 Sup. Ct. 843 (1950).

[42] See, for example, Terry v. Adams, 345 U.S. 461, 97 L. Ed. 1152, 73 Sup. Ct. 809 (1953).

[43] Missouri ex rel. Gaines v. Canada, 305 U.S. 337, 83 L. Ed. 208, 59 Sup. Ct. 232 (1938).

44 Sipuel v. Board of Regents, 332 U.S. 631, 92 L. Ed. 247, 68 Sup. Ct. 299 (1948).

45 Sweatt v. Painter, 339 U.S. 629, 94 L. Ed. 1114, 70 Sup. Ct. 848 (1950).

46 McLaurin v. Oklahoma State Regents, 339 U.S. 637, 94 L. Ed. 1149, 70 Sup. Ct. 851 (1950).

47 Plessy v. Ferguson, 163 U.S. 537, 41 L. Ed. 256, 16 Sup. Ct. 1138 (1896).

48 Brown v. Board of Educ., 347 U.S. 483, 98 L. Ed. 873, 74 Sup. Ct. 686, 38 A.L.R.2d 1180 (1954).

49 Ibid.

50 Letter to the Editor, Birmingham News, June 12, 1954, p. 4, col. 6.

51 Reprinted in the Mobile Press, June 4, 1954.

52 Montgomery Advertiser, May 28, 1954, p. 1, col. 8. The Advertiser registered its own displeasure with Black in sometimes oblique ways. In an editorial attack on Alabama's senior Senator, Lister Hill, on May 19, 1954, the newspaper indicted him on a number of counts including the fact that "Justice Hugo Black is one of his most intimate friends."

53 Bell v. Maryland, 378 U.S. 226, 12 L. Ed. 2d 822, 84 Sup. Ct. 1814 (1964).

54 Id. at 327-28 (dissenting opinion).

55 Id. at 338, 343.

56 Id. at 345 (dissenting opinion).

57 78 Stat. 241, 42 U.S.C. §§ 2000A–2000A-6 [F.C.A. 42 §§ 2000A–2000A-6].

58 Hamm v. City of Rock Hill, 379 U.S. 306, 318-19, 13 L. Ed. 2d 300, 85 Sup. Ct. 384 (1964) (dissenting opinion).

59 Id. at 321.

60 Atlanta Motel v. United States, 379 U.S. 241, 278-79, 13 L. Ed. 2d 258, 85 Sup. Ct. 348 (1964) (concurring opinion); the concurrence, beginning at 268, also applied to Katzenbach v. McClung, 379 U.S. 294, 13 L. Ed. 2d 290, 85 Sup. Ct. 377 (1964).

61 79 Stat. 437, 42 U.S.C. § 2000f [F.C.A. 42 § 200f].

62 South Carolina v. Katzenbach, 383 U.S. 301, 358-59, 15 L. Ed. 2d 769, 86 Sup. Ct. 810 (1966) (concurring in part and dissenting in part).

63 Harper v. Virginia Bd. of Elections, 383 U.S. 663, 666, 16 L. Ed. 2d 169, 86 Sup. Ct. 1079 (1966).

64 The Amendment was interpreted by the Supreme Court in Harman v. Forssenius, 380 U.S. 528, 14 L. Ed. 2d 50, 85 Sup. Ct. 1177 (1965).

65 Id. at 670-80 (dissenting opinion).

66 NAACP v. Overstreet, 384 U.S. 118, 16 L. Ed. 2d 409, 86 Sup. Ct. 1306 (1966).

67 City of Greenwood v. Peacock, 384 U.S. 808, 16 L. Ed. 2d 944, 86 Sup. Ct. 1800 (1966). See also Georgia v. Rachel, 384 U.S. 780, 16 L. Ed. 2d 925, 86 Sup. Ct. 1783 (1966).

68 Brown v. Louisiana, 383 U.S. 131, 139, 15 L. Ed. 2d 637, 86 Sup. Ct. 719 (1966).

69 Id. at 167-68 (dissenting opinion).

70 Adderley v. Florida, 385 U.S. 39, 17 L. Ed. 2d 149, 87 Sup. Ct. — (1966).

71 Id. at 47.

72 *Id.* at 48.

73 *Id.* at 47-48.

74 *Id.* at 55 (dissenting opinion of Douglas, J.).

75 *Id.* at 56.

76 Washington Post, Nov. 15, 1966, p. 1, col. 8.

77 *Ibid.*

78 Newsweek, Nov. 28, 1966, p. 30, col. 1.

79 St. Louis Globe-Democrat, Nov. 14, 1966, p. 9-A, col. 1.

80 See cases cited *supra* notes 53, 58, 60, 62, 65, 69; see also Shuttlesworth v. Birmingham, 382 U.S. 87, 15 L. Ed. 2d 176, 86 Sup. Ct. 211 (1965) (dissenting opinion); Cox v. Louisiana, 379 U.S. 536, 13 L. Ed. 2d 471, 85 Sup. Ct. 453 (1965) (concurring opinion); and Blow v. North Carolina, 379 U.S. 684, 686, 13 L. Ed. 2d 603, 85 Sup. Ct. 635 (1965) (dissenting opinion).

CHAPTER FOUR

The Individual and the Bill of Absolute Rights

————*Irving Dilliard*————

1 The total number may be counted in several ways. Excluding the elevation of sitting Associate Justices to the Chief Justiceship, ninety-eight appointments have been made by Presidents. But one appointee, Robert Harrison of Maryland, "resigned" without sitting; John Rutledge of South Carolina was appointed on two different occasions, though he was not confirmed by the Senate for the second appointment; Charles Evans Hughes served two separate terms, the latter as Chief Justice. Thus there have been only ninety-five individuals who have actually sat as Justices of the Court.

2 Compare John P. Frank, *The New Court and The New Deal,* Chapter Two in this volume, and Stephen Strickland, *Black On Balance,* Chapter Nine in this volume.

3 Bates v. Little Rock, 361 U.S. 516, 528, 4 L. Ed. 2d 480, 488, 80 Sup. Ct. 412 (1960) (concurring opinion of Black and Douglas, JJ.).

4 Speiser v. Randall, 357 U.S. 513, 531, 2 L. Ed. 2d 1460, 78 Sup. Ct. 1332, 1352 (1958) (concurring opinion).

5 Black, *The Bill of Rights,* reproduced in ONE MAN'S STAND FOR FREEDOM: MR. JUSTICE BLACK AND THE BILL OF RIGHTS 31-48 (Dilliard ed. 1963).

6 *Op. cit. supra* note 5, at 33.

7 See Chapter One, Carl B. Swisher, *"History's Panorama and Justice Black's Career,"* p. 8.

8 302 U.S. 419, 423, 82 L. Ed. 336, 58 Sup. Ct. 324 (1938) (dissenting opinion).

9 303 U.S. 77, 83, 82 L. Ed. 673, 58 Sup. Ct. 436 (1938) (dissenting opinion).

10 302 U.S. 112, 82 L. Ed. 141, 58 Sup. Ct. 113 (1937).

11 *Id.* at 116 (dissenting opinion).

12 304 U.S. 458, 82 L. Ed. 1461, 58 Sup. Ct. 1019 (1938).

13 372 U.S. 335, 9 L. Ed. 2d 799, 83 Sup. Ct. 792, 93 A.L.R.2d 733 (1963).

14 309 U.S. 227, 84 L. Ed. 716, 60 Sup. Ct. 472 (1940).

15 304 U.S. 458, 462-63, 82 L. Ed. 1461, 58 Sup. Ct. 1019 (1938).

16 Gideon v. Wainwright, 372 U.S. 335, 9 L. Ed. 2d 799, 83 Sup. Ct. 792, 93 A.L.R.2d 733 (1963).

17 309 U.S. 227, 84 L. Ed. 716, 60 Sup. Ct. 472 (1940).

18 316 U.S. 455, 86 L. Ed. 1595, 62 Sup. Ct. 1252 (1942).

19 *Id.* at 474-77 (dissenting opinion).

20 332 U.S. 134, 91 L. Ed. 1955, 67 Sup. Ct. 1716 (1947).

21 *Id.* at 139.

22 *Id.* at 140-41 (dissenting opinion).

23 367 U.S. 643, 6 L. Ed. 2d 575, 81 Sup. Ct. 1278 (1961). For one explanation of Black's Fourth Amendment posture, see Strickland, Chapter Nine, pp. 256-59.

24 338 U.S. 25, 39, 93 L. Ed. 1765, 69 Sup. Ct. 1434, 7 A.L.R.2d 1280 (1949) (concurring opinion).

25 339 U.S. 56, 66, 94 L. Ed. 653, 70 Sup. Ct. 430 (1950) (dissenting opinion).

26 342 U.S. 165, 174, 96 L. Ed. 183, 72 Sup. Ct. 205, 25 A.L.R.2d 1396 (1952) (concurring opinion).

27 347 U.S. 128, 139, 98 L. Ed. 561, 74 Sup. Ct. 381 (1954).

28 Rochin v. California, 342 U.S. 165, 174, 175, 96 L. Ed. 183, 72 Sup. Ct. 205, 25 A.L.R.2d 1396 (1952) (concurring opinion).

29 347 U.S. 128, 138, 139, 98 L. Ed. 561, 74 Sup. Ct. 381 (1954).

30 *Id.* at 142 (dissenting opinion).

31 *Ibid.*

32 Mapp v. Ohio, 367 U.S. 643, 670, 6 L. Ed. 2d 575, 81 Sup. Ct. 1278 (1961) (concurring opinion of Douglas, J.).

33 Boyd v. United States, 116 U.S. 616, 29 L. Ed. 746, 6 Sup. Ct. 524 (1886) (opinion of Bradley, J.).

34 Mapp v. Ohio, 367 U.S. 643, 661, 6 L. Ed. 2d 575, 81 Sup. Ct. 1278 (1961) (concurring opinion of Black, J.).

35 332 U.S. 46, 91 L. Ed. 1903, 67 Sup. Ct. 1672, 171 A.L.R. 1223 (1947).

36 *Id.* at 68.

37 312 U.S. 287, 299, 85 L. Ed. 836, 61 Sup. Ct. 552, 132 A.L.R. 1200 (1941) (dissenting opinion).

38 *Id.* at 302.

39 Dennis v. United States, 341 U.S. 494, 95 L. Ed. 1137, 71 Sup. Ct. 857 (1951).

40 *Id.* at 581 (dissenting opinion).

41 339 U.S. 382, 94 L. Ed. 925, 70 Sup. Ct. 674 (1950).

42 *Id.* at 448-53 (dissenting opinion).

43 Joint Anti-Fascist Refugee Comm. v. McGrath, 341 U.S. 123, 145-46, 95 L. Ed. 817, 71 Sup. Ct. 624 (1951) (concurring opinion).

44 342 U.S. 485, 96 L. Ed. 517, 72 Sup. Ct. 380, 27 A.L.R.2d 472 (1952). On January 23, 1967, the Court effectively, though not specifically, removed the *Adler* precedent by a five-to-four vote in Keyishian v. Board of Regents, — U.S. —, 17 L. Ed. 2d 629, 87 Sup. Ct. — (1967). Justice Brennan wrote the opinion of the Court, in which Justices Black, Douglas, Fortas and Chief Justice Warren joined.

45 *Id.* at 496-97 (dissenting opinion).

46 354 U.S. 298, 1 L. Ed. 2d 1356, 77 Sup. Ct. 1064 (1957).

47 *Id.* at 339 (concurring in part and dissenting in part).

48 *Id.* at 343-44.

49 360 U.S. 109, 3 L. Ed. 2d 1115, 79 Sup. Ct. 1081 (1959).

50 *Id.* at 160-62 (dissenting opinion).

51 328 U.S. 303, 90 L. Ed. 1252, 66 Sup. Ct. 1073 (1946).

52 384 U.S. 702, 16 L. Ed. 2d 870, 86 Sup. Ct. 1689 (1966).

53 *Id.* at 717 (concurring opinion). See also Yellin v. United States,

374 U.S. 109, 10 L. Ed. 2d 778, 83 Sup. Ct. 1828 (1963); Wheeldin v. Wheeler, 373 U.S. 647, 10 L. Ed. 2d 605, 83 Sup. Ct. 1441 (1963).

54 American Comm. for the Protection of the Foreign Born v. Subversive Activities Control Bd., 380 U.S. 503, 511-12, 14 L. Ed. 2d 39, 85 Sup. Ct. 1148, 1155 (1965) (dissenting opinion).

55 381 U.S. 1, 14 L. Ed. 2d 179, 85 Sup. Ct. 1271 (1965).

56 378 U.S. 500, 518, 12 L. Ed. 2d 992, 84 Sup. Ct. 1659 (1964) (concurring opinion).

57 381 U.S. 1, 22-23, 14 L. Ed. 2d 179, 85 Sup. Ct. 1271 (1965) (dissenting opinion).

58 Dennis v. United States, 341 U.S. 494, 95 L. Ed. 1137, 71 Sup. Ct. 857 (1951).

59 314 U.S. 252, 86 L. Ed. 192, 62 Sup. Ct. 190, 159 A.L.R. 1346 (1941). See also Pennekamp v. Florida, 328 U.S. 331, 90 L. Ed. 1295, 66 Sup. Ct. 1029 (1946); Craig v. Harney, 331 U.S. 367, 91 L. Ed. 1546, 67 Sup. Ct. 1249 (1947); Wood v. Georgia, 370 U.S. 375, 8 L. Ed. 2d 569, 82 Sup. Ct. 1364 (1962).

60 New York Times Co. v. Sullivan, 376 U.S. 254, 11 L. Ed. 2d 686, 84 Sup. Ct. 710, 95 A.L.R. 1412 (1964).

61 Id. at 293.

62 Mills v. Alabama, 384 U.S. 214, 220, 16 L. Ed. 2d 484, 86 Sup. Ct. 1434 (1966).

63 Estes v. Texas, 381 U.S. 532, 14 L. Ed. 2d 543, 85 Sup. Ct. 1628 (1965).

64 Sheppard v. Maxwell, 384 U.S. 333, 16 L. Ed. 2d 600, 86 Sup. Ct. 1507 (1966).

65 Ibid.

66 Estes v. Texas, 381 U.S. 532, 601, 14 L. Ed. 2d 543, 85 Sup. Ct. 1628 (1965).

67 NLRB v. Fruit & Vegetable Packers, Local 760, 377 U.S. 58, 12 L. Ed. 2d 129, 84 Sup. Ct. 1063 (1964).

68 Id. at 79-80 (concurring opinion).

69 Beauharnais v. Illinois, 343 U.S. 250, 267, 96 L. Ed. 919, 72 Sup. Ct. 725 (1952) (dissenting opinion).

70 A Book Named "John Cleland's Memoirs of a Woman of Pleasure" v. Attorney General, 383 U.S. 413, 16 L. Ed. 2d 1, 86 Sup. Ct. 975 (1966); Ginzburg v. United States, 383 U.S. 463, 16 L. Ed. 2d 31, 86 Sup. Ct. 942 (1966); Mishkin v. New York, 383 U.S. 502, 16 L. Ed. 2d 56, 86 Sup. Ct. 958 (1966).

71 Ginzburg v. United States, supra note 70.

72 Id. at 477-78.

73 Freedman v. Maryland, 380 U.S. 51, 61, 13 L. Ed. 2d 649, 85 Sup. Ct. 734 (1965) (concurring opinion).

74 Chambers v. Florida, 309 U.S. 277, 84 L. Ed. 751, 60 Sup. Ct. 549 (1940).

75 385 U.S. 39, 17 L. Ed. 2d 149, 87 Sup. Ct. 242 (1966). See Chapter Three, Daniel M. Berman, The Persistent Race Issue, pp. 87-93, for a detailing of Black's previous dissenting opinions. For a statement of the view that Black's Adderley "formulation is Constitutionally 'inadequate,'" see Kipperman, "Civil Rights at Armageddon—The Supreme Court Steps Back: Adderley v. Florida," Law In Transition Quarterly, Fall 1966 (Vol. III, No. 4), pp. 219-35.

76 361 U.S. 516, 528, 4 L. Ed. 2d 480, 80 Sup. Ct. 412 (1960) (concurring opinion of Black and Douglas, JJ.).

77 Meredith v. Fair, 371 U.S. 828, 9 L. Ed. 2d 43, 83 Sup. Ct. 10, *cert. denied,* 371 U.S. 828, 9 L. Ed. 2d 66, 83 Sup. Ct. 49 (1962).

78 377 U.S. 218, 12 L. Ed. 2d 256, 84 Sup. Ct. 1226 (1964).

79 Colorado Anti-Discrimination Comm'n v. Continental Airlines, 372 U.S. 714, 10 L. Ed. 2d 84, 83 Sup. Ct. 1022 (1963).

80 Gibson v. Florida Legislative Investigation Comm., 372 U.S. 539, 558, 9 L. Ed. 2d 929, 83 Sup. Ct. 889 (1963) (concurring opinion).

81 Louisiana v. United States, 380 U.S. 145, 13 L. Ed. 2d 709, 85 Sup. Ct. 817 (1965); United States v. Mississippi, 380 U.S. 128, 13 L. Ed. 2d 717, 85 Sup. Ct. 808 (1965).

82 Louisiana v. United States, *supra* note 81.

83 Gibson v. Florida Legislative Investigation Comm., 372 U.S. 539, 558-59, 9 L. Ed. 2d 929, 83 Sup. Ct. 889 (1963) (concurring opinion).

84 Durr, *Hugo Black, Southerner: The Southern Background,* 10 AM. U.L. REV. 32, 34 (1961).

85 *Ibid.* That summation is given even fuller force in light of Black's position in two cases decided in the early 50's. In Feiner v. New York, 340 U.S. 315, 321, 95 L. Ed. 295, 71 Sup. Ct. 303 (1951) (dissenting opinion), Black would have allowed a student to use a loudspeaker on a public sidewalk for the purpose of urging Negroes to take direct action to secure their constitutional rights. On the other side of such issues, he would have allowed one Joseph Beauharnais (Beauharnais v. Illinois, 343 U.S. 250, 267, 96 L. Ed. 919, 72 Sup. Ct. 725 (1962) (dissenting opinion)) to publicly distribute leaflets expressing strong views in favor of segregation.

86 Uphaus v. Wyman, 364 U.S. 388, 5 L. Ed. 2d 29, 148, 81 Sup. Ct. 22, 153 (1960).

87 Braden v. United States, 365 U.S. 341, 5 L. Ed. 2d 653, 81 Sup. Ct. 584 (1961).

88 Wilkinson v. United States, 365 U.S. 399, 5 L. Ed. 2d 633, 81 Sup. Ct. 567 (1961).

89 Scales v. United States, 367 U.S. 203, 6 L. Ed. 2d 782, 81 Sup. Ct. 1469 (1961).

90 *In re* Anastaplo, 366 U.S. 82, 6 L. Ed. 2d 135, 81 Sup. Ct. 978 (1962). See also *In re* Summers, 325 U.S. 561, 89 L. Ed. 1795, 65 Sup. Ct. 1307 (1945).

91 For others, see ONE MAN'S STAND FOR FREEDOM (Dilliard ed. 1963).

92 Gideon v. Wainright, 372 U.S. 335, 9 L. Ed. 2d 779, 83 Sup. Ct. 792, 93 A.L.R.2d 733 (1963).

93 *Id.* at 345.

94 378 U.S. 1, 6, 12 L. Ed. 2d 653, 84 Sup. Ct. 1489 (1964).

95 332 U.S. 46, 64, 91 L. Ed. 1903, 67 Sup. Ct. 1672, 171 A.L.R. 1223 (1947).

96 378 U.S. 1, 6-8, 12 L. Ed. 2d 653, 84 Sup. Ct. 1489 (1964).

97 375 U.S. 162, 11 L. Ed. 2d 224, 84 Sup. Ct. 295 (1963).

98 *Id.* at 165.

99 380 U.S. 400, 13 L. Ed. 2d 923, 85 Sup. Ct. 1065 (1965).

100 384 U.S. 1, 16 L. Ed. 2d 314, 86 Sup. Ct. 1245 (1966).

101 381 U.S. 618, 640, 14 L. Ed. 2d 601, 85 Sup. Ct. 1731 (1965) (dissenting opinion).

102 367 U.S. 643, 6 L. Ed. 2d 1081, 81 Sup. Ct. 1684 (1961).

103 Fay v. Noia, 372 U.S. 391, 9 L. Ed. 2d 837, 83 Sup. Ct. 822 (1963).

104 381 U.S. 618, 640, 652-53, 14 L. Ed. 2d 601, 85 Sup. Ct. 1731 (1965) (dissenting opinion).

105 373 U.S. 179, 191, 10 L. Ed. 2d 278, 83 Sup. Ct. 1151 (1963) (dissenting opinion).

106 *Id.* at 191.

107 382 U.S. 406, 419, 15 L. Ed. 2d 453, 86 Sup. Ct. 459 (1966) (dissenting opinion).

108 *Ibid.* The dissent was based on Black's dissent in Linkletter v. Walker, 381 U.S. 618, 640, 14 L. Ed. 2d 601, 85 Sup. Ct. 1731 (1965) (dissenting opinion). See also Johnson v. New Jersey, 384 U.S. 719, 736, 16 L. Ed. 2d 882, 86 Sup. Ct. 1772 (1966) (dissenting opinion).

109 384 U.S. 757, 773, 16 L. Ed. 2d 908, 86 Sup. Ct. 1826 (1966).

110 Boyd v. United States, 116 U.S. 616, 29 L. Ed. 746, 6 Sup. Ct. 524 (1886).

111 384 U.S. 757, 773, 777-78, 16 L. Ed. 2d 601, 85 Sup. Ct. 1731 (1965) (dissenting opinion).

112 382 U.S. 162, 15 L. Ed. 2d 240, 86 Sup. Ct. 352 (1965).

113 384 U.S. 436, 16 L. Ed. 2d 694, 86 Sup. Ct. 1602 (1966).

114 359 U.S. 41, 3 L. Ed. 2d 609, 79 Sup. Ct. 539 (1959).

115 Lamont v. Postmaster General, 381 U.S. 301, 14 L. Ed. 2d 398, 85 Sup. Ct. 1493 (1965).

116 Elfbrandt v. Russell, 384 U.S. 11, 16 L. Ed. 2d 321, 86 Sup. Ct. 1238 (1966). See also Keyishian v. Board of Regents, — U.S. —, 17 L. Ed. 2d 629, 87 Sup. Ct. — (1967).

117 Redmond v. United States, 384 U.S. 264, 265, 16 L. Ed. 2d 521, 86 Sup. Ct. 1415 (1966) (concurring opinion).

118 See Strickland's discussion in Chapter Nine, p. 245.

119 West Virginia State Bd. of Educ. v. Barnette, 319 U.S. 624, 643, 87 L. Ed. 1628, 63 Sup. Ct. 1178 (1943) (concurring opinion).

120 367 U.S. 488, 6 L. Ed. 2d 982, 81 Sup. Ct. 1680 (1961).

121 370 U.S. 421, 8 L. Ed. 2d 601, 82 Sup. Ct. 1261, 86 A.L.R.2d 1285 (1962).

122 United States v. Seeger, 380 U.S. 163, 13 L. Ed. 2d 733, 85 Sup. Ct. 850 (1965). See also Abingdon School Dist. v. Schempp, 374 U.S. 203, 10 L. Ed. 2d 844, 83 Sup. Ct. 1560 (1963); Illinois *ex rel.* McCollum v. Board of Educ., 333 U.S. 203, 92 L. Ed. 649, 68 Sup. Ct. 461, 2 A.L.R.2d 1338 (1948); Everson v. Board of Educ., 330 U.S. 1, 91 L. Ed. 711, 67 Sup. Ct. 504, 168 A.L.R. 1392 (1947); Marsh v. Alabama, 326 U.S. 501, 90 L. Ed. 265, 66 Sup. Ct. 276 (1946); Jones v. Opelika, 316 U.S. 584, 86 L. Ed. 1691, 62 Sup. Ct. 1231 (1943); Minersville School Dist. v. Gobitis, 310 U.S. 586, 84 L. Ed. 1375, 60 Sup. Ct. 1010 (1940); Zorach v. Clauson, 343 U.S. 306, 96 L. Ed. 954, 72 Sup. Ct. 679 (1952).

123 328 U.S. 549, 566, 90 L. Ed. 1432, 66 Sup. Ct. 1198 (1946).

124 369 U.S. 186, 7 L. Ed. 2d 663, 82 Sup. Ct. 691 (1962).

125 376 U.S. 1, 11 L. Ed. 2d 481, 84 Sup. Ct. 526 (1964).

126 *Id.* at 18.

127 *Ibid.*

128 *Ibid.*

129 Reynolds v. Sims, 377 U.S. 533, 12 L. Ed. 2d 506, 84 Sup. Ct. 1362 (1964).

130 *Id.* at 568. See also WMCA v. Lomenzo, 77 U.S. 633, 12 L. Ed. 2d 568, 84 Sup. Ct. 1418 (1964); Maryland Comm. for Fair Representation v. Tawes, 377 U.S. 656, 12 L. Ed. 2d 595, 84 Sup. Ct. 1429 (1964); Davis v. Mann, 377 U.S. 678, 12 L. Ed. 2d 609, 84 Sup. Ct. 1441 (1964); Roman v. Sincock, 377 U.S. 695, 12 L. Ed. 2d 620, 84 Sup. Ct. 1462 (1964); Lucas v. Colorado General Assembly, 377 U.S. 713, 12 L. Ed. 2d 568, 632, 84 Sup. Ct. 1418, 1459 (1964).

CHAPTER FIVE

The Living Constitution and the Court's Role

————*Charles A. Reich*————

1 Cahn, *Justice Black and First Amendment "Absolutes": A Public Interview,* 37 N.Y.U.L. Rev. 553-54 (1962).

2 The Federalist No. 84, at 537 (Lodge ed. 1894) (Hamilton).

3 American Communications Ass'n v. Douds, 339 U.S. 382, 94 L. Ed. 925, 70 Sup. Ct. 677 (1950) (interstate commerce); Dennis v. United States, 341 U.S. 494, 95 L. Ed. 1137, 71 Sup. Ct. 857 (1951) (national defense); *cf.* Roth v. United States, 354 U.S. 476, 1 L. Ed. 2d 1498, 77 Sup. Ct. 1304 (1957) (post office).

4 Wickard v. Filburn, 317 U.S. 111, 87 L. Ed. 122, 63 Sup. Ct. 82 (1942).

5 See Note, *The Bounds of Legislative Specification: A Suggested Approach to the Bill of Attainder Cases,* 72 Yale L.J. 330 (1962), for an analysis of the Court's treatment of the clause and a detailed consideration of how it might be applied functionally to contemporary problems.

6 Bartkus v. Illinois, 359 U.S. 121, 3 L. Ed. 2d 684, 79 Sup. Ct. 676 (1959).

7 *Id.* at 164-66 (dissenting opinion of Brennan, J.).

8 Feldman v. United States, 322 U.S. 487, 88 L. Ed. 1408, 64 Sup. Ct. 1082, 154 A.L.R. 982 (1944).

9 See Knapp v. Schweitzer, 357 U.S. 371, 2 L. Ed. 2d 1393, 78 Sup. Ct. 1302 (1958).

10 United States v. Kahriger, 345 U.S. 22, 97 L. Ed. 754, 73 Sup. Ct. 510 (1953); see Irvine v. California, 347 U.S. 128, 98 L. Ed. 561, 74 Sup. Ct. 381 (1954).

11 Joint Anti-Fascist Refugee Comm. v. McGrath, 341 U.S. 123, 95 L. Ed. 817, 71 Sup. Ct. 624 (1951). See also Kukatush Min. Co. v. United States, CCH Fed. Sec. L. Rep. ¶ 91183 (D.C. Cir. 1962).

12 Barenblatt v. United States, 360 U.S. 109, 3 L. Ed. 2d 1115, 79 Sup. Ct. 1081 (1959). *But cf.* United States v. Icardi, 140 F. Supp. 383 (D.D.C. 1956).

13 See Bailey v. Richardson, 182 F.2d 46 (D.C. Cir. 1950), *affirmed by an equally divided court,* 341 U.S. 918, 95 L. Ed. 1352, 71 Sup. Ct. 669 (1951); Peters v. Hobby, 349 U.S. 331, 99 L. Ed. 1129, 75 Sup. Ct. 790 (1951); Cafeteria Workers, Local 473 v. McElroy, 367 U.S. 886, 6 L. Ed. 2d 1230, 81 Sup. Ct. 1743 (1961).

14 See cases cited *supra* notes 8, 9.

15 See *In re* Groban, 352 U.S. 330, 1 L. Ed. 2d 376, 77 Sup. Ct. 510 (1957); Anonymous v. Baker, 360 U.S. 287, 3 L. Ed. 2d 1234, 79 Sup. Ct. 1157 (1959); Hannah v. Larche, 363 U.S. 420, 4 L. Ed. 2d 1307, 80 Sup.

Ct. 1502 (1960); *cf.* Crooker v. California, 357 U.S. 433, 2 L. Ed. 2d 1448, 78 Sup. Ct. 1287 (1958); Cicenia v. LaGay, 357 U.S. 504, 2 L. Ed. 2d 1523, 78 Sup. Ct. 1297 (1958). In a somewhat similar development, the Court has permitted "civil" powers of search and seizure to be used to gather evidence on which criminal prosecution can be based. Abel v. United States, 362 U.S. 217, 4 L. Ed. 2d 668, 80 Sup. Ct. 683 (1960); *cf.* Frank v. Maryland, 359 U.S. 360, 3 L. Ed. 2d 877, 79 Sup. Ct. 804 (1959).

16 United Pub. Workers v. Mitchell, 330 U.S. 75, 91 L. Ed. 754, 67 Sup. Ct. 556 (1947); Garner v. Board of Pub. Works, 341 U.S. 716, 95 L. Ed. 1317, 71 Sup. Ct. 909 (1951); Adler v. Board of Educ. of the City of New York, 342 U.S. 485, 96 L. Ed. 517, 72 Sup. Ct. 380, 27 A.L.R.2d 472 (1952).

17 *Cf.* Lerner v. Casey, 357 U.S. 468, 4 L. Ed. 2d 1423, 78 Sup. Ct. 1311 (1958); Beilan v. Board of Pub. Educ., 357 U.S. 399, 2 L. Ed. 2d 1414, 1433, 78 Sup. Ct. 1317, 1324 (1958).

18 Konigsberg v. State Bar, 366 U.S. 36, 6 L. Ed. 2d 105, 81 Sup. Ct. 997 (1961); *In re* Anastaplo, 366 U.S. 82, 6 L. Ed. 2d 135, 81 Sup. Ct. 978 (1961). See also Lathrop v. Donohue, 367 U.S. 820, 6 L. Ed. 2d 1191, 81 Sup. Ct. 1826 (1961).

19 Cohen v. Hurley, 366 U.S. 117, 6 L. Ed. 2d 156, 81 Sup. Ct. 954 (1961).

20 See American Communications Ass'n v. Douds, 339 U.S. 382, 94 L. Ed. 925, 70 Sup. Ct. 674 (1950); *cf.* International Ass'n of Machinists v. Street, 367 U.S. 740, 6 L. Ed. 2d 1141, 81 Sup. Ct. 1784 (1961).

21 Regan v. New York, 349 U.S. 58, 99 L. Ed. 883, 75 Sup. Ct. 585 (1955).

22 NAACP v. Alabama *ex rel.* Patterson, 357 U.S. 449, 2 L. Ed. 2d 1488, 78 Sup. Ct. 1163 (1958); Barenblatt v. United States, 360 U.S. 109, 3 L. Ed. 2d 1115, 79 Sup. Ct. 1081 (1959).

23 See C. L. BLACK, THE PEOPLE AND THE COURT 96-100 (1960), for a fully articulated statement of a position similar to Justice Black's. Professor Black's significant book deals with many of the problems considered in this chapter.

24 Bartkus v. Illinois, 359 U.S. 121, 150, 3 L. Ed. 2d 684, 79 Sup. Ct. 676 (1959) (dissenting opinion); Feldman v. United States, 322 U.S. 487, 494, 88 L. Ed. 1408, 64 Sup. Ct. 1082, 154 A.L.R. 982 (1944) (dissenting opinion).

25 Joint Anti-Fascist Refugee Comm. v. McGrath, 341 U.S. 123, 143, 95 L. Ed. 817, 71 Sup. Ct. 624 (1951) (concurring opinion); Peters v. Hobby, 349 U.S. 331, 349, 99 L. Ed. 1129, 75 Sup. Ct. 790 (1955) (concurring opinion); Barenblatt v. United States, 360 U.S. 109, 156-62, 3 L. Ed. 2d 1115, 79 Sup. Ct. 1081 (1950) (dissenting opinion).

26 *In re* Groban, 352 U.S. 330, 337, 1 L. Ed. 2d 376, 77 Sup. Ct. 510 (1957) (dissenting opinion).

27 *Id.* at 344.

28 United Pub. Workers v. Mitchell, 330 U.S. 75, 105, 91 L. Ed. 754, 67 Sup. Ct. 556 (1947) (dissenting opinion); *cf.* Peters v. Hobby, 349 U.S. 331, 99 L. Ed. 1129, 75 Sup. Ct. 790 (1955).

29 Konigsberg v. State Bar, 366 U.S. 36, 56, 6 L. Ed. 2d 105, 81 Sup. Ct. 997 (1961) (dissenting opinion); *In re* Anastaplo, 366 U.S. 82, 97, 6 L. Ed. 2d 135, 81 Sup. Ct. 978 (1961) (dissenting opinion).

30 Green v. United States, 356 U.S. 165, 193, 2 L. Ed. 2d 672, 78 Sup. Ct. 632 (1958) (dissenting opinion).

31 Reina v. United States, 364 U.S. 507, 516, 5 L. Ed. 2d 249, 81 Sup. Ct. 260 (1960) (dissenting opinion).

32 See Joint Anti-Fascist Refugee Comm. v. McGrath, 341 U.S. 123, 143-45, 95 L. Ed. 817, 71 Sup. Ct. 624 (1951) (concurring opinion); Flemming v. Nestor, 363 U.S. 603, 621, 4 L. Ed. 2d 1435, 80 Sup. Ct. 1367 (1960) (dissenting opinion); Communist Party v. Subversive Activities Control Bd., 367 U.S. 1, 146, 6 L. Ed. 2d 625, 81 Sup. Ct. 1357 (1961) (dissenting opinion).

33 See Yates v. United States, 354 U.S. 298, 339, 1 L. Ed. 2d 1356, 77 Sup. Ct. 1064 (1957) (concurring in part, dissenting in part); Rosenberg v. United States, 346 U.S. 273, 296, 97 L. Ed. 1607, 73 Sup. Ct. 1152 (1953) (dissenting opinion).

34 For a fuller treatment of Black's position on the power of judges, see Reich, *Mr. Justice Black and the Living Constitution*, 76 HARV. L. REV. 676-82 (1963).

35 See generally FREUND, THE SUPREME COURT OF THE UNITED STATES (1962).

36 Brown v. Mississippi, 297 U.S. 278, 80 L. Ed. 682, 56 Sup. Ct. 461 (1936).

37 Leyra v. Denno, 347 U.S. 556, 98 L. Ed. 948, 74 Sup. Ct. 716 (1954).

38 Rochin v. California, 342 U.S. 165, 96 L. Ed. 183, 72 Sup. Ct. 205, 25 A.L.R.2d 1396 (1952).

39 Irvine v. California, 347 U.S. 128, 98 L. Ed. 561, 74 Sup. Ct. 381 (1954).

40 Cohen v. Hurley, 366 U.S. 117, 6 L. Ed. 2d 156, 81 Sup. Ct. 954 (1961).

41 Regan v. New York, 349 U.S. 58, 99 L. Ed. 883, 75 Sup. Ct. 585 (1955).

42 Irvine v. California, 347 U.S. 128, 98 L. Ed. 561, 74 Sup. Ct. 381 (1954).

43 Breithaupt v. Abram, 352 U.S. 432, 1 L. Ed. 2d 448, 77 Sup. Ct. 408 (1957).

44 Kingsley Int'l Pictures Corp. v. Regents, 360 U.S. 684, 690-91, 3 L. Ed. 2d 1512, 79 Sup. Ct. 1362 (1959) (concurring opinion).

45 NAACP v. Alabama *ex rel.* Patterson, 357 U.S. 449, 2 L. Ed. 2d 1488, 78 Sup. Ct. 1163 (1959).

46 Barenblatt v. United States, 360 U.S. 109, 3 L. Ed. 2d 1115, 79 Sup. Ct. 1081 (1959).

47 Kingsley Int'l Pictures Corp. v. Regents, 360 U.S. 684, 690, 3 L. Ed. 2d 1512, 79 Sup. Ct. 1362 (1959) (concurring opinion).

48 Reid v. Covert, 354 U.S. 1, 1 L. Ed. 2d 1148, 78 Sup. Ct. 1222 (1957); see Kinsella v. Singleton, 361 U.S. 234, 4 L. Ed. 2d 268, 80 Sup. Ct. 297 (1960) (concurring in majority opinion of Clark, J.); Grisham v. Hagan, 361 U.S. 278, 4 L. Ed. 2d 279, 80 Sup. Ct. 310 (1960) (concurring in opinion of Clark, J.); McElroy v. United States *ex rel.* Guagliadardo, 361 U.S. 281, 4 L. Ed. 2d 282, 80 Sup. Ct. 305 (1960) (concurring in majority opinion of Clark, J.).

49 Reid v. Covert, 354 U.S. 1, 75, 1 L. Ed. 2d 1148, 78 Sup. Ct. 1222 (1957) (concurring opinion of Harlan, J.).

50 McCulloch v. Maryland, 17 U.S. (4 Wheat.) 316, 415, 4 L. Ed. 579 (1819).

51 Griswold, *Foreword: Of Time and Attitudes—Professor Hart and Judge Arnold, The Supreme Court, 1959 Term,* 74 HARV. L. REV. 81, 92

(1960). For an interpretation of "absolutes" in part similar to that suggested here, see C. L. Black, *Mr. Justice Black, The Supreme Court and the Bill of Rights,* Harper's Magazine, Feb. 1961, p. 63.

52 Griswold, *supra* note 51, at 92.

53 Black, *The Bill of Rights,* 35 N.Y.L.U. REV. 865, 880 (1960).

54 See Ullmann v. United States, 350 U.S. 422, 435, 100 L. Ed. 511, 76 Sup. Ct. 497, 53 A.L.R.2d 1008 (1956), for an illustration of a situation in which Congress passed a law despite doubts as to its constitutionality.

55 See Comment, *Passports,* 61 YALE L.J. 116 (1958).

56 See Kent v. Dulles, 357 U.S. 116, 2 L. Ed. 2d 1204, 78 Sup. Ct. 1113 (1958).

57 See Bailey v. Richardson, 341 U.S. 918, 95 L. Ed. 1352, 71 Sup. Ct. 669 (1951); Peters v. Hobby, 349 U.S. 331, 99 L. Ed. 1129, 75 Sup. Ct. 790 (1955); Cole v. Young, 351 U.S. 536, 100 L. Ed. 1396, 76 Sup. Ct. 861 (1956); Service v. Dulles, 354 U.S. 363, 1 L. Ed. 2d 1403, 77 Sup. Ct. 1152 (1957).

58 See generally BROWN, LOYALTY AND SECURITY (1961); Comment, 62 YALE L.J. 954 (1953).

59 In Galvan v. Press, 347 U.S. 522, 531, 98 L. Ed. 911, 74 Sup. Ct. 737 (1954), the Court said, "We are not prepared to deem ourselves wiser or more sensitive to human rights than our predecessors. . . ."

60 Engel v. Vitale, 370 U.S. 421, 8 L. Ed. 2d 601, 82 Sup. Ct. 1261, 86 A.L.R.2d 1285 (1962).

61 *Id.* at 425.

62 369 U.S. 186, 7 L. Ed. 2d 663, 82 Sup. Ct. 691 (1962).

63 347 U.S. 483, 98 L. Ed. 873, 74 Sup. Ct. 686, 38 A.L.R.2d 1180 (1954).

64 Gideon v. Wainwright, 372 U.S. 335, 9 L. Ed. 2d 799, 83 Sup. Ct. 792, 93 A.L.R.2d 733 (1963).

65 Gibbons v. Ogden, 22 U.S. (9 Wheat.) 1, 222, 6 L. Ed. 23 (1824) (Marshall, C.J.).

66 Champion v. Ames, 188 U.S. 321, 375, 47 L. Ed. 492, 23 Sup. Ct. 321 (1903) (dissenting opinion of Fuller, C. J.).

CHAPTER SIX

Federal Taxation: Questions of Power and Propriety

————*Randolph Paul*————

1 KEYNES, THE GENERAL THEORY OF EMPLOYMENT, INTEREST AND MONEY 383-84 (1936).

2 80 CONG. REC. 8809 (1936).

3 Revenue Act of 1936, § 14, 49 Stat. 1655, repealed by Int. Rev. Code of 1939, § 15, 53 Stat. 9.

4 H.R. REP. No. 1681, 74th Cong., 1st Sess. 2 (1935).

5 See PAUL, FEDERAL ESTATE AND GIFT TAXATION 14 (1942).

6 A lurid tale was unfolded before the Joint Committee. In order to siphon assets and income out of the United States, prominent American citizens had deserted the protection and advantages of the established corporate laws of the states in their country to put their assets in corporations established under the corporate laws of Nassau, an insignificant foreign island in the Atlantic Ocean, known principally as a winter pleasure resort, and in corporations established under the laws of other neighboring foreign jurisdictions such as Panama, Newfoundland, and Prince Edward Island. Some American taxpayers were claiming wholly fictitious interest deductions for so-called loans from a company incorporated in the Bahama Islands which masqueraded as an insurance company. Domestic "incorporated pocketbooks," formed to insulate interest and dividends from the individual income tax, had multiplied like mushrooms. The owners of farms, racing stables, and even yachts, had incorporated their pleasures to make them businesses. One wealthy woman supplied her husband with pocket money by having the corporation that owned her country estate employ him as a manager. Multiple trusts were being used to obtain additional personal exemptions and to split income into large numbers of separate units each of which would start with a low tax bracket. Leading cartoonists, violinists, and motion picture actors were resorting to the device of incorporating their personal talents. *Hearings Before the Joint Committee on Tax Evasion and Avoidance,* 75th Cong., 1st Sess. (1937). See Paul, *The Background of the Revenue Act of 1937,* 5 U. CHI. L. REV. 41 (1937).

7 50 Stat. 813.

8 Stone, *The Common Law in the United States,* in THE FUTURE OF THE COMMON LAW 129 (1937).

9 See PAUL, TAXATION IN THE UNITED STATES 279 (1954).

10 *Cf.* Employment Act of 1946, 60 Stat. 23, 15 U.S.C. §§ 1021-24 [F.C.A. 15 §§ 1021-24] (1952).

11 Childs, *The Supreme Court Today,* 176 HARPER'S MAGAZINE 581, 582 (May 1938). Eight years later Childs wrote that Black "worked harder

than perhaps any justice in the history of the court" to "vindicate himself
and to justify in the law his liberal opinions." MCCUNE, THE NINE YOUNG
MEN 33 (1947).

12 See J. P. Frank, *Mr. Justice Black: A Biographical Appreciation,*
65 YALE L.J. 454, 455 (1956). [Black graduated from the University of
Alabama Law School in 1906 after a two-year course. He had switched to
law from medicine after completing, in one year, the course equivalents of
two years at the University Medical School. Ed. note.]

13 The closest John Marshall came to a formal education was a
year's tutoring by a visiting minister and several months' schooling in
Latin at Westmoreland Academy when he was fourteen. Marshall did
spend six weeks attending lectures on the law given at William and Mary
College. See RODELL, NINE MEN: A POLITICAL HISTORY OF THE SUPREME
COURT FROM 1790 TO 1955, at 80 (1955).

14 For instance, Justices Miller and the first Harlan.

15 See J. P. FRANK, MR. JUSTICE BLACK, THE MAN AND HIS OPINIONS
35 (1949).

16 Among other things, while in the Senate he had conducted an
investigation of mail subsidies and the public utility holding company
investigation. This was a fight with a twelve billion dollar industry
which had almost the entire press massed solidly behind it. [See John P.
Frank's discussion in Chapter Two, at 44, 59. Ed. note.]

17 FRANK, *op. cit. supra* note 15, at 62.

18 *Id.* at 47.

19 Three of Roosevelt's eight appointees had been law school professors or deans: Douglas, Frankfurter, and Rutledge.

20 This prior judicial experience exceeded, however, that of six of
the other seven Roosevelt appointees. Twelve of the twenty Justices
appointed between 1897 and 1937 had had prior judicial experience.

21See FRANKFURTER, *The Supreme Court of the United States,* in LAW
AND POLITICS 20, 31 (1939).

Beveridge quotes Schmidt, a writer-contemporary of Chief Justice
Marshall: "Mr. Marshall can hardly be regarded as a learned lawyer.
His acquaintance with the Roman jurisprudence as well as with the laws
of foreign countries was not very extensive. He was what is called a
common lawyer in the best and noblest acceptation of that term." 2
BEVERIDGE, THE LIFE OF JOHN MARSHALL 178 (1916).

22 See FRANKFURTER, *The Zeitgeist and The Judiciary,* in LAW AND
POLITICS 4-5 (1939).

23 See Justice Brandeis' dissenting opinion in Burnet v. Coronado
Oil & Gas Co., 285 U.S. 393, 410-11, 76 L. Ed. 815, 52 Sup. Ct. 443 (1932).

24 See BRANT, STORM OVER THE CONSTITUTION 241 (1936); LLEWELLYN,
THE BRAMBLE BUSH 156 (1930); Douglas, *Stare Decisis,* 49 COLUM. L. REV.
735-36 (1949); Hamilton, *Judicial Process,* in 8 ENCYC. OF THE SOCIAL
SCIENCES 450-51 (1932); Stone, *supra* note 8, at 140.

25 HOLMES, COLLECTED LEGAL PAPERS 181 (1952).

26 HOLMES, THE COMMON LAW 1 (1881). See also J. N. FRANK, COURTS
ON TRIAL 147 (1950); Stone, *Fallacies of the Logical Form in English Law,*
in INTERPRETATIONS OF MODERN LEGAL PHILOSOPHIES 696 (1947).

27 HOLMES, THE COMMON LAW 1 (1881); Justice Stone, dissenting
(with Justices Brandeis and Cardozo) in Morehead v. New York *ex rel.*
Tipaldo, 298 U.S. 587, 633, 80 L. Ed. 1347, 56 Sup. Ct. 918, 103 A.L.R.

1445 (1936). See Lincoln's statement that Supreme Court Justices "have, with others, the same passions for party, for power, and the privilege of their corps." Quoted in RODELL, *op. cit. supra* note 13, at 134. Justice Miller of the Supreme Court once said: "It is vain to contend with judges who have been, at the bar, the advocates of railroad companies, and all the forms of associated capital, when they are called upon to decide cases where such interests are in contest. All their training, all their feelings are from the start in favor of those who need no such influence." *Id.* at 146.

28 Hamilton, *supra* note 24, at 456; see J. N. FRANK, LAW AND THE MODERN MIND 111 (1930).

29 See FREUND, ON UNDERSTANDING THE SUPREME COURT 3 (1949). See also PRITCHETT, THE ROOSEVELT COURT xiii, 14, 282 (1948); Schlesinger, *The Supreme Court: 1947*, Fortune, Jan. 1947, p. 73.

30 This is true because the Constitution was "intended to endure for ages to come, and, consequently, to be adapted to the various *crises* in human affairs." [Emphasis supplied.] McCulloch v. Maryland, 17 U.S. (4 Wheat.) 316, 415, 4 L. Ed. 579 (1819).

31 JACKSON, THE SUPREME COURT IN THE AMERICAN SYSTEM OF GOVERNMENT 54 (1955). See also CURTIS, LIONS UNDER THE THRONE viii, 60-61 (1947).

32 See FRANKFURTER, *The Supreme Court of the United States,* in LAW AND POLITICS 30 (1939).

33 See FRANKFURTER, *Justice Holmes Defines the Constitution,* in LAW AND POLITICS 62 (1939). Even Brandeis, according to his biographer, "was inclined by the pressures and drives of his own nature to translate his own economic and social views into the Constitution itself." MASON, BRANDEIS: A FREE MAN'S LIFE 580 (1956).

34 3 WARREN, THE SUPREME COURT IN UNITED STATES HISTORY 123 (1924). See also Gideon Welles' statement about Evarts as a possible appointee for the Supreme Court. Answering a question from Lincoln, Welles stated that Evarts was "among the foremost at the New York Bar." He went on to say that that was not all: "Our Chief Justice must have a judicial mind, be upright, of strict integrity, not too pliant; should be a statesman and a politician." He then added that by "politician" he did not mean a "partisan." He meant one who was "impressed with the principles and doctrines which had brought this Administration into power"; it was all-important that Lincoln "should have a Judge who would be a correct and faithful expositor of the principles of his Administration and policy after his Administration shall have closed." *Id.* at 125-26.

35 FRANKFURTER, LAW AND POLITICS 66 (1939).

36 *Id.* at 67; see 2 PRINGLE, THE LIFE AND TIMES OF WILLIAM HOWARD TAFT 739 (1939).

37 FRANKFURTER, LAW AND POLITICS 67 (1939); see 2 PRINGLE, *op. cit. supra* note 36, at 739.

38 2 PRINGLE, *op. cit. supra* note 36, at 854.

39 Taft, *Mr. Wilson and the Campaign,* 10 YALE REV. 1, 19-20 (1920).

40 2 PRINGLE, *op. cit. supra* note 36, at 967. Cf. Wilson's letter to Justice Clarke, one of his appointees, when the latter resigned from the Court in 1922: "Like thousands of other liberals throughout the country, I have been counting on the influence of you and Justice Brandeis to restrain the Court in some measure from the extreme reactionary course which it seems inclined to follow. . . . The most obvious and immediate

danger to which we are exposed is that the courts will more and more outrage the common people's sense of justice and cause a revulsion against judicial authority which may seriously disturb the equilibrium of our institutions, and I see nothing which can save us from this danger if the Supreme Court is to repudiate a liberal course of thought and action."

41 *Cf.* McCUNE, THE NINE YOUNG MEN 46 (1947).

42 304 U.S. 405, 424, 82 L. Ed. 1427, 58 Sup. Ct. 969 (1938). For a discussion of this case, see PRITCHETT, THE ROOSEVELT COURT 61 (1948).

43 HUGHES, THE SUPREME COURT OF THE UNITED STATES 68 (1928). As to the function of dissents, and sometimes of separate concurring opinions, see Powell, *And Repent at Leisure,* 58 HARV. L. REV. 930, 943 (1945); PRITCHETT, THE ROOSEVELT COURT 50 (1948); Hamilton, *supra* note 24, at 455.

44 J. N. FRANK, LAW AND THE MODERN MIND 293 (1930).

45 *Cf.* Douglas, *supra* note 24, at 754.

46 17 U.S. (4 Wheat.) 316, 4 L. Ed. 579 (1819).

47 78 U.S. (11 Wall.) 113, 20 L. Ed. 122 (1871).

48 Hamilton, *supra* note 24, at 453. See also *id.* at 455; Cardozo, *Law and Literature,* 14 YALE L.J. 699, 715 (1925); PRITCHETT, THE ROOSEVELT COURT 51 (1948).

49 *Cf.* J. N. FRANK, COURTS ON TRIAL 275 (1950); LLEWELLYN, THE BRAMBLE BUSH 63 (1930).

50 Helvering v. Gerhardt, 304 U.S. 405, 424, 82 L. Ed. 1427, 58 Sup. Ct. 969 (1938).

51 *Ibid.*

52 *Ibid.*

53 *Id.* at 426 (concurring opinion).

54 *Id.* at 427. [That Black is not automatically offended by local taxes indirectly affecting federal property and federal activity is pointed up by City of Detroit v. Murray Corp., 355 U.S. 489, 2 L. Ed. 2d 441, 460, 78 Sup. Ct. 458, 486 (1958), and the companion cases at 466 and 484, decided the same day. Ed. note.]

55 Graves v. New York *ex rel.* O'Keefe, 306 U.S. 466, 486, 83 L. Ed. 927, 59 Sup. Ct. 595, 120 A.L.R. 1466 (1939). See JACKSON, THE STRUGGLE FOR JUDICIARY SUPREMACY 243 (1941).

56 Commissioner v. Harmon, 323 U.S. 44, 49, 57, 89 L. Ed. 60, 65 Sup. Ct. 103 (1944) (Douglas, J., dissenting with Black, J.); *cf.,* the Black dissent in McDonald v. Commissioner, 323 U.S. 57, 65, 89 L. Ed. 68, 65 Sup. Ct. 96, 155 A.L.R. 119 (1944).

57 See J. P. FRANK, MR. JUSTICE BLACK, THE MAN AND HIS OPINIONS 109 (1949).

58 Burnet v. Coronado Oil & Gas Co., 285 U.S. 393, 407-08, 76 L. Ed. 815, 52 Sup. Ct. 443 (1932) (dissenting opinion of Brandeis, J.). Justice Brandeis' protest in this case was a fruitful one. See Helvering v. Mountain Producers Corp., 303 U.S. 376, 82 L. Ed. 907, 58 Sup. Ct. 623 (1938); Oklahoma Tax Comm'r v. United States, 319 U.S. 598, 87 L. Ed. 1612, 63 Sup. Ct. 1284 (1943).

59 New York v. United States, 326 U.S. 572, 590, 90 L. Ed. 326, 66 Sup. Ct. 310 (1946) (Douglas, J., dissenting, with Black, J.). On the subject of stare decisis in general, see Douglas, *supra* note 24; J. N. FRANK, COURTS ON TRIAL 262 (1950).

60 See Burnet v. Coronado Oil & Gas Co., 285 U.S. 393, 406-07, 76 L. Ed. 815, 52 Sup. Ct. 443 (1932) (dissenting opinion of Brandeis, J.). See also CURTIS, LIONS UNDER THE THRONE 56-57 (1947).

61 Douglas, *supra* note 24, at 746-47; *cf.*, FREUND, *op. cit. supra* note 29, at 38.

62 335 U.S. 632, 93 L. Ed. 288, 69 Sup. Ct. 322, 337 (1949).

63 Commissioner v. Estate of Church, 335 U.S. 632, 647, 93 L. Ed. 288, 69 Sup. Ct. 322, 337 (1949). [Compare Black's dissenting opinion, discussed *infra*, in James v. United States, 366 U.S. 213, 222, 6 L. Ed. 2d 246, 81 Sup. Ct. 1052 (1966), especially at 233-34. Ed. note.]

64 281 U.S. 238, 74 L. Ed. 826, 50 Sup. Ct. 286, 67 A.L.R. 1244 (1930).

65 Burnet v. Northern Trust Co., 283 U.S. 782, 75 L. Ed. 1412, 51 Sup. Ct. 342 (1931); Morsman v. Burnet, 283 U.S. 783, 75 L. Ed. 1412, 51 Sup. Ct. 343 (1931); McCormick v. Burnet, 283 U.S. 784, 75 L. Ed. 1413, 51 Sup. Ct. 343 (1931).

66 Int. Rev. Code of 1939, § 811 (c), 53 Stat. 1. See also Estate of Spiegel v. Commissioner, 335 U.S. 701, 93 L. Ed. 330, 69 Sup. Ct. 301 (1949), involving the interpretation of the same provision with reference to a trust with a possibility of reverter.

67 See cases cited note 65 *supra*.

68 Resolution of March 3, 1931, ch. 452, 46 Stat. 1516. See RODELL, NINE MEN: A POLITICAL HISTORY OF THE SUPREME COURT FROM 1790 TO 1955, at 37 (1955).

69 Revenue Act of 1932, § 302(c), 47 Stat. 279.

70 Hassett v. Welch, 303 U.S. 303, 82 L. Ed. 858, 58 Sup. Ct. 559 (1938).

71 309 U.S. 106, 84 L. Ed. 604, 60 Sup. Ct. 444, 125 A.L.R. 1368 (1940), *overruling* Helvering v. St. Louis Union Trust Co., 296 U.S. 39, 80 L. Ed. 29, 56 Sup. Ct. 74, 100 A.L.R. 1239 (1935), and Becker v. St. Louis Union Trust Co., 296 U.S. 48, 80 L. Ed. 35, 56 Sup. Ct. 78 (1935). The taxpayer in the *Hallock* case had created a trust providing that the income from the trust property should be paid to his wife during her lifetime; that upon his death, if she survived him, the corpus of the trust should go to her or other named beneficiaries, but that upon her death, if he survived, the property should revert to himself. The wife survived. The case held, briefly, that the value of the remainder interest should be included in the decedent's gross estate as a transfer intended to take effect in possession or enjoyment at or after the grantor's death. The *Hallock* decision is ably discussed in Eisenstein, *The Hallock Problem: A Case Study in Administration,* 58 HARV. L. REV. 1141 (1945).

72 Commissioner v. Estate of Church, 335 U.S. 632, 643, 93 L. Ed. 288, 69 Sup. Ct. 322, 337 (1949). Justice Black refused to accept the argument that the error of *May v. Heiner* should be continued because of Treasury regulations which had accepted that decision, and the argument that Congress had ratified the doctrine of the case when it passed the Joint Resolution. He also found no merit in the contention that subsequent cases set at rest all questions as to the soundness of the *May v. Heiner* interpretation. See also Commissioner v. Hall's Estate, 153 F.2d 172, 174 (2d Cir. 1946) (dissenting opinion of Frank, J.).

73 Commissioner v. Estate of Church, *supra* note 72, at 644-45.

74 *Id.* at 676 (dissenting opinion of Frankfurter, J.).

75 *Id.* at 676-77.

[76] Estate of Spiegel v. Commissioner, 335 U.S. 701, 93 L. Ed. 330, 69 Sup. Ct. 301 (1949). See note 66 *supra*.

[77] DeWind, *Federal Estate and Gift Taxation,* in 1949 Annual Survey of American L. 225-26.

[78] Treas. Reg. 105, § 81.17 (1949), as amended, T.D. 5741, 1949-2 Cum. Bull. 114.

[79] 63 Stat. 894.

[80] The action of Congress in 1949 has been described by Professor Boris Bittker of the Yale Law School as being based upon the theory that many persons who established trusts relied upon the incorrect decision in *May v. Heiner,* and that the later decision correcting the error of the earlier decision "disappointed their reasonable expectations"—principally their expectation that the error would be perpetuated for all time. Bittker, *Church and Spiegel: The Legislative Sequel,* 59 Yale L.J. 395, 414 (1950). See Paul, Taxation in the United States 533 (1954).

[81] Commissioner v. Estate of Noel, 380 U.S. 678, 680-81, 684, 14 L. Ed. 2d 159, 85 Sup. Ct. 1238 (1965).

[82] Graves v. New York *ex rel.* O'Keefe, 306 U.S. 466, 489, 83 L. Ed. 927, 59 Sup. Ct. 595, 120 A.L.R. 1466 (1939).

[83] Commissioner v. Sansome, 60 F.2d 931, 933 (2d Cir.), *cert. denied,* 287 U.S. 667, 77 L. Ed. 575, 53 Sup. Ct. 291 (1932). *Cf.* Cardozo, Law and Literature 5 (1931); Sage v. Commissioner, 83 F.2d 221, 224 (2d Cir. 1936).

[84] Hanneford v. Silas Mason Co., 300 U.S. 577, 586, 81 L. Ed. 814, 57 Sup. Ct. 524 (1937) (Cardozo, J.).

[85] Commissioner v. Court Holding Co., 324 U.S. 331, 334, 89 L. Ed. 981, 65 Sup. Ct. 707 (1945).

[86] Helvering v. F. & R. Lazarus & Co., 308 U.S. 252, 255, 84 L. Ed. 226, 60 Sup. Ct. 209 (1939).

[87] United States v. Hendler, 303 U.S. 564, 566, 82 L. Ed. 1018, 58 Sup. Ct. 655 (1938).

[88] Smith v. Shaughnessy, 318 U.S. 176, 181, 87 L. Ed. 690, 63 Sup. Ct. 545 (1943).

[89] Helvering v. Sabine Transp. Co., 318 U.S. 306, 312, 87 L. Ed. 773, 63 Sup. Ct. 569 (1943) (dissenting opinion).

[90] Foster v. United States, 303 U.S. 118, 121, 82 L. Ed. 700, 58 Sup. Ct. 424 (1938).

[91] Lochner v. New York, 198 U.S. 45, 76, 49 L. Ed. 937, 25 Sup. Ct. 539 (1905) (dissenting opinion of Holmes, J.); see letter from Oliver Wendell Holmes to Dr. Wu, June 16, 1923, in Justice Oliver Wendell Holmes, His Book Notices and Uncollected Letters and Papers 164-65 (1936).

[92] Court Holding Co., 2 T.C. 531, 539 (1943).

[93] Commissioner v. Court Holding Co., 324 U.S. 331, 334, 89 L. Ed. 981, 65 Sup. Ct. 707 (1945).

[94] United States v. Cumberland Pub. Serv. Co., 338 U.S. 451, 94 L. Ed. 251, 70 Sup. Ct. 280 (1950).

[95] *Id.* at 454-55.

[96] *Id.* at 456.

[97] *E.g.,* Lykes v. United States, 343 U.S. 118, 96 L. Ed. 791, 72 Sup. Ct. 585 (1952) (overruled by Int. Rev. Code of 1954, § 212 (3)); United States v. Lewis, 340 U.S. 590, 95 L. Ed. 560, 71 Sup. Ct. 522 (1951)

(changed by INT. REV. CODE OF 1954, § 1341); Bazley v. Commissioner, 331 U.S. 737, 91 L. Ed. 1782, 67 Sup. Ct. 1489, 173 A.L.R. 905 (1947) (clarified by INT. REV. CODE OF 1954, § 306); Commissioner v. Smith, 324 U.S. 177, 89 L. Ed. 830, 65 Sup. Ct. 591 (1945) (modified by Int. Rev. Code of 1939, § 130A, added by 64 Stat. 942 (1950), now INT. REV. CODE OF 1954, § 421); Magruder v. Supplee, 316 U.S. 394, 86 L. Ed. 1555, 62 Sup. Ct. 1162 (1942) (changed by INT. REV. CODE OF 1954, § 164 (d)); Higgins v. Commissioner, 312 U.S. 212, 85 L. Ed. 783, 61 Sup. Ct. 475 (1941) (overruled by Int. Rev. Code of 1939, § 23(a)(2), 53 Stat. 12, now INT. REV. CODE OF 1954, § 212); Helvering v. Bruun, 309 U.S. 461, 84 L. Ed. 864, 60 Sup. Ct. 631 (1940) (overruled by Int. Rev. Code of 1939, § 22(b)(11), added by 56 Stat. 812 (1942), now INT. REV. CODE OF 1954, § 109); Helvering v. Clifford, 309 U.S. 331, 84 L. Ed. 788, 60 Sup. Ct. 554 (1940) (partially incorporated in INT. REV. CODE OF 1954, §§ 671-78); United States v. Hendler, 303 U.S. 564, 82 L. Ed. 1018, 58 Sup. Ct. 655 (1938) (overruled by Int. Rev. Code of 1939, § 22(b)(9), added by 56 Stat. 811 (1942), now INT. REV. CODE OF 1954, § 108); Helvering v. Bashford, 302 U.S. 454, 82 L. Ed. 367, 58 Sup. Ct. 307 (1937); Groman v. Commissioner, 302 U.S. 82, 82 L. Ed. 63, 58 Sup. Ct. 108 (1937) (overruled by INT. REV. CODE OF 1954, § 368); Koshland v. Helvering, 298 U.S. 441, 80 L. Ed. 1268, 56 Sup. Ct. 767, 105 A.L.R. 756 (1936) (changed by INT. REV. CODE OF 1954, § 305); General Util. & Operating Co. v. Helvering, 296 U.S. 200, 80 L. Ed. 154, 56 Sup. Ct. 185 (1935) (incorporated in INT. REV. CODE OF 1954, § 311).

[98] INT. REV. CODE OF 1954, § 337.

[99] Commissioner v. Brown, 380 U.S. 563, 14 L. Ed. 2d 75, 85 Sup. Ct. 1162 (1965).

[100] Id. at 583-85 (dissenting opinion of Goldberg, J.).

[101] See Paul, Partnerships in Tax Avoidance, 13 GEO. WASH. L. REV. 121 (1945).

[102] See Gregory v. Helvering, 293 U.S. 465, 469, 79 L. Ed. 596, 55 Sup. Ct. 266, 97 A.L.R. 1355 (1935); United States v. Isham, 84 U.S. (17 Wall.) 496, 21 L. Ed. 728 (1873).

[103] Commissioner v. Tower, 327 U.S. 280, 90 L. Ed. 670, 66 Sup. Ct. 532, 164 A.L.R. 1135 (1946).

[104] Commissioner v. Lusthaus, 327 U.S. 293, 90 L. Ed. 679, 66 Sup. Ct. 539 (1946).

[105] Commissioner v. Culbertson, 337 U.S. 733, 93 L. Ed. 1659, 69 Sup. Ct. 1210 (1949).

[106] But "both Amidon [the secretary] and Tower ceased to draw salaries." Commissioner v. Tower, 327 U.S. 280, 286, 90 L. Ed. 670, 66 Sup. Ct. 532, 164 A.L.R. 1135 (1946).

[107] Id. at 286.

[108] Id. at 291.

[109] Commissioner v. Tower, 327 U.S. 280, 292, 90 L. Ed. 670, 66 Sup. Ct. 532, 164 A.L.R. 1135 (1946).

[110] Id. at 288-89.

[111] Id. at 289.

[112] Commissioner v. Culbertson, 337 U.S. 733, 93 L. Ed. 1659, 69 Sup. Ct. 1210 (1949).

[113] In the Lusthaus case the taxpayer owned and operated a retail furniture business with two stores. His wife helped in the stores when needed without compensation. In order to reduce taxes, taxpayer sold

a half interest in the business to his wife and executed a partnership agreement. The wife continued to help out when needed but the taxpayer retained full control of the business. The Court held that the evidence was sufficient to support a finding by the Tax Court that there was no genuine partnership.

[114] Commissioner v. Culbertson, 337 U.S. 733, 738, 93 L. Ed. 1659, 69 Sup. Ct. 1210 (1949).

[115] This premise was, however, disclaimed by the Chief Justice in his majority opinion in the *Culbertson* case, *ibid.* And he and Justice Reed had dissented in the *Tower* and *Lusthaus* cases.

[116] Commissioner v. Culbertson, 337 U.S. 733, 741, 93 L. Ed. 1659, 69 Sup. Ct. 1210 (1949). Or, less politely, "an erroneous reading of the *Tower* opinion." *Id.* at 745.

[117] *Id.* at 742.

[118] See Comment, *Family Partnerships and the Revenue Act of 1951,* 61 YALE L.J. 541 (1952). See also Lifton, *The Family Partnership: Here We Go Again,* 7 TAX L. REV. 461 (1952); Schulman, *Current Tests for Valid Family Partnership Arrangements,* 31 TAXES 447 (1953).

[119] S. REP. No. 781, 82d Cong., 1st Sess. 39 (1951).

[120] Int. Rev. Code of 1939, § 3797(a)(2), as amended, 65 Stat. 511 (1951).

[121] INT. REV. CODE OF 1954, §§ 704(e), 7701(a)(2).

[122] INT. REV. CODE of 1954, § 704 (e) (2).

[123] Int. Rev. Code of 1939, § 51(b), as amended, 62 Stat. 115 (1948) (now INT. REV. CODE OF 1954, § 6013). See PAUL, TAXATION IN THE UNITED STATES 482-83 (1954).

[124] Louis R. Eisenmann, 17 T.C. 1426 (1952).

[125] Theodore D. Stern, 15 T.C. 521 (1950).

[126] Edward D. Sultan, 18 T.C. 715 (1952).

[127] Feldman v. Commissioner, 186 F.2d 87 (4th Cir. 1950).

[128] Stanton v. Commissioner, 189 F.2d 297 (7th Cir. 1951).

[129] SURREY & WARREN, FEDERAL INCOME TAXATION 846 (1954 ed.).

[130] 5 CCH Tax Ct. Mem. 528 (1946), cited in SURREY & WARREN, *op. cit. supra* note 129, at 846.

[131] *Ibid.*

[132] Helvering v. Clifford, 309 U.S. 331, 84 L. Ed. 788, 60 Sup. Ct. 554 (1940). See Edward D. Sultan, 18 T.C. 715, 724-25 (1952).

[133] Commissioner v. Tower, 327 U.S. 280, 291, 90 L. Ed. 670, 66 Sup. Ct. 532, 164 A.L.R. 1135 (1946). In his dissent in the *Lusthaus* case Justice Reed distinguished the *Clifford* case as involving a short term trust rather than a partnership interest which not only was permanently to be the property of the wife, but exposed her to partnership liability. Lusthaus v. Commissioner, 327 U.S. 293, 303, 90 L. Ed. 679, 66 Sup. Ct. 539 (1946). See opinion of Arundell, J., in Edward D. Sultan, 18 T.C. 715, 724 (1952); *id.* at 725 (dissenting opinion of Opper, J.).

[134] Commissioner v. Culbertson, 337 U.S. 733, 739-40, 745-46, 748, 93 L. Ed. 1659, 69 Sup. Ct. 1210 (1949).

[135] S. REP. No. 781, 82d Cong., 1st Sess. 39 (1951). See Comment, 61 YALE L.J. 541, 548 (1952).

[136] 343 U.S. 130, 139, 96 L. Ed. 833, 72 Sup. Ct. 571 (1952) (dissenting opinion). See also Justice Frankfurter's dissent in United States v. Kahriger, 345 U.S. 22, 37, 97 L. Ed. 754, 73 Sup. Ct. 510 (1953).

137 Commissioner v. Wilcox, 327 U.S. 404, 90 L. Ed. 752, 66 Sup. Ct. 546, 166 A.L.R. 884 (1946).

138 Rutkin v. United States, 343 U.S. 130, 141, 96 L. Ed. 833, 72 Sup. Ct. 571 (1952). Similarly, Justice Black protested in McDonald v. Commissioner, 323 U.S. 57, 89 L. Ed. 68, 65 Sup. Ct. 96, 155 A.L.R. 119 (1944), where the Court decided that campaign expenses of a judge were not allowable deduction. The protest was against an oblique attack on abuses in campaign expenditures "by strained statutory construction which permits a discriminatory penalty to be imposed on taxpayers who work for the states, counties, municipalities, or the federal government." The problem "should be attacked squarely by the proper state and federal authorities. . . ." *Id.* at 71 (dissenting opinion). See also "The Effectiveness of Present Federal Tax Statutes and Their Administration," address by Representative Cecil R. King, American Bar Association, Sept. 16, 1952.

139 Rutkin v. United States, 343 U.S. 130, 141-42, 96 L. Ed. 833, 72 Sup. Ct. 571 (1952) (dissenting opinion). "The Bureau as an agency primarily devoted to the problems of general revenue raising is ill-adapted to take on the duties of conducting a criminal investigation job outside the tax field." King, *supra* note 138 at 5.

140 72 CONG. REC. 6214 (1930).

141 Rutkin v. United States, 343 U.S. 130, 142-43, 96 L. Ed. 833, 72 Sup. Ct. 571 (1952).

142 *Id.* at 144. Justice Black mentioned the example that under the Federal White Slave Law men can be imprisoned five years for conduct which many states would not regard as criminal at all. *Ibid.* He might have added the point that gambling—a forbidden activity in many states— is a legitimate activity in Nevada.

143 *Id.* at 145.

144 *Id.* at 147. See United States v. Rutkin, 212 F.2d 641 (3d Cir. 1954); Rutkin v. Reinfeld, 122 F. Supp. 265 (S.D.N.Y. 1954).

145 366 U.S. 213, 6 L. Ed. 2d 246, 81 Sup. Ct. 1052 (1961).

146 *Id.* at 226 (dissenting opinion).

147 *Id.* at 230. [See also Justice Whittaker's dissent—one of the best opinions of his career—in which Black also joined, at 248. Ed. note.]

148 See "Freedom Under Law," Address by Attorney General Brownell, American Bar Association Convention, Aug. 27, 1953.

149 Or, as Member Sternhagen said in a dissenting opinion many years ago, "The revenue act was not contrived as an arm of the law to enforce State criminal statutes by augmenting the punishment which the State inflicts." Burroughs Bldg. Material Co., 18 B.T.A. 101, 105, *aff'd,* 47 F.2d 178 (2d Cir. 1931).

150 See Commissioner v. Heininger, 320 U.S. 467, 88 L. Ed. 171, 64 Sup. Ct. 249 (1943); *cf.,* Lilly v. Commissioner, 343 U.S. 90, 96 L. Ed. 769, 72 Sup. Ct. 497, 27 A.L.R.2d 492 (1952); Commissioner v. Pacific Mills, 207 F.2d 177 (1st Cir. 1953); National Brass Works v. Commissioner, 182 F.2d 526 (9th Cir. 1950); Jerry Rossman Corp. v. Commissioner, 175 F.2d 711 (2d Cir. 1949); Heininger v. Commissioner, 133 F.2d 567, 570 (7th Cir. 1943).

151 See BLOUGH, THE FEDERAL TAXING PROCESS 409, 463 (1952); PAUL, TAXATION FOR PROSPERITY 201 (1947); *cf.,* Paul, *The Use of Public Policy by the Commissioner in Disallowing Deductions,* in MAJOR TAX PROBLEMS OF 1954, U. So. CAL. 1954 TAX INST. 715.

152 Commissioner v. Wilcox, 327 U.S. 404, 408, 90 L. Ed. 752, 66 Sup. Ct. 546, 166 A.L.R. 884 (1946).

153 *Cf.*, Commissioner v. Pacific Mills, 207 F.2d 177 (1st Cir. 1953).

154 Helvering v. City Bank Farmers Trust Co., 296 U.S. 85, 89, 80 L. Ed. 62, 56 Sup. Ct. 70 (1935).

155 Connally v. General Constr. Co., 269 U.S. 385, 391, 70 L. Ed. 322, 46 Sup. Ct. 126 (1926). See also Douglas, J., dissenting in United States v. Harriss, 347 U.S. 612, 628, 98 L. Ed. 989, 74 Sup. Ct. 808 (1954); *cf.*, Commissioner v. Glenshaw Glass Co., 348 U.S. 426, 431, 99 L. Ed. 483, 75 Sup. Ct. 473 (1955), holding that "payments . . . extracted from . . . wrongdoers as punishment for unlawful conduct" retain their character as "taxable income to the recipients."

156 General Util. & Operating Co. v. Helvering, 296 U.S. 200, 206, 80 L. Ed. 154, 56 Sup. Ct. 185 (1935). See also Thomas B. Lilly, 14 T.C. 1066, 1088 (1950) (dissenting opinion of Arundell, J.).

157 See J. N. FRANK, LAW AND THE MODERN MIND 325 (1930); PAUL, TAXATION FOR PROSPERITY 410 (1947).

158 Richardson v. Mellish, 2 Bing. 229, 252, 130 Eng. Rep. 294, 303 (C.P. 1824) (Burroughs, J.).

159 As Holmes once said, "one may criticize even what one reveres." HOLMES, COLLECTED LEGAL PAPERS 194 (1952). To quote another, possibly less eminent Justice of the Court:

It is a mistake to suppose that the Supreme Court is either honored or helped by being spoken of as beyond criticism. On the contrary, the life and character of its justices should be the objects of constant watchfulness by all, and its judgments subject to the freest criticism. The time is past in the history of the world when any living man or body of men can be set on a pedestal and decorated with a halo. True, many criticisms may be, like their authors, devoid of good taste, but better all sorts of criticisms than no criticism at all. The moving waters are full of life and health; only in the still waters is stagnation and death.

I remember seeing in an eastern paper immediately after the decision in the well known income tax case a most extravagant eulogy upon the Supreme Court as a great defender of the rights of the few States against the many and of the accumulation of property against unconstitutional assaults. And when thereafter by that Court the act of Congress denouncing all contracts, combinations and conspiracies in a restraint of trade was held applicable to a combination between railroads to prevent competition in rates, that same paper contained an article expressing the most extraordinary surprise that men supposed to be of ordinary intelligence could be guilty of such a stupid blunder.

The one article could be condensed in a single clause, "a Daniel come to judgment; yea, a Daniel," and the other in the equally short and expressive phrase, "An ass within a lion's skin." Now, it is the inalienable right of every American citizen according to the peculiar construction of his organs of hearing to recognize in the judgments of that Court either the voice of a Daniel or the braying of an ass.

Brewer, *Government by Injunction*, 15 NAT'L CORP. REP. 848-49 (1898).

160 See p. 174, at note 48 *supra*.

161 Douglas, *Stare Decisis*, 49 COLUM. L. REV. 735, 754 (1949).

162 Letter from Thomas Jefferson to Samuel Kerchival, July 12, 1816, quoted in Douglas, *supra* note 161, at 754.

163 Helvering v. Hallock, 309 U.S. 106, 119, 84 L. Ed. 604, 60 Sup. Ct. 444, 125 A.L.R. 1368 (1939).

164 Douglas, *supra* note 161, at 736.

165 Douglas, *supra* note 161, at 746-47. [Compare his dissent in James v. United States, 366 U.S. 213, 222, 6 L. Ed. 2d 246, 81 Sup. Ct. 1052 (1961), especially at 233-34. Ed. Note.]

166 See Hand, *Thomas Walter Swan*, 57 YALE L.J. 167, 169 (1947).

167 *Cf.*, Douglas, *supra* note 161, at 754.

168 See Harrison v. Schaffner, 312 U.S. 579, 85 L. Ed. 1055, 61 Sup. Ct. 759 (1941); Irwin v. Gavit, 268 U.S. 161, 69 L. Ed. 897, 45 Sup. Ct. 475 (1925).

169 See Paul, *The Lawyer as a Tax Adviser*, 25 ROCKY MT. L. REV. 412 (1953).

170 Jaffe, *Mr. Justice Jackson*, 68 HARV. L. REV. 940, 997 (1955).

171 See PAUL, TAXATION IN THE UNITED STATES 698 (1954).

CHAPTER SEVEN

The Development of Antitrust

——*W. Wallace Kirkpatrick*——

Author's Note: David C. Nevins, B.A., University of Minnesota, a student at The National Law Center of the George Washington University where he will graduate in 1967, did a large share of the research for this Chapter and assisted ably in its preparation.

¹ George Gunton, writing in 1888, quoted in STOCKING & WATKINS, MONOPOLY AND FREE ENTERPRISE 257 (1951).

² 24 Stat. 379 (1887), as amended, 49 U.S.C. § 1 [F.C.A. 49 § 1] (1964).

³ 26 Stat. 209 (1890), as amended, 15 U.S.C. § 1 [F.C.A. 15 § 1] (1964).

⁴ Appalachian Coals, Inc. v. United States, 288 U.S. 344, 359-60, 77 L. Ed. 825, 53 Sup. Ct. 471 (1933).

⁵ 26 Stat. 209 (1890), as amended, 15 U.S.C. § 1 [F.C.A. 15 § 1] (1964). For the language of Sections 1 and 2, see note 14 *infra*.

⁶ Board of Trade v. United States, 246 U.S. 231, 238, 62 L. Ed. 683, 38 Sup. Ct. 242, Ann. Cas. 1918D, 1207 (1918).

⁷ Standard Oil Co. v. United States, 221 U.S. 1, 55 L. Ed. 619, 31 Sup. Ct. 502, 34 L.R.A. (n.s.) 834, Ann. Cas. 1912D, 734 (1911); United States v. American Tobacco Co., 221 U.S. 106, 55 L. Ed. 663, 31 Sup. Ct. 632 (1911).

⁸ 26 Stat. 209 (1890), as amended, 15 U.S.C. § 2 [F.C.A. 15 § 2] (1964). This section also condemns the joint act of conspiracy to monopolize.

⁹ For a brief treatment of the "Central Core of Legal Antitrust Concepts" see ATT'Y GEN. NAT'L COMM. ANTITRUST REP. 5-11 (1955). An excellent outline of antitrust is contained in NEALE, INTRODUCTION TO THE ANTITRUST LAWS OF THE UNITED STATES OF AMERICA (1962). The Sherman Act was amended in 1937 to exempt resale price maintenance agreements if legal under state law and in 1955 to increase the criminal penalties. Miller-Tydings Act, 50 Stat. 693 (1937), as amended by 69 Stat. 282 (1955), 15 U.S.C. § 1 [F.C.A. 15 § 1] (1964).

¹⁰ The only significant legislative change has been the 1950 Celler-Kefauver amendment to § 7 of the Clayton Act, the importance of which will be considered *infra*.

¹¹ Arnold, *Antitrust Law Enforcement*, 7 LAW & CONTEMP. PROB. 9 (1940). In 1941 another senior official of the Antitrust Division wrote:

> May it be suggested that a policy of laxity and sporadic enforcement by the Government, a growing belief among the bar that "time and circumstance had drained" the Sherman Act "of vitality," and an inclination on the part of business to forget the Act in the quiet of non-enforcement have so combined as to

313

lessen the effectiveness of the basic law against combinations. It is not suggested that all public officers charged with the enforcement of the Sherman Act have been derelict in their duties, nor that all lawyers have merely told their clients what they wanted to hear, nor that all businessmen have disregarded the Act. It is stated that all three parties to the combination have been sufficiently numerous to almost make a dead letter of that which had been hailed as a charter of freedom for American business.

HODGES, ANTITRUST ACT AND THE SUPREME COURT, 236-37 (1941).

12 Cavers, Introduction to *The Sherman Antitrust Act and its Enforcement—A Symposium,* 7 LAW & CONTEMP. PROB. 1 (1940).

13 *Compare, e.g.,* the regulations of cartels of the West German Republic, C.C.H. COMMON MARKET REPORTER, Vol. 11, *with* the general language in the Sherman Act, note 14, *infra.*

14 "An act to protect trade and commerce against unlawful restraints and monopolies," 26 Stat. 209, as amended, 15 U.S.C. §§ 1, 2 [F.C.A. 15 §§ 1, 2]:

Section 1. Every contract, combination in the form of trust or otherwise, or conspiracy, in restraint of trade or commerce among the several States, or with foreign nations, is declared to be illegal. . . . Every person who shall make any contract or engage in any combination or conspiracy . . . shall be deemed guilty of a misdemeanor, and, on conviction thereof, shall be punished by fine not exceeding fifty thousand dollars, or by imprisonment not exceeding one year, or by both said punishments, in the discretion of the court.

Section 2. Every person who shall monopolize, or attempt to monopolize, or combine or conspire with any other person or persons, to monopolize any part of the trade or commerce among the several States, or with foreign nations, shall be deemed guilty of a misdemeanor, and, on conviction thereof, shall be punished by fine not exceeding fifty thousand dollars, or by imprisonment not exceeding one year, or by both said punishments, in the discretion of the court.

The only amendments to the Sherman Act have been the addition to § 1 permitting resale price maintenance when sanctioned by state law (Miller-Tydings amendment), 50 Stat. 893, as amended, 15 U.S.C. § 1 [F.C.A. 15 § 1] (1964); the increase of the maximum fine from $5,000 to $50,000, 69 Stat. 282, 15 U.S.C. §§ 1, 3 [F.C.A. 15 §§ 1, 3] (1964).

15 Appalachian Coals, Inc. v. United States, 288 U.S. 344, 359-60, 77 L. Ed. 825, 53 Sup. Ct. 471 (1933).

16 Although enforcement policies have changed from time to time, one easy measure of enforcement (although often criticized) is the number of cases filed each year by the Department of Justice. The following table shows the number of such cases filed each year by the Justice Department:

1938—13	1944—25	1950—60	1956—46	1962—94
1939—38	1945—25	1951—49	1957—56	1963—40
1940—92	1946—43	1952—36	1958—59	1964—52
1941—105	1947—33	1953—29	1959—63	1965—40
1942—74	1948—56	1954—34	1960—89	1966—45
1943—38	1949—35	1955—54	1961—60	

17 Justice Black voted with the majority in Moore v. Mead's Fine Bread, 348 U.S. 115, 99 L. Ed. 145, 75 Sup. Ct. 148 (1954) (local operators of interstate bakery subject to antitrust); United States v. First Nat'l Bank & Trust Co., 376 U.S. 665, 12 L. Ed. 2d 1, 84 Sup. Ct. 1033 (1964) (Sherman Act applicable to bank mergers); United States v. El Paso Natural Gas Co., 376 U.S. 651, 12 L. Ed. 2d 12, 84 Sup. Ct. 1044 (1964); Simpson v. Union Oil Co., 377 U.S. 13, 12 L. Ed. 2d 98, 84 Sup. Ct. 1051 (1964) (Sherman Act held to condemn consignment agreements which resulted in price fixing). These cases represent extension of antitrust coverage into new areas. See also, e.g., United States v. National Ass'n of Real Estate Bds., 339 U.S. 485, 94 L. Ed. 1007, 70 Sup. Ct. 711 (1950); International Salt Co. v. United States, 332 U.S. 392, 92 L. Ed. 20, 68 Sup. Ct. 12 (1947); American Medical Ass'n v. United States, 317 U.S. 519, 87 L. Ed. 434, 63 Sup. Ct. 326 (1943); Interstate Circuit, Inc. v. United States, 306 U.S. 208, 83 L. Ed. 610, 59 Sup. Ct. 467 (1939).

Black dissented in McLean Trucking Co. v. United States, 321 U.S. 67, 88 L. Ed. 544, 64 Sup. Ct. 370 (1944) (opinion written by Douglas, J.), maintaining that the Interstate Commerce Commission, although having the statutory authority to except transportation mergers from the antitrust laws, is bound to observe the public interest which is most significantly affected by antitrust philosophy. See also his dissents in United States v. W. T. Grant Co., 345 U.S. 629, 97 L. Ed. 1303, 73 Sup. Ct. 894 (1953); White Motor Co. v. United States, 372 U.S. 253, 9 L. Ed. 2d 738, 83 Sup. Ct. 696 (1963); United States v. Penn-Olin Chem. Co., 378 U.S. 158, 12 L. Ed. 2d 775, 84 Sup. Ct. 1710 (1964). These cases represent occasions in which the majority declined to extend antitrust coverage to new frontiers.

18 Black concurred in the Court's opinion in most of the other major antitrust cases during the last thirty years which developed the meaning of the Sherman Act. At the 1966 term, for example, he agreed with the Court that General Motors' effort to keep its cars out of the hands of so-called "discounters" was a clear antitrust violation since General Motors was acting in concert with its dealers. United States v. General Motors Corp., 384 U.S. 127, 16 L. Ed. 2d 415, 86 Sup. Ct. 1321 (1966).

Earlier, he joined with the Court's majority holding that the New York Stock Exchange was not immune from antitrust standards. Silver v. New York Stock Exch., 373 U.S. 341, 10 L. Ed. 2d 389, 83 Sup. Ct. 1246 (1963). He concurred in Justice Brennan's two opinions for a majority of the Court, holding that du Pont's ownership of a substantial minority of General Motors' stock violated § 7 of the Clayton Act and that divestiture was the only appropriate remedy. United States v. E. I. du Pont de Nemours, 353 U.S. 586, 1 L. Ed. 2d 1057, 77 Sup. Ct. 872 (1957), 366 U.S. 316, 6 L. Ed. 2d 318, 81 Sup. Ct. 1243 (1961). These decisions involved § 7 of the Clayton Act prior to the Celler-Kefauver amendment. Black also supported the majority in all of the significant price-fixing cases, helping to establish the rule that any form of price-fixing is illegal per se. E.g., United States v. Parke, Davis & Co., 362 U.S. 29, 4 L. Ed. 2d 505, 80 Sup. Ct. 503 (1960); United States v. Socony-Vacuum Oil Co., 310 U.S. 150, 84 L. Ed. 1129, 60 Sup. Ct. 811 (1940). See also his opinion in Kiefer-

Stewart v. Joseph E. Seagram & Sons, 340 U.S. 211, 95 L. Ed. 219, 71 Sup.
Ct. 259 (1951).

19 Northern Pac. Ry. v. United States, 356 U.S. 1, 4, 2 L. Ed. 2d 545,
78 Sup. Ct. 514 (1958).

20 322 U.S. 533, 88 L. Ed. 1440, 64 Sup. Ct. 1162 (1944).

21 See dissenting opinion of Chief Justice Stone, 322 U.S. 533, at 572.

22 Chief Justice Stone, 322 U.S. 533, at 562; Justice Frankfurter, 322
U.S. 533, at 583.

23 Dislocation feared by the dissenters has not resulted. Congress reacted to *Southeastern Underwriters* in 1945 by enacting the McCarran
Act, 58 Stat. 33, as amended, 15 U.S.C. § 1011 [F.C.A. 15 § 1011] (1964),
imposing a three year moratorium on the applicability of the antitrust
laws to insurance. Thereafter, the federal antitrust laws should apply to
the insurance business to the extent that it was not regulated by state law.
The Sherman Act was specifically held applicable to any agreement to
boycott, coerce, or intimidate.

24 Timken Roller Bearing Co. v. United States, 341 U.S. 593, 95 L. Ed.
1199, 71 Sup. Ct. 971 (1951).

25 Dissenting opinion of Justice Frankfurter, *supra* note 24, at 605.

26 For example, a Special Committee on the Antitrust Laws and Foreign Trade of the Association of the Bar of the City of New York in 1957
recommended that the Congress give the President power to grant exemption from the antitrust laws to commerce with foreign nations, and suggested further that the President should grant an exemption if he found
that this would further our national security or foreign policy.

27 "We also reject the suggestion that the Sherman Act should not be
enforced in this case because what appellant has done is reasonable in view
of current foreign trade conditions. The argument in this regard seems to
be that tariffs, quota restrictions and the like are now such that the export
and import of antifriction bearings can no longer be expected as a practical matter. . . . The provisions in the Sherman Act against restraints of
foreign trade . . . 'are wholly inconsistent with appellant's argument that
American business must be left free to participate in international cartels,
that free foreign commerce in goods must be sacrificed in order to foster
export of American dollars for investment in foreign factories which sell
abroad.' " 341 U.S. 593, 599, 95 L. Ed. 1199, 71 Sup. Ct. 971 (1951).

28 Fashion Originators' Guild v. FTC, 312 U.S. 457, 85 L. Ed. 949, 61
Sup. Ct. 703 (1941), and Millinery Creators' Guild, Inc. v. FTC, 312 U.S.
469, 85 L. Ed. 955, 61 Sup. Ct. 708 (1941).

29 312 U.S. 457, 85 L. Ed. 949, 61 Sup. Ct. 703 (1941).

30 He went on to say that "among the many respects in which the
Guild's plan runs contrary to the Sherman Act, are the narrowing of the
outlets to which the manufacturers could sell and the sources from which
the retailers could buy, the organized boycott to enforce the program, and
the anti-competitive effects of revealing to the Guild the intimate business
details of its member manufacturers." 312 U.S. 457, at 465.

31 "Action falling within these three categories does not exhaust the
type of conduct banned by the Sherman and Clayton Acts." *Id.* at 466.

32 "The aim of petitioners' combination was the intentional destruction of one type of manufacture and sale which competed with Guild
members. The purpose and object of this combination, its potential
power, its tendency to monopoly, the coercion it could and did practice

upon a rival method of competition, all brought it within the policy of the prohibition declared by the Sherman and Clayton Acts." *Id.* at 467-68.

33 *Id.* at 468.

34 *Id.* at 465.

35 On the authority of the *Fashion Originators' Guild* decision, the Court, speaking very briefly, and again unanimously, through Justice Black, condemned similar boycotting of style pirates in Millinery Creators' Guild v. FTC, 312 U.S. 469, 85 L. Ed. 955, 61 Sup. Ct. 708 (1941).

36 109 F.2d 175 (2d Cir. 1940).

37 114 F.2d 80 (2d Cir. 1940).

38 The explanation for the Second Circuit's different approach in *Fashion Originators' Guild* was that the Supreme Court had handed down its *Socony-Vacuum* opinion, 310 U.S. 150, 84 L. Ed. 1129, 60 Sup. Ct. 811 (1940), in the interim between the two cases. *Socony* had held price-fixing illegal per se, thus rendering irrelevant any inquiry into the economic or business justifications. Relying on *Socony*, the boycott in *Fashion Originators' Guild* was condemned with a per se approach by the Second Circuit.

39 See Kirkpatrick, *Commercial Boycotts as per se Violations of the Sherman Act*, 10 GEO. WASH. L. REV. 302, 317-22 (1942).

40 Justice Black also wrote the Court's opinion in Associated Press v. United States, 326 U.S. 1, 89 L. Ed. 2013, 65 Sup. Ct. 1416 (1945), a case similar to *Fashion Originators' Guild*. In this case, Associated Press' by-laws which facilitated the exclusion of competitors of members of the association were held to be illegal, even though the competition was not destroyed. Justice Black emphasized that the Associated Press had violated the antitrust laws by acting as an extra-governmental agency; through its extra-judicial tribunals it had invaded the areas of governmental responsibilities, with intent to restrain the trade of those who competed with its members. Black did not regard this case as raising first amendment questions, but rather considered it a case involving commercial restraints on the business of publishing newspapers. This was argued by the defendants as a ground for nonapplicability of the antitrust laws to their conduct. Justice Murphy, in a dissenting opinion, worried that the government was for the first time intervening in the dissemination of information.

Once the facts were analyzed sufficiently, Black was satisfied that the effect of the Association's by-laws was to restrict the freedom of non-members to compete effectively. The size and scope of the Associated Press, with its large and celebrated membership, clearly made the restraint significant and illegal.

41 Antitrust's application to labor activities began raising serious problems early in this century when the Court condemned, under the Sherman Act, a union's activities to induce a manufacturer to unionize his plant. Loewe v. Lawlor, 208 U.S. 274, 52 L. Ed. 488, 28 Sup. Ct. 301 (1908). Congress overruled this approach in the Clayton Act, declaring "that the labor of a human being is not a commodity or article of commerce." 38 Stat. 730, at 731, as amended, 15 U.S.C. § 17 [F.C.A. 15 § 17] (1964). The Clayton Act also forbade federal courts to issue any injunction in disputes concerning terms or conditions of employment unless necessary to prevent irreparable injury. This prohibition against labor injunctions was effectively emasculated by a series of Supreme Court decisions. See, *e.g.*, Bedford Cut Stone Co. v. Journeymen Stone Cutters' Ass'n, 274 U.S. 37, 71 L. Ed. 916, 47 Sup. Ct. 522, 54 A.L.R. 791 (1927); Duplex Printing Co. v. Deering, 254 U.S. 443, 65 L. Ed. 349, 41 Sup. Ct.

172, 16 A.L.R. 196 (1921). These decisions led Congress to intervene
again in this field by enacting the Norris-LaGuardia Act, 47 Stat. 70, 29
U.S.C. § 101 [F.C.A. 29 § 101] (1932). The definition of a "labor dispute"
was broadened and federal courts were forbidden to enjoin such "labor
disputes." After the passage of the Norris-LaGuardia Act in 1932, considerable uncertainty existed as to how far labor's immunity from the application of antitrust extended. See text accompanying notes 47 and 48 *infra*.

42 47 Stat. 70, 29 U.S.C. § 101 [F.C.A. 29 § 101] (1964).

43 310 U.S. 469, 84 L. Ed. 1311, 60 Sup. Ct. 982, 128 A.L.R. 1044 (1940).

44 Compare text, page 208 at note 65.

45 312 U.S. 219, 85 L. Ed. 788, 61 Sup. Ct. 463 (1941).

46 Black acquiesced in the opinion written by Justice Frankfurter
which severely limited the application of the antitrust laws to labor's
activities.

47 325 U.S. 797, 89 L. Ed. 1939, 65 Sup. Ct. 1533 (1945).

48 *Id.* at 809-10. A similar approach is reflected in Black's later
opinions in two companion cases—United States v. Employing Plasterers
Ass'n, 347 U.S. 186, 98 L. Ed. 618, 74 Sup. Ct. 452, 456 (1954) and United
States v. Employing Lathers Ass'n, 347 U.S. 198, 98 L. Ed. 627, 74 Sup. Ct.
455 (1954). In these cases the government had charged local groups of
contractors and trade unions agreeing to exclude nonlocal operators from
the Chicago area plastering and lathing business. The trial court dismissed
the complaints, but Black reversed, holding that in these cases the unions
were alleged to have combined with contractor groups, and so were liable
to antitrust sanctions under the *Allen-Bradley* rule. He found enough
restraint on interstate commerce to sustain these complaints.

49 381 U.S. 657, 14 L. Ed. 2d 626, 85 Sup. Ct. 1585 (1965).

50 Local No. 189, Meat Cutters Union v. Jewel Tea Co., 381 U.S. 676,
14 L. Ed. 2d 640, 85 Sup. Ct. 1596 (1965).

51 The majority of the Court, however, found that the contract restrictions sought by the union were intimately tied to wages and hours of
employment, and were thus protected against attack under the antitrust
laws.

52 324 U.S. 293, 89 L. Ed. 951, 65 Sup. Ct. 661 (1945). The defendants
also argued that the 21st amendment to the Constitution, giving states
extensive control over commerce in liquor, immunized them from an antitrust prosecution. But Black briefly disposed of this contention, holding
that there was no real conflict between Colorado's laws and the Sherman
Act's principle.

53 See also United States v. Yellow Cab Co., 332 U.S. 218, 91 L. Ed.
2010, 67 Sup. Ct. 1560 (1947), where the majority reversed the dismissal of
the government's complaint. The trial judge had ruled that no interstate
commerce was restrained, but the Court found an adequate jurisdictional
base in the supplying of cabs and in the transportation of passengers from
one station to another as part of their interstate journey. Black was of the
opinion that the Court should go further and rule that the antitrust laws
also protected the local taxi business since many of the passengers picked
up and dropped off locally were also moving in interstate travel.

54 373 U.S. 934, 10 L. Ed. 2d 691, 83 Sup. Ct. 1534 (1963).

55 Compare FTC v. Bunte Bros., Inc., 312 U.S. 349, 85 L. Ed. 881, 61
Sup. Ct. 580 (1941), where Black joined a dissent written by Justice
Douglas as to the reach of the FTC's powers over business practices within
one state.

56 359 U.S. 207, 3 L. Ed. 2d 741, 79 Sup. Ct. 705 (1959).

57 This opinion was written by a former head of the Antitrust Division.

58 Northern Pac. Ry. v. United States, 356 U.S. 1, 2 L. Ed. 2d 545, 78 Sup. Ct. 514 (1958).

59 356 U.S. 1, at 5. Black's implementation of this view is exemplified in his opinion in Kiefer-Stewart v. Joseph E. Seagram & Sons, Inc., 340 U.S. 211, 95 L. Ed. 219, 71 Sup. Ct. 259 (1951). In the briefest language, citing only *Socony-Vacuum* and quoting just one sentence from that opinion, Black reversed the Circuit Court of Appeals' holding that fixing of maximum prices was not illegal per se. He ruled that any agreements fixing maximum or minimum prices "cripple the freedom of traders and thereby restrain their ability to sell in accordance with their own judgment." *Id.* at 213.

60 United States v. Von's Grocery Co., 384 U.S. 270, 16 L. Ed. 2d 555, 86 Sup. Ct. 1478 (1966); United States v. Pabst Brewing Co., 384 U.S. 546, 16 L. Ed. 2d 765, 86 Sup. Ct. 1665 (1966).

61 See, *e.g.*, *Antitrust in a Coonskin Cap*, Fortune Magazine, July 1, 1966, p. 65. For a specific critique of Black's opinion in *Von*, see *Notes on "Mergers,"* 80 HARV. L. REV. 245-47 (Nov. 1966). The suggestion there is that Black has confused "competition" with "number of competitors."

62 Although a series of railroad cases—United States v. Southern Pac. Co., 259 U.S. 214, 66 L. Ed. 907, 42 Sup. Ct. 496 (1922); United States v. Reading Co., 253 U.S. 26, 64 L. Ed. 760, 40 Sup. Ct. 425 (1920); Northern Sec. Co. v. United States, 193 U.S. 197, 48 L. Ed. 679, 24 Sup. Ct. 436 (1904)—early in the Sherman Act's history held that mergers could be reached by the provisions of that act's first section, the Congress in 1914, when it strengthened the antitrust laws by enacting the Clayton Act, sought to make mergers more vulnerable to early attack by specifically permitting them to be reached under the antitrust laws before the anticompetitive effects became so severe as to amount to a violation of the Sherman Act. However, this new legislation was soon emasculated by Court decisions, and the basic ineffectiveness of the antitrust laws in the merger field was highlighted in United States v. Columbia Steel, 334 U.S. 495, 92 L. Ed. 1533, 68 Sup. Ct. 1213 (1948). A majority of the Court there held that the acquisition by the largest integrated steel company of the major West Coast independent steel fabricator was not an antitrust violation. Justice Black joined in the vigorous dissent in that case written by Justice Douglas. The dissenters were unimpressed with the elaborate analysis of the market and believed that the acquisition was a clear violation of basic antitrust principles.

63 64 Stat. 1125, 15 U.S.C. §§ 18, 21 [F.C.A. 15 §§ 18, 21] (1964).

64 The first case to reach the Supreme Court under the new amendment was Maryland & Virginia Milk Producers' Ass'n, Inc. v. United States, 362 U.S. 458, 4 L. Ed. 2d 880, 80 Sup. Ct. 847 (1960). Black wrote the opinion for a unanimous Court, in which he condemned the association's acquisition of the largest independent milk outlet, producers' major competitor in the area. The opinion spent little time in market study or analysis, since the effect tended so clearly to create a monopoly or restrain trade. Other issues in this case, however, minimized the importance of the opinion as a precedent in the developing law of the application of antitrust to mergers.

65 Brown Shoe Co. v. United States, 370 U.S. 294, 8 L. Ed. 2d 510, 82 Sup. Ct. 1502 (1962).

66 See, *e.g.*, the condemnation of the merger of two natural gas companies even though approved by the appropriate regulatory agency: United States v. El Paso Natural Gas Co., 376 U.S. 651, 12 L. Ed. 2d 12, 84 Sup. Ct. 1044 (1964); the holding that bank mergers were subject to the antitrust laws despite the complicated statutory framework of laws governing banks and their supervising agencies: United States v. Philadelphia Nat'l Bank, 374 U.S. 321, 10 L. Ed. 2d 915, 83 Sup. Ct. 1715 (1963); and, the decision condemning a merger under the Clayton Act because of the likelihood of anticompetitive results from "reciprocity" generated by the acquisition: FTC v. Consolidated Foods Corp., 380 U.S. 592, 14 L. Ed. 2d 95, 85 Sup. Ct. 1220 (1965).

67 384 U.S. 270, 16 L. Ed. 2d 555, 86 Sup. Ct. 1478 (1966).

68 *Id.* at 274. Black then went on to discuss the importance of preserving small and independent competitors: "Thus, where concentration is gaining momentum in a market, we must be alert to carry out Congress' intent to protect competition against ever-increasing concentration through mergers." *Id.* at 277.

69 384 U.S. 270, at 282-83 (dissenting opinion of Stewart, J.).

70 *Id.* at 288.

71 *Id.* at 277-78 (opinion of the Court, by Black, J.).

72 384 U.S. 546, 16 L. Ed. 2d 765, 86 Sup. Ct. 1665 (1966).

73 *Id.* at 549-50.

74 *Id.* at 552-53.

75 Black's unconcern with an elaborate analysis of the "relevant market" concept, especially where such considerations hindered a clear and simple approach to antitrust's application, is reflected by his dissenting votes in three cases where the relevant market concept was so applied as to lead to a holding of no antitrust violation. In Times-Picayune Publishing Co. v. United States, 345 U.S. 594, 97 L. Ed. 1277, 73 Sup. Ct. 872 (1953), the Court held that it was not unlawful for the Times-Picayune newspaper in New Orleans to require advertisers to advertise in both morning and evening editions. Black joined three other dissenting Justices who felt that the market analysis here was unreal and artificial. The subsequent demise of the defendant's competitor-newspaper lends strong support to the dissenters' position. In the *cellophane* case, United States v. E. I. du Pont de Nemours, 351 U.S. 377, 100 L. Ed. 1264, 76 Sup. Ct. 994 (1956), Black joined Warren and Douglas in dissenting from the majority's conclusions as to the "relevant market," when it held that cellophane itself was not a relevant market but only a part of the larger "flexible packaging materials" market. In Tampa Elec. Co. v. Nashville Coal Co., 365 U.S. 320, 5 L. Ed. 2d 580, 81 Sup. Ct. 623 (1961), Black joined Douglas in dissenting without opinion, but in reliance on the district court's opinion; it seems that here Black was unwilling to expand the "relevant market" so as to lead to a holding that tying arrangements did not substantially lessen competition.

This same approach by Black to the simple and effective application of the antitrust laws is shown by his opinion for the Court in FTC v. Morton Salt Co., 334 U.S. 37, 92 L. Ed. 1196, 68 Sup. Ct. 822, 1 A.L.R.2d 260 (1948), where he argued that under the Robinson-Patman Act condemning price discrimination, the Federal Trade Commission need only establish the existence of price discriminations and the reasonable possibility of its lessening competition. He rejected the test of reasonable probability of lessening competition urged by the dissenting Justices.

[76] 323 U.S. 386, 89 L. Ed. 322, 65 Sup. Ct. 373 (1945).

[77] *Id.* at 437.

[78] Black also joined the dissent in this case by Justice Rutledge, which stated:

> The antitrust injunction suit is in form a proceeding in equity. In substance, it is a public prosecution, with civil rather than criminal sanctions, for vindication of public right and for redress and prevention of public injury. To regard the fashioning of appropriate relief in such a suit as identical with the same function in private litigation is to disregard at once the former's statutory origin, its public character and the public interest it protects.
> 323 U.S. 386, at 441-42.

[79] 335 U.S. 303, 93 L. Ed. 24, 69 Sup. Ct. 93 (1948).

[80] 340 U.S. 76, 95 L. Ed. 89, 71 Sup. Ct. 160 (1950).

[81] FTC v. Dean Foods Co., 384 U.S. 597, 16 L. Ed. 2d 802, 86 Sup. Ct. 1738 (1966).

[82] The Court found that this authority existed under the All-Writs Act.

[83] See dissenting opinion, 384 U.S. 597, at 612 (1966).

[84] 38 Stat. 719, 15 U.S.C. § 45 [F.C.A. 15 § 45].

[85] FTC v. Cement Institute, 333 U.S. 683, 92 L. Ed. 1010, 68 Sup. Ct. 793 (1948).

[86] 384 U.S. 316, 16 L. Ed. 2d 587, 86 Sup. Ct. 1501 (1966). "This broad power of the Commission [to declare trade practices unfair] is particularly well established with regard to trade practices which conflict with the basic policies of the Sherman and Clayton Acts even though such practices may not actually violate these laws. *Id.* at 322.

[87] In similar fashion, Black has voted in several cases for interpretations or applications of the Robinson-Patman Act, 49 Stat. 1526, as amended, 15 U.S.C. § 13 [F.C.A. 15 § 13] (1964), which make more effective and competitively meaningful its prohibitions against price discrimination. In Standard Oil Co. v. FTC, 340 U.S. 231, 95 L. Ed. 239, 71 Sup. Ct. 240 (1951) Black joined the dissenters arguing that there must be a showing that the price-discrimination injures competition in order to invoke the defense of "meeting competition." An absolute defense based on "meeting competition" was thought to have the effect of shifting the statutes' purpose of protecting competition. In FTC v. Ruberoid Co., 343 U.S. 470, 96 L. Ed. 1081, 72 Sup. Ct. 800 (1952), Black concurred, specifically noting his feeling that the decree should expressly sanction exemptions for competitive factors. In United States v. Borden Co., 370 U.S. 460, 8 L. Ed. 2d 627, 82 Sup. Ct. 1309 (1962), Black joined the majority in an interpretation of the statute tending to promote competitive factors and discourage size and concentrated power. And, in FTC v. Borden Co., 383 U.S. 637, 16 L. Ed. 2d 153, 86 Sup. Ct. 1092 (1966), Black disagreed with the majority which found a price discrimination unlawful where it was effectuated by selling the same products for a lower price under a private brand name than that charged under a nationally advertised brand.

[88] See, *e.g.*, United States v. Yellow Cab Co., 332 U.S. 218, 91 L. Ed. 2010, 67 Sup. Ct. 1560 (1947).

Black's impatience seems especially acute when procedural snarls
threaten to block antitrust from its goals. For example, in Wallace v.
Tiernan, 336 U.S. 793, 93 L. Ed. 1042, 69 Sup. Ct. 824 (1949), his opinion
for a unanimous Court upheld, against a charge of unreasonable search
and seizure, the government's power to subpoena documents originally
demanded by an illegally constituted grand jury. (Women were excluded
from the grand jury out of an excessive nicety of concern over the limited
toilet facilities.) Likewise, Black, in dissent, has argued for allowing a
third party to intervene in a suit seeking dissolution because he felt it
would facilitate complete resolution of the antitrust issue. See Sutphen
Estates, Inc. v. United States, 342 U.S. 19, 23, 96 L. Ed. 19, 72 Sup. Ct. 14
(1951). And, in Theatre Enterprise v. Paramount Film Distrib. Corp., 346
U.S. 537, 98 L. Ed. 273, 74 Sup. Ct. 257 (1954), Black, again dissenting,
urged that a private plaintiff be permitted to use a previous finding of
concerted activity to establish a prima facie violation, notwithstanding the
fact that the majority found the previous finding to involve a different
place and time.

Black's desire for an effective and complete disposition of every antitrust case is evidenced in several other cases. See, *e.g.,* FTC v. Minneapolis-Honeywell Regulator Co., 344 U.S. 206, 97 L. Ed. 245, 73 Sup.
Ct. 245 (1952) (dissenting opinion); Shenandoah Valley Broadcasting, Inc.
v. American Soc'y of Composers, 371 U.S. 540, 9 L. Ed. 2d 508, 83 Sup. Ct.
519 (1963); United States v. Wayne Pump Co., 317 U.S. 200, 87 L. Ed. 184,
63 Sup. Ct. 191 (1942); United States v. National City Lines, Inc., 337
U.S. 78, 93 L. Ed. 1226, 69 Sup. Ct. 955 (1949).

89 See, *e.g.,* Sola Elec. Co. v. Jefferson Elec. Co., 317 U.S. 173, 87 L. Ed.
165, 63 Sup. Ct. 172 (1942), holding a patent licensee is not estopped,
because of his license, from asserting that a price-fixing clause violated the
Sherman Act; Besser Mfg. Co. v. United States, 343 U.S. 444, 96 L. Ed.
1063, 72 Sup. Ct. 838 (1952) approving a district court's order for compulsory licensing and fixing royalties by arbitration; Walker Process
Equip., Inc. v. Food Mach. & Chem. Corp., 382 U.S. 172, 15 L. Ed. 2d 247,
86 Sup. Ct. 347 (1965). See also Katzinger Co. v. Chicago Metallic Mfg.
Co., 329 U.S. 402, 91 L. Ed. 380, 67 Sup. Ct. 421, 424 (1947), and United
States Gypsum Co. v. National Gypsum Co., 352 U.S. 457, 1 L. Ed. 2d
465, 77 Sup. Ct. 490 (1957).

90 304 U.S. 175, 82 L. Ed. 1273, 58 Sup. Ct. 857 (1937).

91 *Id.* at 185-86. Black appreciated the frightening anticompetitive
results of a patent pool where the members sought to divide among themselves the various fields in which the invention could be applied. He
continued:

Although the patent laws contemplate and authorize but one
patent monopoly for one invention, many separate patents
authorizing single patent monopolies are merged in this "patent
pool." Thus, all these separate patent monopolies are combined
and in many respects are made to function as one. The record
shows that from this larger combination—completely outside the
conception in the patent statutes of single and separate monopolies—allotments of submonopolies are made in the respective
"fields," from which emanate in turn other monopolies.

304 U.S. 175, at 187.

92 See, Ethyl Gasoline Corp. v. United States, 309 U.S. 436, 84 L. Ed.
852, 60 Sup. Ct. 618 (1940); United States v. Univis Lens, 316 U.S. 241,

86 L. Ed. 1408, 62 Sup. Ct. 1088 (1942); United States v. Masonite Corp., 316 U.S. 265, 86 L. Ed. 1461, 62 Sup. Ct. 1070 (1942); United States v. Bausch & Lomb Optical Co., 321 U.S. 707, 88 L. Ed. 1024, 64 Sup. Ct. 805 (1944); United States v. United States Gypsum Co., 333 U.S. 364, 92 L. Ed. 746, 68 Sup. Ct. 525 (1948); United States v. New Wrinkle, Inc., 342 U.S. 371, 96 L. Ed. 417, 72 Sup. Ct. 350 (1952).

[93] See, *e.g.*, Black's concurring opinion in Mercoid Corp. v. Mid-Continent Inv. Co., 320 U.S. 661, 88 L. Ed. 376, 64 Sup. Ct. 268 (1944). In his opinion here Black stated:

> At least since Adam Smith wrote unhampered competition has not generally been considered immoral. While there have been objections to the Sherman Anti-Trust Act . . . few if any of the objectors have questioned its morality.

320 U.S. 661, at 673. See also Mercoid Corp. v. Minneapolis-Honeywell Regulator Co., 320 U.S. 680, 88 L. Ed. 396, 64 Sup. Ct. 278 (1944); Transparent-Wrap Mach. Corp. v. Stolses & Smith Co., 329 U.S. 637, 91 L. Ed. 563, 67 Sup. Ct. 610 (1947) (dissenting opinion); and United States v. Singer Mfg. Co., 374 U.S. 174, 10 L. Ed. 2d 823, 83 Sup. Ct. 1773 (1963).

[94] 324 U.S. 370, 89 L. Ed. 1006, 65 Sup. Ct. 741 (1945).

[95] 333 U.S. 287, 92 L. Ed. 701, 68 Sup. Ct. 550 (1948).

[96] 339 U.S. 827, 94 L. Ed. 1312, 70 Sup. Ct. 894 (1950).

[97] *Id.* at 838.

[98] 376 U.S. 225, 11 L. Ed. 2d 661, 84 Sup. Ct. 784 (1964).

[99] 376 U.S. 234, 11 L. Ed. 2d 669, 84 Sup. Ct. 779 (1964).

[100] 376 U.S. 225, 230-31 (1964).

[101] 365 U.S. 127, 5 L. Ed. 2d 464, 81 Sup. Ct. 523 (1961).

[102] See text accompanying notes 42-49.

[103] 325 U.S. 821, 89 L. Ed. 1954, 65 Sup. Ct. 1545 (1945). A related facet of this labor limitation involves the determination of whether the group involved is composed of employees or of independent businessmen, a determination that is often quite difficult. In Milk Wagon Drivers Union, Local 753 v. Lake Valley Farm Products, Inc., 311 U.S. 91, 85 L. Ed. 63, 61 Sup. Ct. 122 (1940), the question was whether milkwagon drivers who bought milk and resold it to retail stores were employees or independent entrepreneurs. Black held that they were employees, partly because they assumed no business risk since the dairies had agreed to take back all unsold milk, and partly because the drivers had joined a rival union. Accordingly, there was a controversy involving the employer-employee relationship and hence a "labor dispute" within the meaning of the Norris-LaGuardia Act. The result was that no injunction might issue because the prohibition on the federal courts against issuing injunctions in cases involving a "labor dispute" applies to injunctions restraining violations of the Sherman Act as well as to any other statute.

See also Columbia River Packers Ass'n v. Hinton, 315 U.S. 143, 86 L. Ed. 750, 62 Sup. Ct. 520 (1942), which involved the question of defining a "non-labor group," where Black spoke for the Court.

Black joined an 8-1 majority in the *grease peddlers* opinion, Los Angeles Meat & Provision Drivers' Union, Local 826 v. United States, 371 U.S. 94, 9 L. Ed. 2d 150, 83 Sup. Ct. 162 (1962), written by Stewart. As in *Columbia River Packers,* this opinion held that union membership conferred no antitrust immunity on independent businessmen. Douglas alone vigorously dissented on the ground that economically and realistically

these "independent businessmen" were actually employees. See also
United Bhd. of Carpenters v. United States, 330 U.S. 395, 91 L. Ed. 973,
67 Sup. Ct. 775 (1947), where Black voted against the government; the
Court holding that there could be no liability under antitrust, for a union,
without clear proof that the members of the union authorized the action
which precipitated the charge of a violation.

104 Hughes v. United States, 342 U.S. 353, 96 L. Ed. 394, 72 Sup. Ct.
306 (1952).

105 Pittsburgh Plate Glass Co. v. United States, 360 U.S. 395, 3 L. Ed.
2d 1323, 79 Sup. Ct. 1237 (1959).

106 *Id.* at 401.

107 372 U.S. 29, 9 L. Ed. 2d 561, 83 Sup. Ct. 594 (1963).

108 377 U.S. 95, 12 L. Ed. 2d 152, 84 Sup. Ct. 1082 (1964).

109 32 Stat. 903, 15 U.S.C. § 32 [F.C.A. 15 § 32] (1964).

110 377 U.S. 95, at 115. Black's dissenting opinion in St. Regis Paper
Co. v. United States, 368 U.S. 208, 7 L. Ed. 2d 240, 82 Sup. Ct. 289 (1961),
reflects the same concern for the protection of the rights of private citizens.
In *St. Regis,* he objected to a decision compelling a company to submit
copies of reports the company had made to the Census Bureau to the Federal Trade Commission; Black thought that the statutes which gave protection to a company submitting census reports was broad enough to prevent any other branch of the government from obtaining such information.

This same philosophy is also reflected in Black's dissenting vote in
Cheff v. Schnackenberg, 384 U.S. 373, 16 L. Ed. 2d 629, 86 Sup. Ct. 1523,
1537 (1966), where the majority upheld a sentence of six months' imprisonment for contempt, without a jury trial, for a violation of a Court of
Appeals order to cease and desist pending review of an order of the
Federal Trade Commission. Douglas' dissenting opinion, which Black
joined, argued that there was no reason or justification for classifying as
"petty," contempts punished by less than six months, and accordingly,
approving such punishment without a jury trial.

CHAPTER EIGHT

The Federal Civil Rules and the Pursuit of Justice

————*George Kaufmann*————

1 370 U.S. 626, 8 L. Ed. 2d 734, 82 Sup. Ct. 1386 (1962).
2 The Act provided as follows:

That the Supreme Court of the United States shall have the power to prescribe, by general rules, for the district courts of the United States and for the courts of the District of Columbia, the forms of process, writs, pleadings, and motions, and the practice and procedure in civil actions at law. Said rules shall neither abridge, enlarge, nor modify the substantive rights of any litigant. They shall take effect six months after their promulgation, and thereafter all laws in conflict therewith shall be of no further force or effect.

SEC. 2. The court may at any time unite the general rules prescribed by it for cases in equity with those in actions at law so as to secure one form of civil action and procedure for both: *Provided, however,* that in such union of rules the right of trial by jury as at common law and declared by the seventh amendment to the Constitution shall be preserved to the parties inviolate. Such united rules shall not take effect until they shall have been reported to Congress by the Attorney General at the beginning of a regular session thereof and until after the close of such session.

Act of June 19, 1934, 48 Stat. 1064; superseded by 28 U.S.C. § 2072 [F.C.A. 28 § 2072].
3 302 U.S. 783 (1937).
4 323 U.S. 821 (1944). Mr. Justice Frankfurter also dissented, stating that since the members of the Supreme Court no longer try criminal cases, the Court "is not an appropriate agency for formulating the rules of criminal procedure for the district courts." He also objected that serious questions, apparently of a constitutional nature, lurk in the promulgation of any rule of criminal procedure and that such issues are best decided in litigation between parties. The latter argument was prescient. See Singer v. United States, 380 U.S. 24, 13 L. Ed. 2d 630, 85 Sup. Ct. 783 (1965). See also the objections to the 1966 Amendments to the Federal Rules of Criminal Procedure authorizing the Court to require defendants to give certain information to the prosecutor before the trial, a procedure which at least arguably violates the privilege against self-incrimination. Statement of Mr. Justice Douglas, 383 U.S. 1089, at 1090-93. On the same

day that this rule was promulgated, the Court denied rehearing of an order denying certiorari to review a state conviction raising this question. Frazier v. California, 383 U.S. 931, 384 U.S. 946 (1966). Petitioner in that case had urged that it would be preferable to decide the constitutional questions, "in the normal course of the Court's adjudicatory function, rather than in adopting rules of criminal procedure." Petition for Certiorari, No. 755, Oct. Term, 1965, p. 24, n.33; see also *id.*, Petition for Rehearing, pp. 6-7.

5 346 U.S. 946 (1954).

6 *Ibid.* He objected to the new rules also because they restricted appellate review and improperly limited the rights of persons other than the parties before the Court to file briefs. 346 U.S. 947 (1954).

7 Statement of Mr. Justice Black, 1961, 368 U.S. 1012.

8 Statement of Mr. Justice Black and Mr. Justice Douglas, Jan. 21, 1963, 374 U.S. 865-66.

9 Statement of Mr. Justice Black, Feb. 28, 1966, 383 U.S. 1032.

Mr. Justice Black has long insisted upon strict adherence to the constitutionally prescribed separation of powers: See, *e.g.*, Youngstown Sheet & Tube Co. v. Sawyer, 343 U.S. 579, 96 L. Ed. 1153, 72 Sup. Ct. 834 (1952); United States *ex rel.* Toth v. Quarles, 350 U.S. 11, 100 L. Ed. 8, 76 Sup. Ct. 1 (1955); Joint Anti-Fascist Refugee Comm. v. McGrath, 341 U.S. 123, 142, at 144-45, 95 L. Ed. 817, 71 Sup. Ct. 624 (1951) (concurring opinion); Irvine v. California, 347 U.S. 128, 139, at 142, 98 L. Ed. 561, 74 Sup. Ct. 381 (1954) (dissenting opinion); Barenblatt v. United States, 360 U.S. 109, 134, at 153-62, 3 L. Ed. 2d 1115, 79 Sup. Ct. 1081 (1960) (dissenting opinion); Zemel v. Rusk, 381 U.S. 1, 20, 14 L. Ed. 2d 179, 85 Sup. Ct. 1271 (1965) (dissenting opinion).

10 23 U.S. (10 Wheat.) 1, 6 L. Ed. 253 (1825).

11 Hanna v. Plumer, 380 U.S. 460, 471, 14 L. Ed. 2d 8, 85 Sup. Ct. 1136 (1965).

12 Mississippi Publishing Corp. v. Murphree, 326 U.S. 438, 442, 90 L. Ed. 185, 66 Sup. Ct. 242 (1946).

13 312 U.S. 1, 85 L. Ed. 479, 61 Sup. Ct. 422 (1941).

14 *Id.* at 14.

15 *Id.* at 17 (dissenting opinion of Frankfurter, J.).

16 *Ibid.* The *Sibbach* case had an interesting aftermath in Schlagenhauf v. Holder, 379 U.S. 104, 13 L. Ed. 2d 152, 85 Sup. Ct. 234 (1964). There a physical examination was required of a *defendant,* who while accepting the *Sibbach* precedent as to plaintiffs, contended that since a defendant is in court involuntarily, a different result should follow. The Court rejected this contention, only Mr. Justice Douglas thinking *Sibbach* distinguishable. Mr. Justice Black filed an interesting separate opinion in *Schlagenhauf.* Accepting the *Sibbach* precedent, he emphatically concurred in the Court's rejection of the distinction between the rights of plaintiffs and the rights of defendants to be free of physical examination. But he went further and disagreed with some of the limitations which the Court placed on the physical examination to which the defendant in that case could properly be subject, buttressing his views with a detailed explanation of the potential value of such an examination to the plaintiff. Schlagenhauf v. Holder, *supra* at 123-24. In sharp contrast to his opinion is that of Justice Douglas, who was concerned with the great potential of

blackmail in allowing a plaintiff to subject the defendant to physical examination or suffer judgment to be entered against him. *Id.* at 126.

17 Some of his more important constitutional opinions in which the right to jury trial was controlling, or significant to his conclusion, are: Duncan v. Kahanamoku, 327 U.S. 304, 90 L. Ed. 688, 66 Sup. Ct. 606 (1946); United States v. Lovett, 328 U.S. 303, 90 L. Ed. 1252, 66 Sup. Ct. 1073 (1946); United States *ex rel.* Toth v. Quarles, 350 U.S. 11, 100 L. Ed. 8, 76 Sup. Ct. 1 (1956); Reid v. Covert, 354 U.S. 1, 1 L. Ed. 2d 1148, 77 Sup. Ct. 1222 (1957) (plurality opinion); Sacher v. United States, 343 U.S. 1, 20, 90 L. Ed. 717, 72 Sup. Ct. 451 (1952) (dissenting opinion); Green v. United States, 356 U.S. 165, 193, 2 L. Ed. 2d 672, 78 Sup. Ct. 632 (1958) (dissenting opinion); United States v. Barnett, 376 U.S. 681, 724, 12 L. Ed. 2d 23, 84 Sup. Ct. 984 (1964) (dissenting opinion); United States v. Gainey, 380 U.S. 63, 74, 13 L. Ed. 2d 658, 85 Sup. Ct. 754 (1965) (dissenting opinion); Jackson v. Denno, 378 U.S. 368, 401, 12 L. Ed. 2d 908, 84 Sup. Ct. 1774 (1964) (dissenting in part).

Justice Black's respect for the jury system has also influenced his interpretation of statutes. See, *e.g.,* Moore v. Illinois Cent. R.R., 312 U.S. 630, 85 L. Ed. 1089, 61 Sup. Ct. 754 (1941). *In re* Michael, 326 U.S. 224, 227, 90 L. Ed. 30, 66 Sup. Ct. 78 (1946); Romero v. International Terminal Operating Co., 358 U.S. 354, 388, 3 L. Ed. 2d 368, 79 Sup. Ct. 468 (1959) (dissenting opinion); Mitchell v. De Mario Jewelry Co., 361 U.S. 288, 297, 4 L. Ed. 2d 323, 80 Sup. Ct. 332 (1960) (joining dissenting opinion); Pennsylvania R.R. v. Day, 360 U.S. 548, 554, at 560-63, 3 L. Ed. 2d 1422, 79 Sup. Ct. 1322 (1959) (dissenting opinion); Republic Steel Corp. v. Maddox, 379 U.S. 650, 659, particularly at 664, 13 L. Ed. 2d 580, 85 Sup. Ct. 614 (1965) (dissenting opinion). There is also, of course, a large body of personal injury cases in which he has insisted on giving the jury broad scope; see, *e.g.,* Tiller v. Atlantic Coastline R.R., 318 U.S. 54, 87 L. Ed. 610, 63 Sup. Ct. 444 (1943); Wilkerson v. McCarthy, 336 U.S. 53, 93 L. Ed. 497, 69 Sup. Ct. 413 (1949); Brown v. Western Pac. R.R., 338 U.S. 294, 94 L. Ed. 100, 70 Sup. Ct. 105 (1949); Dice v. Akron, C. & Y.R.R., 342 U.S. 359, 96 L. Ed. 398, 72 Sup. Ct. 312 (1952); Southern R.R. v. Jackson, 375 U.S. 837, 11 L. Ed. 2d 65, 84 Sup. Ct. 77 (1963) (dissent from denial of certiorari).

18 319 U.S. 372, 396, 87 L. Ed. 1458, 63 Sup. Ct. 1077 (1943) (dissenting opinion). Black's understanding of the early history of trial by jury is disputed in Henderson, *The Background of the Seventh Amendment,* 80 HARV. L. REV. 289 (1966).

19 374 U.S. 866-67 (1963).

20 In Associated Press v. United States, 326 U.S. 1, 89 L. Ed. 2013, 65 Sup. Ct. 1416 (1945), Justice Black affirmed the granting of summary judgment in an important antitrust case, rejecting "the contention of the appellants that there were genuine disputes as to material facts and that the case therefore should have gone to trial." *Id.* at 5. He agreed that the rule authorizing summary judgments ". . . should be cautiously invoked to the end that parties may always be afforded a trial where there is a bona fide dispute of facts between them." *Id.* at 6. But he found that restrictive arrangements which the appellants had admitted were sufficient to support the entry of a judgment entered against them. Other instances in which Justice Black has approved the granting of summary judgment by the District Courts include Northern Pac. Ry. v. United States, 356 U.S. 1, 2 L. Ed. 2d 545, 78 Sup. Ct. 514 (1958); Kennedy v. Silas Mason Co., 334

U.S. 249, 257, 92 L. Ed. 1347, 68 Sup. Ct. 1031 (1948) (noting, in dissent, that a judgment of the Court of Appeals which had reversed a summary judgment should in turn be reversed); White Motor Co. v. United States, 372 U.S. 253, 275, 9 L. Ed. 2d 738, 83 Sup. Ct. 696 (1963) (joining in a dissent from a reversal of a summary judgment in an antitrust case).

21 See 374 U.S. at 867-68.

22 See Beacon Theatres v. Westover, 359 U.S. 500, 3 L. Ed. 2d 988, 79 Sup. Ct. 948 (1959); Dairy Queen, Inc. v. Wood, 369 U.S. 469, 8 L. Ed. 2d 44, 82 Sup. Ct. 894 (1962). In these cases the question was whether a District Court had power to order the trial of equitable claims before legal claims, where the effect would be to deny trial by jury on the common issues in the suit. Justice Black said, *inter alia,* that one of the reforms of the Federal Rules was to allow legal and equitable causes of action to be tried jointly and that the District Courts' actions were inconsistent with their obligation to preserve the right to trial by jury. *Cf.* Fitzgerald v. United States Lines, 374 U.S. 16, 10 L. Ed. 2d 720, 83 Sup. Ct. 1646 (1963), where Justice Black held for the Court that where a claim for maintenance and cure (normally triable by the Court) was joined with a Jones Act claim (triable by a jury) both must be submitted to the jury when they arise out of one set of facts.

23 370 U.S. 626, 8 L. Ed. 2d 734, 82 Sup. Ct. 1386 (1962).

24 370 U.S. 626, at 628-29.

25 291 F.2d 542 (7th Cir. 1961).

26 370 U.S. 626, at 630-33.

27 *Id.* at 635.

28 See 291 F.2d 542 (7th Cir. 1961), particularly at 543; and Justice Black's discussion, 370 U.S. 626, at 638-39.

29 The absence of findings also made it impossible to determine whether the District Court's feeling that the suit was obviously without merit was a factor in its decision—either as an additional reason for believing that plaintiff would not wish to go to trial (but was preserving the suit for its nuisance value), or as minimizing, in the Court's mind, the severity of the sanction of dismissal. It is a nice question whether this would be a proper consideration on either ground; if not, and if the District Court had explained with particularity the basis of its decision, a remand to the District Court to reconsider on the basis of valid criteria would have been required. See Platt v. Minnesota Min. & Mfg. Co., 376 U.S. 240, 244-45, 11 L. Ed. 2d 674, 84 Sup. Ct. 769 (1964).

30 See Phelps Dodge Corp. v. NLRB, 313 U.S. 177, 85 L. Ed. 1271, 61 Sup. Ct. 845, 133 A.L.R. 1217 (1941); S.E.C. v. Chenery Corp., 318 U.S. 80, 87 L. Ed. 626, 63 Sup. Ct. 454 (1943); 332 U.S. 194, 91 L. Ed. 1995, 67 Sup. Ct. 1575 (1947).

31 370 U.S. 626, at 643.

32 *Id.* at 646 (dissenting opinion).

33 The *Link* opinion was anticipated in Black's 1954 memorandum dissenting from the adoption of the Supreme Court's own revised rules, and especially in that part quoted in the text at page 222.

34 Statement of Mr. Justice Black and Mr. Justice Douglas (Jan. 21, 1963), 374 U.S. 865, 868.

35 Statement of Mr. Justice Black (Feb. 28, 1966), 383 U.S. 1032, 1034-37. He has followed these views in dissenting from denials of certiorari in several cases: Bertman v. J. A. Kirsch Co., 377 U.S. 995, 12 L. Ed. 2d 1047, 84 Sup. Ct. 1913 (1964); Lord v. Helmandollar, 383 U.S. 928, 15

L. Ed. 2d 847, 86 Sup. Ct. 929 (1966); Riess v. Murchison, 383 U.S. 946 (1966); Beaufort Concrete Co. v. Atlantic States Constr. Co., 384 U.S. 1004, 16 L. Ed. 2d 1018, 86 Sup. Ct. 1908 (1966). Most recently he dissented from the Supreme Court's dismissal of an appeal which had been filed out of time. Pittsburgh Towing Co. v. Mississippi Valley Barge Line Co., 385 U.S. 32, 17 L. Ed. 2d 31, 87 Sup. Ct. 195 (1966).

36 *Supra* note 35.

37 383 U.S. 363, 15 L. Ed. 2d 807, 86 Sup. Ct. 845 (1966).

38 383 U.S. 1004, at 1006.

39 383 U.S. 363, at 373.

40 303 U.S. 197, 82 L. Ed. 745, 58 Sup. Ct. 507 (1938).

41 *Id.* at 200.

42 For a subsequent application of the rule by Black in a case similar to *Maty*, see Tiller v. Atlantic Coastline R.R., 323 U.S. 574, 581, 89 L. Ed. 465, 65 Sup. Ct. 421 (1944).

43 373 U.S. 934, 10 L. Ed. 2d 691, 83 Sup. Ct. 691 (1963).

44 *Id.* at 935 (dissenting opinion). See also Lathrop v. Donohue, 367 U.S. 820, 865, 6 L. Ed. 2d 1191, 81 Sup. Ct. 1826 (1961) (dissenting opinion).

45 355 U.S. 41, 47-48, 2 L. Ed. 2d 80, 78 Sup. Ct. 99 (1957).

46 Compare United States v. 93.970 Acres of Land, 360 U.S. 328, 332, 3 L. Ed. 2d 1275, 79 Sup. Ct. 1193 (1959), where Justice Black, speaking for a unanimous Court, held that the Federal Rules of Civil Procedure do away with the common-law doctrine of election of remedies.

47 See Conley, 355 U.S. 41, at 45-56; United States v. Employing Plasterers, 347 U.S. 186, 98 L. Ed. 618, 74 Sup. Ct. 452 (1954); Glus v. Brooklyn Eastern Terminal, 359 U.S. 231, 3 L. Ed. 2d 770, 79 Sup. Ct. 760 (1959); Beacon Theatres v. Westover, 359 U.S. 500, 3 L. Ed. 2d 988, 79 Sup. Ct. 948 (1959).

48 See, *e.g.,* Polk Co. v. Glover, 305 U.S. 5, 10, 83 L. Ed. 6, 59 Sup. Ct. 15 (1938) (dissenting opinion of Black, J.).

49 312 U.S. 552, 85 L. Ed. 1037, 61 Sup. Ct. 719 (1941).

50 *Id.* at 556. He continued:

> For our procedural scheme contemplates that parties shall come to issue in the trial forum vested with authority to determine questions of fact. This is essential in order that parties may have the opportunity to offer all the evidence they believe relevant to the issues which the trial tribunal is alone competent to decide; it is equally essential in order that litigants may not be surprised on appeal by final decision there of issues upon which they have had no opportunity to introduce evidence.

Similar considerations underlie a series of opinions by Justice Black interpreting Rule 50(b). These held the Courts of Appeals are without power to direct the District Courts to enter judgments in favor of the appellant notwithstanding a jury verdict, unless the appellant had followed his motion for directed verdict with a timely motion for judgment in the trial court. Cone v. West Virginia Pulp & Paper Co., 330 U.S. 212, 91 L. Ed. 849, 67 Sup. Ct. 752 (1947); Globe Liquor Co. v. San Roman, 332 U.S. 571, 92 L. Ed. 177, 68 Sup. Ct. 246 (1948); Fountain v. Filson, 336 U.S. 681, 93 L. Ed. 971, 69 Sup. Ct. 754 (1949) (opinion per curiam);

Johnson v. New York, N.H. & H.R.R., 344 U.S. 48, 97 L. Ed. 77, 73 Sup. Ct. 125 (1952). In *Johnson* the railroad had filed a motion for directed verdict in its favor, but the judge, reserving decision on that motion, submitted the case to the jury. The jury entered a verdict for the plaintiff, which the railroad moved to set aside. No motion for judgment notwithstanding the verdict was made. The district court denied the motion to set aside the verdict, and also denied the motion for directed verdict which it had previously denied. The Court of Appeals, holding that the motion for directed verdict should have been granted, reversed, an order which the parties interpreted as directing the trial court to enter judgment for the railroad. See 344 U.S. 48, at 49. A 5-4 majority of the Supreme Court held that *Cone* precluded the Court of Appeals from imposing this duty on the trial court. The railroad attempted to distinguish *Cone* on the ground that the district judge had reserved decision on the motion for directed verdict, but Justice Black observed that this contention "not only flies in the teeth of the Rules' unambiguous language but if sustained would undermine safeguards for litigants some of which have been pointed out in prior cases," *id.* at 51. He then carefully traced the history of Rule 50(b), concluding, "Rule 50(b) as written and as construed by us is not difficult to understand or to observe. Rewriting the rule to fit counsel's unexpressed wants and intentions would make it easy to reintroduce the same type of confusion and uncertainty the rule was adopted to end." *Id.* at 53. It is somewhat ironic that an opinion so soundly justified by fairness and practicality should be characterized in dissent as a return to the hypertechnicalities of common-law pleading associated with the name of Baron Parke, 344 U.S. 48, at 62.

51 Hormel v. Helvering, *supra* note 49, at 557. Justice Black has generally taken a broad view of appealability. See, *e.g.*, Gillespie v. United States Steel Corp., 379 U.S. 148, 152-54, 13 L. Ed. 2d 199, 85 Sup. Ct. 308 (1964); McCullough v. Kammerer Corp., 331 U.S. 196, 91 L. Ed. 1365, 67 Sup. Ct. 1165 (1947); Dickinson v. Petroleum Corp., 338 U.S. 507, 516, 94 L. Ed. 299, 70 Sup. Ct. 322 (1950) (dissenting opinion); Baltimore Contractors v. Bodinger, 348 U.S. 176, 185, 99 L. Ed. 233, 75 Sup. Ct. 249 (1955) (dissening opinion); Morganton v. Royal Ins. Co., 337 U.S. 254, 261, 93 L. Ed. 1347, 69 Sup. Ct. 1067 (1949) (dissenting opinion).

52 371 U.S. 215, 9 L. Ed. 2d 261, 83 Sup. Ct. 283 (1962).

53 *Id.* at 217.

54 370 U.S. 626, 633-34.

55 375 U.S. 384, 11 L. Ed. 2d 404, 84 Sup. Ct. 397 (1964).

56 Wolfsohn v. Hankin, 376 U.S. 203, 204, 11 L. Ed. 2d 636, 84 Sup. Ct. 699 (1964) (dissenting opinion).

57 Brinkerhoff-Faris Trust & Savings Co. v. Hill, 281 U.S. 673, 678, 74 L. Ed. 1107, 50 Sup. Ct. 451 (1930).

58 Lord v. Helmandollar, 348 F.2d 780, 782, n.3 (D.C. Cir. 1965).

59 Lord v. Helmandollar, 383 U.S. 928, 15 L. Ed. 2d 847, 86 Sup. Ct. 929 (1966).

60 Pittsburgh Towing Co. v. Mississippi Valley Barge Line Co., 385 U.S. 32, 34, 17 L. Ed. 2d 31, 87 Sup. Ct. 195 (1966).

61 It is certainly true that some court clerks believe that court rules were instituted for their own convenience and insist on readings which promote the interests of neither the court nor the parties. This is perhaps particularly prevalent in state jurisdictions where the clerks have a political

base independent of the court, and the office of the clerk is regarded as a source of patronage rather than an aid to the processing of lawsuits.

62 Lewis v. Roberts, 267 U.S. 467, 69 L. Ed. 739, 45 Sup. Ct. 357, 37 A.L.R. 1440 (1924). Discussed in Introduction, p. xxiii. Black's law partner was Crampton Harris.

63 See, *e.g.*, Adkins v. DuPont & Co., 335 U.S. 331, 93 L. Ed. 43, 69 Sup. Ct. 85, 11 A.L.R.2d 599 (1948); Betts v. Brady, 316 U.S. 455, 474, 86 L. Ed. 1595, 62 Sup. Ct. 1252 (1942) (dissenting opinion); Gideon v. Wainwright, 372 U.S. 335, 9 L. Ed. 2d 799, 83 Sup. Ct. 792, 93 A.L.R.2d 733 (1963).

64 363 U.S. 207, 4 L. Ed. 2d 1170, 80 Sup. Ct. 1222 (1960).

65 *Id.* at 224 (dissenting opinion).

66 Farmer v. Arabian American Oil Co., 379 U.S. 227, 235, 13 L. Ed. 2d 248, 85 Sup. Ct. 411 (1964).

67 Polizzi v. Cowles Magazines, Inc., 345 U.S. 663, 667, 671-72, 97 L. Ed. 1331, 73 Sup. Ct. 900 (1953) (Black, J., concurring in part and dissenting in part). See also Cameron v. Johnson, 381 U.S. 741, 742, at 753, 14 L. Ed. 2d 715, 85 Sup. Ct. 1751 (1965) (dissenting opinion).

68 In Anderson v. Yungkau, 329 U.S. 482, 91 L. Ed. 436, 67 Sup. Ct. 428 (1947), Mr. Justice Black joined a seven-man majority which construed Rules 25(a) and 6(b) of the Federal Rules of Civil Procedure to bar a suit against the executors of defendants because the executors had not been substituted within two years after the death of the original parties. Suits pending against these defendants had been delayed by mutual consent, while a test case on which their liability would be based was wending its way through the courts. Through no lack of diligence, the plaintiff did not learn of the death of the original parties until after the expiration of the two-year period. Nonetheless, the Court held that the District Court was without power to extend the two-year period prescribed in Rule 25(a) for the substitution of parties. A strong technical argument could be made—and was made in dissent—that Rule 6(b) impliedly granted such discretion to the District Court. But the majority chose to read Rule 25(a) as a statute of limitations and supported its decision with the policy argument that a contrary rule would interfere in the administration of estates by state courts. Thus, the severe adverse impact of delay upon the defendant was thought sufficient to bar the plaintiff from any relief on a claim which had been recognized by the Supreme Court and where the plaintiff was not at fault. *Cf.* Snyder v. Buck, 340 U.S. 15, 95 L. Ed. 15, 71 Sup. Ct. 93 (1950), where Justice Black was one of four dissenters from a decision that a suit against a government official abates if within six months after he leaves office his successor is not substituted as a party. In *Snyder,* the defendant left his office while his appeal from the decision favorable to the plaintiff was pending. The result, as the majority candidly put it, was, "Petitioner loses her judgment and must start over." 340 U.S. 15, at 22. In 1962 the Rules were amended to alter the result of the *Snyder* case. 368 U.S. 1012, at 1015. See the opinion of Justice Douglas dissenting from this action, *id.* at 1012-14.

69 370 U.S. 626, at 634, n.10 (emphasis in original).

70 384 U.S. 1004, 16 L. Ed. 2d 1018, 86 Sup. Ct. 1908 (1965).

71 *Id.* at 1005-06.

72 See Black's opinion in Johnson v. New York, N.H. & H.R.R., 344 U.S. 48, 53, 97 L. Ed. 77, 73 Sup. Ct. 125 (1952). *Cf.* F.T.C. v. Minneapolis-Honeywell Regulator Co., 344 U.S. 206, 97 L. Ed. 245, 73 Sup. Ct. 245

(1952). There the Court dismissed as untimely the government's petition for certiorari, where there was doubt as to when the judgment of the court below has become "final." Justice Black dissented, saying: "But in arguing over 'finality' we should not ignore the fact that Congress has declared that this type of proceeding should be reviewable both in the Court of Appeals and here. We frustrate that declaration when review is denied a litigant because of his failure to guess right when confronted in August 1951 with a puzzle, the answer to which no one could know until today." *Id.* at 216-17.

73 Plant Economy, Inc. v. Mirror Insulation Co., 308 F.2d 275, 278 (3d Cir. 1962).

74 Daniels v. Allen, decided *sub nom.* Brown v. Allen, 344 U.S. 443, 482-87, 97 L. Ed. 469, 73 Sup. Ct. 397 (1953).

75 *Id.* at 552. See also dissenting opinion of Justice Frankfurter in which Justices Black and Douglas joined. *Id.* at 550.

76 372 U.S. 391, 9 L. Ed. 2d 837, 83 Sup. Ct. 822 (1963).

77 See Heflin v. United States, 358 U.S. 415-18, n.7, 3 L. Ed. 2d 407, 79 Sup. Ct. 451 (1959); Fallen v. United States, 378 U.S. 139, 12 L. Ed. 2d 760, 84 Sup. Ct. 1689 (1964). But the Court has not always been as generous as Justice Black would wish. See, *e.g.,* United States v. Robinson, 361 U.S. 220, 4 L. Ed. 2d 259, 80 Sup. Ct. 282 (1960) (dissent); Berman v. United States, 378 U.S. 530, 12 L. Ed. 2d 1012, 84 Sup. Ct. 1895 (1964) (dissenting opinion); Santana v. United States, 385 U.S. 848 (1966) (dissenting opinion).

78 370 U.S. 626, at 633-34.

79 *Id.* at 645-48 (dissenting opinion).

80 The value of the cause of action may also be measured in terms of what the plaintiff can obtain as a settlement. That value, however, depends on the parties' assessment of the costs of litigation and the plaintiffs' chances of a recovery. It would hardly be an appropriate function of the Rules to so increase the costs of defending even a non-meritorious suit, that the price which the defendant is willing to pay to be rid of the suit will be greater.

81 Such a test would in effect deprive the district courts of their power to enter an involuntary dismissal for failure to prosecute.

82 Two examples should suffice to make the point. In Braden v. United States, 365 U.S. 431, 5 L. Ed. 2d 653, 81 Sup. Ct. 584 (1961) counsel abandoned, in his brief on the merits, an issue which was subsequently found to be meritorious and to require the dismissal of an indictment. See Russell v. United States, 369 U.S. 749, 754, n.7, 8 L. Ed. 2d 240, 82 Sup. Ct. 1038 (1962). On the same day that *Link* was decided, the Court decided Glidden Co. v. Zdanok, 370 U.S. 530, 8 L. Ed. 2d 671, 82 Sup. Ct. 1459 (1962). There, as Justice Harlan observed in the prevailing opinion, petitioner's counsel had failed to raise in the petition for certiorari a substantial question of law which was before the Court in another case at the time the petition in *Glidden* was filed, and which, if raised, would have resulted in a decision in petitioner's favor, 370 U.S. 530, at 537, n.8.

83 *In re* McConnell, 370 U.S. 230, 236, 8 L. Ed. 2d 434, 82 Sup. Ct. 1288 (1962). See also Cammer v. United States, 350 U.S. 399, 100 L. Ed. 474, 76 Sup. Ct. 456 (1956); Sacher v. United States, 343 U.S. 1, at 14 (dissenting opinion). For other evidence of Justice Black's vigorous defense of the independence of the bar, see, in addition to the cases already cited, Konigsberg v. State Bar, 353 U.S. 252, 273, 1 L. Ed. 2d 810, 77 Sup. Ct.

722 (1957); Holt v. Virginia, 381 U.S. 131, 14 L. Ed. 2d 290, 85 Sup. Ct. 1375 (1965); Cohen v. Hurley, 366 U.S. 117, 131-35, 6 L. Ed. 2d 156, 81 Sup. Ct. 954 (1961) (dissenting opinion); Lathrop v. Donohue, 367 U.S. 820, 865, 6 L. Ed. 2d 1191, 81 Sup. Ct. 1826 (1961) (dissenting opinion). For indications of intemperate treatment of lawyers by judges, see, *e.g.*, Sacher v. United States, 343 U.S. 1, 90 L. Ed. 717, 72 Sup. Ct. 451 (1952), particularly the excerpts from the trial record in the appendix to Justice Frankfurter's dissenting opinion, 343 U.S. at 42-90; Offut v. United States, 348 U.S. 11, 99 L. Ed. 11, 75 Sup. Ct. 11 (1954); *In re* Sawyer, 360 U.S. 622, 3 L. Ed. 2d 1473, 79 Sup. Ct. 1376 (1959), and the *McConnell* case, *supra*.

84 Pittsburgh Towing Co. v. Mississippi Valley Barge Line Co., 385 U.S. 32, 34, 17 L. Ed. 2d 31, 87 Sup. Ct. 195 (1966) (dissenting opinion of Black, J.).

85 Nor would it be advisable to leave discipline in such situations to the bar itself. There would be a great danger that all but the most grievous blunders would be condoned, with the result that the procedural rules would atrophy. Unequal application would perhaps be even more likely than if such discipline were undertaken by the judiciary. There would also be the question of how proceedings before the bar committee would be instituted. If there is no sanction against the client, he would have no reason to institute charges, since discipline of opposing counsel would not benefit him; the other party would do so only out of vindictiveness. Indeed, counsel for the latter would in most instances discourage his client from seeking recourse before the bar association against another attorney. And while courts may appropriately, in cases of repeated misconduct by counsel, refer them to the bar committee for disciplinary action, the objections stated in the text militate against such reporting as a matter of regular practice.

86 Dilliard, Chapter Four, p. 107.

87 A striking example is Justice Black's dissenting opinion in National Equip. Rental, Ltd. v. Szukhent, 375 U.S. 311, 11 L. Ed. 2d 354, 84 Sup. Ct. 411 (1964). The Szukhents, Michigan farmers, had leased some farm equipment from National, a corporation whose principal place of business was New York. After the Szukhents had defaulted on payments due under the lease, National brought suit against them in the United States District Court for the Southern District of New York. Service of process on the Szukhents was made by sending the summons and complaint to one Florence Weinberg, who immediately transmitted these papers to the Szukhents. The Szukhents did not know Florence Weinberg, but the lease agreement under which suit was brought contained the provision that "the lessee [the Szukhents] hereby designates Florence Weinberg, 47-21 Forty-first Street, Long Island City, N.Y., as agent for the purpose of accepting service of any process within the State of New York." The question in the Supreme Court was whether service on the Szukhents in this manner was valid. This, in turn, depended upon whether she was "an agent authorized by appointment . . . to receive service of process" within Rule 4(d)(1) of the Federal Rules of Civil Procedure. A majority of the Court had little difficulty in determining that she was such an agent. The majority indicated that the question was one to be decided by federal rather than state law but determined that the result would be the same in either event. They noted that it had long been settled law "that parties to a contract may agree in advance to submit to the jurisdiction of a given court, to permit

notice to be served by the opposing party, or even to waive notice all together." 375 U.S. at 315-16. Moreover, the agency was valid because it effectuated its purpose—the receipt of notice of the lawsuit by the Szukhents. Finally, the Court rejected the contention that the agency was invalid because of a conflict of interest on Weinberg's part, pointing out that ". . . such a contention ignores the narrowly limited nature of the agency here involved. . . . An agent with authority so limited can in no meaningful sense be deemed to have had an interest antagonistic to the respondents [the Szukhents], since both . . . petitioner and the respondents had an equal interest in assuring that, in the event of litigation, the latter be given that adequate and timely notice which is a prerequisite to a valid judgment." *Id.* at 317-18.

Three justices joined in a dissenting opinion by Mr. Justice Brennan. They agreed that federal law should be applied but would have adopted standards narrowing the concept of agency for the purpose of Rule 4(d)(1). They would have denied validity to the appointment of an agent whose interest conflicted with those of his principal; would have required that the appointment expressly provide that the agent transmit the process forthwith, and, finally, where the appointment of the agency was in a printed form contract, they would have required proof that the potential defendant understandingly consented to be sued outside his state of residence. It is difficult to see what relation the second and third requirements have to do with the existence of a principal-agent relationship; nor did Mr. Justice Brennan meet the majority's point that there was in fact no conflict of interest in the Szukhents' case.

Mr. Justice Black dissented separately. In the first part of his opinion he contended that state law should apply in determining whether Weinberg was an agent of the Szukhents even as it determined rights and liabilities under the lease agreement. It would seem, however, that the interest of uniformity militates in favor of a general federal rule as to agency, particularly since the Rules themselves make explicit the circumstances in which they refer to state law, *e.g.,* Rule 4(d)(7). But Mr. Justice Black objected to the Court's decision even on the assumption that federal law applied. He thought that because Mrs. Weinberg was the wife of one of the company's officers and was under its supervision, there was a conflict of interest nullifying the agency; he also agreed with Justice Brennan that to come within the rule a contract must expressly require that notice be given by the agent. But Mr. Justice Black had a more fundamental objection. He believed that parties should not be held to have waived the right to be sued in their own state on the basis of contracts drawn by other parties. 375 U.S. at 324-29. Indeed, Justice Black thought that the Szukhents' right to be sued in their home state was of constitutional dimension and pointed to cases holding, in other contexts, that the waiver of constitutional rights is not to be lightly implied. Of course, if the defendants had a constitutional right not to be sued in New York, Rule 4(d)(1) could not authorize process against them in New York. However, Justice Black's constitutional argument runs counter to long accepted principles cited by the Court (at 316) as well as to the modern trend to expand the jurisdiction which states might exercise over nonresidents. Mr. Justice Black has played an important role in this development of the law. See particularly his opinions to the Court in McGee v. International

Life Ins. Co., 355 U.S. 220, 2 L. Ed. 2d 223, 78 Sup. Ct. 199 (1957), and Travelers Health Ass'n v. Virginia, 339 U.S. 643, 94 L. Ed. 1154, 70 Sup. Ct. 927 (1950). See also his opinion in Hanson v. Denckla, 357 U.S. 235, 256, 2 L. Ed. 2d 1283, 78 Sup. Ct. 1228 (1958), where he dissented from a holding by a five-man majority that a Delaware corporate trustee could not constitutionally be served in Florida where the grantor and many of the beneficiaries of the trust were domiciled. It should be noted, however, that Justice Black has taken a narrower view of constitutional jurisdiction where suit is filed against a nonresident individual in a noncommercial context. See, particularly, Vanderbilt v. Vanderbilt, 354 U.S. 416, 1 L. Ed. 2d 1456, 77 Sup. Ct. 1360 (1957), following Justice Black's concurring opinion in Armstrong v. Armstrong, 350 U.S. 568, 575, 100 L. Ed. 705, 76 Sup. Ct. 629 (1956), and emphatically reaffirmed by him in Simons v. Miami Beach First Nat'l Bank, 381 U.S. 81, 88-89, 14 L. Ed. 2d 232, 85 Sup. Ct. 1315 (1965) (concurring opinion).

Justice Black repeatedly contended that the agreement was not genuine and was unfair to the Szukhents. For example, in 375 U.S. at p. 328 he said:

This Court should reject any construction of Rule 4(d)(1) or formulation of federal standards under it to help powerful litigants to achieve by unbargained take-it-or-leave-it contracts what Congress has consistently refused to permit by legislation.

However, there was nothing in the record regarding the relative bargaining powers of the parties. Unless it be assumed that the company had monopolistic control of the market of farm equipment leasing, this was no "take-it-or-leave-it" contract—the Szukhents could have "left it" simply by contracting with some other company. Even if the industry were monopolistic, and there is conspiracy of all leasing companies to insist on contracts with lessees which provide that suit would be brought in the companies' home states, one would have to assume that no such companies were located in Michigan, where Justice Black believed the Szukhents were entitled to be sued. A hypothesis quite contrary to that implicit in Mr. Justice Black's opinion seems at least equally reasonable: namely, that the Szukhents chose National Equip. Rental because they could get the most attractive terms for rental and that National was able to provide these terms in part because it had by contract protected itself from the expense of bringing suit in foreign jurisdictions. However, whichever hypothesis is correct, the most serious objection to Mr. Justice Black's position is that he seeks to utilize the Rules of Civil Procedure to effectuate antitrust policies, or, more broadly, his views of fair commercial dealing. But as Mr. Justice Black himself has often recognized, the purpose of the Rules of Civil Procedure is different, though no less worthy— the just, speedy and inexpensive determination of every action. Rule 1.

CHAPTER NINE

Black on Balance

————*Stephen Parks Strickland*————

1 J. P. FRANK, MR. JUSTICE BLACK: THE MAN AND HIS OPINIONS 139 (1949).

2 Scott, *Personality Parade,* Parade, Nov. 7, 1965, p. 2.

3 Cahn, *The Firstness of the First Amendment,* 65 YALE L.J. 464, 470 (1956).

4 ONE MAN'S STAND FOR FREEDOM: MR. JUSTICE BLACK AND THE BILL OF RIGHTS 25 (Dilliard ed. 1963).

5 CLAYTON, THE MAKING OF JUSTICE: THE SUPREME COURT IN ACTION 40, 48, 118, 122, 219-20 (and elsewhere) (1964).

6 ONE MAN'S STAND FOR FREEDOM: MR. JUSTICE BLACK AND THE BILL OF RIGHTS (Dilliard ed. 1963), hereinafter cited as Black-Dilliard.

7 *Id.* at 24.

8 Chapter One, p. 9.

9 J. P. FRANK, MR. JUSTICE BLACK: THE MAN AND HIS OPINIONS (1949); Black-Dilliard, *op. cit. supra* note 6; WILLIAMS, HUGO L. BLACK: A STUDY IN THE JUDICIAL PROCESS (1950). In addition to these works, there is also the personal memoir of Black's niece, Hazel Black Davis, UNCLE HUGO: AN INTIMATE PORTRAIT OF MR. JUSTICE BLACK, which was privately printed in 1963.

10 Black-Dilliard, *op. cit. supra* note 6, at xiii. See also Dilliard's re-iteration of this conviction in Chapter Four of this volume, especially at pages 97-98.

11 *The Supreme Court: The Limits That Create Liberty and the Liberty That Limits Create,* Time, Oct. 9, 1964, p. 48.

12 Black-Dilliard, *op. cit. supra* note 6, at 31.

13 *Id.* at 467-83.

14 339 U.S. 382, 94 L. Ed. 925, 70 Sup. Ct. 674 (1950).

15 *Id.* at 411-12.

16 *Id.* at 446-49 (dissenting opinion).

17 Dennis v. United States, 341 U.S. 494, 95 L. Ed. 1137, 71 Sup. Ct. 857 (1951).

18 *Id.* at 579 (dissenting opinion).

19 *Id.* at 581.

20 323 U.S. 214, 89 L. Ed. 194, 65 Sup. Ct. 193 (1944).

21 *Id.* at 218.

22 *Id.* at 219-20.

23 Letter from J. Vernon Patrick to writer, March 19, 1965. Black said in Speiser v. Randall, 357 U.S. 513, 531, 2 L. Ed. 2d 1460, 78 Sup. Ct.

1332, 1352 (1958) (concurring opinion): "I happen to believe that . . . our Nation cannot be imperiled by mere talk."

24 WILLIAMS, *op. cit. supra* note 9, at 188.

25 See, *e.g.,* Duncan v. Kahanamoku, 327 U.S. 304, 90 L. Ed. 688, 66 Sup. Ct. 606 (1946). In that case Black held for the Court that the convictions of certain civilians in Hawaii by military courts were invalid despite the Territorial Governor's proclamation of martial law after the attack on Pearl Harbor. Emphasizing that the phrase "martial law" was not intended as an excuse to supplant the court system with military tribunals, Black thus upheld and reinforced *Ex parte Milligan,* decided in 1866. See also *Ex parte* Kawato, 317 U.S. 69, 87 L. Ed. 58, 63 Sup. Ct. 115 (1942).

26 Beauharnais v. Illinois, 343 U.S. 250, 267, 96 L. Ed. 919, 72 Sup. Ct. 725 (1952) (dissenting opinion).

27 Wieman v. Updegraff, 344 U.S. 183, 192, 97 L. Ed. 216, 73 Sup. Ct. 215 (1952) (concurring opinion).

28 Smith v. California, 361 U.S. 147, 155, 4 L. Ed. 2d 205, 80 Sup. Ct. 215 (1959) (concurring opinion).

29 Thornhill v. Alabama, 310 U.S. 88, 84 L. Ed. 1093, 60 Sup. Ct. 1093 (1940).

30 312 U.S. 287, 299, 85 L. Ed. 836, 61 Sup. Ct. 552, 132 A.L.R. 1200 (1941) (dissenting opinion).

31 Giboney v. Empire Storage & Ice Co., 336 U.S. 490, 93 L. Ed. 834, 69 Sup. Ct. 684 (1949).

32 *Id.* at 499.

33 Milk Wagon Drivers Union, Local 753 v. Meadowmoor Dairies, Inc., 312 U.S. 287, 316-17, 85 L. Ed. 836, 61 Sup. Ct. 552, 132 A.L.R. 1200 (1941).

34 Black-Dilliard, *op. cit. supra* note 6, at 477-78.

35 Minersville School Dist. v. Gobitis, 310 U.S. 586, 84 L. Ed. 1375, 60 Sup. Ct. 1010, 127 A.L.R. 1493 (1940).

36 319 U.S. 624, 87 L. Ed. 1628, 63 Sup. Ct. 1178, 147 A.L.R. 674 (1943) (concurring opinion of Black and Douglas, JJ.).

37 330 U.S. 1, 91 L. Ed. 711, 67 Sup. Ct. 504, 168 A.L.R. 1392 (1947).

38 *Id.* at 18.

39 *Ibid.*

40 Engel v. Vitale, 370 U.S. 421, 8 L. Ed. 2d 601, 82 Sup. Ct. 1261, 86 A.L.R.2d 1285 (1962).

41 A notable exception is Dean Erwin Griswold of the Harvard Law School. See Griswold, *Absolute Is in the Dark: A Discussion of the Approach of the Supreme Court to Constitutional Questions,* 8 UTAH L. REV. 167 (summer 1963), reprinted in CONG. REC. 22143-48 (daily ed. Sept. 19, 1966).

42 Engel v. Vitale, 370 U.S. 421, 435, 8 L. Ed. 2d 601, 82 Sup. Ct. 1261, 86 A.L.R.2d 1285 (1962).

43 343 U.S. 306, 96 L. Ed. 954, 72 Sup. Ct. 679 (1952).

44 Engel v. Vitale, 370 U.S. 421, 443, 8 L. Ed. 2d 601, 82 Sup. Ct. 1261, 86 A.L.R.2d 1285 (1962) (concurring opinion of Douglas, J.). See also Justice Douglas' book, THE BIBLE AND THE SCHOOLS (1966). Apparently offered mainly in defense of the Court's decision in *Engel v. Vitale,* Douglas provides a survey of Supreme Court decisions and a more general history of the meaning of "freedom of religion" and "establishment of religion." But he also hints at his current tendency toward a new absolut-

ism, saying, among other things: "[Christianity] does not need state subsidies, nor state privileges, nor state prestige. . . . What the Roman
Catholics, the Baptists, or the Presbyterians can command of the public
treasury or in other public support, so in time can the Moslems or the
Mormons as they grow politically stronger. The noncomformist . . . pays
the price when public institutions he supports promote sectarian purposes." *Id.* at 58. These thoughts are offered in connection with what
Douglas admits are "unsettled constitutional questions," primarily
prompted by recent federal aid to education legislation permitting the
lending of public funds to parochial institutions of higher education.
Chapter VI, pages 54-59.

For an attack on the "absolute test" as an approach to the Establishment
Clause and Free Exercise Clause, see *Liberties in Conflict*, Book Week,
Nov. 6, 1966, p. 5, a review by Sidney Hook of Thomas I. Emerson's book,
TOWARD A GENERAL THEORY OF THE FIRST AMENDMENT (1966).

45 Illinois *ex rel.* McCollum v. Board of Educ., 333 U.S. 203, 96 L. Ed.
649, 68 Sup. Ct. 461, 2 A.L.R.2d 1338 (1948); Zorach v. Clauson, 343 U.S.
306, 315, 96 L. Ed. 954, 72 Sup. Ct. 679 (1952) (dissenting opinion).

46 Everson v. Board of Educ., 330 U.S. 1, 91 L. Ed. 711, 67 Sup. Ct.
504, 168 A.L.R. 1392 (1947). See also the more recent case of Chamberlain
v. Dade County, 377 U.S. 402, 12 L. Ed. 2d 407, 84 Sup. Ct. 1272 (1964),
for further evidence of Black's cautious delineation—in this case joining
Douglas—of which practices are acceptable, and which are not, under the
Establishment Clause.

47 332 U.S. 46, 68, 91 L. Ed. 1903, 67 Sup. Ct. 1672, 171 A.L.R. 1223
(1947) (dissenting opinion). For support for Black's reading of the Fourteenth Amendment's history, see BRANT, THE BILL OF RIGHTS (1965), especially Chapters 27 & 28. *Cf.* Willard Hurst, *The Role of History,* in
SUPREME COURT AND SUPREME LAW (Cahn ed.) (1954).

48 *Id.* at 59 (concurring opinion of Frankfurter, J.).

49 *Id.* at 69, 89, 90-92 (dissenting opinion).

50 CLAYTON, *op. cit. supra* note 5, at 231.

51 372 U.S. 335, 9 L. Ed. 2d 799, 88 Sup. Ct. 792, 93 A.L.R.2d 733
(1963).

52 316 U.S. 455, 474, 86 L. Ed. 1595, 62 Sup. Ct. 1252 (1942) (dissenting opinion).

53 Time, *supra* note 11, p. 56.

54 342 U.S. 165, 176, 96 L. Ed. 183, 72 Sup. Ct. 205, 25 A.L.R.2d
1396 (1952) (concurring opinion). Irving Dilliard describes Black's and
the Court's difficulties with the Fourth Amendment in Chapter Four of
this volume, pp. 106-09. Justice Black's former law clerk, David J. Vann,
suggests that Black's differences over Bill of Rights issues with both the
Holmes and Frankfurter schools is that they wish to extend the Fourth
Amendment's "reasonableness" standard to the other Amendments, "a
process which Justice Black has strenuously opposed throughout his career
on the Court." Letter from Mr. Vann to writer, March 18, 1965. That
Black continues to be more tolerant than some of his colleagues of what
local law enforcement officers consider to be "reasonable search and
seizure" is manifested in his Feb. 1967 opinion for the Court in Cooper
v. California, — U.S. —, 18 L. Ed. 2d 243.

55 Adamson v. California, 332 U.S. 46, 67-68, 91 L. Ed. 1903, 67 Sup.
Ct. 1672, 171 A.L.R. 1223 (1947) (concurring opinion of Frankfurter, J.).

56 *Id.* at 89 (dissenting opinion of Black, J.).

57 *Id.* at 124 (dissenting opinion of Murphy, J.).

58 381 U.S. 479, 14 L. Ed. 2d 510, 85 Sup. Ct. 1678 (1965).

59 *Id.* at 485.

60 *Id.* at 486-92 (concurring opinion of Goldberg, J.).

61 381 U.S. 479, 501, 14 L. Ed. 2d 510, 85 Sup. Ct. 1678 (1965) (concurring opinion of Harlan, J.).

62 *Id.* at 509-10 (dissenting opinion of Black, J.).

63 *Ibid.*

64 22 U.S. (9 Wheat.) 1, 6 L. Ed. 23 (1824).

65 25 U.S. (12 Wheat.) 419, 6 L. Ed. 678 (1827).

66 53 U.S. (12 How.) 299, 13 L. Ed. 996 (1859).

67 J. P. FRANK, MR. JUSTICE BLACK: THE MAN AND HIS OPINIONS 154 (1949).

68 Gwin, White & Prince, Inc. v. Henneford, 305 U.S. 434, 83 L. Ed. 272, 59 Sup. Ct. 325 (1939).

69 *Id.* at 454 (dissenting opinion).

70 325 U.S. 761, 89 L. Ed. 1915, 65 Sup. Ct. 1515 (1945).

71 *Id.* at 789 (dissenting opinion).

72 FRANK, *op. cit. supra* note 67, at 154. Charlotte Williams confirms this opinion in a table which shows that in cases involving the right of a state to tax or regulate business (from the 1938 through the 1946 Court terms) Black voted in 92 per cent of those cases to uphold that right. Justice Murphy was next with an 85 per cent consistency, followed closely by Justice Douglas with 84 per cent. WILLIAMS, HUGO L. BLACK: A STUDY IN THE JUDICIAL PROCESS 175 (1950).

73 338 U.S. 25, 39, 93 L. Ed. 1782, 69 Sup. Ct. 1359 (1949).

74 *Id.* at 40, 41.

75 380 U.S. 693, 14 L. Ed. 2d 170, 85 Sup. Ct. 1246 (1965).

76 *Id.* at 703 (concurring opinion). But compare Mapp v. Ohio, 367 U.S. 643, 6 L. Ed. 2d 1081, 81 Sup. Ct. 1684 (1961) (concurring opinion).

77 334 U.S. 558, 92 L. Ed. 1574, 68 Sup. Ct. 1148 (1948).

78 *Id.* at 562.

79 Ginsburg v. United States, 383 U.S. 463, 477-78, 16 L. Ed. 2d 31, 86 Sup. Ct. 942, 969 (1966) (dissenting opinion).

80 Cox v. Louisiana [No. 24], 379 U.S. 536, 13 L. Ed. 2d 471, 85 Sup. Ct. 453 (1965); [No. 49], 379 U.S. 559, 13 L. Ed. 2d 487, 85 Sup. Ct. 476 (1965) (Black, J., concurring in No. 24 and dissenting in No. 49). *Id.* at 575.

81 *Id.* at 581-84.

82 See also United States v. California, 381 U.S. 139, 14 L. Ed. 2d 296, 85 Sup. Ct. 1401 (1965). In this case, Black, joined by Justice Douglas, dissented, and defended the right of California to claim, under the Submerged Lands Act, the historic boundaries of her offshore lands, which right the Court majority denied. *Id.* at 210 (dissenting opinion).

83 Miller and Howell, *Interposition, Nullification, and the Delicate Division of Power in the Federal System,* 5 EMORY J. PUB. L. 36, 37 (1956).

84 *Id.* at 36.

85 301 U.S. 1, 81 L. Ed. 893, 57 Sup. Ct. 615, 108 A.L.R. 1352 (1937).

86 *Id.* at 30.

87 *E.g.*, Milk Wagon Drivers Union, Local 753 v. Meadowmoor Dairies, Inc., 312 U.S. 287, 299, 85 L. Ed. 836, 61 Sup. Ct. 552, 132 A.L.R. 1200 (1941) (dissenting opinion).

88 WILLIAMS, *op. cit. supra* note 72, at 85. Miss Williams explains the limits of Black's sympathy for certain union activities, saying it is not labor unions but the individual laborer who has Black's keenest interest. *Id.* at 104-29 *passim*. In *Lincoln Fed. Labor Union v. Northwestern Iron & Metal Co.*, for example, Black, speaking for the Court, upheld North Carolina and Nebraska laws challenged by the unions which forbade employers "to enter into contracts or agreements obligating themselves to exclude persons from employment because they are or are not labor union members." 335 U.S. 525, 528, 93 L. Ed. 212, 69 Sup. Ct. 251, 6 A.L.R. 453 (1949). Such a position on those forerunners of the "right to work" laws in no wise endeared Black to organized labor. See also Black's Feb. 1967 dissent in Vaca v. Sipes, — U.S. —, 17 L. Ed. 2d 129, 209.

89 379 U.S. 306, 13 L. Ed. 2d 300, 85 Sup. Ct. 384 (1964).

90 *Id.* at 318 (dissenting opinion).

91 Kilpatrick, *A Conservative View: Belated Tribute to Justice Black,* Birmingham News, Feb. 12, 1965, p. 11.

92 Karmin, *Justice Black: Recent Opinions Hint at a More Conservative Philosophy,* Wall St. J., Nov. 2, 1965, p. 18.

93 *Marital Privacy* (editorial), Washington Post, June 8, 1965, p. A18.

94 WILLIAMS, *op. cit. supra* note 72, at 85.

95 *Ibid.*

96 *Id.* at 88.

97 *Ibid.*

98 *Ibid.*

99 For examples of Black's specific reliance on Madison in cases of various categories, see his opinions in Bridges v. California, 314 U.S. 252, 86 L. Ed. 192, 62 Sup. Ct. 190, 159 A.L.R. 1346 (1941); Everson v. Board of Educ., 330 U.S. 1, 91 L. Ed. 711, 67 Sup. Ct. 504, 168 A.L.R. 1392 (1947); Yates v. United States, 354 U.S. 298, 1 L. Ed. 2d 1356, 77 Sup. Ct. 1064 (1957); Barenblatt v. United States, 360 U.S. 109, 3 L. Ed. 2d 1115, 79 Sup. Ct. 1081 (1959); Communist Party v. Subversive Activities Control Bd., 367 U.S. 1, 6 L. Ed. 2d 625, 81 Sup. Ct. 1357 (1961); Engel v. Vitale, 370 U.S. 421, 8 L. Ed. 2d 601, 82 Sup. Ct. 1261, 86 A.L.R.2d 1285 (1962); Wesberry v. Sanders, 376 U.S. 1, 11 L. Ed. 2d 481, 84 Sup. Ct. 526 (1964); and Chapman v. California, — U.S. —, 18 L. Ed. 2d 241 (1967).

100 For an excellent discussion of Madison's initial lack of commitment to a written Bill of Rights and his subsequent persuasion by Jefferson, see Cahn, *The Firstness of the First Amendment,* 65 YALE L.J. 464 (1956). Cahn relates Black's position to this history of the First Amendment.

101 Communist Party v. Subversive Activities Control Bd., 367 U.S. 1, 137, 6 L. Ed. 2d 625, 81 Sup. Ct. 1357 (1961) (dissenting opinion).

102 ONE MAN'S STAND FOR FREEDOM: MR. JUSTICE BLACK AND THE BILL OF RIGHTS 47 (Dilliard ed. 1963).

103 *Id.* at 26. See further, Chief Justice Warren's Introduction to *Mr. Justice Black: Thirty Years in Retrospect,* 14 U.C.L.A.L. REV. 397-98 (No. 2, 1967).

Table of Cases

Cases listed in *italics* are discussed in some detail. Those listed in ordinary type are merely cited. References are to pages and, where appropriate, to notes pertaining to page references immediately preceding them.

Index

References are to pages. A small "n" or "nn" refers to comment in the footnotes compiled in this book commencing on page 275.

351